IRISH HOUSES AND CASTLES 1400–1740

Irish houses and castles
1400–1740

Rolf Loeber

Edited by Kevin Whelan and Matthew Stout

FOUR COURTS PRESS

Set in 10.5 on 12.5 point Ehrhardt for
FOUR COURTS PRESS LTD
7 Malpas Street, Dublin 8, Ireland
www.fourcourtspress.ie
and in North America for
FOUR COURTS PRESS
c/o IPG, 814 Franklin Street, Chicago, IL, 60622.

A catalogue record for this title
is available from the British Library.

ISBN 978-1-84682-820-1

Printed in England
by CPI Antony Rowe, Chippenham, Wilts.

Contents

Illustrations

FIGURES

TABLES

Abbreviations

AC	*Annála Connacht: the annals of Connacht AD 1224–1544*, ed. and trans. A.M. Freeman (Dublin, 1944)
AFM	*Annala rioghachta Eireann; Annals of the kingdom of Ireland by the Four Masters*, ed. J. O'Donovan, 7 vols (Dublin, 1851)
Anal. Hib.	*Analecta Hibernica* (Dublin, 1930–)
Arch. Sur. Down	*An archaeological survey of county Down* (Belfast, 1966)
Archiv. Hib.	*Archivium Hibernicum: or Irish historical records* (Maynooth, 1912–)
Atlas of Irish rural landscape	F. Aalen, K. Whelan & M. Stout (eds), *Atlas of the Irish rural landscape*, second edition (Cork, 2011)
AU	*Annals of Ulster/Annála Uldh (to A.D. 1131)* eds & trans., W. Hennessey & B. MacCarthy, 4 vols (Dublin, 1887–1901)
BL, Add. MSS	British Library, Additional Manuscripts
Bodl.	Bodleian Library, Oxford University
Breifne	*Breifne: Journal of Cumann Seanchais Bhreifne* (Breifne Historical Society) (Cavan, 1958–)
Cal. Carew MSS	*Calendar of Carew manuscripts preserved in the archiepiscopal library at Lambeth 1515–1574*, eds J. Brewer & W. Bullen, 6 vols (London, 1867–73)
Cal. pat. rolls, of Henry VIII etc.	*Calendar of the patent and close rolls of Chancery in Ireland the reigns of Henry VIII, Edward VI, Mary and Elizabeth*, ed. J. Morrin, 3 vols (Dublin, 1861–3): 1514–75, 1576–1603, 1625–33
Cal. pat. rolls, James I	*Irish patent rolls of James I: facsimile of the Irish Records Commissioners calendar prepared prior to 1830* (Dublin, 1966)
CARD	*Calendars of ancient records of Dublin*, ed. J. Gilbert, 18 vols (Dublin, 1889–1922)
CELT	Corpus of Electronic Texts, University College Cork
Clogher Rec.	*Clogher Record* (Monaghan, 1953–)
CSPD, 1547–80 [etc.]	*Calendar of state papers preserved in the Public Record Office, domestic series, 1547–1695*, 81 vols (London, 1856–1972)
CSPI	*Calendar of state papers relating to Ireland 1509–1670*, 24 vols (London, 1860–1911).
CTP	*Calendar of treasury papers*
DIB	*Dictionary of Irish biography*, eds J. McGuire & J. Quinn, 9 vols (Cambridge, 2009)

DNB	*The dictionary of national biography*, eds L. Stephen & S. Lee, 66 vols (London, 1885–1901; reprint with corrections, 22 vols (London, 1908–9)
EHR	*English Historical Review* (Oxford, 1886–)
Fiants Henry VIII etc.	*The Irish fiants of the Tudor sovereigns: during the reigns of Henry VIII, Edward VI, Philip & Mary, and Elizabeth I*, ed. J.J. Digges La Touche, 4 vols (Dublin, reprint, 1994)
Fiants Eliz.	'Calendar and index to the fiants of the reign of Elizabeth'. Appendices to 11th–13th, 15th–18th & 21st–22nd Reports of the Deputy Keeper of the Public Records in Ireland (Dublin, 1879–90)
GO	Genealogical Office of Ireland
Hist. Ire.	*History Ireland* (Bray/Dublin, 1993–)
HMC	Historical Manuscripts Commission
IESH	*Irish Economic and Social History Journal* (Dublin, 1974–)
IHS	*Irish Historical Studies* (Dublin, 1938–)
Ir. Arch. & Dec. Studies	*Irish architectural and decorative studies,* Irish Georgian Society (Dublin, 1998–)
Ir. Geneal.	*The Irish Genealogist*, Irish Genealogical Research Society (London, 1937–)
Ir. Geog.	*Irish Geography,* Geographical Society of Ireland (Dublin, 1944–)
Ir. Georgian Soc. Bull.	*Quarterly Bulletin of the Irish Georgian Society* (Celbridge, 1958–66; Dublin, 1966–)
Ir. Sword	*The Irish Sword: Journal of the Military History Society of Ireland* (Dublin, 1949–)
JCHAS	*Journal of the Cork Historical and Archaeological Society* (Cork, 1892–)
JGAIIS	*Journal of the Galway Archaeological and Historical Society* (Galway, 1900–)
JKAS	*Journal of the County Kildare Archaeological Society* (Dublin, 1891–)
JRSAI	*Journal of the Royal Society of Antiquaries of Ireland* (Dublin, 1854–: appeared under varying titles before 1892)
Misc. Ir. An.	*Miscellaneous Irish annals AD 1114–1437*, ed. S. Ó hInnse (Dublin, 1947)
NAI	National Archives of Ireland, Bishop Street, Dublin
NHI	*A new history of Ireland,* 9 vols (Oxford, 1976–2005)
NGI	National Gallery of Ireland
NLI	National Library of Ireland
NMAJ	*North Munster Antiquarian Society Journal* (Limerick, 1936–)
NMI	National Museum of Ireland
ODNB	*Oxford dictionary of national biography*, eds H. Matthew & B. Harrison, 60 vols (Oxford, 2004)

OS	Ordnance Survey
PRIA	*Proceedings of the Royal Irish Academy* (Dublin, 1836–)
PRO	Public Record Office, London
QUB	Queen's University Belfast
RIA	Royal Irish Academy
SP, Hen. VIII	*State papers of Henry VIII*, 11 vols (London, 1830–52)
Studia Hib.	*Studia Hibernica* (Dublin, 1961–)
TCD	Trinity College, Dublin
TNA	The National Archives, London, United Kingdom.
Topog. dict. Ire.	S. Lewis, *A topographical dictionary of Ireland*, 3 vols (London, 1837)
UCC	University College Cork
UCD	University College Dublin
UJA	*Ulster Journal of Archaeology* (Belfast, 1853–)

Acknowledgments

Author's acknowledgements

Chapter one: I am greatly indebted to Magda Stouthamer-Loeber for her consistent support of my Irish studies over the past thirty years, including her comments on an early draft of this chapter. In addition, I owe much to stimulating discussions with Elizabeth FitzPatrick, Matthew Stout, Kevin Whelan and Joep Leerssen, and to the attendees at the meetings on Gaelic settlement in Trinity College, Dublin, September 1997 and at All Hallows College, Dublin in February 1999. Elizabeth FitzPatrick and Kevin Whelan helped considerably with editing this chapter. I am very grateful to Matthew Stout for the maps that accompany the text.

Chapter two: Dedicated to John H. Andrews and David B. Quinn in gratitude for their inspiration and encouragement. This chapter is the product of many years of part-time study, which was encouraged by colleagues and friends. First, I am enormously indebted to my wife Magda Stouthamer-Loeber for her unfailing interest in this field of inquiry. Second, I am very grateful to Harman Murtagh for suggesting that I write this essay and for his patient support. Kevin Whelan has made valuable comments at various stages and played a pivotal role as consulting editor in guiding the essay to final publication. The following individuals also provided advice, comments and help: John Andrews, Paddy Bowe, Michael Byrne, Nicholas Canny, Maurice Craig RIP, Aidan Clarke, Ann Crookshank RIP, David Dickson, N.W. English RIP, William Garner, The Knight of Glin RIP, Desmond Guinness, Bob Hunter RIP, David Johnson, Mr and Mrs W.S. Johnston, Hugh Kearney RIP, Paul Kerrigan, Michael MacCarthy-Morrogh, Edward McParland, William O'Sullivan, Michael Perceval Maxwell, David Quinn RIP and Lucille Stark. I am grateful for the assistance of numerous libraries. Without the help of many hospitable owners of properties, this study would not have been possible. Special thanks to Stephen Hannon of the Department of Geography, UCD, for his painstaking work on the maps, and to David Miller and Mark Samber who laid their foundations. I appreciate the support of the Group for the Study of Irish Historic Settlement. John Andrews, David Quinn, William O'Sullivan and Kevin Whelan made valuable comments on an earlier draft.

Chapter three: This chapter is dedicated to Maurice Craig, RIP (*ob.* 2011), a friend, mentor, poet and an inspiring historian of architecture and bookbinding. I am indebted to many individuals who have helped me over the years in my architectural history studies of seventeenth-century Ireland, especially Maurice Craig, Mairtín D'Alton, Jane Fenlon, James Lyttleton, Harman Murtagh, Edward McParland and Terence Reeves-Smyth. Special thanks to Magda Stouthamer-Loeber and Anne Mullen Burnham for their useful comments on earlier drafts.

Chapter four: I dedicate this chapter to my wife, Magda, whose comments were by far the best stimulation that I received. I am indebted to the Hon. Desmond Guinness for his encouragement, and for his help in making it possible for me to work in Ireland. I also acknowledge assistance from Maurice Craig RIP in drawing my attention to Cromwellian architecture, and kind suggestions from Edward McParland, William O'Sullivan RIP and Miss M. Griffith from Trinity College, Dublin. Without the assistance of the staff of the Interlibrary Loan Department of Queen's University Library, Kingston, Ontario, this study would never have materialised. I am particularly grateful to Dr Richard Van Allen for improving the manuscript. I acknowledge the kind advice of Pierre Duprey for the reconstruction of Burton House and I am indebted to Anne Crookshank RIP for some of the information on Burton House.

Chapter five: A draft of this chapter was first presented to the Irish Georgian Society in St Catherine's Church, Dublin on 17 September 1974. The research was supported by a Leverhulme Trust Fellowship. I am especially grateful to Desmond Guinness and John Harris for their encouragement, and to Maurice Craig RIP for his valuable comments. Without the kind help of numerous owners of houses, ministers and caretakers of churches and librarians, this paper would never have been completed.

Chapter six: We are greatly indebted to Magda Stouthamer-Loeber for her comments on earlier drafts and for her work on the Egmont papers, Maurice Craig RIP, the Knight of Glin RIP, David Griffin, Edward McParland, Harman Murtagh, Jeremy Williams RIP and the owners of many country houses. We extend special thanks to Honora Faul for her help with access to the drawing collection at the NLI. Due to the substantial number of houses discussed, limitations of space made it impossible to cite references for each one.

Editors' acknowledgements

We, Kevin Whelan and Matthew Stout, edited this volume as a tribute to our lamented friend Rolf. We are grateful to the following: to publishers Four Courts Press and editors Patrick Duffy, David Edwards and Eliabeth FitzPatrick for permission to reprint chapter 1, which originally appeared as R. Loeber, 'An architectural history of Gaelic castles and settlements 1370–1600' in P.J. Duffy, D. Edward & E. FitzPatrick (eds), *Gaelic Ireland c.1250–c.1650: land, lordhip and settlement* (Four Courts Press, Dublin, 2001), pp 271–313; to publishers Group for the Study of Irish Historic Settlement, and their then publications editor Kevin Whelan for permission to reprint chapter 2, which originally appeared as R. Loeber, *The geography and practice of English colonisation of Ireland from 1534 to 1609* (Group for the Study of Irish Historic Settlement, Athlone, 1992); to publishers Spire Books and editor Olivia Horsfall Turner for permission to reprint chapter 3, which originally appeared as R. Loeber, 'The early seventeenth-century Ulster and Midlands plantations, part 1; Pre-plantation architecture and building regulations' and 'Part II: The new

Rolf Loeber and Magda Stouthamer-Loeber.

architecture' in O. Horsfall Turner (ed.), *'Theatre of empire': the seventeenth-century architecture of Britain and her colonies* (New York, Spire Books, 2012), pp 73–99, 101–37; to publishers The Irish Georgian Society and their Executive Director, Donough Cahill, for permission to reprint chapter 4, which originally appeared as R. Loeber, 'Irish country houses and castles of the late Caroline period: an unremembered past recaptured', *Ir. Georgian Society Bull.*, xvi (1973), pp 1–69, and chapter 5, which originally appeared as R. Loeber, 'Early Classicism in Ireland: architecture before the Georgian era', *Architectural Hist.*, xxii (1979), pp 49–63; and to publishers Four Courts Press, editors Raymond Gillespie and Roy Foster, and co-author Livia Hurley for permission to reprint chapter 6, which originally appeared as R. Loeber & L. Hurley, 'The architecture of Irish country houses 1691–1739: continuity and innovation' in R. Gillespie & R. Foster (eds), *Irish provincial cultures in the long eighteenth century: essays for Toby Barnard* (Four Courts Press, Dublin, 2012), pp 201–19. For assistance during the preparation of this volume, we are grateful to the following: Margaret Arriola and Robert Black for sterling technical assistance; Lisa Scholey for preparing the index; and everyone at Four Courts Press. Others who helped included Michael Byrne, Donough Cahill, Vandra Costello, George Cunningham, George Gossip, Livia Hurley, William Laffan, Niall McCullough, Harman Murtagh, Tony Roche, Katharine Simms and Martin Timoney.

CHAPTER ONE

An architectural history of Gaelic castles and settlements 1370–1600

INTRODUCTION

THE EXISTING ARCHITECTURAL HISTORY of the later medieval and early modern periods in Ireland is largely based on the colonial architectural remains of the British rather than those of the native Gaelic population.[1] Of fifteen volumes on castles and settlements in Ireland published over the last half-century, only four specifically deal with Gaelic architecture,[2] despite the fact that Ireland, by the early modern period, had become 'the most castellated part' of Great Britain and Ireland.[3]

Why is it necessary to address Gaelic architecture in particular? The Gaelic Irish inhabited a culture with its own traditions, literature and laws. In the late medieval period, the Gaelic Irish still controlled a significant part of the country that had never been infiltrated by the English, and they had also recovered extensive districts from the English settlers. This distinctive cultural heritage extended to Gaelic architecture and settlements and it deserves to be studied both in and of itself and in a comparative manner. The highest single expenditure of Irish lords and their freeholders in their lifetime consisted of building a castle (a few built several castles). In the early seventeenth century, Mathew De Renzy estimated that the 'meanest' castle cost at least £600 or £700.[4] The significant number of

---

1 Gaelic architecture in this chapter refers to buildings of the native Irish, excluding Anglo-Normans or their descendants. Thus, castles of such families as the Barrys, Fitzgeralds, Burkes, and Stauntons are not included in this review, even if they adopted Irish habits. Irish architecture of Gaels who immigrated from Scotland is included.   2 T. Barry, *The archaeology of medieval Ireland* (London, 1987); B. de Breffny, *Castles of Ireland* (London, 1977); C. Cairns, *Irish towerhouses: a county Tipperary case study* (Athlone, 1987); M. Craig, *The architecture of Ireland* (London, 1982); J. Healy, *The castles of County Cork* (Cork, 1988); D.N. Johnson, *The Irish castle* (Dublin, 1985); P. Kerrigan, *Castles and fortifications in Ireland 1485–1945* (Cork, 1995); H. Leask, *Irish castles and castellated houses* (Dundalk, 1946); R. Loeber, 'The geography and practice of English colonisation in Ireland 1534–1609' in this volume, pp 35–111; T. McNeill, *Anglo-Norman Ulster: the history and archaeology of an Irish barony 1177–1400* (Edinburgh, 1980); T. McNeill, *Castles in Ireland: feudal power in a Gaelic world* (London, 1997); K. O'Conor, *The archaeology of medieval rural settlement in Ireland* (Dublin, 1998); A. O'Sullivan, *The archaeology of lake settlement in Ireland* (Dublin, 1998); M. Salter, *Castles and strong houses of Ireland* (Malvern, 1993); D. Sweetman, *The medieval castles of Ireland* (Cork, 1999). Castles are listed in the valuable county archaeological inventories published by the Archaeological Survey of Ireland.   3 S. Duffy, *Ireland in the Middle Ages* (New York, 1997), p. 166. See the map of towerhouses in Ireland, England and Scotland in M.W. Thompson, *The decline of the castle* (Cambridge, 1987), p. 23.   4 PRO, SP 46/90, f. 143.

I

castles built by the Gaelic Irish between 1370 and 1600 demonstrated considerable concentration of wealth in the country.

The neglect of Gaelic domestic architecture partially stems from the lack of interest of architectural historians in Gaelic buildings and culture, and partially from an under-utilisation of source material and surviving physical remains. A major issue in the study of Gaelic architecture is that documentary sources are sparse, when compared with those available to study the architecture of English settlers in Ireland. There are no known building plans and elevations by Gaelic craftsmen. Estate papers and land surveys are very rare, while diaries and correspondence about buildings are lacking. Contracts with architects and craftsmen have not survived. Regulations governing carpentry are known only from a lost tract, *Bretha Luchtine*.[5] Topographical drawings of buildings in their landscape setting by Gaelic artists are also non-existent. A further problem is the blasé use of English documentation concerning Gaelic society. Such documentation was inevitably biased in favour of English civilisation, sometimes exhibited a clear anti-Irish bias and always requires independent confirmation.[6] In addition, English scribes, ignorant of the Irish language, frequently mangled Irish family and place names. Lastly, Irish terms for building types do not always correspond with those in English.

Architectural historians studying Gaelic architecture must investigate other material, such as native annals and bardic poems.[7] Other useful sources include English topographical surveys, letters by English administrators, soldiers and travellers, and topographical drawings by non-Irish draftsmen. It is also possible to construct 'property pedigrees' of successive occupancies of Gaelic sites by using property deeds, letters patent, pardons and other mostly English documents relating to landownership.[8] The available data has never been systematically mined to advance knowledge of Gaelic castles and settlement in the medieval period.

The relative scarcity of Gaelic documentation forces us to utilise English records. Such records, however, are primarily available during periods of reconquest or settlement. Thus, they are less detailed and abundant for the fourteenth and fifteenth centuries than for the sixteenth and seventeenth centuries. Although scholars have made extensive use of the six-inch Ordnance Survey maps and letters, reliance solely on these sources is insufficient, because many Gaelic settlement sites were not necessarily recorded in them.[9]

Complementary approaches include the study of the morphology of existing buildings, archaeological excavations of sites known for their Gaelic settlement,

---

5 K. Simms, 'The brehons of later medieval Ireland' in D. Hogan & W.N. Osborough (eds), *Brehons, serjeants and attorneys* (Dublin, 1990), pp 51–76. Regulations governing smiths, whose work was necessary for the portcullis, yetts and other ironwork of towerhouses, were spelled out in *Bretha Goibnenn*.   6 C. Brady, 'The decline of the Irish kingdom' in M. Greengrass (ed.), *Conquest and coalescence* (London, 1991), pp 94–115.   7 The annals provide more coverage for Ulster and Connacht than for Munster, and none for Leinster.   8 R. Loeber, 'Geographical calendar of landownership in Ely O'Carroll in the sixteenth and seventeenth centuries', unpublished document, deposited at the Offaly Historical Society, Tullamore (Offaly).   9 P. O'Flanagan, 'Surveys, maps and the study of rural settlement development' in D. Ó Corráin (ed.), *Irish antiquity* (Cork, 1981), pp 320–6.

Figure 1.1 Parkes Castle, County Leitrim. This castle on the shores of Lough Gill was completed by Roger Parkes in 1610 as a fortified manor house occupying the site of an earlier Uí Ruairc castle. Parkes retained the earlier bawn but demolished the towerhouse to insert his three-storey manor, with its mullioned windows and diamond-shaped chimneys. Two round flankers defend the bawn. An arched entrance through a gate building leads into the courtyard (National Monuments Service).

geophysical and remote sensing techniques to investigate sites prior to excavation, and the scientific dating of surviving timbers in castles.[10] Irish archaeology has favoured exploration of Anglo-Norman and later British plantation sites over Gaelic sites, of which amazingly few have been excavated, notably Dunboy Castle (Cork) and Parke's Castle (formerly Newtown, Leitrim) (Figure 1.1). This essay addresses the following deceptively simple questions concerning Gaelic castles and settlements between 1370 and 1600: (i) What are the arguments for and against the study of Gaelic castles and settlements? (ii) Are there differences between Gaelic and English castles? (iii) What is the historical context of castle building during the Gaelic revival and conquest? (iv) How common were conflicts within and between Gaelic lordships? (v) What is known about the distribution of castles? (vi) When were Gaelic castles built? (vii) Are there unique architectural features of Gaelic castles? (viii) Which social strata in Gaelic society built castles? (ix) How important were chiefry castles? (x) Who built multiple castles? (xi) Were castles strategically situated?

Architectural terms in Irish and English
In discussing these topics, it is necessary to highlight Irish architectural terms used in original sources, which have not always been well understood or properly

---

10 These arguments were made by M. MacCurtain in 'A lost landscape: the Geraldine castles and towerhouses in the Shannon estuary' in J. Bradley (ed.), *Settlement and society in medieval Ireland* (Kilkenny, 1988), pp 429–44.

translated into English. Caislén or caistel refers to a castle but the castle could have been constructed of stone, timber or a combination of both. Túr means a tower. Crannóg, referring to an artificially constructed island in a lake, only appears in the sources after 1200, but lake settlements generally date back to the sixth and seventh centuries.[11] The term inis usually refers to an island site. Both crannóg and insí were used as places of refuge. Longphort (longport, longpurt, longpuirt), as distinct from castles, are frequently referred to in thirteenth- and fourteenth-century sources, and the word is conventionally translated to mean 'fortress' or 'stronghold'. An early fourteenth-century poem dedicated to Aodh Ó Domhnaill advised him to construct a longphort above Loch Ree.[12] Ráth generally refers to an earthen rampart fort.[13] It has a more specific reading as an earthen rampart surrounding a chief's residence and by extension it is sometimes used to refer to the enclosed dwelling.[14] Irish annals of 1590 mention the 'cúirte, caisteoil agus sostabha sabhaile' ('courts, castles and comfortable seats') of the chief Mac Cochlainn,[15] but it is ambiguous what these distinctions actually meant. A surge in additional building-related vocabulary in the Irish language occurred in the fourteenth and fifteenth century, coinciding with the increase in Gaelic castle building.[16]

English sources often used their own terms to distinguish buildings of the Irish. For instance, the now archaic term fortalice, meaning fortress, was used as early as 1180.[17] A large castle, such as Birr (Offaly), was characterised in an English document in 1622 as a 'castle and fortilage',[18] probably referring to its stone castle set within a fort-like enclosure. The English colonist Robert Cowley distinguished between 'piles, holdes, and strong houses' of the Irish in 1537.[19] Possibly, piles refer to towerhouses or tall castles in general, holds to fortresses and strong houses to dwellings with defensive features, but their distinctive features and the general acceptance of these terms in Ireland needs to be further explored. An English traveller in north Wexford in 1634 noted 'as handsome an Irish hall' 'as I ever saw in this kingdome',[20] but we lack descriptions or drawings to reveal its distinctively Irish features. Finally, English sources occasionally refer to wooden castles. A 'wooden castle' remained almost constantly in the hands of the O'Connor family from at least 1564 to 1622 at Derrymullin (probably now Millgrove in east Offaly).[21] Again, we lack records that might help us to visualise this type of structure.

11 A. O'Sullivan, 'Crannógs in late medieval Gaelic Ireland, *c.*1350–*c.*1650' in P. Duffy, D. Edwards & E. FitzPatrick (eds), *Gaelic Ireland c.1250–c.1650: land, lordship and settlement* (Dublin, 2001), 397–417.   12 Cited in J. Leerssen, *Mere Irish and fíor-Ghael* (Cork, 1997), p. 163.   13 O'Conor, *Archaeology*, pp 77, 79, 82, 84.   14 RIA, *Dictionary of the Irish language* (Dublin, 1990), p. 501.   15 *AFM*, v, 1349; vi, 1893.   16 K. Simms, 'Native sources for Gaelic settlement: the house poems' in Duffy, Edwards & FitzPatrick (eds), *Gaelic Ireland*, pp 246–67.   17 K. O'Conor, 'The later construction and use of motte and bailey castles in Ireland: new evidence from Leinster', *JKAS*, 17 (1987–91), pp 13–29; Cairns, *Irish towerhouses*, p. 9.   18 *Cal. pat. rolls, Ire., James I*, p. 467.   19 *S.P. Hen. VIII*, ii, p. 452.   20 R. Loeber & M. Stouthamer-Loeber, 'The lost architecture of the Wexford plantation' in K. Whelan (ed.), *Wexford: history and society* (Dublin, 1987), pp 173–200.   21 BL, Add. MS 4756, f. 82v; *Cal. Carew MSS, 1589–1600*, p. 192; *Cal. pat. rolls, Ire., James I*, p. 490.

Why study Gaelic castles and settlements?

An alleged impediment to the study of Gaelic settlements has been the opinion that Gaelic society was so unstable and impermanent that it is futile to seek its architecture. Two factors are frequently cited to demonstrate that the Irish were not used to building or were living under conditions that discouraged permanent residences: the nomadic migration with cattle in the summer months to hill pastures (buaile or booleying), and periodic redistribution of lands among family groups. This has led to the mistaken belief that Gaelic society produced few permanent settlements.

There are too many accounts of transhumance to discount it, but this was a feature only of the lower strata of Gaelic society. Richard Stanihurst recognised this already in 1584: 'There is a certain forcible and widespread opinion in many minds that the Irish have cast off all humanity, that they wander scattered and dispersed through very dense woods, and generally that they live unrestrainedly in rough and uncivilised fashion. But those who defame them thus are manifestly wrong'. He then praised Irish lords who had 'fixed dwelling-places to which a great number of guests flock daily'.[22] Camden described their castles as 'no more than towers, with narrow loop-holes rather than windows; to which adjoins a hall made of turf, and roofed over with thatch, and a large yard fenced quite round with a ditch and hedge to defend their cattle from thieves'.[23]

The second issue, the periodic redistribution of lands, is regarded as running counter to the stability necessary for settlement and building. Sir John Davies, in his *A discovery of the true causes why Ireland was never entirely subdued* (1612), claimed that two factors discouraged building: the custom of tanistry and the periodic redistribution of lands (often referred to in English sources as gavelkind, a term used in Kent and Wales). These two customs caused great 'uncertainty of estates' and 'hath been the true cause of such desolation and barbarism in this land', preventing the Gaelic Irish from making 'any provisions for posterity' because their estates were 'so uncertain and transitory in their possession'.[24]

While periodic redistribution of lands could take place, it was not a general feature of every Irish lordship during the later medieval and early modern period. In Mayo, redistribution and fractional ownership of castles was common, and this practice could even assign various rooms in a castle to different individuals.[25] In an agreement of 1584 among the Kennedys of Lower Ormond (north Tipperary), the castle and small bawn of Ballycapple was assigned to the senior and 'worthiest' (richest) of the family. This person also enjoyed the use of the great bawn but he had to share it with any other co-heir. If this co-heir did not build inside the bawn, then

22 C. Lennon, 'Richard Stanihurst (1547–1618) and Old English identity', *IHS*, xxi (1978–9), pp 121–43, at p. 133, citing R. Stanyhurst's *De rebus in Hibernia gestis* (Antwerp, 1584). 23 Thompson, *Decline of the castle*, p. 24. 24 J. Davies, *Historical tracts* (London, 1786), ed. G. Chalmers, pp 136–7; H. Pawlisch, *Sir John Davies and the conquest of Ireland* (Cambridge, 1985), pp 60–1. 25 M. O'Dowd, *Power, politics and land: early modern Sligo 1568–1688* (Belfast, 1991), pp 69–72; W. O'Sullivan (ed.), *The Strafford inquisition of County Mayo* (Dublin, 1958). County designations are used in this chapter to facilitate knowledge of locations; counties in several Gaelic areas were not established until the sixteenth century.

his share would remain at the disposal of the senior member.[26] It is unclear, however, to what extent co-ownership inhibited the building and maintenance of castles, and whether the density of castle building was inversely related to the degree to which periodic redistribution and fractional ownership prevailed.

The extent of redistribution has probably been exaggerated. Redistribution of lands primarily occurred within the derbfine (the four-generation group eligible for leadership roles within a leading family) and not within the kin group as a whole.[27] English documents asserted that lordship lands were re-divided among its principal members at the transition to a new tánaiste. However, this re-division applied solely to the lands of the dominant family, excluding lands of inferior families, who were free and whose lands were their own by right. The resulting system, at least under the MacMahons and their freeholders in Monaghan, exhibited considerable stability with properties remaining in the possession of the same family over long periods.[28] Moreover, since mensal and demesne lands were attached to the position of the chieftainship and not to a particular family, these lands and the chiefry castle were presumably shielded from any redistribution. The same may have applied to the castle and demesne attached to the position of tánaiste.[29] Furthermore, church lands (on which many freeholders dwelt) were excluded from periodic re-distribution. In conclusion, many types of lands were obviously not subject to periodic redistribution, and investments in building could be made and safeguarded.

In those areas subjected to periodic redistribution of lands, at least two outcomes were possible concerning buildings. Nicholls remarks that 'It is difficult to see how such frequent, even annual, redistributions could have been possible if the normal dwelling houses of the Irish were permanent ones'. It is debatable whether this conclusion also applies to the dwellings of the middle and upper classes. Another possibility was that re-division, as it concerned buildings, applied to structures in an abstract or legalistic way (that is, one person held a right to one-fifth of a castle, his brother held another fifth, etc.), and that this share could easily be transferred following the death of a chief and the subsequent redistribution of properties. Nicholls explains: 'As regards the inconvenience caused by the yearly divisions, however, we must not forget that in many cases the co-heirs would have grouped their habitations together in some central or fortified place, a castle or earthen fort'.[30]

Several areas in Ireland did not experience periodic redistribution of lands. In those areas, rules of inheritance were much closer to those accepted in England. Among Sligo families in the sixteenth and early seventeenth centuries, there is no evidence of annual or even regular redistribution of land. Instead, the land was

26 K.W. Nicholls, 'Gaelic landownership in Tipperary from surviving Irish deeds' in W. Nolan & T. McGrath (eds), *Tipperary: history and society* (Dublin, 1985), pp 92–103; J. Graham, 'Rural society in Connacht 1600–1640' in N. Stephens & R. Glasscock (eds), *Irish geographical studies* (Belfast, 1970), pp 192–208.   27 G.A. Hayes-McCoy, 'Gaelic society in Ireland in the late sixteenth century', *Historical Studies*, iv (1963), pp 45–61, at p. 54.   28 P.J. Duffy, 'Patterns of landownership in Gaelic Monaghan in the late sixteenth century', *Clogher Rec.*, x (1981), pp 304–22, at pp 315, 317.   29 K. Simms, *From kings to warlords* (Woodbridge, 1987), p. 129.   30 K.W. Nicholls, *Land, law and society in sixteenth-century Ireland* (Dublin, 1978), pp 3–26, at pp 18–19.

held by different branches of the main ruling family, and inheritance routinely occurred within each branch without reference to other branches. Inheritance was most often from father to son (primogeniture), but other family members, notably younger sons, could rent land cheaply from the head of the family.[31] In the late sixteenth century, the Dublin government sought to impose primogeniture on those areas where traditional succession was still accepted. The 1590s land settlement in Monaghan stopped short of confiscation. Instead, it abolished Gaelic overlordship and established inheritance by primogeniture under English law.[32]

In conclusion, the redistribution of lands was not widespread and even where it did occur, it did not affect all lands. Further, the evidence of large-scale castle building by Gaelic families from the fifteenth century onward, and the hundreds of castles lived in by the Irish, inevitably contributed 'to an impression of permanence and stability'.[33]

Differences between Gaelic and Anglo-Norman castles

Several architectural historians have asserted that Gaelic towerhouses were not distinct from the towerhouses built by families of Anglo-Norman origin. The towerhouse represented a 'national' building type that was indiscriminately built by both the Irish and the Anglo-Normans.[34] Although this may be the case for the overall appearance of towerhouses, it is far from clear whether this conclusion equally applied to details of craftsmanship and modes of construction, which have been poorly studied.[35] It is certain that the physical context and ownership of Gaelic castles and settlements differed from their Anglo-Norman counterparts.

There are several reasons why Gaelic architecture in Ireland should be studied in its own right and in a comparative manner. Firstly, Gaelic towerhouses formed part of a territorial organisation based on a landholding system that differed fundamentally from the geography of Anglo-Norman settlements. The Anglo-Norman landscape with its caputs, manors and subinfeudation represented a feudal system in which all landownership was ultimately derived from the English king. The geography of Gaelic castles needs to be understood in the context of a radically different and more fragmented landholding system consisting of the lands of many different lineages. In each case, lordship lands, including those assigned to the chieftain and the tánaiste, remained the collective property of a lineage group. However, inferior families living under the dominant family were free and held their property as their

31 O'Dowd, *Early modern Sligo*, pp 69–72.   32 P.J. Duffy, 'The territorial organisation of Gaelic landownership and its transformation in County Monaghan 1591–1640', *Ir. Geog.*, xiv (1981), pp 1–26; P.J. Duffy, 'The evolution of estate properties in south Ulster 1600–1900' in W. Smyth & K. Whelan (eds), *Common ground* (Cork, 1988), pp 84–109.   33 O'Dowd, *Early modern Sligo*, p. 19.   34 Craig, *Architecture*, p. 96; Cairns, *Towerhouses*, p. 9.   35 M. McKenna, 'Evidence for the use of timber in medieval Irish towerhouses: a regional study in Lecale and Tipperary', *UJA*, xlvii (1984), pp 171–4. An in-depth study of architectural fabric remains fraught with problems. Many Gaelic castles, especially in strategic locations, were later occupied and modified by settlers, who thereby obliterated or modified original features. A further complication is that Irish craftsmen were likely employed by both natives and settlers. Gaelic magnates may have copied the building practices of settlers and the reverse may also have occurred.

own by right.[36] Secondly, the siting of Gaelic Irish castles was dictated by security needs of both the principal family and its individual members, particularly its chieftain and tánaiste. Thirdly, in contrast to Anglo-Norman settlements of manors and churches, many Gaelic chieftains built a principal castle and added an adjacent ecclesiastical foundation. Finally, there were undoubtedly significant architectural differences between the castles of the Gaelic Irish and the Anglo-Normans.

An architectural history of Gaelic buildings can proceed on several fronts: the study of surviving architectural remains, the identification of former sites through documentation[37] and archaeological investigations.[38] A further line of inquiry should be historical documentation of the genealogy of different family branches according to current standards of genealogy.[39] When matched with other historical evidence, accurate genealogy can clarify the successive occupants of sites.[40]

Finally, with a few exceptions, writing on Irish castles has been preoccupied with stone structures and has neglected wooden castles and other dwelling types of the ruling Gaelic families.[41] Given the abundance of domestic sites without known stone castles, the challenge remains to establish the precise domestic living conditions of a significant segment of the upper and middle classes in Gaelic society.

CASTLE BUILDING DURING THE GAELIC REVIVAL

The Anglo-Norman conquest of Ireland, initiated in the twelfth century, was never completed. Most of Ulster (Donegal, Tyrone, Fermanagh, Leitrim, Cavan) saw little or no Anglo-Norman settlement. Similarly, a few areas further west, notably Clare, largely escaped Anglo-Norman incursions.[42] In several districts infiltrated by the Anglo-Normans, the conquest caused displacements of the Irish. The O'Byrnes and O'Tooles, driven from the plains of Kildare, were forced high into the mountains of Wicklow. The O'Flahertys, displaced from east Galway, seized a new territory west of Lough Corrib (Galway), while the O'Sullivans, forced out of Tipperary, retreated to south-west Cork and Kerry.[43]

The Anglo-Norman advance slowed appreciably in the thirteenth century and subsequently the Irish regained large portions of their former lands in all four

36 Duffy, 'Territorial organisation', p. 7; Duffy, 'Patterns of landownership', p. 315; M. MacCurtain, *Tudor and Stuart Ireland* (Dublin, 1972), p. 40.   37 J.H. Andrews, 'The mapping of Ireland's cultural landscape 1550–1630' in Duffy, Edwards & FitzPatrick (eds), *Gaelic Ireland*, pp 153–80; K. Simms, 'Native sources for Gaelic settlement' in Duffy, Edwards & FitzPatrick (eds), *Gaelic Ireland*, pp 246–67.   38 K. O'Conor, 'The morphology of Gaelic lordly sites in north Connacht' in Duffy, Edwards & FitzPatrick (eds), *Gaelic Ireland*, pp 329–45.   39 K.W. Nicholls's work is exemplary: see, e.g., his 'The Kavanaghs 1400–1700', *Ir. Geneal.*, v (1974–9), pp 435–47, 573–80, 730–4.   40 O'Conor, 'Motte and bailey castles', p. 16; O'Conor, 'The morphology of Gaelic lordly sites'.   41 Not discussed are cabins lived in by the lower classes: see the sources listed by K.W. Nicholls, 'Gaelic society and economy in the high Middle Ages' in *NHI*, ii, p. 403.   42 W. Butler, 'The policy of surrender and regrant', *JRSAI*, iii (1913), p. 104; McNeill, *Anglo-Norman Ulster*, Fig. 15.   43 Butler, 'Surrender and regrant', p. 105. The architecture of the displaced families in their new territories apparently has not been studied.

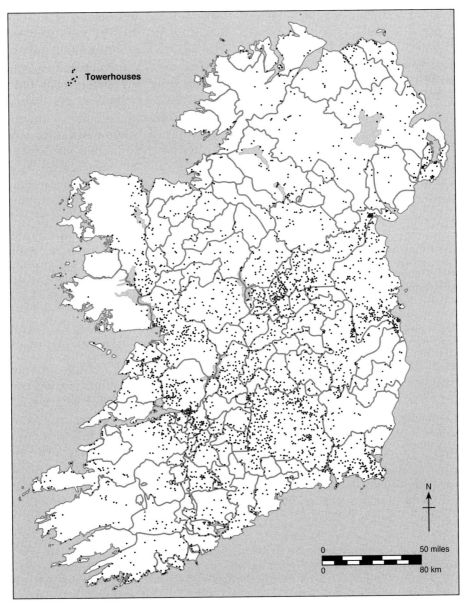

Figure 1.2 Distribution of towerhouses in Ireland (based on Figure 71 in Aalen, Whelan & Stout (eds), *Atlas of the Irish rural landscape*).

provinces. The Irish advanced eastward in Leinster towards Kildare and reoccupied large parts of Laois and Offaly, and eventually captured the Anglo-Norman strongholds of Dunamase and Lea (Laois).[44] By the mid thirteenth century, the Butlers had relinquished control of north Tipperary to the Irish. In all, the Butlers

44 O'Conor, 'Motte and bailey castles', p. 21; S. Ellis, *Reform and revival* (New York, 1984), pp 59–60.

lost half of their lordship.[45] In Wicklow, the Anglo-Norman settlements of Newcastle, Kilcommon and Kilpipe were abandoned and allowed to become ruins.[46] By the beginning of the sixteenth century, the English colony in Leinster had contracted to a Z-shaped swathe of land, stretching from Greencastle (Down) to Waterford city.

The expulsion of English settlers was more complete in Connacht and Ulster. In Connacht, the royal castles of Roscommon and Rinndown were finally deserted in the 1350s.[47] In Ulster, several Gaelic chiefs gained notoriety by expelling English settlers. For example, Aodh Buí Mac Brian Ballagh Ó Néill, who died in 1444, was eulogised as 'the only man (in his own days) that most planted of English lands against their wills that was in Ireland'. The O'Reilly pedigree boasts that Thomas McMahon O'Reilly levelled eighteen castles of the Anglo-Norman Tuites, although this might have been hyperbolic. The densest Anglo-Norman settlements in Antrim and Down were also overrun by the Irish.[48] In addition, the O'Dowds in Sligo and the O'Kellys in Galway ousted settlers.[49] The retreat of the Anglo-Normans in Munster was less complete. In the fourteenth century, the MacCarthys, together with the Barretts, repossessed Muskerry in Cork, the former Cogan lordship.[50] However, a large portion of lowland Limerick and north Kerry remained nominally under Anglo-Norman control.

In summary, by the reign of Henry VIII, two-thirds of Ireland was back in the hands of the Gaelic Irish.[51] This remarkable Gaelic revival posed a major frontier problem to the Dublin government by blurring the distinction between the *terra pacis* (land of peace) and the *terra guerre* (land of war).[52] The shifts in borders probably caused a major adjustment between the different lordships in their incessant competition for an extended sphere of influence. The extensive reconquest of territories must have been accompanied by a dramatic increase in income (and therefore the ability to build) of the ruling Gaelic families, because usually the territory conquered by the chief 'became the property of that chief to distribute as he pleased'.[53] The change may also have triggered major scrambles for resources within dominant families and lordships. Generally, an Irish lord fought not for possession of land but for dominion over people on whom he could enforce payment of tribute and services.[54]

---

45 Barry, *Medieval Ireland*, pp 171–3, 197, citing C. Empey, 'The Butler lordship in Ireland 1185–1514' (PhD, TCD, 1970); J. Lydon, 'The problem of the frontier in medieval Ireland', *Topic: a Journal of the Liberal Arts*, xiii (1967), pp 9–14; P.J. Duffy, 'The nature of the medieval frontier in Ireland', *Studia Hib.*, xxii–xxiii (1982–3), pp 21–38.   46 L. Price, 'The Byrnes in County Wicklow in the sixteenth century', *JRSAI*, iii (1933), pp 224–42, at p. 235.   47 Barry, *Medieval Ireland*, pp 171–3; see also *AFM*, iii, 563.   48 *Miscellany of the Irish Archaeological Society* (Dublin, 1844), p. 203; McNeill, *Anglo-Norman Ulster*, pp 119–20; Davis, *Castles of County Cavan*, p. 77; C. Parker, 'Cavan: a medieval border area' in R. Gillespie (ed.), *Cavan* (Dublin, 1995), p. 43.   49 Butler, 'Surrender and regrant', p. 104.   50 D. Ó Murchadha, 'Gaelic land tenure in county Cork: Uíbh Laoghaire in the seventeenth century' in P. O'Flanagan & C. Buttimer (eds), *Cork: history and society* (Dublin, 1993), pp 213–48.   51 W. Butler, *Confiscation in Irish history* (Dublin, 1917), p. 9.   52 Lydon, 'Frontier in medieval Ireland', p. 10.   53 Butler, 'Surrender and regrant', p. 104; J. O'Donoghue, *Historical memoirs of the O'Briens* (Dublin, 1860), p. 129.   54 K. Simms, 'Warfare in the medieval Gaelic lordships', *Ir. Sword*, xi (1975–6), pp 98–108.

The situation for many Gaelic lordships altered dramatically in the early sixteenth century when the Dublin government embarked on a series of punitive military campaigns followed by settlements and the introduction of English law. Whereas in the preceding century, Gaelic conflicts were conducted largely within and between family dynasties, except for an occasional incursion by a Lord deputy and his army, the expansion of English power outside the Pale now became a routine feature and provoked another series of conflicts, starting in the sixteenth century.[55]

Conflicts within and between Gaelic lordships

Figure 1.3 shows the distribution of Gaelic lordships in the later medieval period. The lordships varied greatly in size: among the largest were those of Mac Cárthaigh Mór in Kerry and Úi Néill in Tyrone (whose territories incorporated lesser lordships, not shown in Figure 1.3). Many smaller lordships were concentrated in the present counties of Tipperary and Offaly and in north-east Connacht. The distribution of lordships (Figure 1.3) may make it appear that a lordship was merely a geographic entity. The opposite was true: the term Irish lordship 'must not be conceived as a closed and defined territory but rather as a complex of rights, tributes and authority'.[56]

Gaelic society was characterised by incessant strife between rivals and successors within ruling kin groups, and the constant jostling for hegemony between various branches. These conflicts influenced the building and siting of castles within lordships. As an example of the persistence of conflict, over one-third (39%) of known ruling members of Cenel nEogain (Úi Néill) died at the hands of kinsmen or in internecine warfare in the period from 879 to 1607.[57] Rivalry within families was common, often leading to a permanent alienation of people from rights to their ancestral property.[58] In the late fourteenth and early fifteenth centuries in south Connacht, permanent divisions occurred among the principal lordly families. The MacDonaghs split into two separate lordships, Tirerrill and Corran, while the O'Haras bifurcated into the O'Hara Reagh and the O'Hara Boy. An annalist referred to the death of O'Hara, 'halfe king' of the western part of Luyny in 1449. The O'Dowds were also weakened by internal division and the territory of Carbury was divided among four branches of the O'Connors.[59] The chieftainship of Annaly (modern Longford) was split in two in 1445. Another division took place in 1489, once again creating two parts, one headed by the Ó Fearghail Bán, the other by Ó Fearghail Buí, who governed the lands north and south of Granard respectively.[60]

Further to the south-east, the Byrnes of Wicklow were divided into two branches, the Gabhal Dunluing and the Sliocht Donnchaidh.[61] Across the mountains, the division between the Úi Braonáin (O'Brennans) of Fassadinin (north Kilkenny)

---

55 Loeber, 'Geography and practice', this volume, pp 35–111; Ellis, *Reform and revival*, pp 661ff.   56 K.W. Nicholls, *Gaelic and gaelicised Ireland in the Middle Ages* (Dublin, 1972).   57 Cited in McNeill, *Anglo-Norman Ulster*, p. 104.   58 Simms, *Kings to warlords*, pp 58–9.   59 O'Dowd, *Early modern Sligo*, p. 19; *Miscellany*, p. 222.   60 *AFM*, iv, 941, 949, 1173. The main seats of the Ó Fearghail Bán were Boat, also known as Ban, Tully and Moat. The Ó Fearghail Buí resided at Tendick and Ardenragh: D. Gallagher, 'The plantation of Longford 1619–41' (MA, UCD, 1968), App. I–III.   61 Price, 'Byrnes in County Wicklow', p. 225.

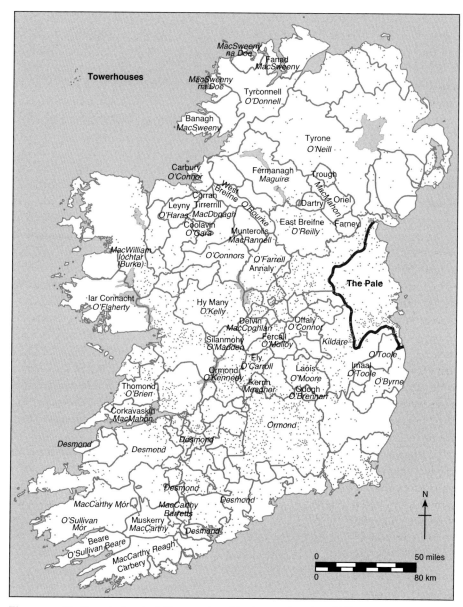

Figure 1.3 Gaelic and other lordships mentioned in the text (based on K.W. Nicholls, 'Lordships, *c.*1534', *NHI*, iii, Map 1).

prompted the formation of four branches. The primary branch did not own most land but occupied the area of greatest strategic and agricultural value, which was also safely distant from the unstable border area. Each of the four clans occupied its own centre.[62] In addition, several midland lordships were split into different

---

62 W. Nolan, *Fassadinin: land, settlement and society in south-east Ireland 1600–1850* (Dublin, 1979), pp 31–2.

branches. For example, the O'Melaghlin, chief of Clan-Colman (Westmeath) and overlord of Delvin MacCoghlan, partitioned the MacCoghlan lordship into three sub-lordships in the early sixteenth century.[63]

Many partitions took place in other lordships. By 1541, a government document noted the two O'Carrolls and the two O'Kennedys.[64] Two O'Molloys were established as chiefs in 1454 to govern Ferceall in south-western Offaly, one residing at Broughal, the other at either Ballyboy or Eglish.[65]

Conflicts and subsequent division of territories were not limited to smaller lordships. In 1385, after an intense conflict between two contestants, the O'Conor lordship in Connacht was divided in two, one headed by O'Conor Roe, the other by O'Conor Don. The O'Conor Don was then known as 'half king of Connaught'.[66] Whereas the main O'Conor seat had been Roscommon castle (built by the Anglo-Normans, but taken over by the O'Conors), the O'Conor Don resettled at Ballintober Castle (another Anglo-Norman stronghold), while the O'Conor Roe seated himself at Tulsk.[67]

Similarly, the powerful Úí Néill of Tyrone splintered into several branches, each with its own nucleus of settlement. The branch known as Clann Airt Óig was seated in the barony of Strabane (Tyrone), with fortresses at Castlederg and the crannóg of Loch Laoghaire, and later, Strabane castle.[68] An older branch, the Sliocht Airt, held its lands in the barony of Omagh with its stronghold of the same name. Another power base was the castle at Dungannon (in the barony of the same name), which contained lands of the richest agricultural potential and the highest population density.[69] Although partitions in many lordships could be enduring, some were temporary. For example, the distinction between the three MacCoghlan branches ceased in the second half of the sixteenth century when one family became dominant and produced a lineage of chieftains who ruled the whole lordship.[70]

Divisions of kingdoms and lordships had major consequences. Although the original chiefry castle may have been retained by one contestant, the other contestant built or occupied a chiefry castle as his principal residence (this must have had legal ramifications because castles of a chief, legally speaking, belonged to a lineage rather than to an incumbent under Gaelic law).

We can also assume that territorial defences would have to be redrawn when a lordship was divided. However, it is not clear to what extent internal defences

63 *AFM*, v, 1455; B. Mac Cuarta, 'Mathew De Renzy's letters on Irish affairs 1613–1620', *Anal. Hib.*, xxxiv (1987), pp 109–82, at p. 159.   64 *S.P.*, *Hen. VIII*, part 3, pp 348–50.   65 *AFM*, ii, 991.   66 C. O'Conor Don, *The O'Conors of Connaught* (Dublin, 1891), pp 150–1.   67 Ibid., p. 149.   68 Andrews, 'Mapping Ireland's cultural landscape', Fig. 2, p. 160.   69 Ibid., Plate 1, p. 163. P. Walsh, *The will and family of Hugh O'Neill, earl of Tyrone* (Dublin, 1930), pp 68–9; H. Morgan, *Tyrone's rebellion* (Dublin, 1993), pp 90–1; *AFM*, v, 1449; P. Robinson, 'The plantation of Co. Tyrone in the seventeenth century' (PhD, QUB, 1974), p. 70, Map 2.7. The earl of Tyrone's 'house' at Dungannon is noted in 1543 (*Calendar of the manuscripts of the marquis of Salisbury* (London, 1883), i, p. 21), but the castle was already in existence in 1505 (*AFM*, v, 1281).   70 L. Cox, 'The Mac Coghlans of Delvin Eathra', *Ir. Geneal.*, iv:6 (1973), pp 534–46, at pp 538–9; K.W. Nicholls, 'The MacCoghlans' in *Ir. Geneal.*, vi:4 (1983), pp 445–60, at p. 448.

between two lordships were needed once the major conflict had been resolved by the division. Still, defences were needed to thwart external attacks. In addition, some re-orientation of settlement may have been required, for either commercial or cultural reasons, particularly when two sites for the inauguration of lords and other community functions were needed.[71] An additional reason for castle building arose when branches or entire lineage groups were ousted from their ancestral lands. Gaelic lords occasionally expelled freeholders from their territory. Tadhg Ó Conchubhair (Teige O'Conor) and his kinsmen defeated the sons of Brian Ballagh in 1462, which was followed by their banishment and subsequent resettlement in Annaly (Longford), where O'Ferrall gave them lands for their cattle.[72] Similarly, the descendants of Maelmora of Mullagh (Cavan) were banished from their country and their lands were taken over by the O'Reillys. The *Annals of the Four Masters* recount that the sons of Glasny O'Reilly subsequently settled on this territory and built a castle there.[73] Sometimes those who had been banished were allowed to return, as happened to Felim Ó Ruairc (O'Rourke), whose castle at Castletown was demolished by Hugh O'Donnell in 1487. However, O'Donnell permitted Ó Ruairc to return to his country to make peace among the men of Breifne, and 'the country' (that is, the local people) was compelled to rebuild their castle. It must have been made fairly strong because it was retaken only after a long siege.[74]

That defences continued to be necessary is clear from the events that followed the division of the O'Conor Connacht kingdom in 1385. Ó Conchobhair Rua (O'Conor Roe) built the castle of Tulsk (Roscommon) in 1406 but it was demolished by hostile external forces in the following year. Subsequently, it was rebuilt, since the annals note that the castle and its 'prison' were demolished by the Burkes in 1485, but it must have been restored again because it was unsuccessfully besieged by O'Donnell in 1490.[75] The re-divisions in Sligo (and probably elsewhere) increased stability 'with the sub-branches of each ruling family becoming possessed of more definable territories and retaining the same land over centuries'.[76]

Can the friction within and between lordships explain the construction of towerhouses in Ireland? Lydon's explanation for the Anglo-Norman areas points to this: 'With the gradual growth of disorder, especially in areas not within the reach of Dublin, it became necessary for the manorial lords (and, presumably, for Gaelic lords) to be far more defense-conscious than had been the case in more settled times'.[77] Prior to the introduction of stone castles around 1400, the Irish lords relied on natural rather than man-made defences. However, wooden castles were built and used in medieval Gaelic Ireland. A study of their sites may force us to revise our explanations about the transition to stone castles.

---

71 For a general review of inauguration sites, which were sometimes situated near a chiefry castle, see E. FitzPatrick, 'The practice and siting of royal inauguration in medieval Ireland' (PhD, TCD, 1997), i, p. 104.   72 *AFM*, iv, 1019.   73 *AFM*, iv, 1135. I have been unable to identify this site.   74 *AFM*, iv, 1151, 1153.   75 *Misc. Ir. An.*, p. 181; *AC*, 401; *AFM*, iv, 1133, 1181, 1189, 1253; vi, 1937.   76 O'Dowd, *Early modern Sligo*, p. 19; *Miscellany*, p. 222.   77 J. Lydon, *Ireland in the later Middle Ages* (Dublin, 1973), p. 8.

Castle distribution

This section concerns the distribution of castles in the Gaelic areas of Ireland and focuses on regional differences. Unless specified, castles include both stone and wooden structures.[78] The map in *Atlas of the Irish rural landscape*, based on the Sites and Monument Records, also included documented sites, which is important because so many castles have disappeared in modern times (Figures 1.2–1.3). If we exclude those parts of Ireland that remained under the firm control of the English (the Pale around Dublin, counties Kildare and Kilkenny, and most of north Limerick), large numbers of towerhouses were situated in the Gaelic and Gaelicised parts of Ireland. Once existing, known and possible examples are mapped, the largest concentrations appear in the centre of the country, in Tipperary, Offaly and Laois (which were partly in Gaelic hands). Other sizeable concentrations occurred in Clare and Galway. By comparison, Ulster exhibits a much lower density of towerhouses. The value of this map (Figure 1.2) clearly lies in incorporating possible sites, because conclusions based solely on surviving specimens are unreliable. Certain areas had very few towerhouses, particularly south-central Ulster, consisting of Cavan, Fermanagh and Monaghan.[79] In addition, north Wexford and most of Wicklow had a particularly low density of towerhouses. The same was the case for large portions of Kerry, west Galway and west Mayo.

These conclusions align with contemporary information about the distribution of castles in certain areas. In Clare, an English survey in 1584 listed a staggering 165 castles, virtually all in Gaelic Irish hands. The survey may even have been an underestimate because 195 ruins and known sites were counted three centuries later, which may include castles built after 1584.[80] Many castles mentioned in the 1584 list were towerhouses, but it is unclear whether this was universal. Some were remarkable. In 1540, Edmund Sexton described Ballyvercolloman (Ballymaccolman) and Clonideralagh (Clonderlaw), two castles of the chief MacMahon in west Clare, as 'the fairest houses in Ireland'. The latter was characterised in 1682 as 'a very ancient castle and a house of great hospitality'.[81] Several other areas dominated by the Gaelic Irish had impressive numbers of castles. Lists for Mayo and Roscommon, dated 1573–4, itemise 136 and 69 castles, respectively.[82] A much smaller area, Ely O'Carroll, had forty-five castles around 1600.[83] South of Ely O'Carroll lay the barony of Ikerrin in north Tipperary; its archaeological survey listed sixteen castles, twelve occupied by the Gaelic Irish, principally the O'Meaghers.[84] Just north of

---

78 Craig, *Architecture of Ireland*, p. 95; Leask, *Irish castles*, pp 153–61; C. Ó Danachair, 'Irish towerhouses and their regional distribution', *Béaloideas*, xlv–xlvii (1974–9), pp 158–63; G. Stout & M. Stout, 'Early landscapes: from prehistory to Plantation' in Aalen, Whelan & Stout (eds), *Atlas of the Irish rural landscape*, Fig. 71. Cairns's map of stone castles in Co. Tipperary did not distinguish them by Gaelic lordships (*Irish towerhouses*, p. 4). **79** Craig, *Architecture of Ireland*, p. 94. **80** Leask's count of 225 castles may have included later structures (*Irish castles*, p. 154). **81** B. Ó Dalaigh (ed.), *The stranger's gaze: travels in County Clare 1534–1950* (Ennis, 1998), pp 4, 64. The castle was later demolished. **82** Leask, *Irish castles*, p. 159; Nicholls, 'Gaelic society', p. 406. **83** R. Loeber, 'The changing borders of the Ely O'Carroll lordship' in W. Nolan & T. O'Neill (eds), *Offaly: history and society* (Dublin, 1998), pp 287–318, see Fig. 9.2. **84** G. Stout, *Archaeological survey of the barony of Ikerrin* (Roscrea, 1984), pp 124–37.

Ikerrin, De Renzy counted twenty-eight castles in Delvin MacCoghlan in the early seventeenth century.[85] These contemporary counts, however, do not define castles or differentiate them from a variety of other structures.

Several areas exhibited a low density of stone castles. Bodley's survey of Maguire country (modern Fermanagh) in 1609 showed only four ruined castles (Enniskillen, Lisnaskea, Iniskeen, Belleek). These towerhouses were of recent vintage.[86] Enniskillen castle, seat of the Maguire chieftain, was probably the largest. Bodley's survey also confirmed the low density of castles in Tyrone, where ten castles were depicted, all occupied by the ruling Uí Néill. Prominent members of less dominant families living under the Uí Néill continued to reside in timber or wattle structures inside sod bawns. A powerful leader such as Ó Donghaile (O'Donnelly) occupied a ringfort, Fort O'Donnalie (later known as Castlecaulfield), shown on an early seventeenth-century map.[87]

Starting in the late 1610s, the Dublin government undertook several plantations in the Midlands, including Offaly, Longford and Leitrim, and in the south-east in Wexford and Wicklow. Pre-plantation surveys constitute unique records of Gaelic land division and settlement prior to the introduction of settlers and the building of their dwellings. A few pre-plantation surveys of south-west Offaly survive. One covers the barony of Ballyboy, which partly coincided with O'Molloy country. The map showed only four towerhouses, but recorded a substantial number of other settlements.[88] By contrast, Longford had a moderate number of castles: the pre-plantation survey in the 1620s record fifty-one towerhouses. A description of the county around this time mentions that 'manie of the principall natives have good ancient castles, and most have bawnes about them, but they are somewhat ruinous'.[89]

Architectural historians have calculated the density of castles per square mile and then compared the figures for different counties.[90] While it is illuminating to make quantitative comparisons, these exercises should calibrate landscape features (notably mountains, woods, lakes and bogs), because such characteristics limited habitable lands. Density levels remain to be computed for Gaelic lordships, and ideally should take into account other settlements of the later medieval period (crannógs, ringforts, moated sites).

There may be several reasons for these pronounced regional differences in the density of castles and other settlements. Areas that contained different, sometimes warring, branches of the same lineage needed reinforced dwellings more than areas that were homogeneous and peaceful. A low density of towerhouses in a given territory may also reflect a lack of resources in that area. In Monaghan, the absence

85 Mac Cuarta, 'De Renzy's letters', 128, 136, 139, 157, 176–7. 86 J.D. Johnston, 'The plantation of County Fermanagh 1610–1641: an archaeological and historical study' (MA, QUB, 1976), pp 11, 105. Known castles, notably Pettigoe and Lisgoole, are not shown on Bodley's map whose accuracy is debatable. 87 Robinson, 'Plantation of Co. Tyrone', pp 72–5; *AFM*, v, 1405; Andrews, 'Mapping Ireland's cultural landscape', p. 163; H. Bagenal, 'Marshal Bagenal's description of Ulster, anno 1586', *UJA*, ii (1854), pp 137–60. Higher counts for Tyrone may include British settlers' castles (Cairns, *Irish towerhouses*, p. 6). 88 PRO, MPF 268. 89 BL, Cotton, 1 Aug., i (14–48), ii (25, 26, 28); BL, Add. MS 4756, f 127v. 90 Craig, *Architecture of Ireland*, p. 95.

of castles and towerhouses indicates relative poverty.[91] However, any correlation between the density of stone castles and the wealth of a lordship (expressed, for example, in terms of armies maintained by Gaelic lords) is imperfect.[92] For instance, the largest armies in Ulster were under O'Neill and O'Donnell, but their territories contained relatively small numbers of stone castles. Another interpretation is that the building of stone castles was less common in heavily wooded areas such as north Wexford or the O'Molloy country in Offaly (baronies of Ballyboy, Ballycowan and Eglish), where the construction of wooden castles was presumably less costly than stone ones. There is no compelling single explanation for differences in the density of stone castles in Ireland; diverse explanations may apply to different regions.

Dating Gaelic castles

Architectural historians propose that castle building in stone by the Gaelic inhabitants post-dates the building of stone castles by Anglo-Norman settlers. Cairns stated that 'the towerhouse began in the fourteenth century as a form of Anglo-Norman settlement, and was adopted in the fifteenth century by Gaelic chieftains'.[93] As early as 1612, a similar conclusion was already voiced by Sir John Davies: the Irish 'never built any houses of brick or stone, some few religious houses excepted, before the reign of King Henry the Second' (*ob.* 1189). When the Gaelic Irish 'saw us [the English] build castles upon their borders, they have only, in imitation of us, erected some few piles for the captains [chieftains] of the country'.[94] How does this assertion compare with the documented evidence?

The heyday of Anglo-Norman castles was in the twelfth century and the first quarter of the thirteenth century.[95] The first 'castles' built by the Gaelic Irish were constructed in the twelfth century (this conclusion may need revision as fresh information becomes available). In 1125, well before the Anglo-Normans penetrated Connacht, the 'Connachtmen' erected three castles (caislen) at Dún Leodhar (Ballinasloe, Galway), Galway town and Cuil-maeile (Collooney, Sligo), but it is probable that these and several other early castles were constructed of timber.[96] Twenty-one years earlier, the Cullinane family had constructed a castle at Castlelyons in Cork.[97]

A few Gaelic castles were constructed of stone prior to the early fourteenth century. Ruaidhrí Ó Conchubhair (Roderic O'Connor) built a stone castle in 1161 which was considered a novel and extraordinary edifice and characterised as 'the

---

91 Duffy, 'Territorial organisation', p. 2.   **92** L. Price, 'Armed forces of the Irish chiefs in the early sixteenth century', *JRSAI*, lxii (1932), pp 201–7. I am indebted to Kevin Whelan for this source.   **93** Cairns, *Irish towerhouses*, p. 9; Leask, *Irish castles*, p. 75; T. Wood, *An inquiry concerning the primitive inhabitants of Ireland* (Cork, 1821), pp 254–6: he mentions some exceptions on p. 256.   **94** Davies, *Historical tracts*, p. 137.   **95** There is a useful survey listing castles up to 1216 in G.H. Orpen, 'Motes and Norman castles in Ireland', *EHR*, xii (1907), pp 228–54, 440–67. A survey of Anglo-Norman castles after that date is much needed, but see MacCurtain, 'Geraldine castles', pp 429–44; P. Holland, 'The Anglo-Normans and their castles in County Galway' in G. Moran & R. Gillespie (eds), *Galway: history and society* (Dublin, 1996), pp 1–25; G. Cunningham, *The Anglo-Norman advance into the south-west Midlands of Ireland 1185–1221* (Roscrea, 1987).   **96** *AFM*, ii, 1021; Leask, *Irish castles*, p. 6   **97** Wood, *Primitive inhabitants of Ireland*, p. 256.

wonderful castle'.[98] The great house of Aodh Ó Conchubhair (Hugh O'Connor) at Cloonfree (Roscommon), according to a praise poem, was built by a mason shortly prior to 1306, but it had been planned by Aodh himself. However, the poet described the house as a 'brugh slatach', suggesting that the main building was not a masonry structure but one made of rods or wattle-and-daub. In the same period, the first known stone castle in Clare was built at Ennis between 1283 and 1306 by the chief Torlogh O'Brien. A poem in translation recounts:

> Torlogh, for wealth royal seats renowned,
> Who first a fortress built of stone did found;
> In Ennis town upon the western side,
> It braves all force so strongly fortified.[99]

Thus some stone castles were constructed by Irish lords before the early fourteenth century. However, the chronology of the Gaelic towerhouses built of stone remains obscure and it cannot be calibrated against a chronology of earlier Irish defensive residences. Earlier structures may have included moated sites, fortalices, rectangular earthworks and ringforts, and these are not discussed here.[100]

Architectural historians identify a 'hiatus' in the Anglo-Irish building of major stone castles in Ireland from the end of the first quarter of the fourteenth century into the following century.[101] Alongside this hiatus for domestic architecture, few ecclesiastical buildings can be dated to the second half of the fourteenth century, with a major lacuna existing for half a century. The same conclusion applies to Gaelic castle building: only a handful of castles were built in the last quarter of the fourteenth century.

Before that, several Irish chieftains had exchanged their native residences for stone castles originally built by Anglo-Norman lords. The O'Conor Don occupied Ballintober Castle (Roscommon); the O'Connor Sligo lived at Sligo Castle (Sligo) from at least 1371 onward, while the O'Reillys became resident at Clogh Oughter Castle (Cavan) sometime before 1369.[102] In the course of this change, the Irish must have mastered siege techniques, initially without the use of guns. In summary, several Irish chieftains and their descendants were already highly familiar with stone castles before they embarked on building towerhouses.

A remarkable renaissance in Gaelic activity took place during the fourteenth and fifteenth centuries, which encompassed castles, friaries and parish churches.[103] Appendix 1.1 lists Gaelic castles and structures from between 1370 and 1600 for which there is evidence of the year of building or an ultimate date of construction as recorded in the annals, other written sources, or through archaeological investigation.[104] Documentation of dates of building (or rebuilding) between

---

98 Wood, *Primitive inhabitants of Ireland*, p. 256, does not specify its location.   99 O'Donoghue, *O'Briens*, p. 119.   100 Cairns, *Irish towerhouses*, p. 9; Barry, *Medieval Ireland*, pp 85–8.   101 Ibid., p. 68.   102 O'Conor, *O'Conors*, p. 149; *AFM*, iii, 647, 653.   103 R. Stalley, 'Irish Gothic and English fashion' in J. Lydon (ed.), *The English in medieval Ireland* (Dublin, 1984), pp 65–86, at pp 79–80.   104 I excluded vague references to, for example, 'a sixteenth-century castle'. I also excluded references to castles noted in annals and contemporary sources but lacking their builder's name or other means to estimate a building date.

Figure 1.4 Clogh Oughter Castle, County Cavan, occupied before 1369 by the Ó Raghallaigh (O'Reilly) family.

1370 and 1600 exists for seventy-nine structures, which is a mere fraction of all known Gaelic castles. Very few Gaelic castles are documented for the first three-quarters of the fourteenth century.[105] There were notable geographical differences in the construction of castles. Almost all datable castles built between 1377 and 1440 were located west of a diagonal line running from Clare to Longford.[106] This chronology conforms with the heyday of the building of friaries, many founded by castle building chieftains, and which also largely took place west of this diagonal (there are some exceptions).

The first castle noted in this list is Lissardowlin (Longford), built in 1377 by Seán Ó Fearghail (John O'Farrell), Lord of Annaly. Two other castles were also built between 1377 and 1400. The first twenty-five years of the fifteenth century saw the building of sixteen castles. Following this peak, castle building remained stable up to 1600, at an average of almost seven castles per quarter century (range: six to ten). Thus, castle building and founding of friaries coincided in the west of Ireland, where they were often accomplished by the same individuals.

The relatively late development of castle building east of the diagonal line is confirmed by dated castles in Delvin MacCoghlan (west Offaly): with few exceptions, these date from Elizabethan times. The MacDonnells built castles along the Antrim coast, sometimes on older foundations, from 1540 to 1590. The influx of Scots into the area began slightly earlier: English state papers recorded the settlement of Scots in Ulster in 1542, and relate that they 'purchaseth castles and piles upon the sea co[a]ste there', which redefined Ulster as a border area between England and

---

105 But see Cairns, *Irish towerhouses*, p. 27.   **106** H. Leask, *Irish churches and monastic buildings* (Dundalk, 1978), iii, pp 89ff; A. Gwynn & R. Hadcock, *Medieval religious houses, Ireland* (Dublin, 1970); S. Duffy (ed.), *Atlas of Irish history* (Dublin, 1997), p. 45.

Scotland.[107] In addition, the Scots built new castles: two were constructed by Sorley Boy MacDonnell and his brother Colla in the late 1540s or early 1550s, and two more by Sir James MacDonnell in 1560, all in north Antrim.

The conclusion that castle building emerged first in the west of Ireland requires qualification. Firstly, castles continued to be built in the west after the 1440s; secondly, castles were built to the east of the diagonal at a relatively early date in a few instances. Thus, conclusions about temporal and geographical trends of castle building should only be advanced with considerable caution. The list of documented castles is small and probably unrepresentative (for example, castles in Clare are over-represented). However, dating is important because it can open up comparative studies of dated structures with undated ones, leading to the approximate dating of some of the latter. In addition, morphological and structural changes took place over more than two centuries of castle building which can be further explored in future studies.

Finally, the absence of dated castles in some areas can be linked to other information. For example, we know that the O'Connor lordship of east Offaly was in decline from the second half of the fifteenth century. Many of its castles were destroyed in the first half of the next century; a 1560s map showed the former lordship pockmarked by ruined castles.[108] Only a single instance is known of a castle newly built by the O'Connor chieftain before 1537, when it was captured and destroyed by the English.[109]

In summary, these records counter the assertion that Gaelic castle building started in the late fourteenth century and was adopted in the fifteenth century by Gaelic chieftains. Instead, some stone castles were built by the Gaelic Irish as early as the twelfth and thirteenth centuries. A Gaelic revival in castle building initially occurred during the last quarter of the fourteenth century but it accelerated in the first decades of the fifteenth century and then persisted at a slightly lower rate until the end of the sixteenth century. It is less clear, however, how the building of castles in Gaelic areas compared to castle building in English-dominated areas during these centuries.

Distinctive architectural features of Gaelic castles
The study of unique architectural features of Gaelic castles is still in its infancy and as a consequence the following statements should be regarded as highly tentative. The Irish never built large keepless castles with multiple wall towers of the type represented by Roscommon and Ballymote (Sligo).[110] Compared to Anglo-Norman

107 *S.P., Hen. VIII*, iii, p. 432. M. Perceval-Maxwell, *The Scottish migration to Ulster in the reign of James I* (London, 1973), p. 21; Hill, *MacDonnells of Antrim*, pp 36ff; H. Kearney, *The British Isles: a history of four nations* (Cambridge, 1989), p. 103.   **108** E. Curtis (ed.), 'The survey of Offaly in 1550', *Hermathena*, xx (1929), pp 312–52: C. Ó Cleirigh, 'The O'Connor Faly lordship of Offaly 1395–1513', *PRIA*, xcvi:4, C (1996), pp 87–102, at pp 97–100; F. Fitzsimons, 'The lordship of O'Connor Faly 1520–1570' in Nolan & O'Neill (eds), *Offaly*, pp 207–42; J.H. Andrews & R. Loeber, 'An Elizabethan map of Leix and Offaly: cartography, topography and architecture' in Nolan & O'Neill (eds), *Offaly*, pp 243–85, Plate 8.1 on p. 263.   **109** *CSPI, 1509–73*, p. 27.   **110** Leask, *Irish castles*, p. 69. Leask stated that Ballintubber (Ballintober) was built *c.*1300 by the O'Conors but it was actually built by Richard de Burgh (O'Conor, *Archaeology of rural settlement*, p. 76).

castles, Gaelic castles had some unique structural features. In Ulster, and possibly elsewhere, a Gaelic towerhouse often had a mural staircase running in the thickness of the wall around two sides of the tower, in contrast to the usual circular newel stairs (although these can certainly be seen in Gaelic castles).[111] A castle type emerged in the Gaelic Midlands, probably in the sixteenth century, without main vault(s), with wooden floors throughout, but protected by a narrow vaulted area on the ground floor near the entrance, presumably to prevent attackers from setting fire to the castles during a siege (for example, Castle Armstrong and Esker, both in Offaly).[112] Furthermore, bartizans protruding from the corners halfway up the wall (for example, Ballymalis in Kerry and Aughnanure in Galway) mostly appear in Gaelic areas.[113]

The issue of stylistic differences between Gaelic and Anglo-Norman architecture should be considered. When English authority waned in late medieval Ireland, respect for English fashions in ecclesiastical architecture waned with it. Thus, whereas the Perpendicular style of architecture flourished in the Pale, ecclesiastical architecture developed in a more independent Decorated form in Gaelic Ireland.[114] Many Irish friaries were built during the fifteenth and sixteenth centuries close to their seats under the sponsorship of Gaelic chiefs. Stylistic links between decorations used in ecclesiastical and domestic Gaelic architecture remain to be studied and these need to be compared to similar links in English areas. Regional styles definitely emerged, particularly in Antrim where the MacDonnells built castles in the second half of the sixteenth century 'after a design typical of the coastal castles of the Scottish Highlands', which 'in some cases [was] copied by native Irish, who, by alliance with the Antrim Scots, maintained a footing there'.[115] A final distinction concerns the crannógs that were typical of Gaelic Ireland in the northern third of the island.[116] Thus, several architectural features distinguish Gaelic from English towerhouses, and require further study. Better ranges of dates need to be assigned to 'late' elements of castles. Examples include wooden floors in the absence of vaults, stylistic features of carved decorations, types of embrasures (different for cross-bows and muskets),[117] gun ports, fireplaces instead of a central hearth, chimney stacks, and the presence of gables and discontinuous wall-walks.

The architectural study of Gaelic castles should be considered against the backdrop of the architecture that it replaced. With so few comparative studies available,[118] it is hard to judge the extent to which stone castles represented

---

111 A. Rowan, *North-west Ulster* (London, 1979), 27–8. However, newel stairs were also inserted into castles built by the Irish.　112 N. Fennelly, 'An analysis of the towerhouses in a County Offaly study area' (MA, UCC, 1997), p. 231. Narrow vaulting is also evident in several churches in the area. Examples are Kilbride (in Kilcoursey) and Rathlihen (in Ferceall) which have vaulting for that part of the church in which the priest lived: E. FitzPatrick & C. O'Brien, *The medieval churches of County Offaly* (Dublin, 1998), pp 114, 127, 135–6.　113 Craig, *Architecture of Ireland*, p. 99.　114 Stalley, 'Irish Gothic', pp 85–6.　115 H.C. Lawlor, *Ulster: its archaeology and antiquities* (Belfast, 1928), p. 149.　116 O'Sullivan, 'Crannógs in late medieval Gaelic Ireland'. In a rare instance, the Anglo-Normans built crannógs (O'Conor, *Archaeology of rural settlement*, p. 80). There is a national map of crannógs in *Atlas of rural Ireland*, p. 49.　117 Lawlor, 'Ulster archaeology', p. 129.　118 T. O'Keeffe, *Barryscourt Castle and the Irish towerhouse* (Dublin, 1997), pp 12–13.

improvements in domestic comfort or defensive features, compared to earlier structures such as crannógs or wooden castles. Given that halls adjoining Gaelic stone castles were often constructed of mud and wattle, it is quite possible that older building traditions persisted.

Gaelic social strata and castle building

A more nuanced understanding of Gaelic castle building and the siting of castles can be gained by considering social strata in Gaelic society. There were three types of rulers: first, an overlord whose authority over several other lordships was on a provincial level (for example, the chief O'Neill); second, the ur-rí, or sub-king, supreme in his own area, but who owed duties to an overlord; third, the lord of a tuath, paramount within his tuath, but who owed duties to the ur-rí.[119] At each level, the lord lived in a timber, wattle or mud house within a fortified enclosure, or resided in a stone castle.

Architectural historians have rarely established the hierarchical organisation of Gaelic settlements and castles, first on the level of the provincial overlord, second on the level of a sub-king and third on the level of an individual lordship. On the last level, passes into a lordship had to be protected against intrusion from other lordships. On the second and also perhaps the first level, a lord could possess and ward castles outside of his own lordship by gaining possession of castles in inferior lordships. Thus, a network of castles could exist within and outside of a lordship, presented schematically in Figure 1.4.

Castles outside dominant lordships   Under O'Donnell's rule, his overlordship was imposed on other family groups through the occupation of castles and annual visits to repress opposition. In 1539, a year after the chief had captured Sligo Castle, Manus O'Donnell, a man of Renaissance qualities, concluded an agreement with Thady O'Conor Sligo concerning the government of the town of Sligo: O'Donnell stipulated that he was to have the 'small tower' of Sligo in which he would place his own officers 'and keep his own documents',[120] presumably leaving the greater castle of Sligo in O'Conor's hands. In a similar manner, the lords of Tyrone maintained a fort and constable at Castle Roe inside O'Cahan's territory to manage O'Neill's share of the lucrative Bann fishery.[121] Thus, territorial expansion by an Irish lord was accompanied by the acquisition and selective occupation of castles for strategic or economic reasons.[122]

The process by which territorial dominance took place, leading to the establishment of castles outside a lord's territory, is not always clear. A survey of Clare castles in 1584 provides significant insights into individuals who owned multiple castles both

119 Hayes-McCoy, 'Gaelic Ireland', p. 48.   **120** Cited in O'Conor, *O'Conors*, pp 180–1; B. Bradshaw, 'Manus "The magnificent": O'Donnell as renaissance prince' in A. Cosgrove & D. McCartney (eds), *Studies in Irish history* (Dublin, 1997), pp 15–36.   **121** Morgan, *Tyrone's rebellion*, p. 88.   **122** C. Breen, 'The maritime cultural landscape in medieval Gaelic Ireland' in Duffy, Edwards and FitzPatrick (eds), *Gaelic Ireland*, pp 418–35; MacCurtain, 'Geraldine castles', p. 439; *AU*, iii, 175, for another example.

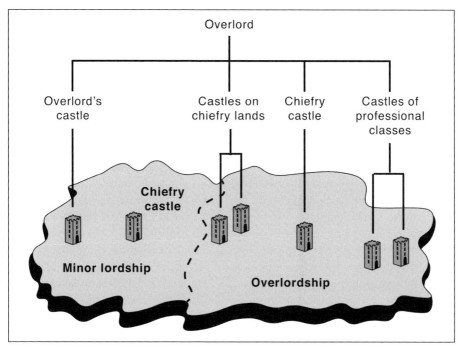

Figure 1.4 A schematic representation of castle ownership and location.

inside and outside their core territory. The earl of Thomond and his son held eleven castles dispersed over half of the baronies in the county. These included the major castles of Clonroad, Bunratty and Clare. Significantly, several remaining castles were situated in baronies dominated by other chiefs, as, for example, in the barony of Dangan West, dominated by the Mac Conmara (MacNamaras).[123]

A similar network of castles could be found at the level of sub-lords. O'Connor Sligo, despite his subjugation by, and loss of a castle to, the O'Donnells, retained his own strategic network of castles, as well as castles in every other lordship that he dominated. Installing wardens to safeguard castles outside his lordship was necessary to exercise more permanent control.[124] When subjugated families became more independent, they presumably were in a position to repossess these castles.

Castles and settlements in a lordship There are several ways of examining the distribution of castles within lordships. One is to map castles as a function of geographic features. A more useful exercise is to examine the functional relationships between castles. For instance, how many castles were 'owned' by a chieftain, and what was his relationship to the individuals living in them? How many castles had come to him by confiscation from weaker families within the lordship? Did a chieftain actively build castles for his dependents? Did gallowglasses, poets and chroniclers build their own castles? What was the relationship between the buildings

123 *AFM*, v, 1563, 1641; P. White, *History of Clare and the Dalcassian clans of Tipperary, Limerick and Galway* (Dublin, 1893), p. 394. 124 O'Dowd, *Early modern Sligo*, pp 18, 22, 66.

of the dominant lord and those of inferior families living in the same tuath? Sir John Davies argued that only chieftains built stone castles in Gaelic society in the early seventeenth century, and that no other 'particular person' ever built 'any stone or brick house for his private habitation'.[125]

At the beginning of the seventeenth century, there were at least forty-five castles in the lordship of Ely O'Carroll, of which nineteen (42%) were on the O'Carroll demesne.[126] Dymmok observed in 1599 that Ely O'Carroll had 'small piles of little importance, the chiefest whereof is Limwaddon [Leap Castle]'. This chiefry castle, although large in comparison to other surviving towerhouses in the lordship, was probably trumped by Birr Castle, which dates back to the Anglo–Norman period. The precise function of the many castles on the O'Carroll demesne lands remains unclear. It is likely that members of the O'Carroll family occupied many castles on the chief's demesne lands.[127] At least some tánaistí held their own castles. For example, the tánaiste Seán Ó Néill died at Ceann Aird (Kinard, close to the present Caledon in Tyrone).[128] Each tánaiste, similar to each lord, had property assigned to him in demesne by virtue of his office.[129]

In the case of the MacCoghlan lordship of Delvin MacCoghlan in west Offaly, it is possible to partially reconstruct how the chieftain acquired castles from a weaker branch of the family. When De Renzy listed the castles of Sir John MacCoghlan in the early seventeenth century, he included, amongst others, Raghra, Kilcummin and Fadden. These castles originally belonged to the Sliocht Feargal branch of the MacCoghlans and they must have been seized following their banishment from the lordship in the early sixteenth century.[130]

In several lordships, we know that the professional classes, including the brehons, chroniclers and superior craftsmen, lived in their own ringforts or castles close to the chiefry castle and sometimes held their own freeholds.[131] By the end of the sixteenth century, a strong freeholder interest had emerged in several Gaelic lordships.[132] Butler concluded that 'the chiefs came to have under them large bodies of dependents, who were somewhat in the position of feudal vassals, and who were not connected by ties of blood with the original clan'. For example, at the beginning of the seventeenth century, Donnell Gallocar (Domhnall Ó Gallchobhair), one of O'Donnell's chief counsellors, resided in a 'fort' at Ballakit (presumably in Donegal).[133]

Some freeholders were members of the dominant family, but most belonged to subordinate families who rendered economic and military services to the principal lords.[134] In Ely O'Carroll, ancient non-ruling families, such as the McGillefoyles,

125 Davies, *Historical tracts*, p. 137.   126 Loeber, 'Ely O'Carroll', Fig. 9.2. The 42% of castles on demesne lands reflected the fact that the demesne lands constituted 40% of all profitable lands in Ely O'Carroll.   127 J. Dymmok, *A treatice on Ireland* (Dublin, 1843), p. 15. The castle had been conveyed by the O'Carroll family to the earl of Ormond in 1594: E. Curtis (ed.), *Calendar of Ormond deeds* (Dublin, 1943), vi, p. 76.   128 Walsh, *O'Neill*, p. 63.   129 Hayes-McCoy, 'Gaelic society', p. 48.   130 Mac Cuarta, 'De Renzy letters'; Cox, 'MacCoghlans', pp 29, 539.   131 Hayes-McCoy, 'Gaelic Ireland', p. 49.   132 Brady, 'Decline', p. 102; Pawlisch, *Sir John Davies*, p. 79.   133 Butler, 'Surrender and regrant', p. 102; G. Hill, *Plantation papers* (Belfast, 1889), i, p. 145.   134 Duffy, 'Territorial organisation', p. 7.

enjoyed freehold status and lived in a castle.[135] The numbers of freeholders within a lordship could be sizeable. At the time of the plantation in north Wexford in the early seventeenth century, 667 individuals claimed freehold out of an estimated population of 15,000.[136] The plantation of counties Longford and Leitrim listed 142 and 151 natives, respectively, who received lands, which included a few Old English and even fewer New English.[137] The term 'freeholder' in Gaelic Ireland represented attempts by English officials to calibrate the Gaelic system to English landholding structures.[138] While their numbers in Gaelic areas varied widely, freeholders constituted a substantial portion of the upper strata in Gaelic society.

Within a lordship, some were more protected than others from the encroachment of ruling families. For example, the dominant family in Fermanagh was Mag Uighir (Maguire). The smaller lineage groups, however, were more numerous as holders of spiritual lands, usually as erenaghs, which may have shielded them from total domination by the Maguires.[139] Some freeholders built castles on the church lands, which could then function as buffer zones between rival chiefs, because they carried with them the right of sanctuary,[140] and thereby could offer lands and residency for less powerful families. In Ely O'Carroll, Liscloony Castle was built by Melaghlin O'Dalaghan in 1556, whose family originally had come into Delvin as 'churchmen'. In 1620, this castle was described as built 'uppon a church wall', and a 'fine and stately seat of a castle … English-like seated with a fine parke neare it and goodly meddows belonging to it uppon the Shenen side'.[141] One castle in Clare was owned in 1584 by Charles Cahane (Keane) 'by inheritance', in his function as coarb to a monastery.[142]

In some lordships, tax-free land was set aside for poets, historians and gallowglasses (professional soldiers of Scottish origin).[143] Several Mac Suibhne (MacSweeneys), gallowglasses under O'Donnell held castles on the coast of Donegal, such as Doe Castle and Rathmullan Castle, which was Mac Suibhne Fanad's principal residence.[144] In Clare, Eoghan Mac Suibhne (Owen MacSwyne) owned three castles in 1584 under Sir Donel O'Brien.[145] A surviving gallowglass castle at Tinnakill (Laois) was built by John Carragh MacDonnell about 1450.[146]

Little is known about the housing of the professional classes such as brehons, physicians, coarbs and poets. When John MacClancy, chief brehon to the earl of

---

135 It is unclear to what extent an interrelated network of castles existed within a lordship. While some chiefry castles may have been protected by other castles, this remains unproven.   136 Butler, 'Surrender and regrant', p. 103.   137 TCD, MS 672, f. 129v; BL, Add. MS 4756, f. 130.   138 Duffy, 'Territorial organisation', p. 8.   139 Johnston, 'Fermanagh', p. 7.   140 Robinson, 'Plantation of Co. Tyrone', p. 62.   141 *AFM*, v, 1543; Mac Cuarta, 'De Renzy's letters', pp 170, 173, 176. De Renzy, in contrast to the Four Masters, assigned the building of the castle to Lochlainn Óg Ó Dalaghan. The present ruins date from the late seventeenth century: see C. O'Brien & P. Sweetman, *Archaeological inventory of County Offaly* (Dublin, 1997), pp 175–6.   142 White, *History of Clare*, pp 208, 396.   143 Simms, *Kings to warlords*, p. 87; G.A. Hayes-McCoy, *Scots mercenary forces in Ireland 1565–1603* (Dublin, 1937).   144 G.A. Hayes-McCoy (ed.), *Ulster and other Irish maps c.1600* (Dublin, 1964), p. 27; *AFM*, v, 1335. Niall Mór Mac Suibhne (MacSweeney) died in 1524 at his castle of Rahin (Donegal) (*AFM*, v, 1375).   145 White, *History of Clare*, p. 397.   146 Borrowes, 'Tennekille Castle'.

Desmond, died in 1578, his eulogy claimed that 'there was no son of a lay brehon in Ireland in this time who had better tillage or a better house than he'.[147] The Ó Cléirigh family of hereditary chroniclers and historians were freeholders in Donegal for several centuries. Tadhg Cam Ó Cléirigh (*ob.* 1492) had three famous sons and annalists, Tuathal, Giolla Riabhach and Diarmaid, 'by whom the stone houses were erected at Cull Barrainn' (Kilbarron). The new building presumably replaced an earlier mud or timber building, because their grandfather, Diarmaid of the 'Three Schools', had maintained schools of literature, history and poetry there.[148] Remains on the site consist of the Ó Cléirigh gatehouse, keep and bawn, situated on a precipitous promontory on the seacoast.[149]

Chiefry castles   Two types of castles were especially contested and besieged: castles on the borders between major lordships (such as, for example, Sligo Castle and Ballyshannon, between counties Sligo and Donegal), and chiefry castles. A chiefry castle was most likely to be besieged by native contestants or English forces seeking to dislodge and then kill the chieftain. It is therefore unsurprising that Irish chieftains were among the first to build stone castles for their protection. Many dated castles (Appendix 1.1) were built by Gaelic chieftains. Thus, chieftains rather than lesser freeholders spearheaded the development of castle building in Ireland from the late fourteenth century onwards. Currently, we lack published lists of the main castles in which the various chiefs lived. Even this superficially simple topic is fraught with complications. Although there was considerable continuity of the chief's residence across different generations of chiefs, the designated chiefry castle might change in certain cases following conflicts between different members of the ruling family and the division of territories. Chiefry castles were often the largest structures. Examples include Leap Castle of the Carroll chiefs, and Blarney Castle, seat of the Mac Cárthaigh Mór, reflecting the peak of wealth within each lordship. There must be a correlation between the sophistication of a chiefry castle and the wealth generated from demesne lands. For example, Mac Cárthaigh Mór held at least half of his lordship as demesne lands.[150] In Ely O'Carroll, 40% of all profitable lands belonged to the chief's demesne, and much of it had a higher value than the remaining lands.[151]

Warfare externally (between lordships) and internally (through succession conflicts) ensured that the chief (but also the tánaiste) needed to live in a highly defensible castle. Leap Castle was built on an impregnable position on a high rocky ridge and defended on its sloping side by several lines of earthworks and towers, traces of which remain.[152] When the castle was taken by the earl of Kildare in 1516, an Irish annalist noted 'there was scarcely any castle of that period better fortified and

---

147 *AFM*, v, 1711.   148 P. Walsh, *The Ó Cléirigh family of Tír Conaill* (Dublin, 1938), p. 33.   149 B. Lacy, *Archaeological survey of County Donegal* (Lifford, 1983), pp 359–60.   150 Hayes-McCoy, 'Gaelic Ireland', p. 55.   151 Loeber, 'Ely O'Carroll', p. 300. At the beginning of the seventeenth century, Sir John MacCoghlan controlled 20 out of 62 (32%) ploughlands in Delvin MacCoghlan (PRO, SP 46/90, f. 131).   152 N.D. Atkinson, 'The plantation of Ely O'Carroll' (MA, TCD, 1955), p. 5.

defended'.[153] The lower portion of Blarney Castle was built with 3.7m thick walls,[154] presumably strong enough to withstand battery by cannons, and that thickness must also have impeded the undermining of the structure in the course of a siege. The first known siege of a castle by cannon in Ireland took place at Balrath (Westmeath) in 1488; others quickly followed, including the chiefry castle of the O'Conors at Tulsk (Roscommon) in 1498.[155] Chiefry castles were not built to withstand cannon warfare, and at best were fortified with embankments, such as those at Leap Castle.

Feuds within a lordship sometimes forced chiefs to reside in different strongholds. For example, Maolrunaidh Ó Cearbhuill is described as of Clonlisk (Offaly), but he resided more commonly at Modreeny in Ormond (north Tipperary), an area into which the O'Carrolls expanded in the sixteenth century.[156]

Builders of multiple castles Some Gaelic chieftains, because of their territorial and economic power and their strategic needs for protection, were among the most prolific castle builders inside their lordships. For example, Turlough MacCoghlan, chief of the MacCoghlans, built the castles of Fadden and Kincora in west Offaly before 1520.[157] Sir John MacCoghlan, of a different branch of the MacCoghlans, died in 1590 and the annals eulogised him: 'there was not a man of his property who had better furnished or more commodious courts, castles and comfortable seats'.[158] According to a late eighteenth-century report, Delvin MacCoghlan 'abounds with ruins of the MacCoghlan's castles, all have Latin inscriptions showing that they were built in Elizabethan times'.[159] Although this may be an overstatement, the MacCoghlan chieftain certainly exerted direct control over several castles. In the early seventeenth century, John MacCoghlan owned at least eight and possibly eleven of twenty-eight castles in the area.[160]

A chieftain's desire for castle building within a lordship had several motivations, such as the need for comfort and accommodation for himself and his wife, and protection for his kin group. Some building of stone castles was undertaken to replace residences on an island or a crannóg. Shortly before the end of the fourteenth century, the O'Reilly chief moved his principal residence from the island fortress of Clogh Oughter (originally an Anglo-Norman castle) to the more accessible castle at Tullymongan, close to Cavan town. A 1591 plan shows Tullymongan as a square towerhouse; it was considered sufficiently important to be confiscated and reused as part of the plantation of Ulster in the early seventeenth century.[161]

---

153 *AFM*, v, 1337. **154** Leask, *Irish castles*, pp 113, 115. **155** G.A. Hayes-McCoy, 'The early history of guns in Ireland', *JGAHS*, xviii (1938–9), pp 43–65. **156** Nicholls, 'Gaelic landownership in Tipperary' in Nolan & McGrath (eds), *Tipperary*, pp 92–103; Loeber, 'Ely O'Carroll'. **157** *AFM*, v, 1341, 1345. Kincora was built on the site of an older castle of alleged Anglo-Norman origin; its bawn was built by Séamus Óg Mac Cochlainn (Mac Cuarta, 'De Renzy's letters', p. 122, p. 177; Fennelly, 'Towerhouses in Co. Offaly', p. 179). **158** *AFM*, v, 1349; vi, 1893. The text has been translated as 'mansions, castles and good dwelling houses' (Cox, 'MacCoghlans', p. 540). **159** C. Coote, *General view of the agriculture and manufactures of the King's County* (Dublin, 1801), p. 103. **160** Mac Cuarta, 'De Renzy's letters', pp 128, 136, 139, 157, 176–7. **161** Davies, 'Castles of County Cavan', p. 89; *AU*, iii, 47; Hill, *Plantation of Ulster*, p. 412. The castle and adjacent monastery were burnt by the English in 1468 *(AFM,* iv,

Women's jointure was recognised in Gaelic society,[162] and this could extend to castles and lands. Two date stones testify that Coole Castle (Offaly) was built by Sir John MacCoghlan for his wife. The castle was probably constructed in two stages, with the second stage in 1575 (according to the date stone in the upper chamber). As recorded on another stone (since removed), it was built for Sir John's wife, Sabia (Sadhb) O'Dallaghan, 'on condition that she should have it for [her] lifetime, and afterwards each of her sons according to their seniority'. The towerhouse shows finely carved decoration of a quality not often replicated elsewhere, and appropriately Sir John left it in his will of 1590 to his wife.[163] Another example of a woman occupying a castle is depicted on a late sixteenth-century map of Munster. It shows the castle of Iwogh (Castle Lough?) occupied by the mother of the earl of Clancarty (a Mac Carthaigh Mór).[164] The 'chiefe house' of O'Donnell's mother in the early seventeenth century was near Lough Foyle, at a site called M'Gevyvelin (now Mongavlin, Donegal) (Figure 1.6).[165]

In rare cases, Irish chieftains were forced to construct successive castles for their own protection. The history of Brian O'Connor, chief of Ua Conchobair Failghe (O'Connor Faly) in east Offaly in the first half of the sixteenth century, is illustrative. His castle and 'chieff place' at Monasteroris in east Offaly, 'estemyed the strongist holde withyn the Iryshry', was successfully besieged with cannon by the English in 1521. Ó Conchobair (Connor) subsequently moved his household further west and by 1537 he had built a towerhouse and bawn in a 'great marsh' at Daingean in the same county, fortified behind 'great ditches and waters'. This castle, considered by the English 'of such strength as we have not hitherto seen the like in this land', was in turn besieged with cannon and taken by the English in 1537, after which O'Connor was again forced to flee and establish himself and his followers even further west. A government survey of 1550 noted that at Inchelough carr (now the drained lake of Lough Coura in west Offaly), 'there is a fast i[s]land that no man can cume unto but by bo[a]te & reputed for a verye fast place, having a greate wo[o]d & moche mo[o]re & bogge, where O'Connor had his chiefe refuge all the tyme of his exile, where are two messuages [buildings]'.[166]

Sometimes, as part of a strategic retreat, Gaelic lords destroyed their own castles to prevent the structures falling into the hands of their enemies.[167] Dungannon Castle (Tyrone), Hugh O'Neill's 'principal house', which he had 'well builded' and covered with lead, and for which he purchased furniture in London in 1590,

1057). The O'Reillys repaired the castle and the monastery afterwards, since their chief Turlough O'Reilly died at the castle in 1487 (*AFM*, iv, 1147; v, 1263). Cavan Castle, presumably the same site, was reduced by the earl of Kildare in 1514 (*AC*, 625). **162** O'Dowd, *Early modern Sligo*, p. 73. **163** Mac Cuarta, 'De Renzy's letters', p. 139, describes the two wives; for John MacCoghlan's will, see J. Monahan, *Records relating to the diocese of Ardagh and Clonmacnoise* (Dublin, 1886), pp 62–4. **164** *Cal. Carew MSS* 625, f. 27. **165** Hill, *Plantation papers*, p. 144. **166** *S.P. Hen. VIII*, iii, pp 76, 79, 441; *CSPI, 1509–73*, pp 26–7; Curtis, 'Offaly in 1550', pp 312–52; PRO, MPF 268, f. 260; Kerrigan, *Castles and fortifications*, pp 3, 30; Hayes-McCoy, 'Guns in Ireland', p. 56. On Brian O'Connor, see Fitzsimons, 'O'Connor Faly', pp 207–42. For the round castle on the former island in Lough Cara, see Fennelly, 'Towerhouses in Co. Offaly', pp 133–4. **167** *AC*, 613.

Figure 1.6 Mongavlin Castle, County Donegal (NLI).

was pulled down by him five years later to prevent its capture by the Lord deputy Russell.[168] An English eyewitness, observing from a safe distance, reported that the stone castle stood 'very stately and high', but by noon the next day 'it was so low that it could scarcely be discerned'.[169] In addition, O'Neill destroyed Sligo Castle and another thirteen castles, including the residences of O'Hagan and O'Quinn.[170] Hugh O'Neill then retreated to 'his island habitation' at Creeve Lake in the same county and, subsequently, to other lake dwellings.[171]

The ability of Irish chieftains to construct castles rested on the customary duties of tenants to provide labour service to build and maintain their chief's residences.[172] A listing of the duties and customs due to the Ó Raghallaigh (O'Reilly) in 1585, paid by 'the gentill and others of the barony of the Cavan', included 'all manner of chardgis [charges] both for workmen, stofe [stuff], and labourers, and victualls, for the buildinge and maintaininge of his castell of the Cavan, and all other necessary ro[o]mes and offices about the same'.[173] De Renzy claimed that the castles built

168 *Description of Ireland and the state thereof as it is at this present in anno 1598*, ed. E. Hogan (Dublin, 1878), p. 22; H. Morgan, 'The end of Gaelic Ulster: a thematic interpretation of events between 1534 and 1610', *IHS*, xxvi (1988), pp 8–32. **169** Hayes-McCoy, *Ulster and other Irish maps*, p. 8. Plate 5 shows a ruined castle and its bawn. The hall, presumably built of timber and probably standing within the bawn, is not visible because it was burnt in 1597. **170** *AFM*, vi, 1991; Morgan, *Tyrone's rebellion*, p. 186; P. Walsh (ed.), *The life of Aodh Ruadh Ó Domhnaill transcribed from the book of Lughaidh Ó Clerigh* (Dublin, 1948), p. 111. **171** P. Walsh (ed.), *The Flight of the earls by Tadhg Ó Cianáin* (Dublin, 1916), p. 7. **172** O'Dowd, *Early modern Sligo*, p. 20. **173** *AFM*, v, 1806.

by MacCoghlan in Delvin (Offaly) were built 'uppon the countrie charge as their custom is, so that he laid out no monie'.[174] Manus MacMahon, chief of Farney (south Monaghan) in the fifteenth century, employed English hostages as forced labour to build his bawn. The annals refer to a palisade round his stronghold, suggesting an earthen rampart topped by stakes.[175]

Strategic location of castles

It has been stated that castles in Tipperary and Ely O'Carroll were not built at strategic positions.[176] However, there is abundant evidence that castles in Gaelic Ireland were strategically positioned and formed part of defensive and sometimes offensive strategies.

There are many examples of Gaelic chieftains building castles in response to threats from neighbouring lordships. In 1526, Conchubhair Ó Néill (Con O'Neill) unsuccessfully sought to hinder the building by Manus O'Donnell of a castle at Portnatrynod (Tyrone) on the Foyle, which must have threatened O'Neill, whose main seat at Strabane lay on the other side of the river. O'Donnell considerably strengthened his position in the next year by building his castle at Lifford, which also faced Strabane. This castle consisted of 'works of stone, wood, and boards',[177] indicating that it was partly constructed of stone and timber. The poet Tadhg Dall Ó hUiginn (1550–1591) lauded it in a poem as 'the delightful, lofty building' with 'its wondrous, handsome, firm walls, its smooth marble. Beloved is the castle in which we used to spend awhile at chess playing, awhile with the daughters of the men of Bregia, awhile with the fair books of the poets'.[178] Brian O'Connor Sligo built Bundrowes Castle in 1420 to prevent Niall O'Donnell from encroaching into north Connacht. O'Donnell retaliated three years later by building a castle at nearby Ballyshannon.[179] Leitrim Castle was built by Brian Ó Ruairc in 1540, clearly as a defense against the 'wars' waged against him 'on all sides', while an island castle at Lough Scur was erected by Seán Mac Raghnaill (John Reynolds) probably for security reasons in 1570. Maolochlainn Ó Ceallaigh (Melaghlin O'Kelly) built three castles (Gallagh, Garbally, Monivea) in east Galway sometime prior to 1504. The castles constituted a threat to the Burkes, and Ulick Mac William Burke demolished them in that year.[180]

Territorial defences could be complex because of geographical features. The territory of the O'Maddens, situated in Offaly and Galway, straddled the Shannon. Their main castles were at Cloghan in Lusmagh (west Offaly) and Lismore in east Galway.[181] The geography of this unusual lordship made it paramount to secure the fords across the Shannon. Until at least 1542, the O'Maddens held two passes and

174 Mac Cuarta, 'De Renzy's letters', p. 123.   **175** I am indebted to Katharine Simms for this reference from *Clogher Rec.*, 4 (1960–2), p. 128.   **176** Cairns, *Irish towerhouses*, p. 11.   **177** *AC*, 659, 665; *AFM*, v, 1391, 1479, 1487, 1597.   **178** D. Quinn, *The Elizabethans and the Irish* (Ithaca, 1966), p. 74; *Topog. dict. Ire.*, ii, p. 217; H. Wood (ed.), *The chronicle of Ireland 1584–1608 by Sir James Perrot* (Dublin, 1933), p. 61. There is an early seventeenth-century plan in the PRO (*CSPI, 1600–1*, p. 92).   **179** *AFM*, iv, 859.   **180** *AFM*, v, 1275, 1311.   **181** The absence of a vault suggests that it must be a late towerhouse.

castles across the Shannon at Meelick and Banagher,[182] which were so strategic that the government took them over later. Although the MacCoghlans, living north of Lusmagh, did not have lands across the Shannon, they secured passes across the river with castles. In the early seventeenth century, De Renzy gave detailed descriptions of the strategic location of those castles in MacCoghlan country protecting fords across the Shannon (from south to north: Beál Átluid, Banagher and Raghra).[183]

Natural barriers played an important role in the strategic siting of castles. Sometimes, a castle was situated next to a pass or tóchar (anglicised togher) through bogs, and these were called 'togher' castles in north-west and east Offaly.[184] The castle of Barnacor (near Shrule, Longford), was apparently built to defend the pass of the River Inny in co-operation with Lot's castle on the opposite bank.[185]

The strategic significance of some castles is not clear and their locations may have been governed by economic or other factors. For instance, in at least two areas, strings of castles were situated along the banks of rivers. One group of castles, some belonging to MacCoghlan and others to freeholders, festooned the north bank of the Brosna (Moystown, Coole, Kincora, Gallen, Ballyclare, Ballyshiel, Kilcolgan, Lemanaghan, Lisderg).[186] Likewise, in Longford, a string of eleven castles lined the Inny along the border with Westmeath. Remarkably, the border further north with Westmeath was virtually devoid of castles, and this was also true for the border with Leitrim.[187] For that reason, the strategic intent of the castles strung along the Inny is obscure. The question remains whether co-ordination existed between different families within a common lineage group in the strategic building of castles. Not all castles were located on borders. Castles were often concentrated in the most fertile areas of the country.[188] O'Neill castles in Tyrone were clearly strategically placed within the lowland centres of population.[189]

Figure 1.2 shows that towerhouses were concentrated along the coasts in those counties with a low density of towerhouses, such as Kerry, Mayo, Donegal and Antrim.[190] Coastal defences, possibly protecting fisheries, were necessary because attacking parties arrived in long boats by sea.[191] The shores of many lakes in Ulster and Connacht were dotted with castles. This was certainly the case in Sligo (Ballindoon, Templehouse), where the O'Garas built their castles on the shores of Lough Gara. Crannógs and lake islands offered effective places of refuge in times of war or raids.[192] In Longford, however, there were surprisingly few castles along the Shannon.[193] An understanding of the strategic siting of castles in Gaelic Ireland needs to consider both the type and function of land resources.

182 *S.P., Hen. VIII*, iii, p. 361; A.M. Freeman (ed.), *The composition book of Conought* (Dublin, 1936), p. 75. 183 Mac Cuarta, 'De Renzy's letters', p. 169. 184 In Delvin MacCoghlan, the following castles were situated on the edge of bogs: Stonestown, Kilcummin, Corracollin and Castletown. 185 *Topog. dict. Ire.*, ii, p. 555. 186 Mac Cuarta, 'De Renzy's letters', pp 169–70, 172, 174–5. 187 BL, Cotton, 1 Aug, i (14–48); ii (25, 26, 28). 188 Barry, *Medieval Ireland*, p. 189; Fennelly, 'Towerhouses in Co. Offaly', p. 225. 189 Robinson, 'Plantation of Ulster', p. 75. 190 *Atlas of rural landscape*, Fig. 67. 191 *AFM*, v, 1475. 192 O'Dowd, *Early modern Sligo*, pp 8–9. 193 BL, Cotton, 1 Aug., i (14–48); ii (25, 26, 28).

CONCLUSION

The architectural history of Gaelic buildings remains elusive. For instance, as O'Conor has remarked, 'the dating of the initial phase of towerhouse construction to the early fourteenth century is by no means proven' and it may very well have happened earlier. Secondly, towerhouses and earthworks existed together and it is quite plausible that mottes continued to be built during the period when stone and wooden castles were constructed.[194] Space inhibits a review of the abundant evidence on other building types erected in Gaelic lordships, such as mottes and crannógs. In addition, there is a need for detailed study of Gaelic wooden castles, polygonal enclosure castles, hall castles, watchtowers, long houses, halls and fortifications.

A study of Gaelic society cannot rest solely on knowledge of castle sites. Early seventeenth-century plantation documents make it clear that there were many more substantial Irish landowners than can be accounted for by known castle sites. Studies of the type and distribution of the residences of non-castle owning freeholders are lacking. Only by incorporating their presence in settlement studies can we gain a more comprehensive understanding of Gaelic Ireland.

Regional studies are needed for particular lordships, as well as the border areas between them, examining the chronology, distribution and function of castles and castle sites. Further archaeological excavations are required on specific sites within Gaelic lordships, particularly chiefry castles, whether at provincial, subordinate or tuath level. In addition, archaeological investigations need to focus particularly on subsidiary buildings within bawns.[195] Excavations of sites of known wooden castles and the exploration of villages close to castle sites are also welcome. Interpretations of Gaelic architecture should incorporate study of the contemporary cultural context. In the fifteenth and sixteenth centuries, many chiefs and their immediate families enjoyed prosperity, as can be judged from their castle building, church endowments, investments in leases and lands,[196] and sponsorship of a vigorous cultural revival of Gaelic poetry, history and genealogy.[197]

Furthermore, Gaelic castles and settlements require to be studied in their contemporary geographical context of place names, as well as landscape features such as bogs, lakes and rivers that have been altered considerably down to the present. The rich English sources for Gaelic landscape and settlements, particularly in the late sixteenth and seventeenth centuries, largely remain untapped. Only through the use of more extensive sources, combined with careful fieldwork, can the function and strategic position of Gaelic castles and settlements be properly appreciated.

194 O'Conor, 'Motte and bailey castles in Ireland', p. 17.   195 Barry, *Medieval Ireland*, pp 189–90.
196 Lennon, *Sixteenth-century Ireland*, p. 35.   197 Simms, *Kings to warlords*, p. 17.

Appendix 1.1: Dated Gaelic castles from the fourteenth to the late sixteenth centuries

Site	County	Builder	Date	Source
Lissardowlin	Longford	Séan Ó Fearghail	1377	*AFM*, iv, 669; *AC*, 349
Daingean Uí Bhigín	Clare	Cúmhéadha Mac Conmara	*c.*1380	Westropp, 351
Newtown	Clare	Lochlainn Mac Conmara	1380	Westropp, 351
Parke's Castle	Leitrim	Ó Ruairc	early 15c	Barry, 189
Rossroe	Clare	Síoda Mac Conmara	pre 1402	Westropp, 351
Granard	Longford	Uilliam Ó Fearghail	1405 (rebuilt?)	*Misc. Ir. An.*, 175
Barry	Longford	Cathal Ó Fearghail	1405 (rebuilt?)	*Misc. Ir. An.*, 175
Tirlickeen	Longford	Ross Ó Fearghail	1406	*Misc. Ir. An.*, 181
Áth na Sluaidhe (Ballinasloe)	Galway	Eoghan Ó Ceallaigh	1406	*Misc. Ir. An.*, 181
Tulsk	Roscommon	Ó Conchobhair Rua	1406	*Misc. Ir. An.*, 181
Ballindoon	Sligo	Conor MacDonough	1408	*AFM*, iv, 797
Colloony	Sligo	Murrough MacDonough	1408 (rebuilt)	*AFM*, iv, 797
Enniskillen	Fermanagh	Aodh Mag Uidhir (Maguire)	*c.*1415–20	Salter, 149
Ballicottle	Sligo	Donnell O'Dowd	1417	O'Rorke, ii, 420.
Killtoghert	Leitrim	Tadhg Ó Ruairc & others	1419	*AC*, 447
Caisleán na mallacht	Roscommon?	Uilliam Ó Ceallaigh	1418/19	*AFM*, iv, 837; *AC*, 439–40; *AU*, iii, 77
Bundrowes	Leitrim	Brían Ó Conchubhair	1420	*AFM*, iv, 843; *AU*, iii, 83
Lough Dargan	Sligo	Conor MacDonough	1422	*AFM*, iv, 857
Ballyshannon	Donegal	Niall Ó Domhnaill	1423	*AFM*, iv, 859; *AU*, iii, 93
Inch	Donegal	Neachtan Ó Domhnaill	1430s	Salter, 152
Ballymarkahan	Clare	Domhnall Mac Shéan Mac Conmara	*c.*1430	Westropp, 351
Garrycastle	Offaly	Feidhlim McCoghlan?	before 1436	Nicholls, 'MacCoghlans', 448
Drishane	Cork	Mac Cárthaigh	*c.*1436–50	Healy, 329
Firtane (Rosslara)	Clare	Ruaidhrí Mac Conmara	1440/1480	Westropp, 351
Garruragh	Clare	Donnchadh Mac Ruaidhrí Mac Conmara	1440/1480	Westropp, 351
Blarney	Cork	Cormac Mac Cárthaigh	1446 (date stone)	Leask, 113; Healy, 21–5
Tullyvin	Cavan	Eoghan Rua Ó Raghallaigh	*c.*1450	Davies, 99
Tinnakill	Laois	Séan Carrach Mac Domhnaill	*c.*1450	Borrowes, 37
Donegal	Donegal	Aodh Rua Ó Domhnaill	1470s?	Salter, 145; *AFM*, v, 1283
Chomhaid	Clare	Tadhg Ó Briain	before 1466	O'Conor, *O'Conors*, 145
Bunratty	Clare	Maccon Mac Síoda Mac Conmara	*c.*1450–67	Salter, 98
Dromline	Clare	Seán Fionn Mac Conmara	pre 1467	Westropp, 351; *AFM*, vi, 1945
Knappogue	Clare	Seán Fionn Mac Conmara	pre 1467	Westropp, 351; *AFM*, vi, 1945
Ballymulcassell	Clare	Conor na Sróna O Briain	pre 1470	Westropp, 351
Bealnafirverna	Clare	Toirrdhealbhach Ó Briain	pre 1480	Westropp, 351
Danganbrack	Clare	Séan Mac Conmara	1487	Westropp, 351
Castletown	Leitrim	Feidhlim Ó Ruairc	1487 (rebuilt)	*AFM*, iv, 1151
Coolreagh	Clare	Pilíb Mac Conmara	1487	Westropp, 351
Ralahine	Clare	Tadhg Mac Conmara	1490	Westropp, 351
Dunboy	Cork	Ó Súilleabháin	*c.*1490	Barry, 190; Healy, 183–91
Moghane	Clare	Domhnall Mac Conmara	*c.*1490	Westropp, 351
Ballyhennan	Clare	Aodh Mac Conmara	*c.*1490	Westropp, 351
Carrigafoyle	Kerry	Conor Liath Ó Conchubhair	*c.*1490	MacCurtain, 435
Ballydivlin	Cork	Ó Mathúna (Mahony)	1495	Healy, 167–8
Lough Ateriff	Fermanagh	Pilíb Mag Uidhir (Maguire)	1500	*AFM*, iv, 1257.
Gallagh	Galway	Maolseachlainn Ó Ceallaigh	pre 1504	*AFM*, v, 1275, 1311
Garbally	Galway	Maolseachlainn Ó Ceallaigh	pre 1504	*AFM*, v, 1275, 1311
Monivea	Galway	Maolseachlainn Ó Ceallaigh	pre 1504	*AFM*, v, 1275, 1311
Clonony	Offaly	Domhnall Mac Rossa Mac Cochlainn	*c.*1509	Cox, 21; PRO, SP 46/90, ff 34, 38

Site	County	Builder	Date	Source
Faddan	Offaly	Toirrdhealbhach Mac Cochlainn	pre 1520	*AFM*, v, 1349
Kincora	Offaly	Toirrdhealbhach Mac Cochlainn	pre 1520	*AFM*, v, 1349
Milltown	Clare	Domhnall Mac Conmara	c.1520	Westropp, 351
Dún Guaire	Galway	Ó hEidhin (Hynes)	c.1520	Johnson, Plate 28
Doe	Donegal	Ó Coinn (Quin)	1520–35	Salter, 144
Portnatrynod	Tyrone	Manus Ó Domhnaill	1526	*AC*, 659; *AFM*, v, 1353, 1385
Lifford	Donegal	Manus Ó Domhnaill	1527	*AC*, 665
Daingean	Offaly	Ua Conchobair Failghe	1521–37	*CSPI, 1509–73*, 26–7
Leitrim	Leitrim	Brian Ó Ruairc	1540	*AC*, 713; *AFM*, v, 1459
Banagher	Offaly	Tadhg Ó Cearbhaill	1544 (rebuilt)	*AFM*, v, 1489
Kenbane	Antrim	Colla MacDonnell	c.1547	Salter, 153; Lawlor, 150; McNeill, 112
Kilcummin	Offaly	Edmund (O'Connor) Fay	c.1548 (rebuilt)	Nicholls, 'MacCoghlans', 450
Dunanainey	Antrim	Somhairle Buí Mac Domhnaill	c.1550	Lawlor, 149–50
Liscloony	Offaly	Maolseachlainn O'Dalaghan	1556	*AFM*, v, 1543
Red Bay	Antrim	James MacDonnell	c.1560	Lawlor, 151–2
Clogh	Antrim	James MacDonnell	c.1560	Lawlor, 151–2
Lackan	Sligo	Mac Fhirbhisigh	1560	Ó Muraíle, 42
Benburb	Tyrone	Seán Ó Néill	pre 1567	*UJA*, 2 (1854), 148
Lough Scur	Leitrim	Seán Mac Raghnaill	1570	*JRSAI*, 13 (1908), 389
Coleraine	Derry	Uí Néill	1570 (rebuilt)	Hill, *MacDonnell*, 131
Coole	Offaly	Séan Mac Cochlainn	1571 (rebuilt)	*JRSAI* (1913), 225
Belturbet	Cavan	Aodh Conalach Ó Raghallaigh	pre 1583	Davies, 91; O'Hart, i, 722
Bellanacargy	Cavan	Aodh Conalach Ó Raghallaigh	pre 1583	Davies, 99; O'Hart, i, 722
Ballynacarriga	Cork	Randal Mac Cárthaigh?	1585 (inscription)	Lewis, i, 151; Healy, 226–7
Newcastle	Down	Mac Aonghusa (Maginnes)	1588 (inscription)	Lawlor, 147; *Arch. Sur. Down*, 262
Dunluce	Antrim	MacDonnell	1593–6 (rebuilt)	Lawlor, 134
Craigue	Tipperary	O.H. (Hogan family)	1594 (inscription)	Cairns, 16
Strabane	Tyrone	Toirrdhealbhach Luineach Ó Néill	pre 1595	Walsh, 71; Morgan, 91
Dungannon	Tyrone	Aodh Ó Néill	pre 1595 (rebuilt)	Morgan, 186; HMC, *Salisbury*, i, 21

CHAPTER TWO

The geography and practice of English colonisation in Ireland 1534–1609

You see, my Lord, all those goodly lands ... were once my ancestor's, and I meane to have them agayne; for now the time is come that we shall be righted of the wronges heretofore done unto us.

> *Felim Mac Giolla Phádraig, chief of the*
> *Mac Giolla Phádraigs in Upper Ossory, 1598*

All those countries which lyinge neare unto any mountaines or Irishe desertes, had bene planted with Englishe [in the Middle Ages], were shortly displanted and lost ... the overrunning and waisting of the realme ... was the begynning of [all the] other evills which sythence have afflicted that lande, and opened a ways unto the Irishe to recover their possession, and to beate out the Englishe which had formerlie wonne the same.

> *Edmund Spenser, 1597*

And what can be more honorable to princes, than to inlarge the bounds of their kingdomes without injurie, wrong & bloodshed; and to frame them from a savage life to a civill government, neither of which the Spaniards in their conquests have performed.

> *John Hooker, 1586*

Let us, therefore, use the persuasions which Moses used to Israel ... and tell them [future settlers in east Ulster] that they shall goe to possesse a lande that floweth with milke and hon[e]y, a fertile soile truly if there be any in Europe.

> *Thomas Brett, 1572*

Those who take other men's lands cannot hope for heaven.

> *Patrick Tanck[ard] of Castletown, Meath, sixteenth century*

Fubún fúibh, a shluagh Gaoidheal,	Irishmen, your actions are shameful
ní mhaireann aoinneach agaibh;	not one of you has life in him;
Goill ag comhroinn bhur gcríche;	foreigners divide your ancestral land among themselves
re sluagh síthe bhur samhail.	you are like a host of ghosts.

> *Anonymous, sixteenth century*

INTRODUCTION

Historians concerned with English colonial expansion in Ireland during the sixteenth century have prioritised colonial theories (based on contemporary tracts) rather than the actual settlement process. Typically writers on colonial theories neglect the selection of settlement sites, the nature of changing frontiers separating settlers from the native inhabitants, the relationship between military forts and subsequent plantations, government schemes for the extensive introduction of settlers, and the impact of government incentives on private plantations.[1] As a result, the study of English expansion and settlement and how it became embedded in the Irish landscape is neglected. Likewise, architectural historians focus more on stylistic themes in surviving examples of castles and residences rather than on their colonial context and geographic distribution.[2] Moreover, their understandable concern for surviving structures has neglected sources documenting lost architecture. The latter are indispensable in creating a comprehensive picture of how the change in landownership generated a network of colonial settlements.

This survey's main aim is to document the sequence, expansion and methods of English settlement from 1534 to 1609 in its geographic context. A subsidiary aim is to explore the settlements themselves, their architecture, agricultural enclosures and local industries, and to challenge the assertion that the sixteenth century witnessed 'no notable architectural development'.[3] A final aim is to illustrate the changing role of the Old English and New English in the creation of plantations. The former were the descendants of settlers who had come to Ireland mostly during the Norman period, while the latter were new arrivals from the sixteenth century onward.[4] The political and military history of the period is underplayed, as it can be easily found in standard sources.[5]

The year 1534 coincided with the installation of 'an English-manned and military-based administration in Dublin', and the beginning of the Reformation, which was formally acknowledged by the Irish parliament two years later.[6] In 1609, the government's plans for the plantation of west Ulster consolidated. The chosen period starts when the government in Dublin had ceased to control most of the country, two-thirds being in the hands of the Irish or Gaelicised Old English.[7] Between 1534 and 1609, the English government re-asserted control, generating internal borders between the English and the Gaelic or Gaelicised areas (often characterised as frontiers) that shifted slowly westward, with collateral movements to the south and the north. The increase in English-controlled territory facilitated

1 J.H. Andrews, 'Plantation Ireland: a review of settlement history' in T. Barry (ed.), *A history of settlement in Ireland* (London, 2000), pp 140–57. For theoretical colonial approaches, see D. Quinn, *The Elizabethans and the Irish* (Ithaca, 1966); D. Quinn, 'Ireland and sixteenth-century European expansion', *Historical Studies*, i (1958), pp 20–32; N. Canny, 'The ideology of English colonisation: from Ireland to America', *William & Mary Quarterly*, xxx (1973), pp 575–98; B. Bradshaw, 'Sword, word and strategy in the Reformation in Ireland', *Hist. Jn.*, xxi (1978), pp 475–502. 2 Leask, *Irish castles and castellated houses*; Craig, *Architecture of Ireland*. Nothing is available on Irish architecture of the period comparable to M. Airs, *The making of the English country house 1500–1640* (London, 1975). For a broader perspective on these changes, see G. Parker, *The military revolution: military innovation and the rise of the West 1500–1800* (Cambridge, 1988). 3 G.A. Hayes-McCoy, 'The completion of the Tudor conquest', *NHI*, iii, p. 137. 4 The term 'Old English' did not come into use until the 1590s. Contemporary terms include 'Anglo-Hiberni', 'English-Irish' and 'English of Irish birth'; see C. Brady, 'Spenser's Irish crisis: humanism and experience in the 1590s', *Past & Present*, cxi (1986), p. 24; N. Canny, *The formation of the Old English elite in Ireland* (Dublin, 1975), p. 2. 5 *NHI*, iii; N. Canny, *From Reformation to Restoration: Ireland 1534–1660* (Dublin, 1987); M. McCurtain, *Tudor and Stuart Ireland* (Dublin, 1972). 6 D. Quinn & K.W. Nicholls, 'Ireland in 1534', *NHI*, iii, p. 1. 7 W. Butler, *Confiscation in Irish history* (Dublin, 1917), p. 9.

immigration from England, Wales and Scotland, on a scale that matched emigration to the North American colonies.[8] In the process, government control expanded gradually to cover a significant part of the island.

Settlements are here defined as a fort, castle or manor house. Usually, this included a church and a village as well, but limited space does not allow for a systematic recording here. A settlement was often a hub of commerce through a regulated or informal market, and a centre for law enforcement through a court leet and a court baron.[9] The survival of buildings is haphazard, and therefore upstanding remains should not be considered as adequate indicators of the contemporary settlement pattern. Moreover, as one travels through the Irish countryside, the succession of buildings of different ages and styles conceals the location of former frontier areas, or where English control of land expanded or contracted. An attempt has been made here to reconstruct the movement of frontiers. This chapter documents the earliest dates of settlement, which for the New English was either the first year of their known residence on a property, or the year in which the property was granted or leased to them. For the Old English already resident in Ireland, sites that they acquired and/or built away from their main or original place of residence are shown. Only a proportion of buildings owned by settlers are firmly dated from surviving remains or from documentary sources (appendix 2.1). This chapter combines documentary and field evidence to present an analysis of how English colonialism re-established a firm grip on the Irish countryside. Many structures shown on the maps are only known from contemporary sources as they have disappeared above the ground. Sites are likely missing but these omissions, however common, are unlikely to distort the description of the distinct avenues by which English expansion advanced.

The scattering of sites implies, but does not show, the actual size of estates that came into English hands. A mapping of these estates would have been desirable, but this falls beyond the scope of this chapter. The maps show the main estate sites, rather than the surrounding farms (with the exception of the large seignories in Munster, where main tenants are indicated whenever possible). To show the progress of colonial advance, the period from 1534 to 1609 will be discussed in sections of one or more decades at a time, but these intervals are arbitrary; the accompanying maps summarise settlements from 1534 to 1609.

Fluctuations of English control

There were fundamental differences between settlers and natives in their justifications of landownership.[10] Gaelic and Anglo-Norman rights clashed, while religion served

8 For North American immigration, see T. Rabb, *Enterprise and empire* (Cambridge, MA, 1967), pp 57–68; C. Shammas, 'English commercial development and American colonisation 1560–1620' in K. Andrews, N. Canny & P. Hair (eds), *The westward enterprise* (Liverpool, 1978), p. 153.   9 Length restrictions make it impractical to give sources for all the sites marked on the accompanying maps.   10 The quotations are from the following sources: *Chronicle of Ireland 1584–1608*, p. 150; E. Spenser, *A view of the present state of Ireland*, ed. W. Renwick (London, 1934), pp 19–23; J. Hooker, 'The description, conquest, inhabitation, and troublesome estate of Ireland 1586' in R. Holinshed, *The chronicles of England, Scotland and Ireland* (London, 1574), ii, pp iii–v; [T. Brett], *A letter sent by T[homas] B[rett] gentleman… conteining a large discourse of the peopling*

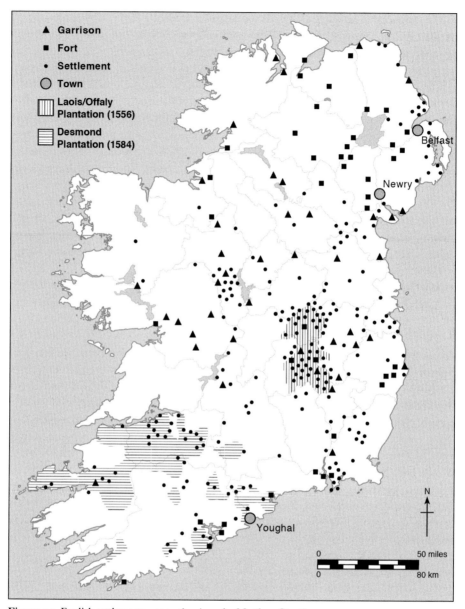

Figure 2.1 English settlements 1534–1609 (map by Matthew Stout).

alternatively as a condemnation of those seizing land from its rightful owners, or
to establish biblical precedents as a justification for doing just that. The Anglo-
Norman infiltration of Ireland, initiated in the second half of the twelfth century,
was accompanied by an extensive building programme that covered most of the

and inhabiting the c[o]untrie called Ardes (London, 1572), reprinted in G. Hill, *MacDonnells of
Antrim* (Belfast, 1873), pp 405–15; W. O'Sullivan, 'Medieval Meath manuscripts', *Ríocht na Midhe*,
vii:4 (1985–6), p. 18; Leerssen, *Mere Irish and fíor-Ghael*, p. 205.

country. Several areas escaped Anglo-Norman settlement, notably the north-west of the island. From the thirteenth century onwards, Anglo-Norman rule declined and large territories were eventually regained by the Irish. In the fourteenth century, the Irish recovered much of north-west Tipperary, Laois and Carlow, and the greater part of Ulster. Similarly, the O'Farrells of Longford, the O'Kellys of Galway and the O'Dowds of Sligo rose and expelled the settlers. By the 1350s, several royal castles, such as Roscommon in Connacht, had been abandoned by the English.[11] They were not recovered until three centuries later. To defend the Pale (the area around Dublin over which the English government exercised more direct control), its inhabitants constructed a ditch in the mid fifteenth century, planned to run from Ardee (Louth) to the port of Dalkey (Dublin), but it may never have been completed (Figure 2.2a). Piles (earthwork enclosures) and towerhouses were also built in the border areas, encouraged by a 1429 government subsidy of ten pounds, extended in 1441 to the building of towerhouses along the Corock river in south-west Wexford. Many towers around the Pale perimeter, in Kildare, Meath and Louth, and south of the Liffey bordering on the Wicklow mountains, date from this period, and these protected Anglo-Norman settlements from Gaelic incursions.[12]

Under the seventh and eighth earls of Kildare (Thomas, 1430–78; Gerald, 1456–1513), a renewed expansion took place, starting with the recovery of Rathangan (Kildare) in 1459; by 1500, the O'Connors had been pushed further westward, losing the strongholds of Morett and Lea in Laois. Fortifications were erected in Kildare, particularly at key border points, notably at Castledermot (1485), where there had been a medieval walled town, and Powerscourt (1500) in Wicklow. In the early sixteenth century, the earl of Kildare's justices administered English law from Carbury Castle in Kildare near the Laois border. When the eighth earl died in 1513, a Gaelic annalist wrote that 'in power, fame and estimation, he exceeded all the Gaill [foreigners], conquered more territory from the Gaeil [Irish], built more castles for the Gaill, rased more castles of the Gaeil, particularly on the borders'. A map of Leinster (1520–30) showed Kildare castles at Maynooth, and along or near the 'frontier' Barrow (from north to south) at Rathangan, Woodstock, Athy, Kilkea and Castledermot. A subsequent earl of Kildare, however, revolted between 1534 and 1536; in 1536, the border county of Kildare was 'much waste and void of inhabitants' 'which is the greatest decay of this country. But would God that it would please the King's Highness to send Englishmen to inhabit here … for unto that there is no way to the reformation of this land'.

In the 1530s, a dangerous situation for English control over Ireland had arisen. The net outflow of English and Irish to England reached a critical level, driven by the plague, famine and particularly endemic warfare in the border areas. The decline of Anglo-Norman power was facilitated because many Anglo-Norman families had

11 B. Graham, *Anglo-Norman settlement in Ireland* (Athlone, 1985). See also listing of lost properties in Connacht (1574?) in *Cal. Carew MSS 1601–1603*, pp 471–6; Barry, *Medieval Ireland*, pp 1–7, 197; R. Glasscock, 'Moated sites and deserted boroughs and villages: two neglected aspects of Anglo-Norman settlement in Ireland' in Stephens & Glasscock (eds), *Irish geographical studies*, pp 279–301. 12 Barry, *Medieval Ireland*, pp 181–3, 188; B. Colfer, 'Anglo-Norman settlement in county Wexford' in K. Whelan (ed.), *Wexford history and society* (Dublin, 1987), p. 91. For the definition of pile, see D. Grose, *The antiquities of Ireland*, ed. R. Stalley (Dublin, 1991), i, p. xxx.

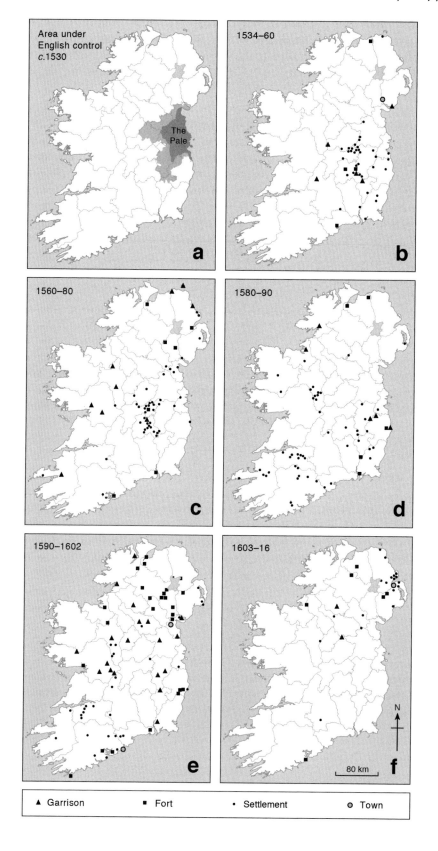

▲ Garrison   ■ Fort   • Settlement   ⊙ Town

become Irish in their customs, language and apparel. Weak English rule in Ireland produced a secondary threat in that France and Spain might contemplate invading Ireland as a launching pad to invade England itself. A third threat was the infiltration of unruly Scots into the north of Ireland.

Ownership of, and control over, Irish land had become a critical question at the beginning of the sixteenth century. Government control was largely confined to the Pale area around Dublin and the smaller Wexford Pale consisting of the baronies of Forth and Bargy in the south-east corner of the county (both were named after the Pale of Calais in French, the small corner of France to which the English had been driven back). Beyond these territories lay 'marches' or frontier areas, some occupied by 'degenerate [Old] English' as in Westmeath. Other border areas, notably Wicklow, were controlled by the Gaelic Irish, and had only a much thinner buffer of English borderers. In addition, the earls of Ormond and Desmond, of Anglo-Norman descent, reigned over vast tracts, including palatinates in Tipperary and Kerry, not under the direct control of the Dublin government. Lastly, the port towns on the south and west coasts had become isolated; the English government almost entirely lost control over these cities, which became virtually autonomous jurisdictions controlled by wealthy merchant dynasties.

The Pale had shrunk back to a radius of 48km around Dublin. In 1515, this area (Figure 2.2a) was surrounded by a string of towns and other strongholds. (Towns walled during the Middle Ages are asterisked). From north to south, the border sites were Carlingford,* Dundalk,* Ardee* (Louth), Kells,* Athboy* (Meath), Kilcock, Clane, Naas,* Kilcullen,* Ballymore Eustace (Kildare), Tallaght to Dalkey (south Dublin). By 1537, the Dublin Pale had shrunk further at its northern boundary, and ran from Drogheda via Navan and Maynooth to Tallaght in the south. The situation was precarious, and for the inhabitants of the Dublin Pale, the fate of Calais (surrendered to the French in 1557) hung menacingly over them. The only known representations of the defenders of the Pale are the stone effigies of knights in armour at border sites such as Ballymore Eustace and Kilcullen (Kildare) and Athboy (Meath). These represent a sculptural tradition that expired on the borders of the Pale in the late sixteenth century.

In 1541, King Henry VIII of England was proclaimed King of Ireland, an upgrade from his former title as Lord of Ireland. By this move, the King undertook the political unification of Ireland, where formerly a state of jurisdictional partition had existed between those of English and Irish race. Several avenues were open to the government to regain control over the country, some of which concerned direct action by the government. First among these was granting legal title to Irish-held land through the policy of 'surrender and regrant', a legal procedure allowing Irish chiefs to hold their lands directly from the crown. This method, as it did not necessarily lead to colonisation or infiltration, will not be highlighted here. A second strategy intruded local or regional officers into areas that had not experienced English government control and English law for decades or even centuries. This

Figure 2.2 (left) Chronology of early English colonisation 1534–1616 (maps by Matthew Stout).

strategy was often accompanied by the building of fortifications for garrisons. A third more intrusive strategy focused on boosting crown lands by the resumption and confiscation of the lands of absentees, attainted 'traitors' and monasteries, and then regranting them to loyal subjects for resettlement. This strategy often required the grantees to reside on the property, to build according to certain specifications, and to lease only to English tenants, who would then form the core of a local militia.

Other policies, although encouraged and condoned by the government, relied on private initiative. Gentlemen adventurers were permitted to organise an armed conquest of a particular territory. Another strategy allowed the discovery by private parties, often through devious and nefarious means, of lands allegedly 'concealed' from the crown, which then could be regranted to prospective settlers. A final plan involved the transplantation of the native inhabitants to remote impoverished areas, thereby freeing up their lands for settlers. Such a strategy, although rarely used, was implemented by having private participants do the 'dirty' work. In practice, although some areas saw a single strategy applied, other areas saw a succession or a combination of plans, such as the introduction of forts and the installation of administrative officers, followed by plantation grants to settlers.

The military and civic settlements resulting from a change in English colonial policy in Ireland in the sixteenth century left a permanent impression on the landscape. Scores of castles and fortified houses were built, dozens of fortifications were erected and communications were improved through the cutting of passes through woods and the building of bridges, some fortified. [13]

1534 TO 1560

In 1534, Sir William Skeffington replaced the rebellious earl of Kildare as Lord deputy, and this formed a turning point by initiating an unbroken line of English Lord deputies, and permanently excluding the Old English as potential governors of Ireland (Figure 2.2b). Colonisation during this period was relatively benign, compared with later periods, and it was limited to the confiscation of properties, the strengthening of the Pale border and the introduction of English seneschals. In Laois and Offaly, two principal fortified garrisons were built, which subsequently formed the core of a government-sponsored plantation. Elsewhere, the crown re-established its right to certain castles, and helped to strengthen the corridor along the Barrow connecting the Dublin Pale with loyal areas to the south. The Dublin government also encouraged or condoned private initiatives by the restored earl of Kildare and the earl of Ormond to expand territories under their control.

The decades from the 1530s to the 1550s were characterised by three forms of confiscation – seizure of the property of the house of Kildare, confiscation of the lands of major absentee landholders, and the first series of suppressions of the monasteries. The rebellion of the earl of Kildare (1534–6) allowed the government to seize his vast estates, including the marches on the western border of the Dublin

13 For the latter, see *Cal. pat. rolls, James I*, pp 83–4, 107.

Pale. Portlester, an estate on the western border of Meath, was granted in 1547 to the soldier Francis Herbert, a member of a Dublin merchant family. More settlers were introduced on other Kildare lands. In addition, the government used confiscation of these lands to promote the building of several castles to protect the Pale at its weakest points. This 'door' to the Dublin Pale consisted of several passes through the bogs and woods of Allen, wedged in between the Boyne and Barrow. Here, four 'towers' recommended by the Dublin government were built or repaired in 1540 at Castlejordan, Kinnafad, Kishavanny and Ballinure.[14] Surviving fortifications at Castlejordan date from this period, including a keep, originally with two round towers – similar to Ballyadams (Laois) – situated within an enclosure, protected by a highly unusual pointed flanker with two small round towers facing the bridge.

Further confiscations took place after the Act of Absentees (1536) that covered vast estates in Ireland held by absentee English lords, notably the Duke of Norfolk, the earl of Wiltshire, and the earl of Shrewsbury, who had failed to recruit and protect tenants of English stock and had instead leased lands to Gaelic tenants. It is not known, however, whether these confiscations introduced English settlers.

The first series of suppressions of Irish monasteries was directed against sites in the border areas that were alleged to 'nourish rebels'. Initially, a plan developed by Sir Patrick Finglas in 1534 called for the suppression of monasteries on the lands of the McMurrough Kavanaghs in Leinster (north Wexford) and the introduction of 'lords and gents out of England'; Finglas also advocated granting the abbeys lying on the border with the Irish to 'good English captains', who would keep the turbulent Irish in order. New plans in 1535–6, advancing well beyond the monastic lands, targeted the lands of the O'Tooles and the O'Byrnes in Wicklow, and sought the destruction or banishing of the septs. If implemented, this ambitious project could have linked the Dublin and the Wexford Pales, but no further action was undertaken, presumably because of the military scale of the challenge and prohibitive costs.[15]

In 1536 and 1541, acts for the limited suppression of monasteries were introduced in the Irish parliament. The first commission was completed in 1539–40, when 'voluntary' surrenders of 38 monastic communities were enrolled in the Dublin Court of Chancery. In the same period, the mendicant communities were suppressed, in total, 51 houses in 37 centres, primarily in the border areas. For example, the preceptory of Kilteel (Kildare) passed into the hands of Thomas Alen and his wife – these lands were 'situated in the marches near the Irish enemies, the Tholes [O'Tooles], where resistance and defence are necessarily required'. Remains at Kilteel include a fifteenth-century five-storeyed towerhouse and gateway, surrounded by elaborate earthworks, which reinforced the Pale ditch at a vulnerable point where it turned east in the direction of the coast.[16]

14 *Fiants Henry VIII*, 84; Quinn, *Elizabethans*, p. 3; J.P. Prendergast, *The Cromwellian settlement of Ireland* (Dublin, 1922), p. 246: *Cal. Carew MSS 1575–1588*, p. 91; *CSPI, Henry VIII*, iii (part 3), p. 241; *Cal. pat. rolls, Eliz.*, ii, pp 47–8, 84. The castles were soon joined by a fort at Ticroghan.   **15** Bradshaw, *Revolution*, p. 123; Bradshaw, *Dissolution*; P.H. Hore, *History of the town and county of Wexford*, 6 vols (London, 1901), vi, pp 117–18; *Cal. Carew MSS 1515–1574*, pp 85, 95.   **16** Bradshaw, *Dissolution*, pp 45, 64, 70, 75–7, 184; *Cal. pat. rolls, Henry VIII*, ii, p. 77: Barry, *Medieval Ireland*, pp 181–3.

Several groups profited from grants of monastic property, especially the New English (twenty grantees), closely followed by the Old English gentry. In areas not directly under government control, monastic properties were usually handed over to the local lord, such as Desmond in Munster and Ormond in Kilkenny and Tipperary. The Old English of the Dublin region mostly obtained properties within the Pale, and some along its borders. Properties in the most strategic positions, however, tended to be allocated to New English military officers. In Westmeath in 1550, the soldier Francis Digby was granted the abbey of Kilbeggan with its land, lying 'upon the borders and in danger of dayly spoilinge' because it was a 'good place for horsemen to lye on, and doo service yf the enemies shulde approche'.[17] In the same county in 1562, Captain William Piers, constable of Carrickfergus Castle (Antrim), received a grant of the monastic lands of Tristernagh more than 130km away, which must have caused him logistical problems. He was prohibited from setting any land except to 'English by both parents, or persons born within the English pale'. This provision proved unworkable in this distant district, and Piers was freed from this restriction seven years later. Remains at Tristernagh include a small late sixteenth-century fortified chapel, which may have been built by Piers; this structure was strategically placed at the sole road into the abbey, the only point not surrounded by bogs.[18]

Another example of a monastery occupied by a military officer was the former Norman stronghold and abbey of Durrow (Offaly). The property was granted for twenty-one years to Nicholas Herbert in 1561. Six years later, Herbert complained that this site, surrounded by woods and bogs, was exposed to daily robberies and spoils and that the only way to avoid this hazard was to build 'strongholds and castles well manned'. In return for a fee farm, he offered to build two 'warrlyke castles for him and his sonnes to inhabit in'. The Queen stipulated that these castles were to be built within two years. Durrow was certainly inhabited subsequently, and the Herberts likely built a castle at nearby Lismoyny on a ford across the Brosna (on the Offaly/Westmeath border), later characterised as situated 'upon a great strait, and the chief entrance into Fercall'. Durrow's hazardous location was proved when it was burned by the Irish in 1582 and it temporarily fell into the hands of the MacGeoghegans in 1599. As the property was monastic, the MacGeoghegans observed canon law and returned its ownership to the Catholic church.[19]

Little is known about the actual adaptation of monasteries for secular use, but surviving descriptions indicate that abbey towers occasionally served as refuges in case of attacks. Moreover, abbeys, unlike towerhouses, had the great advantage of

17 Bradshaw, *Dissolution*, pp 99, 136, 138, 184, 192–4, 200; *Cal. pat. rolls, Henry VIII*, i, pp 232–3. 18 *Eleventh report of the deputy keeper of the public records in Ireland* (1879), p. 82; *Twelfth report of the deputy keeper of the public records in Ireland* (1880), p. 27; Gwynn & Hadcock, *Medieval religious houses*, p. 196. For a similar grant to Andrew Brereton of the house of friars at Athlone in 1570, see H. Murtagh, 'Tudor, Stuart and Georgian Athlone' (PhD, NUI, 1986), p. 42. 19 *Cal. pat. rolls, Henry VIII*, i, pp 471, 515; PRO, SP 63/22/176v; *CSPI, 1600–1601*, p. 227; *CSPI, 1625–1632*, p. 65; *CSPI, 1574–1585*, p. 361; *De L'Isle and Dudley MSS*, ii, p. 418; *CSPI, 1599–1600*, p. 217.

large living quarters that could be used in more peaceful times for residence, garrison and storage. The government turned the church of the Cluniac monks at Athlone into a store, and converted the conventual buildings into a house for John Crofton, escheator general for Connacht. When the Irish attacked it in 1572, the defenders retreated into the abbey's tower. Monastic buildings, even within the Dublin Pale, were regarded as places of refuge, serving as a protection for individuals living in its neighbourhood.[20] The grants of monasteries to the New English or the Old English did not all lead to settlements, especially in outlying areas. Thomas Alen received a grant of St Mary's Abbey at Ferns (Wexford) in 1538; fifteen years later, Alen had yet to take possession, because these lands were situated among the Irish and as a consequence were waste and uninhabited.[21]

The suppression of the monasteries in Ireland was a forerunner of later plantations, but it differed from the latter in several respects. Suppression did not generate wholesale expropriation on an ethnic basis. Properties were usually granted for twenty-one years to individuals, normally without conditions to plant the land with a specified number of English settlers, or to displace the Irish natives. The government also did not generally stipulate that the grantee must build fortified dwellings and towns as nuclei for settlements. The granting of monastic properties largely followed ethnic lines, with the Gaelic Irish excluded in favour of the Old English and the New English. The largest grants went to the New English. Edward Moore received a grant of the monastic lands of the Cistercian abbey at Mellifont (Louth): according to later surveys, it consisted of 51,000 acres (21,000ha), six castles, 600 messuages and cottages, and numerous impropriations of churches.[22]

The transfer of the monastic lands was accompanied by the stiffening of government control along the borders of the Pale through the creation of the counties of Westmeath (1542), Carlow (1550, when some parts were transferred to Kilkenny), Laois (1556) and Offaly (1556).[23] Shiring had several functions: establishment of a county town with a gaol and session house, formalisation of county administration (including a sheriff, justices of the peace, tax collectors and an escheator to hold inquisitions), and delineation and mapping of the physical features of each county.

Strengthening the Pale border
The medieval border of the Dublin Pale continued to be penetrated by raiding parties. As late as 1582, the situation around Dundalk was characterised as 'such disorders of spoiling, robbing, and murdering of his Majesty's good subjects by

---

20 Murtagh, 'Athlone', p. 54. At Tintern (Wexford), the living quarters were partly in the steeple of the abbey while a stair turret was added for this purpose at Abbeylara (Longford); see also T. McNeill, 'The stone castles of northern County Antrim', *UJA*, xlvi (1983), p. 127; Gwynn & Hadcock, *Medieval religious houses*, pp 111, 134, 140, 271.   21 Gwynn & Hadcock, *Medieval religious houses*, p. 176; Bradshaw, *Dissolution*, p. 76.   22 Gwynn & Hadcock, *Medieval religious houses*, p. 140; 'A certificate of the state and revenues of the bishopricke of Meath and Clonemackenosh [Clonmacnoise] (1622)' in C. Elrington (ed.), *The whole works of the most Rev James Ussher D.D.* (Dublin, 1847), i, pp liii–cxxv. Other large grants went to Anthony Brabazon and Henry Draycott.   23 Bradshaw, *Dissolution*, p. 199; *NHI*, ix, Map 45.

the men of the Fews [Armagh], Farney, MacMahon's country, the Dartreys [Monaghan], and O'Reilly's country [Cavan], as is pitiful as is to be heard'.[24] A 1427 statute had encouraged the building of small castles or towers, 20 x 16 feet (6.1m x 4.9m) and 40 feet high (15.2m), through offering a subsidy of £10.[25] In the mid sixteenth century, the Dublin government reinstated subsidies for castle building in border areas. The new regulations in Ireland followed similar measures instituted in 1535 for the frontier area between England and Scotland.[26] In Ireland, the new subsidy consisted of a reward of £10 and the 'freedom' of one ploughland, which guaranteed exemption from certain levies. For example, with this subsidy, James Dowdall received a grant of lands in 1552 on condition that he would build a castle at Castletown-Cooley in north Louth within three years 'on the borders and marches of the Irish, which should be a great key, and defence'.[27] In the next two decades, more castles were built in this area, although it is unclear whether they enjoyed the same subsidy. From 1556 onwards, grantees were required to reside at border castles as, for example, Mathew King, who was granted a lease in 1556 of Castlerickard, a former Anglo-Norman manorial village on the western perimeter of Meath near the strategic Boyne. In an apparently rare instance, Sir John Barnewall, Lord Trimleston, was granted borderland on condition that a village was to be erected for the better defence of the existing castle and to protect the English against the incursions of the O'Connors.[28]

In south Meath, John Parker, master of the rolls, who had organised the defence of Carrickfergus, obtained the rule of the border land near Ticroghan in 1553, where he was also granted lands. Parker was to repair 'a ditch that reacheth from the Castle of Secroighan [Ticroghan] to the Boyne, which in times past was made for the defense of the country' (undoubtedly a reference to the former Pale ditch). The fort here is no longer visible on the surface but its outline appears with remarkable clarity in aerial photographs (Figure 2.3).[29] Equally important as the border strongholds were the walled towns on the periphery of the Pale, but the financially strapped government left it to these towns themselves to further strengthen their defences. Further south, the Alen family of Norfolk occupied monastic properties in County Kildare on the border at Kilteel and at Alenscourt (St Wolstans), granted in the 1530s and early 1540s. The government was also stimulating the colonisation of Wicklow. Powerscourt (Wicklow), the former stronghold of the earl of Kildare, was re-edified in 1536, and granted the next year to a Palesman, Peter Talbot, along with other manors in that area.

---

24 Cited in J. D'Alton & J. O'Flanagan, *The history of Dundalk* (Dublin, 1864), pp 121–2.   **25** Leask, *Castles*, p. 77. An earlier statute stipulated minimal internal dimensions of 15 x 12 feet (4.6m x 3.7m).   **26** M. Lindsay, *The castles of Scotland* (London, 1986), pp 29–30.   **27** *Cal. pat. rolls, Henry VIII*, i, p. 291; see also RIA, MS 24.D.4 for an order *c*.1558 to assist E. Balff of the Gregge in Meath to build a border castle.   **28** *Cal. pat. rolls, Henry VIII*, i, pp 7, 361; B. Graham, 'Anglo-Norman settlement in Meath', *PRIA*, lxxv C:11 (1975), pp 223–49 at p. 247.   **29** *Cal. pat. rolls, Henry VIII*, p. 321; M. Moore, *Archaeological inventory of County Meath* (Dublin, 1987), p. 183; F.E. Ball, *The judges of Ireland 1221–1921*, 2 vols (London, 1926), i, p. 206; P. Kerrigan, 'Seventeenth-century fortifications, forts and garrisons in Ireland: a preliminary list', *Ir. Sword*, xiv:44–5 (1980), p. 144. He dates the earthworks from the mid seventeenth century, however.

Figure 2.3 Ticroghan, County Meath. John Parker, master of the rolls, guaranteed to repair a section of the Pale ditch that ran from Ticroghan to the Boyne. A large fort, locally called 'Queen Mary Castle', can be traced at this site. The rectangular earthwork fort, 101 square metres on the inside, has projecting bastions, sufficient to accommodate a large garrison (Bing maps).

James Goodman, of a south Dublin family from Loughlinstown near Killiney, was given a grant of land near Castlekevin in Wicklow some time before 1547. He was to reside on the lands for the 'defence of the castle and for the more quiet rule and government of the people'. In 1541, however, both the manors of Powerscourt and Castlekevin were granted to the native O'Tooles, on condition that they and their tenants would adopt English dress and language, and build houses for the farmers.[30] Closer to Dublin were English planters such as the Wolverstons from Suffolk, who settled at Stillorgan, and the Travers family who occupied monastic lands at Monkstown. Aside from the Wolverstons, other families from East Anglia settled in the marches of the Dublin Pale around this period, such as the Alens, the Wingfields and the Phipos, but it is not clear whether they came singly or were part of some broader scheme. The

---

30 W. Fitzgerald, 'The manor and castle of Powerscourt', *JKAS*, vi:2 (1909–11), pp 131–6; *CSPI, 1509–1573*, p. 89; *Cal. pat. rolls Henry VIII*, i, p. 141; Ball, *Dublin*, i, p. 87.

southern part of the marches contained much church and monastic land, and a few royal manors. The royal manors were not used for plantations, but the archbishop's manor of Tallaght, often threatened by the Irish, saw the introduction of English tenants. Archbishop Browne (*ob.* 1554) established his relatives here, and before 1553 he leased the property to the military officer Sir Ralph Bagenal.[31]

Fortified garrisons, and initial grants in Laois and Offaly

Government control was tenuous or absent westward beyond Kildare, an area difficult to traverse because of its dense woods and multitude of bogs and lakes. To improve government control, Lord deputy Bellingham founded two fortified garrisons between 1546 and 1548, called Fort Governor (later Philipstown, now Daingean, Offaly) and Fort Protector (later Maryborough, now Portlaoise, Laois). Fort Governor replaced a newly built O'Connor stronghold, situated in a morass and surrounded by great ditches and waters. The initial intention was to confiscate land in the immediate vicinity of the forts, and lease it to the soldiers to make the forts self-financing. The soldiers apparently took their role as farmers much less seriously than their military function. The construction of the forts was partly financed through the levy of a cess on the Old English inhabitants of the Pale.[32]

Fort Protector and Fort Governor survived subsequent troubles when the O'Moores and the O'Connors revolted. Once their rising was suppressed, the native inhabitants were reduced to one-third of their former territories, the remaining two-thirds going to new planters, who arrived in two waves in Laois and Offaly.[33] A first wave of settlements took place under the third deputyship of St Leger (1553–6), when the government was prepared to grant freeholds in Laois and Offaly to residents from the Dublin Pale and to soldiers who had been instrumental in suppressing the local rebellion. Letters patent were issued from 1551 onward to twenty-nine planters in Laois and to eleven in Offaly. The letters patent included the clause that planters must reside on their estate, arm their tenants, and exclude the O'Moores and O'Connors. In choosing grantees, St Leger sought to strike a balance between New English, Old English and loyal Gaelic Irish proprietors. An initial major handicap was that the leases were for only twenty-one years, similar in duration to those on monastic properties. As a consequence, not all grantees occupied their lands. Nevertheless, several sites were planted as far west in Offaly

31 Ball, *Dublin*, i, p. 117; (part 3), p. 8; *CSPI, 1509–1573*, p. 152; see map in P. O'Sullivan (ed.), *Newcastle Lyons: a parish of the Pale* (Dublin, 1986), p. 13. 32 *CSPI, 1509–1573*, p. 27; PRO, MPF 277; N. Canny, *The Elizabethan conquest of Ireland* (Hassocks, 1976), pp 34–5; N. Canny, 'The permissive frontier: the problem of social control in English settlements in Ireland and Virginia 1550–1650' in Andrews, Canny & Hair (eds), *Westward enterprise*, p. 23; *Cal. Carew MSS 1575–1588*, p. 88. Provision for settlers was possibly made in the barony of Shillelagh (Wicklow), but I have not been able to confirm this (D. White, 'The reign of Edward VI in Ireland', *IHS*, xiv:55 (1965), pp 204, 210). 33 The following is based on R. Dunlop, 'The plantation of Leix and Offaly 1556–1622', *EHR*, vi:21 (1891), pp 61–96; Quinn, 'Edward Walshe', pp 307–10; Canny, *Elizabethan conquest*, pp 35–44; G. Hayes-McCoy, 'Conciliation, coercion and the Protestant Reformation 1547–71', *NHI*, iii, pp 79ff; D. White, 'Tudor plantations in Ireland before 1571' (PhD, TCD, 1968), p. 196.

as Bracklin and Kilclonfert (both east of Durrow Abbey), and at Ballyburley, which were noted in 1557 by St Leger's successor Sussex. Aside from Kilclonfert and Ballyburley, government soldiers were stationed in other castles as well: Edenderry and Monasteroris (Offaly), Stradbally, Ballybrittas and Ballyknockan (Laois).[34] The plantation suffered in 1557 when many sites were burned by the Irish. Even though planters were obliged to build houses for their tenants, such structures have not been identified.

The plantation in Laois and Offaly had been implemented ahead of the area being shired; this situation was remedied in 1557 when Queen's (later Laois) and King's (later Offaly) counties were created. The earlier forts were renamed after the reigning monarchs (Fort Governor as Philipstown and Fort Protector as Maryborough).[35] A decade earlier, native seneschals had been replaced by English ones in Wicklow under the Lord deputyship of Bellingham (1548–9); three administrative zones were created, corresponding to areas inhabited by the O'Byrnes, O'Tooles and Kavanaghs. No major strongholds with large garrisons were founded in Wicklow, unlike the situation in the Midlands.

The Barrow corridor

Another strategic step was the strengthening of the corridor along the Barrow connecting the Dublin Pale with the loyal areas further south, where several castles had fallen into the hands of the government after the attainder of the earl of Kildare. At the end of the sixteenth century, the adventurer and soldier Sir Thomas Lee, who constructed Castle Rheban along the river, stressed that this corridor, once properly fortified, would divide the province into Lower and Upper Leinster (the former consisting of Dublin, Carlow and Wexford; the latter consisting of Kilkenny, Laois and Offaly). Aside from safeguarding the route to the south, the strengthening of the passes across the Barrow severed the rebellious O'Byrnes in lower Leinster from the equally rebellious O'Connors and the O'Moores in upper Leinster.[36] Therefore, the string of strongholds along the river was essential to preventing Irish lordships from joining forces to overthrow the English. From north to south, the corridor included the castle of Rathangan, the strategically situated monastery of Evan (Monasterevan), rebuilt from 1549 onward, and a bridge at Belan across the Barrow that was to be fortified in 1552–3 with a castle at one end and a tower at the other. To the south lay Woodstock, separated from Belan by a large bog. The gun embrasures at this castle, facing the former river crossing, date from 1536, when it was rebuilt, showing the change in warfare caused by the introduction of artillery.[37]

---

34 *Cal. Carew MSS 1515–1574*, p. 267. **35** Ellis, *Tudor Ireland*, pp 233, 235; E. Hickey, 'The Wakelys of Navan and Ballyburly', *Ríocht na Midhe*, v:4 (1974), p. 9; *De L'Isle and Dudley MSS*, i, p. 366. **36** Sir Thomas Lee, 'The discovery and recovery of Ireland [*c*.1600]', Folger Library, Washington DC, MS Add. 586, ff 52r–9v; W. Fitzgerald, 'Castle Rheban', *JKAS*, ii (1896–8), p. 173. **37** G.A. Hayes-McCoy, 'The early history of guns in Ireland', *JGAHS*, xviii (1938), pp 43–65. A drawing of Woodstock in 1795 named it Seymour Castle (TCD, MS 942, i, f. 52); see also E. Jope, 'Moyry, Charlemont, Castleraw and Richhill: fortification to architecture in the north of Ireland', *UJA*, xxiii (1960), Plate xxiv.

Below Woodstock lay the bridge and castle at Athy, strengthened at the same time, and noted in 1600 as the only way to cross the Barrow from Kildare into Laois. South of Athy, there were the castles of Carlow and Leighlin. In 1536 and 1548, construction at Leighlinbridge (Carlow) took place at another strategic crossing of the Barrow of the road to the south. This probably included the construction of a large walled enclosure, 340 feet x 250 feet (104m x 76m), to house the garrison, with a keep (surviving) and a round tower diagonally placed at two corners.[38] Thus, the Barrow corridor was protected by an impressive array of improved castles, which increased in strategic importance after the adjoining Laois plantation was created in the early 1550s. Lands in Carlow near the garrisons of Leighlinbridge and Carlow town were earmarked for a plantation in 1552, but there is no evidence that settlement actually took place in that decade.[39]

Re-establishment of crown castles

In south Leinster, the Dublin government was active in regaining control during the first half of the sixteenth century. The attainder of the earl of Kildare in 1536 prompted the confiscation of Maynooth Castle (Kildare), which remained crown property reserved for the Lord deputy until restored to the Kildares in 1552. To the south, the government declared several castles as crown property in 1543. Almost all had been built in Anglo-Norman times, but had been lost to the Irish, such as Clohamon, Enniscorthy and Ferns (Wexford), and Ballyloughan and Clonmullen (Carlow). From 1559 onwards, the status of several castles was further transformed; Ferns, Enniscorthy, Carlow, Monasterevan, Roscommon, two new forts in Laois and Offaly, and Athlone were reserved to the Lord deputy. According to an inscription on his (now lost) tomb in St Catherine's, Dublin, Sir Edward Brabazon was responsible for the winning of Athlone, and became the first Englishman to settle again in Connacht.[40]

Another early planter occupying crown land was Captain Nicholas Heron. He received grants of the castle of Ferns in 1558 and the abbey at this site in 1561, to which he added in 1565–6 the friary and the manor of Enniscorthy, 10km south of Ferns, where he was the first to make a determined attempt to occupy crown land. Around this time, Colonel Roberts started manufacturing sword blades at ironworks near Enniscorthy. Further south, the ancient silver mines continued to be worked at Clonmines. A workhouse for smelting silver ore was built there in 1552 by Joachim Gundelfiniger, a German mining engineer who had been brought over to develop the mines.[41]

---

38 *Cal. pat. rolls, Henry VIII*, i, pp 266, 302–3. Belan is also spelled Belin. P. Kerrigan, 'Irish castles and fortifications in the age of the Tudors, part I', *An Cosantóir*, 4 (1984), p. 202; *Cal. Carew MSS 1515–1574*, p. 96; J. Feehan, *Laois: an environmental study* (Ballykilcavan, 1983), p. 424; *De L'Isle and Dudley MSS*, i, p. 380. Information on Leighlinbridge kindly provided by Paul Kerrigan.   39 *Cal. Carew MSS 1515–1574*, pp 232–3.   40 *Cal. pat. rolls, Henry VIII*, i, p. 43; [W. Fitzgerald], 'Maynooth Castle', *JKAS*, i (1891–5), p. 230; H. Goff, 'English conquest of an Irish barony' in Whelan (ed.), *Wexford*, p. 126; W. FitzGerald, 'The house and demesne of Monasterevin', *JKAS*, iv:3 (1903–5), p. 256; NLI, MS 392, f. 39. I am indebted to Jane Costello for translating the Latin inscription on Brabazon's tomb.   41 Goff, 'English conquest', pp 127–8; E. McCracken, 'Supplementary list of Irish charcoal-burning ironworks', *UJA*, xxviii (1965), pp 132–6 at p. 134; Hore, *Wexford*, vi, p. 247.

The earl of Kildare in Counties Down and Offaly

From the 1550s onwards, the strategy of the Dublin government was to grant whole territories or baronies in the border areas to local lords to recover territories without the expense of conquest by government forces. One of these areas was Lecale in south Down, which was described in the sixteenth century as almost an island, totally bare and devoid of wood, with access through 'one way (overland only), which is less than two miles in length'. In 1549, Lecale had been granted to an Englishman Andrew Brereton. It was described in 1553 as 'for English freeholders and good inhabitants is as civil as few places in the English pale'.

After the restoration of the house of Kildare by Queen Mary (1553–8), the earl of Kildare resumed his traditional role as defender of the marches, as his forebears had done for many centuries. The Queen granted the territory of Lecale to him and his countess; in 1566, Elizabeth ordered him to recover it from Shane O'Neill and to 'have regard to ke[e]pe the Englyshe pale in strength to withstande his incursion', but he had failed to inhabit it by 1570. Notwithstanding, the earl was also granted the barony of Geashill in Offaly in 1569, another frontier area, west and beyond the plantation of Offaly, but closer to Kildare's core strength in the Dublin Pale.[42]

The earls of Ormond in Counties Kilkenny and Tipperary

The earls of Ormond, nominal owners of much of Kilkenny and the palatinate of Tipperary, had suffered a gradual erosion of the area under their control in the fourteenth and fifteenth centuries. After the Kildare revolt, the government, now lacking the former support of the earls of Kildare in the border areas, turned instead to the Butlers. The heir, Lord James Butler, was sent to inspect the Calais Pale and to study the English response to the threat of expulsion from French soil. On his return to Ireland, he was assigned custody of a string of strategically placed crown castles in Carlow and Wexford. The Butlers remained responsible for the security of the border area where the Barrow divided Carlow and Wexford and where the Kavanaghs dominated. It was also here that the Butlers were later granted monastic properties such as Duiske Abbey near Graiguenamanagh (Kilkenny), lying 'upon the borders' between Kilkenny and Carlow, and Holy Cross Abbey, situated on the western border which then ran through the middle of Tipperary. There is no evidence that these abbeys were converted to secular purposes. However, James's successor, Thomas, tenth earl of Ormond, instituted building leases in the border areas; in 1549, he leased lands at Listerlin (south Kilkenny) to a local priest, on condition that within five years he would build 'a tymbre castell glased and covered with sclate, a backhouse, a frenchkyll [French kiln], plante and graifte a good orcherde of apples, peeres, and stone fruyte, and make a dowe [dove] house, and a me[a]dowe for haye and mounde or compace [encompass] the chiefe dwellyng place with a wall of gre[e]ne soddes so as it shal[l] be defensible'.[43]

---

42 T. Ó Laídhin (ed.), *Sidney state papers 1565–1570* (Dublin, 1962), pp 27, 127; [H. Bagnall], 'The description and present state of Ulster 1586', *UJA*, ii (1854), p. 153; BL, Add. MS 4756, f. 82v; *Cal. Carew MSS 1515–1574*, p. 242. White ('Reign of Edward VI', p. 204) stated that Brereton's occupation did not lead to a settlement. **43** T. Barry, *Medieval moated sites of south-east Ireland* (Oxford, 1977), p. 27; Bradshaw, *Constitutional revolution*, p. 122; Ó Laidhin (ed.),

There was also pressure to create more strongholds on the southern border of the earl's palatinate of Tipperary, facing Waterford and the Desmond lands of his enemy, the earl of Desmond. Here a line of castles bordered the Suir, most of which are not datable. An exception is the 1547 lease from Lady Ormond to one of the Butlers, with the clause that a castle was to be built on the lands of Brittas: 'the same castle to be of thre[e] loftes besides the ro[o]fe, and the same substancially builded; the first loft to be with a vault and to be xiii fo[o]te hy, and the other ii loftes to be every of them x fote hy, and the ro[o]fe to be substancially covered with slate and the gutters with gutterstone well embateled, and to be furnisshed with a chymney in every of the ii overloftes'; a substantial barbican was to be included for defence,[44] and an iron grate (a yett)[45] for the gate.[46] The contract specified that this castle was to be modelled on the existing one at Pollywherie (Poulakerry) and this castle may represent a typical building for this area. With the exception of its chimneys, however, the castle was traditional, invoking prototypes reaching at least as far back as the fourteenth century. It is not known whether new settlers were introduced in this area.

An isolated property of the Ormonds was the barony of Arklow (Wicklow), an ancient inheritance of the Butlers recovered from the Kavanaghs in 1525 by James, ninth earl of Ormond. In 1543, he granted the lordship and the three shires to John Travers, master of the ordnance. Travers, whose main residence was at Monkstown in south Dublin, was bound to defend the lordship and to endeavour to win back Ormond's lands in Leinster from the Irish. In 1544, Travers was also granted the friary at Arklow by the Dublin government. Travers was an unusual choice as a tenant for Ormond, because the earl generally favoured Old English and native Irish tenants over New English ones.[47] Settlements in the Arklow barony, however, are not known to have taken place at this time.

There were widespread confiscations in the decades from the 1530s to the 1550s, even though government officials respected legal details. Most confiscated properties belonged to former Irish monasteries or to the Old English rather than to the Gaelic Irish. The subsequent granting of border monasteries to soldiers produced spearheads into the Gaelic lands, and were occupied virtually everywhere by the New English. The north-west border of the Pale was strengthened through a state-subsidised programme, but how widespread its impact was remains unknown, and there is no evidence that the same programme was instituted for the Wexford Pale. The Old English of the Pale were primarily entrusted with the defence of the northern Pale, but they were restrained from occupying the newly freed advance

---

Sidney papers, p. 46; R. Stalley, *The Cistercian monasteries of Ireland* (New Haven, 1987), p. 227; E. Curtis (ed.), *Ormond deeds* (Dublin, 1943–70), v, p. 27. A moated site at Listerlin was removed in the nineteenth century (Barry, *Medieval moated sites*, p. 190).   **44** A barbican is a fortified outpost or gateway, such as an outer defense to a castle, or any tower situated over a gate or bridge used for defensive purposes. Barbicans were normally built outside the main line of defences.   **45** A yett (Old English and Scots word for gate) is a grille of latticed wrought-iron bars used for defensive purposes in castles and towerhouses.   **46** Curtis, *Ormond deeds*, v, pp 22–3; Cairns, *Towerhouses*, p. 4.   **47** Curtis, *Ormond deeds*, iv, pp 102, 256–7: Gwynn & Hadcock, *Medieval religious houses*, p. 221; Bradshaw, *Dissolution*, p. 192.

positions on the frontier. They played a lesser role in the Dublin marches towards Wicklow, where the New English became a dominant force.

The building of castles along the Pale borders, however, still left a permeable frontier; this generated a need for strongholds within the Pale: witness the fortified dwellings constructed in this period at Athcarne and Bective Abbey (Meath). Only a limited attempt was made to revive the old Pale ditch, but even this barrier was not sufficiently secure to keep out the Irish. Finally, the initiation of the plantation of Laois and Offaly, with their government forts as nuclei, proved a conceptual and geographic breakthrough. In contrast to the confiscation of monasteries, however, the introduction of land grants in Laois and Offaly had a shaky legal basis, unratified by any act of the Irish parliament. In this area, the Old English were given short shrift in favour of New English and even Gaelic Irish settlers. Later, the relatively advantageous position of the Gaelic Irish was terminated for centuries to come, while the Old English were still permitted to play a minor role for some time.

1560 TO 1590

The nature of the border areas was transformed with the erosion of Old English influence, where formerly the earl of Kildare and Viscount Baltinglass had served as a buffer between the Dublin government and the Gaelic lordships.[48] The Dublin government now came more often into abrasive conflict with rebellious Irish in its efforts to colonise the border areas. In the 1560s and the 1570s, colonisation activities peaked, leading to extensive settlements outside the two Pales (Figure 2.2c). These settlements emanated from several converging approaches to colonisation. The former method of confiscation of monasteries was expanded, construction of castles along the Pale was continued, together with strengthening of the seneschalships and other local administrative offices in Westmeath and Wicklow, the barony of Idrone in Carlow was recovered through legal proceedings, and the government-sponsored plantation in Laois and Offaly was augmented. The most violent colonial expansion was attempted through grants of land to Englishmen in Ulster to be conquered from the Irish and the Scots, not unlike grants issued by the English crown for conquests in North America. In Ireland, these grants resulted from the attainder of Shane O'Neill by parliamentary act in 1569, freeing up large parts of Ulster for colonisation.[49] To the south, the earl of Ormond considerably expanded the territory under his control in Kilkenny and Tipperary.

Further strengthening of the Pale
The programme of castle building in the Dublin Pale, spurred on by continued pressure from the Irish lordships, was encouraged by the government during the late

---

48 K. Bottigheimer, 'Kingdom and colony: Ireland in the westward enterprise 1536–1660' in Andrews, Canny & Hair (eds), *Westward enterprise*, p. 51. **49** Shammas, *American colonisation*, pp 158–61; R.D. Edwards, *Ireland in the age of the Tudors* (London, 1977), pp 120–1.

1560s to the 1580s, but its scale remains unclear, and it is not known how long the subsidy for castle building was effective. Louth gained several new castles, almost all built by the Old English, at Haggardstown, Dowdstown and Edmondstown (the latter was situated on the east bank of the Lagan, facing Monaghan). Government stipulations for Haggardstown were specific: the grantee, a Dublin merchant, was to make a double ditch, and build within it a stone wall and a gatehouse or tower of lime or clay and stone within four years for the defence of the area.[50]

A new style of oblong castle emerged during this period, as occurred in Wexford, in which a tower and castle were combined into a longer and more commodious fortified house (later called a 'hall type fortified house'). Late sixteenth-century examples in the Dublin Pale include Darver (Louth), and the still surviving Robertstown (north Meath on the Cavan border). In 1567, Alexander Barnewall of Robertstown received a grant of the commandery of Kilmainhambeg, lying even closer to the Cavan border, on condition that he would build a fortification within two years 'for the strengthening [of] those borders of the country against O'Reyley and MacMahon'. Thomas Fleming, Lord Slane, settled furthest west in Monaghan itself, trying to maintain a supply route between Slane (his main seat in Meath) and his castle near Carrickmacross in 1561. Further south, towards the Meath and Offaly borders, two castles were built at Ballina and Clonagh (Kildare). Close by in the same county, Henry Cowley was regranted Carbury Castle in 1569 on condition that he would rebuild with lime and stone the bawn at Clonkeen and a watchtower at another (unidentified) location within four years.[51]

Seneschalships in Westmeath and Wicklow
In another development in Leinster during the late 1570s and early 1580s, the last remaining areas were shired (Longford in the west, Wicklow and parts of Wexford to the south). In this way, county seats were established, county administrations were founded and English law was introduced.

One of the early settlements in Westmeath was in the hands of Thomas LeStrange, a wealthy Norfolk man, who had served as the sub-constable and captain of Athlone in 1577, and justice and keeper of the peace in County Westmeath in 1578, a post that he held intermittently for years. In 1566, he was constable of Roscommon Castle, but he was deprived of that position after losing the castle to the Irish. He received, however, in compensation a grant of Athleague in the same county. From 1564 onwards, he had his 'chief dwelling place' near the former

50 V. Buckley, *Archaeological inventory of County Louth* (Dublin, 1986), pp 92, 96; a sketch of Dowdstown in Huntington Library, Palo Alto, California, MS HAM, Oversize box 9; *Cal. pat. rolls, James I*, p. 12; Ó Laidhin (ed.), *Sidney papers*, p. 50; C. Lennon, *The lords of Dublin in the age of Reformation* (Dublin, 1989), p. 250.   **51** T. Wright, *Louthiana* (London, 1748), Plates 3 and 4; *Cal. pat. rolls, Henry VIII*, i, p. 515; *Fiants, Eliz. 1245–1347*; E.P. Shirley, *The history of the county of Monaghan* (London, 1879), p. 43; *Cal. pat. rolls, Eliz.*, ii, p. 117. Several other castles along the Dublin Pale border appear in a list of places to be garrisoned in 1642, indicating that the datable castles in the text comprise only a fraction of all post-medieval castles built to defend the Pale (*Ormonde MSS*, n.s., i, pp 49–50).

Norman De Lacy stronghold of Ballymore Loughsewdy (Westmeath) on the road from the Dublin Pale to Athlone. The settlement was burned by the Irish in 1572, except LeStrange's 'house and castle'. It is probably significant that the church of the Augustinian priory at this location in the reign of Henry VIII was designated as the new cathedral for the diocese of Meath, a dramatic move westward from its earlier location at Trim. There was a regular market at Ballymore Loughsewdy, where merchants from Dublin purchased hides, sheep fell and yarn. LeStrange lost his life in 1580 at the hands of the Irish, but the settlement, which included 'artisans and English mechanics', continued under his Irish son-in-law Sir James Shaen, known as a 'man faythfully devoted to the Queen and state'.[52]

The supply line to Ballymore, and through it westward to Athlone, was guaranteed by the strengthening of Mullingar that occurred in 1567. In this shire town, a 'faire strong house' and prison were built to serve the justices of the assizes. Further east, the road via Delvin to Athboy was improved by Anglo-Irish families, who built a bridge across the Deel in 1584. Christopher Nugent, fourteenth baron Delvin, lived at Clonyn (near Delvin), closer to the Pale perimeter. He observed in 1591 that his favourite occupation, aside from reading books, was building.[53]

Sometime after 1566, Francis Agard, one of the seneschals in Wicklow, re-occupied Newcastle. In 1569, he urged the government to provide him with five or six gunners to keep this 'wide house', where he was willing to 'adventure his carcase' against the local Irish. He likely built the surviving remains on this large site, originally occupied in Anglo-Norman times. As seneschal of the O'Byrne and adjoining countries, Agard preserved a relative peace. To strengthen the English presence, he suggested walling Arklow as a 'meanes both to replenishe the towne with people, and to drawe maney artisans, and other mecanicall persons [craftsmen], to dwell there, when they may be assured to remayne in saffetye within walles'. His death in 1577 interrupted this plan; Arklow and Wicklow, although having earthwork ramparts, remained unwalled and exposed to attack.[54]

Idrone in County Carlow

The most spectacular transfer of land in this period occurred in west Carlow. An inquisition was held in 1568 showing that the Kavanaghs wrongfully held 'by the strong hand' the whole barony of Idrone, an area 11km by 26km, granted in the Middle Ages to the Carews. The action was brought by Sir Peter Carew from Devon, the first person to attempt to revive ancient English titles in territories in

---

52 Murtagh, 'Athlone', pp 46–7; A. Longfield, *Fitzwilliam accounts* (Dublin, 1960), p. 122; *CSPI, 1509–1573*, p. 477; *Cal. pat. rolls, Eliz.*, ii, p. 12; *Anal. Hib.* xx (1958), p. 17; F. Moryson, *An itinerary* (Glasgow, 1907–8), ii, p. 352: Dymmock, *Treatise of Ireland*, pp 64, 149; [Perrot], *Chronicle*, p. 112. **53** PRO, SP 62/22/180v; *Fiants, Eliz.* 932. A 1567 building plan for Mullingar is in PRO, SP 63/22/62; I am indebted to N.W. English for the information on Deel bridge situated near Rockview (Westmeath) at a disued road; J. Lodge, *The peerage of Ireland*, ed. M. Archdall (Dublin, 1789), iv, p. 174. **54** Canny, *Elizabethan conquest*, p. 34; G. Orpen, 'Novum Castrum McKynegan: Newcastle, Co. Wicklow', *JRSAI*, viii (1908), pp 137–8: *CSPI, 1509–1573*, pp 416–17: A. Collins (ed.), *Letters and memorials of state* (London, 1746), i, p. 159; Kerrigan, 'Irish castles, part 2', p. 276.

Meath and Carlow and in the province of Munster, held for several centuries by Irish or Old English families. Having won his battles in a Dublin court, first against the Old English family of Cheevers in the Dublin Pale, then against the Kavanaghs in Leinster, Carew assumed formal possession of the barony of Idrone.

The Dublin government in effect pandered to Carew's fishing in ancient records by giving him unrestricted access to documents in their possession. In 1570, the Queen recommended that Carew be granted the castle of Leighlinbridge, where the road to the south crossed the Barrow. The surrounding town with its seventy houses had been burned by Piers Butler in the preceding year. Carew agreed to guard it at his own cost, and to maintain ten English horsemen there; 'it is apparent that the planting of our English good subjects there is very profitable for the regiment of that realme'. As constable of the castle, he used it as his residence, fortified it and equipped it with culverins (a light long-barrelled cannon used to bombard targets from a distance). He planned 'the plantinge of Englishe men yn this countrie for the makinge and buylding of townes which shal[l] be replenished with all sortes of English artyficers'. However, he assigned leaseholds to the principal gentlemen of the Kavanaghs, and remained on good terms with tenants who did not cause him trouble.

Holinshed remarked that he divided the barony into manors and instituted court barons in each of them. His hospitality was well known, keeping almost one hundred persons in his household, aside from forty horsemen and one hundred kernes ready at his command to chase and pursue 'such as lay upon the frontiers of his country'.[55] This was particularly necessary since the occupation of Idrone was perceived by the east Kilkenny Butlers as a threat, as this settlement had been established within their ancestral sphere of influence.

Records concerning the introduction of English settlers in Idrone are sparse. Carew built a town at Leighlinbridge, introduced artisans there, and further strengthened the Barrow corridor. The barony of Idrone was surveyed in 1569 in anticipation of the plantation, and this map was subsequently published in Mercator's atlas; no other sixteenth-century plantation in Ireland achieved this status. Four years after Carew's death in 1575, however, 'a greate parte' of unwalled Leighlinbridge was burned by the Butlers, as was the town of Carlow.[56] The Barrow corridor remained vulnerable.

The second wave of grants in Laois and Offaly
By 1564, the second wave of letters patent had been issued for the plantation in Laois and Offaly, seven years after the Irish parliament had ratified the confiscation and plantation. These grants of lands were in 'fee farm' (conferring the right to hold a freehold estate on payment of an annual rent – farm is an archaic word for

---

55 *Cal. pat. rolls, Henry VIII*, i, p. 519; J. Prendergast, 'The plantation of the barony of Idrone, County Carlow', *Kilkenny & South East Ire. Arch. Soc. Jn.*, ii (1859), pp 400–28; iii (1860), pp 20–44, 69–80, 171–88, 196–208; *CSPI, 1509–1573*, p. 416; Ó Laidhin (ed.), *Sidney papers*, pp 134–5; Canny, *Elizabethan conquest*, p. 68; P. Bagenal, *Vicissitudes of an Anglo-Irish family 1530–1800* (London, 1925), p. 73.   56 Prendergast, *Idrone*, p. 422; PRO, MPF 70; Collins, *State papers*, i, pp 216, 230; Canny, *Elizabethan conquest*, p. 145.

rent – thus establishing a landlord-tenant relationship between the parties) rather than leases for years, which further consolidated the settlements. Twice as many grants (88) were issued in this second wave compared to the first wave, and included most of the former grantees: 51 in Offaly and 37 in Laois. Half the grantees were soldiers (five of whom came from Scotland and four from Wales). Most settlers were Catholic. One-third were New English, while another third were Irish, and only 17% of the settlers came from the Dublin Pale. Even in this diluted form, the plantation expressed a novel approach by relying heavily on new blood, but also on co-operation among individuals from diverse backgrounds. The extent of the land grants amounted to half of Laois and one-third of Offaly. The O'Connors and the O'Moores, the original inhabitants, were forced to transplant to the west, with the O'Moores moving to west Offaly adjoining the Shannon. The western parts of both counties were not included. Some lands were also excluded, such as O'Dunne's country in Iregan and O'Dempsey's country in Clanmalier (Laois).[57]

Conditions for the new settlers in the plantation did not include clauses to build; instead clauses prohibited intermarriage and the use of Brehon law, and prescribed the use of the English language, dress and manner of life. Plantation conditions failed to specify the number of English tenants to be introduced. A survey of east Offaly of 1550 listed many existing castles in the area, albeit often in ruins. New dwellings are known in only a few cases. Francis Cosby constructed a large house out of the fabric of the friary at Stradbally (Laois). Surviving examples of new settler castles include Timahoe, Garron and Shrule (Laois), and possibly Clonmore (Offaly). Some buildings (Timahoe, Garron) were built on an oblong plan rather than the traditional square template. Timahoe, for example, measured 40 feet x 78 feet (12.2m x 23.8m).[58]

It is remarkable that the new plantation estates were grouped within a radius of 10km of the two plantation forts at Philipstown and Maryborough; those near Philipstown were situated north and west of the fort only. Other plantation estates in Offaly centred around Edenderry and Monasteroris. In Laois, another concentration was situated along the Barrow, the strategic north-south corridor, where a third fort was built by the government in 1560 at Blackford.[59] In addition, several castles were erected or rebuilt by settlers in this area as at Shrule (1576) and Monksgrange (1588), both by the Hartpole family. The two plantations were quite separated with only a few strongholds connecting the passage from Maryborough to Philipstown. In the absence of an analysis of the townlands granted under the plantation scheme, it is impossible to estimate the contiguity of lands granted to the settlers in each of the two counties. The plantation relied heavily on agriculture;

---

57 Ellis, *Tudor Ireland*, p. 235: Canny, *Elizabethan conquest*, p. 36; Butler, *Confiscation*, pp 15–16, 35. I have identified most but not all of the plantation sites. **58** E. Curtis, 'The survey of Offaly in 1550', *Hermathena*, xiv (1930), pp 312–52; A.P. Smyth, *Celtic Leinster* (Blackrock, 1982), frontispiece; TCD, MS 1209, f. 9; *JRSAI*, liv (1924), pp 34, 42–3; Gwynn & Hadcock, *Medieval religious houses*, p. 259; *Cal. pat. rolls, Eliz.*, ii, pp 47–8. Garron Castle is known from a drawing by Beranger (RIA, MS 3 C 30, f. 48), but its exact location in Laois is unclear. **59** *Cal. Carew MSS 1575–1588*, p. 93.

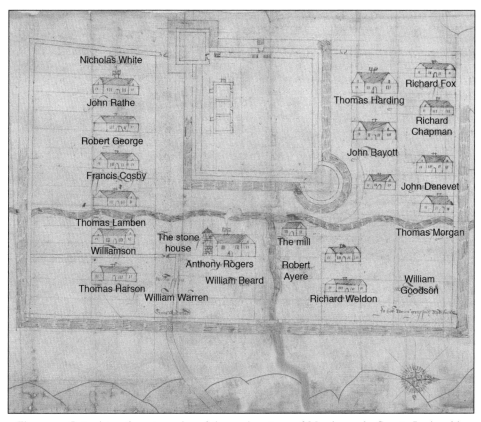

Figure 2.4 Late sixteenth-century plan of the garrison town of Maryborough, County Laois, with names superimposed. The millrace channel followed the original route of the Triogue (judging from an earlier 1571 map). These bounds also align with the approach road from the Dublin direction – the 1571 map indicates that it may originally have crossed the Triogue on that alignment. With the creation of the approach via Bridge Street, the area immediately north, already with some building in 1571, was further infilled. A striking feature of the map is the vivid depiction of the esker ridge to the south of the town. The listing of settlers' names is dominated by West Country English and Welsh families – Cosby, Ayers, Williamson, Morgan, Harding, Harson and Rogers (National Archives, London: MPF 1/277).

only in isolated instances did industry emerge, as at Dysert, where an ironworks was started in the late sixteenth century.[60]

Small villages arose under the protective shadow of the two forts at Maryborough and Philipstown, which were incorporated in 1569–70. Their charters stipulated that the burgesses must fortify each borough with ditches and stone walls for their defence. A contemporary plan of Maryborough, prior to 1570, depicted a walled area of 415 feet x 350 feet (127m x 107m), with a castle on one corner and a blockhouse diagonally opposite.[61] It probably served both as a town and as a cattle enclosure. A

60 E. McCracken, 'Charcoal-burning ironworks in seventeenth- and eighteenth-century Ireland', *UJA*, xx (1957), pp 123–38 at p. 132.   **61** *Cal. pat. rolls, Henry VIII*, p. 220; *Fiants, Eliz.* 1500; PRO, MPF 277; TCD MS 1209, f. 10, published in N. McCullough & V. Mulvin, *A lost tradition: the nature of architecture in Ireland* (Dublin, 1987), p. 42.

late sixteenth-century plan of Maryborough (Figure 2.4) showed a smaller walled enclosure (270 feet x 255 feet, 82m x 78m) with the fort on one side, and a wet moat around the perimeter wall enclosing several dwellings. Not surprisingly, the names of the resident inhabitants were mostly English. Some grantees, such as Francis Cosby, an anglicised Irishman, had a house in this town.[62]

It is difficult to estimate the population of planters in Laois and Offaly. The planters, who owed the services of 174 horsemen, 46 foot soldiers and 35 gallowglasses, may have comprised 500 English in total.[63] In the absence of a census of the plantation, this estimate does not take into account the many Irish settlers. The importance of the Laois/Offaly plantation should not be underestimated: it formed a model for virtually every other plantation that followed, in Munster in the late sixteenth century, and Ulster and Leinster in the early seventeenth century (with the significant difference that the later plantations stipulated more explicitly the introduction of specific numbers of English tenants). The Laois/Offaly plantation had a dramatic existence. Eighteen separate risings took place between 1563 and 1603. As early as 1575, Sidney reported that Laois and Offaly 'are much spoyled and wasted, by the race and offspringe of the old natyve inhabiters'. The O'Connors in Offaly, who focused especially on Englishmen rather than the Old English, 'burned the last of the Englishmen that were without castles'. Not all of the settlers had defensive strongholds available to them and the plantation was consequently highly vulnerable.[64]

Ulster

Lord deputy Sidney's main aim was to overthrow Seán Ó Néill (Shane O'Neill), head of the vast Tyrone lordship in Ulster. The brutal murder of O'Neill in 1567 paved the way for the creation of the counties of Antrim and Down (and probably also Armagh) in 1570–1. This was a prelude to several attempts to introduce new settlements. Sidney's second aim was to expel the Scots, who had infiltrated the eastern part of the province, and reoccupy their land.

Newry   Among the most influential settlements in Ulster was Newry (Down), 21km north of Dundalk, just north of the Pale. Sir Nicholas Bagenal, marshal of the army, was granted monastic and other lands here from 1550–2 onwards, including the castles and manors of Carlingford and Greencastle, and the friary in Carlingford. At Newry, he built an oblong towerhouse (28 feet x 48 feet, 8.5m x 14.6m) resembling structures in the Dublin Pale, whence its builders probably came (Figure 2.5). It was clearly more a fortified house than a castle as it enjoyed large windows and only a partially vaulted basement, but it still carried battlements. Bagenal also erected a church and a large town.[65]

---

62 PRO, MPF 277. I am indebted to Paul Kerrigan for information about Philipstown and Maryborough.   63 White, *Tudor plantations*, ii, p. 406.   64 Butler, *Confiscation*, p. 16; Collins, *Letters of state*, i, p. 83; Dunlop, 'Leix and Offaly', p. 79; *CSPI, 1574–1585*, p. 3.   65 *Cal. pat. rolls, Henry VIII*, i, pp 228–9; Stalley, *Cistercian monasteries*, p. 249; *CSPI, 1509–1573*, p. 192.

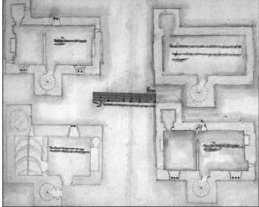

Figure 2.5 Elevation and plans of Sir Nicholas Bagenal's residence at Newry, Co. Down, a sophisticated design of the late sixteenth century, depicting the transition from towerhouse to fortified house (National Archives, London: MPF 83).

Sir Henry Sidney was impressed when he visited Newry in 1575:

> I found such good policy and order in the country where the Marshal dwelleth, his lands so well manured, his tenants so well cherished, and maintained, the towns so well planted with inhabitants, and increased in beauty and building, as he is much to be commended, as well that he useth his tenants to live so wealthily under him, as his own bounty and large hospitality and housekeeping, so able and willing to give entertainment to so many, and chiefly to all those that have occasion to travel to and fro northwards, his house lying in the open highway to their passage.

In 1579, Bagenal petitioned to have his town walled with stone, having already trenched and fortified it within a rampart of earth. This did not take place at that time; Bagenal was killed in 1598 in a military expedition. Before his death, however, he acquired the barony of Idrone from the Carew heir for his son Dudley, thereby indicating his wealth as a planter. As late as 1607, Newry was referred to as a 'frontier town' desperately in need of a town wall.[66]

The Carrickfergus enclave   A second isolated stronghold was at Carrickfergus (Antrim). During the Lord deputyship of Sir Anthony St Leger (1540–8), his secretary John Parker established a small colony near Carrickfergus, and also organised its defences. The town had once been the centre of the earldom of Ulster; its bailiwick was now confined to a radius of less than 8km, known as the County of Carrickfergus. In 1557, plans were revived to fortify its harbour and those of Carlingford, Strangford, Olderfleet, the Bann and Lough Foyle, but only after settlers had been first planted. This scheme was not executed, but an artillery

---

66 Collins, *Letters of state*, i, pp 75, 189; *Salisbury MSS*, xiv, p. 451.

blockhouse in Carlingford Lough, possibly built in 1569–70, resembled Henry VIII's Brownsea Castle at Poole Harbour in England.[67]

In Carrickfergus, three lines of defence protected the colony: on the outer perimeter were peel towers, then came the town defences, and the last resort was towerhouses within the town and its royal castle. These outer defences were not maintained in the sixteenth century. The town's defences were improved by entrenching the friary in 1566. Inside the town, the castle was provided with gun ports between 1561 and 1567. Inhabitants criticised its defences, judging them so inadequate that private towerhouses were still being erected in the town in the 1550s and 1560s, one by the constable of the government castle, Captain William Piers. In 1574, an earthwork rampart was built around the town on the orders of Lord deputy Sidney after Brian Mac Feilim Ó Neill had attacked and destroyed much of the settlement, with only the castles remaining unburned. A round bulwark for cannons, revealed through excavations, may date from this period. The scared inhabitants eventually fled in 1575, leaving only six householders 'of any countenance'. The town recovered, however; a 1570s report noted that over five hundred ploughs were active in its surrounding area. A new town wall was planned but it was not built until 1596. As Carrickfergus rose from its ashes, its government was gradually taken over by the New English; Captain William Piers became its mayor in 1572 and he and his son held this post another four times in the following decade.[68]

Further private campaigns of conquest Elizabeth took a personal interest in Ulster because the earldom belonged to her as her inheritance, but she never enjoyed effective control over the province. She was not willing to wage war at the cost of the government to acquire Ulster lands. In 1565–6, a private campaign led by Arthur Champemoun of Devon, accompanied by a group of West Country gentry, attempted unsuccessfully to gain control of the area east of the Bann. Shane O'Neill, head of the Tyrone lordship, was murdered in the following year. The anticipated break-up of the Tyrone lordship was not sanctioned by the London government; instead, Shane's son of the same name succeeded, and he was recognised as its ruler. The difference was, however, that those O'Neills who had expanded into east Ulster (east of the Bann and Lough Neagh) were forced to resettle within the confines of the traditional Tyrone lordship. This, theoretically at any rate, freed up land for resettlement by English planters.[69]

67 Ellis, *Tudor Ireland*, p. 145; Ball, *Judges*, i, p. 205. Parker also developed industries; Kerrigan, 'Irish castles, part 2', p. 203; *De L'Isle and Dudley MSS*, i, p. 413; *Arch. Sur. Down*, pp 228–9. **68** P. Robinson, *Carrickfergus* (Dublin, 1986), pp 2–3; R. Gillespie, *Colonial Ulster: the settlement of east Ulster 1600–1641* (Cork, 1985), p. 68; Kerrigan, 'Irish castles, part 2', p. 275; Collins, *Letters of state*, i, p. 77: *De L'Isle and Dudley MSS*, ii, p. 27; *Twelfth report of the deputy keeper of the public records in Ireland* (1880), p. 27; *Cal. pat. rolls, James I*, p. 122; M. Gowen, 'Seventeenth-century artillery forts in Ulster', *Clogher Rec.*, x (1979–80), p. 240; S. M'Skimmin, *The history and antiquities of Carrickfergus* (Belfast, 1823), pp 315–16. **69** Canny, *Reformation to Restoration*, p. 81; Canny, *Elizabethan conquest*, pp 71–2.

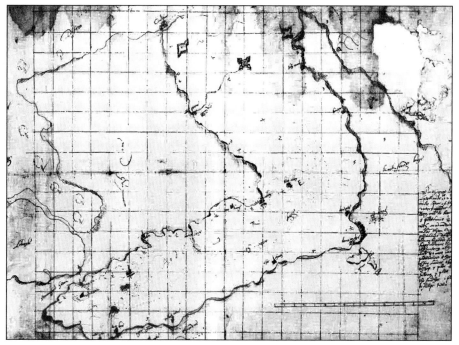

Figure 2.6 Map of the Ards, County Down, associated with the colonisation scheme of Sir Thomas Smith. The 'Great Ardes' is roughly represented by present-day north Down, as far south on the Ards peninsula as the Blackstaff river (at Salt Water Brigg). The 'Little Ardes' is the area south of the Blackstaff, contained within a line from Salt Water Brigg through Glastry where this river begins, and then in a straight line along the modern road from Glastry school to Ballyhalbert (NLI, MS 2656, f. 20).

In 1568, Lord deputy Sidney persuaded local native owners that they should hand over the castle and manor of Belfast, in return for the government building a bridge over the Lagan, cutting passes, defending woodcutters, and protecting shipping. Subsequently, however, such conciliatory techniques were no longer used in Ulster. Instead, Elizabeth relied on the ability of private armies to conquer territories, to eject the interloping Scots and to destabilise Irish landownership, in the anticipation that the adventurers and their soldiers would then be able to establish private plantations as their reward. Suggestions had been made to fortify the Bann to stop the Scots moving from Clandeboy to Tyrone, but the government garrisoned and later fortified only Coleraine at the mouth of the river. In 1567, the Queen observed that the best way of preventing the Scots from settling in Ireland was to expel them and 'by planting the sea coast of the same with English subjects', under the charge of 'some gentlemen of good howses within our realme heere'. Four years later, these plans assumed a firmer shape when Elizabeth approved proposals for military expeditions of conquest to be led by the Englishmen, Sir Thomas Smith, Thomas Chatterton and Captain Nicholas Malby; soon after, the Queen granted Walter Devereux, first earl of Essex, permission for a similar venture.[70]

70 *CSPI, 1509–1573*, p. 391; Canny, 'Ideology', pp 577, 594; Gillespie, *Colonial Ulster*, p. 44; Ó Laidhin (ed.), *Sidney papers*, pp 70–3; R. Dunlop, 'Sixteenth-century schemes for the plantation

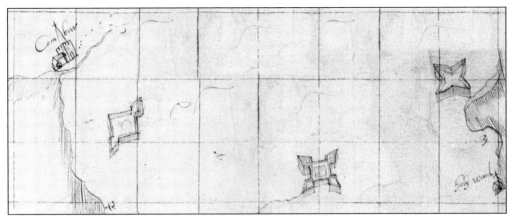

Figure 2.7 Detail of three proposed forts protecting the entry into the Ards peninsula.

Sir Thomas Smith was assigned the territory of the Clandeboy O'Neills in the Little and the Great Ards, comprising 60,000 acres (24,000ha). In 1572, Smith published a pamphlet in London and advertised his plans to invade the country and to conquer it 'with the sworde', thus alerting and alarming the native inhabitants.[71] Upon the conquest, the soldiers would first raise strong garrisons along the border with the Irish. A contemporary plan of the Little and Great Ards, associated with Smith's colonisation plans, showed three such proposed border forts, one between Belfast and Holywood, a second near Clandeboy, and a third closer to Comber and Newtownards (Figures 2.6–2.7).[72]

Once the seashore and the frontier had been safeguarded, the soldiers would be removed five miles (8km) into the country to build another 'fortresse'. As soon as the conquest had been completed, the soldiers could be decommissioned and set to work as husbandmen. Each foot soldier was to receive one ploughland of 120 acres (49ha), while each horseman was to get double that. Smith, greatly influenced by Roman examples of colonisation, also proposed to build a town called 'Elizabetha' in honour of the Queen. He equipped two expeditions into the Ards, which encountered so much native resistance that they proved a threat to both the Gaelic Irish and the 'degenerate English' alike. Eventually, Smith's son was killed and the venture ended. Although his men were aided by some of the Old English of Lecale and the Little Ards, permanent settlements never materialised. It is unlikely that the planned forts were ever built.

In 1573, the first earl of Essex mobilised a large expeditionary force from England to claim other parts of north-east Ulster. He proposed to bring over 1,200

of Ulster', *Scottish Hist. Rev.*, xxii (1924), pp 116–26.   71 D. Quinn, 'Sir Thomas Smith (1513–77) and the beginning of English colonial theory', *Am. Phil. Soc. Proc.*, lxxxix:4 (1945), pp 543–60; M. Dewar, *Sir Thomas Smith: a Tudor intellectual in office* (London, 1964); H. Morgan, 'The colonial venture of Sir Thomas Smith in Ulster 1571–1575', *Hist. Jn.*, xxviii (1985), pp 261–78; Robinson, *Plantation of Ulster*, pp 48–9; *De L'Isle and Dudley MSS*, p. 13.   72 NLI, MS 2656, f. 20, published in Hayes-McCoy (ed.), *Ulster and other Irish maps*, Plate xx; J. Hogan & N. McNeill O'Farrell (eds), *The Walsingham letter-book, or register of Ireland, May 1578 to December 1579* (Dublin, 1959), pp 83–4.

men and gentlemen adventurers, but he arrived with only 212 horse and 228 foot, some of whom were tenants of his English estate. The aim was to conquer the northern half of Clandeboy (most of south Antrim, exclusive of the area around Carrickfergus), where he planned to build and fortify towns, and to introduce husbandmen. His proposal was based on a hierarchically ordered commonwealth, consisting of a detailed division of the land into shires, hundreds, manors and towns. In each of the three areas, two principal places would be well built for 'strength and commodit(i)e' and these would be assigned to barons. These places were not be located further apart than twelve miles (19km); each undertaker was to retain fifty persons in his household, and as many tenants 'for the defense of ye sayd places'. The earl also promised to build castles to protect the areas granted to him, and that he would man them with constables and soldiers for seven years. He planned a corporate town at Belfast, on the southern tip of the vast area granted to him. An earthen fort built in this period at Skegoneill near the present city may be associated with this quixotic enterprise.[73]

In 1574, gentlemen soldiers in Essex's army were promised particular areas in Ulster as an incentive for them to win the land; the settlements were to be arranged in a string along the coast, undoubtedly to thwart further Scottish incursions into the area. Essex's campaign was aimed at dislodging the Scots already living there, and it culminated in the horrific slaughter of the entire population of Rathlin Island off the north coast of Antrim in 1575. A garrison was positioned here, but like a similar one at Dunluce, it was abandoned by the government in 1576 because it was difficult to 'victual'. During his campaign in the north, Essex also protected his western flank by building a fort on the Armagh bank of the Blackwater in 1573. It faced Tyrone and, indirectly, Ó Néill, then at the apex of his power, controlling the present counties of Tyrone, south Derry and north Armagh. A major disadvantage of this fort was its remoteness from the Pale. An intermediate supply point at Armagh was strengthened in 1575 by the building of a fort. Following an explosion of the magazine stored in St Columba's church, however, the fort remained unfinished and the garrison was withdrawn. Soon the fort on the Blackwater was attacked and overrun. Before that, however, Essex boasted (extravagantly) that he was 'advancing the pale' as far as the Blackwater.[74]

Closer to the Pale, Essex had also been granted extensive lands in the peninsula of Lecale (Down), formerly in the hands of the earl of Kildare, who had failed to plant it. In 1575, Sidney commented that these lands were waste, 'but nowe on the mendinge hand, and far the better since the earl of Essex had it, and that by his plantinge of tenauntes, and placinge of soldiours; so that it doth verye well defende itselfe'. The next year, however, Essex died. Lecale was the only positive result of

73 Dunlop, *Ulster*, pp 124–5; *Bath MSS*, v, p. 241; *Salisbury MSS*, v, pp 241–3; Kerrigan, 'Fortifications', p. 8; 'Description and present state of Ulster 1586', p. 153; Shirley, *Monaghan*, pp 51–2.   **74** Dunlop, *Ulster*, pp 52, 200, 206; Canny, 'Ideology', p. 580; Collins, *Letters of state*, i, p. 77. The fort at Rathlin was probably Bruce's castle (McNeill, *Castles of Antrim*, p. 105); Hayes-McCoy (ed.), *Ulster and other Irish maps*, p. 14; Andrews, 'Geography', p. 182; J. Curl, *The Londonderry plantation 1609–1914* (Chichester, 1986), p. 9.

Essex's ventures in Ulster, which otherwise failed miserably. Some of his soldiers stayed behind and played a role in later plantations there. Sidney's account in 1575 further showed the disarray resulting from half-hearted colonisation methods by other adventurers and their armies. Chatterton was bound to plant before 1579, but remained in England and, in the process of getting a plantation started, was thought to have 'utterly undone himself'. His lands were waste, with 'neither house, pile, or castle left standing in it, but only a little soorie [sorry] fort, pitched of soddes and thurves [turfs], that he buylt there for his streingth and defence' (this fort was situated in south Armagh, facing Newry). Likewise, McCartan's country (the barony of Kinelarty, west of Lecale in Down), granted to Captain Nicholas Malby, was 'all desolate and waste, full of thieves, outlaws and unreclaymed people'.[75]

Malby and Essex negotiated an exchange of lands in Roscommon and Monaghan, respectively. After this first wave of unsuccessful colonisation attempts, the Queen ordered a grant of lands in Ulster to be drawn in 1579 for Captain William Piers, constable of Carrickfergus Castle and seneschal of Clandeboy. Her grant was probably in response to Piers's proposal for the settlement of the Little Ards, prepared after Sir Thomas Smith's failure to colonise the whole peninsula. Piers planned to 'separate the said c[o]untrye from the reste of the great Ardes by [three] fortes', on a line from Ballyhalbert to Kircubbin. He requested a grant for a commercial company with monopoly rights, who as a 'bodye pollytyque' would build a walled town. He also sought 300 soldiers, so that he could expel the Scots. Piers held the lands in 1586, when they were described as 'a fertile champion [lowland] country'.[76] It is unclear whether these forts were built, or whether he was able to attract settlers.

The outcome of land grants in Ulster during the decades of the 1570s and 1580s was singularly disastrous and did not result in an expulsion of the Irish. Only Newry and Carrickfergus endured as isolated English footholds. [77]

Connacht

1570 saw the shiring of Connacht as the first step towards increased English control. A few years earlier, Sir Henry Sidney improved access to the province by building a nine-arched stone bridge across the Shannon at Athlone. It featured a bust of Queen Elizabeth and two effigies of himself as a statement that the crown and its deputy intended to stay put. One inscription was a biblical warning to the native inhabitants and settlers to pay taxes to church and state: 'give. to. Cesar. that. w[hich]. is. Cesars. and. to. God. that. whiche. is. gois. [*sic*] mat[thew].22'.[78]

---

75 *De L'Isle and Dudley MSS*, ii, p. 27; J.H. Andrews, 'Mapping the past in the past' in C. Thomas (ed.), *Rural landscapes and communities* (Blackrock, 1986), p. 51: Shirley, *Monaghan*, pp 61–2; *Maps of the escheated counties in Ireland 1609* (Southampton, 1861). **76** John Dalway and Sir Moses Hill were among the soldiers with Essex's expedition (M'Skimmin, *Carrickfergus*, pp 316, 319). The three planned forts were at Blackstaff, another at a nearby bridge, and at Talbotstown (*De L'Isle and Dudley MSS*, ii, pp 87–91). Piers had already proposed settlements on the Ulster coast in 1565 (Canny, *Elizabethan conquest*, pp 70–1); 'Description and present state of Ulster 1586', pp 153–4. **77** Gillespie, *Colonial Ulster*, p. 49. **78** Murtagh, 'Athlone', pp 49–51: W. Fitzgerald, 'The sculptured stones from the bridge of Athlone', *JRSAI*, v:3 (1915), pp 115–22 at p. 120.

Another key stronghold was at Ballinasloe in Galway, situated on the main route from Athlone to Galway, where a bridge had been built over the Suck by 1579. Subsequently, Sir Anthony Brabazon was placed at this location. His father-in-law Sir Nicholas Malby had acquired forfeited estates in this neighbourhood.[79]

The initial infiltration of English settlers into Roscommon occurred prior to 1576 as a result of the confiscation of the monasteries. This settlement, however, did not fare well. A 1574 report stated that many settlers had been displaced by Irish rebels. In the same year, Sidney described the country near Roscommon as 'for twenty miles of length as fruitful and pleasant a country as in England or Ireland, all utterly waste through the wars'.[80]

A good deal is now known about these settlers, who arrived mostly in south Roscommon in the late 1570s and early 1580s.[81] Some initial colonists had come with Sir Edward Fitton (the first Lord President of Connacht) in 1569, such as Edward Mostian, who settled at Killeglin. The most important planter was Sir Nicholas Malby (*ob.* 1584), Fitton's successor in 1578. After his failure to create a settlement in Ulster, he had led a military campaign in Connacht in the winter of 1576–7, resulting in the submission of the Mac-an Iarlas and their allies. Malby obtained a grant of crown and monastic land around Roscommon town, totalling over 17,000 acres (6,900ha), making it the second largest estate in Connacht after that of the earl of Clanricard. In 1578, Malby proposed to the Queen to build walls around Athlone and Roscommon. A 1581 draft of a layout of Roscommon, probably by the English engineer John Easton, shows a plan of parallel streets at evenly spaced distances, defended by two round bulwarks for cannons.

Malby also remodelled Roscommon Castle and made it English-like by piercing the heavy walls with a multitude of regularly placed transom-and-mullion windows. In Malby's words, 'I am become a great builder at Roscommon'. He also introduced several dozen settlers, to whom he gave estates within a radius of 6.4km around Roscommon. The settlers were mostly of English stock; some had fought with Malby in Ulster, but they included faithful Irish soldiers as well. There was no indication that the planters secured strategic passes across the Shannon into Leinster or into Galway, although some crossings across the Suck (as well as that at Ballinasloe) were reinforced by castles as, for example, Sir Thomas LeStrange's at Athleague. Here the ruins of a fortified house survive with two wings surrounding a small courtyard, but it is unclear whether the remains date from the sixteenth or seventeenth century.

One purchaser of lands in this area was Thomas Dillon, who acquired the strategic castle at Curraghboy, lying on the road between Athlone and Roscommon.[82] Contemporary and earlier documents indicate that about forty settlers had planted in the county, a conclusion reinforced by Sir Richard Bingham's comment in 1593

79 *Anal. Hib.*, vi (1934) p. 366; Collins, *Letters of state*, i, p. 106.   **80** *De L'Isle and Dudley MSS*, ii, p. 44; *Cal. Carew MSS 1525–1574*, p. 475; *Description of Ireland 1598*, p. 154.   **81** T. Cronin, 'The Elizabethan colony in Co. Roscommon' in H. Murtagh (ed.), *Irish midland studies: essays in commemoration of N.W. English* (Athlone, 1980), pp 107–20; T. Cronin, 'The foundations of landlordism in the barony of Athlone 1566–1666' (MA, UCG, 1976), p. 31; PRO, MPF 95; *Walsingham letter-book*, p. 47.   **82** Cronin, 'Elizabethan colony', p. 114.

that the area around Athlone was 'well peopled with English'. It is difficult to specify which architectural remains represent this colonial advance, but a single-storey house at Dundonnell, situated within a round – possibly earlier – earthwork, could be linked to the settlement.[83] Some colonists lived in castles, either newly built or pre-existing; other settlements were housed inside earthen forts, some presumably with timber dwellings. A later document speaks of the settlement as containing forty-four castles, nineteen earthen forts and eight abbeys.[84]

The Roscommon plantation was remarkable in its link with the Lord Presidency of Connacht, and its otherwise private investments without direct support from the Dublin government. The safety of the urban settlements, however, was far from guaranteed. At Malby's urgent request, the Queen consented only to the building of a wall at Roscommon, but this was not accomplished, possibly because of Malby's death in 1584. Some construction of gate towers had occurred at Athlone by 1578, but the town remained unwalled until the 1620s.[85]

Munster

English rule over Munster was strengthened with the introduction of the Lord Presidency in 1571; unlike Connacht, however, successive Lord Presidents did not actively promote or participate in settlements. Instead, new settlements were initiated by sheriffs and private individuals.

The abbey at Owney (also known as Abington, Limerick) was leased in 1562 to Piers Walsh, whose family erected a handsome house near the ancient buildings. According to Lord deputy Mountjoy in 1601, it was strategically situated; 'there is no other good passage [from Tipperary into Limerick] but by the nearby abbey of Ownhie'. The 'Hospital' in the parish of Aney (Limerick) was granted to William Apsley, sheriff of the county, who lived there in 1578.[86] Further west in Kerry, the town of Dingle expanded, probably because of its commerce based around rich fishing resources. Stone castles were erected here in 1565 and 1586. In 1585, Elizabeth signed a warrant for the incorporation of the town with similar privileges to Drogheda, and granted £300 towards erecting walls around the settlements: this work was never executed.[87]

The largest plantations in this period took place south of Cork, near Tracton Abbey, which had been granted to the earl of Desmond. In the late 1560s, the earl leased a substantial part of the surrounding barony of Kerrycurrihy, including the castle of Carrigaline, to Sir Warham St Leger. In this venture, Sir Richard Grenville later joined him, probably bringing his followers from England to Munster. The government sanctioned the plantation, because Grenville was appointed sheriff of County Cork. The settlement proceeded so well that its leaders made grandiose plans to expand their hold on the province. Before June 1569, St Leger, Grenville and twenty-five other Englishmen formed a corporation to undertake the conquest

83 Murtagh, 'Athlone', p. 90.   84 *Cal. Carew MSS 1575–88*, pp 136–7.   85 Murtagh, 'Athlone', pp 59–60.   86 Gwynn & Hadcock, *Medieval religious houses*, pp 126, 336; *CSPI, 1601–1603*, p. 12; *Cal. Carew MSS 1575–1588*, p. 143.   87 J. Cuppage (ed.), *Archaeological survey of the Dingle peninsula* (Ballyferriter, 1986), p. 380; *Cal. pat. rolls, Eliz.*, ii, p. 105.

of south-west Munster. The Gaelic areas were targeted rather than the Desmond lands, to be won by a force of 3,000 soldiers, who would repel 'the wild and rebel enemy'. After the anticipated victory, the soldiers would metamorphose into settlers. The corporation promised to generate trade and commerce, especially through the fishing industry around Baltimore (Cork); a final draft delimited a huge tract to be conquered lying between the mouth of the Shannon and Cork harbour. The project was touted as securing the coast from future invasions. However, this scheme, planned slightly earlier than similar ones in Ulster, was never approved by the Queen.

These ambitious plans may have precipitated the outbreak of the revolt in 1569. The Kerrycurrihy settlement suffered badly when Fitzmaurice and his followers stormed Tracton Abbey, killing seventeen people, and spoiled the castle of Carrigaline, Fitzmaurice's birthplace. A document outlining Munster colonisation plans cynically welcomed the rebellion, correctly predicting that colonisation would provoke more rebellions and that consequently all lands should fall to the crown 'within the space of tenne yeres' 'by office, attaynder or otherwise'.

A second proposal for conquest in Munster was formulated in 1573; as well as St Leger, it included Sir John of Desmond, brother to the earl of Desmond. This was the first and last time that the Old English in Munster were drawn into a colonisation scheme directed at their Gaelic neighbours. This plan was again rejected in London. Significantly, however, Jerome Brett, an associate of St Leger in Munster, became the military commander for Sir Thomas Smith's conquest of the Ards in Ulster in 1574.[88]

Tipperary and Kilkenny

Visiting Tipperary in 1567, Sidney found that 'the inhabitants of the towns of Clonmel, Cashel and Fedart [Fethard] did not durst to go outside of the walls because of fear that they would be robbed or killed'. He described the countryside as an 'unmeasurable tracte of lande nowe waste and uninhabited', as a result of slaughter and famine, which 'of late yeares, was well tilled and pastured'. Thomas, ninth earl of Ormond, moved the central control of his estate from Kilkenny to this area, where he added a splendid 'Elizabethan' mansion to his castle at Carrick-on-Suir (1565–6), which survives to this day. He instigated a policy of regaining lost lands formerly in the hands of his ancestors. In 1578, he urged the Dublin government to help him regain possession of the territory of Arra, west of Nenagh (north Tipperary), which, according to him, was wrongfully occupied by the Mac Briens. He also reclaimed ancestral lands in north-west Tipperary including the recovery of Nenagh Castle and Dromineer Castle (1591–3) from the O'Kennedys. Several contracts concluded in the sixteenth century between Ormond and chiefs of Irish lordships (O'Dwyers, O'Meaghers, O'Mulrians) attest to the earl's expansion of control. In north Tipperary, he relied on Old English tenants such as the

88 Canny, *Elizabethan conquest*, p. 82; P. Piveronus, 'Sir Warham St Leger and the first Munster plantation', *Éire-Ireland*, xiv (1979), pp 24–5; Quinn, 'Smith', p. 559.

Cantwells, Purcells and Butlers. Piers Butler built a huge bawn with tall walls at Ballynakill (near Roscrea) about 1580, measuring 137m x 73m, which protected the large stock of cattle on the surrounding lands.[89]

Similarly, the Mac Briens and the O'Mulrians were seen as enemies along the western border of Tipperary. The earl built small castles at Ballysheeda and Farneybridge to repel the O'Mulrians. The surge westward was also evident from other Old English families establishing strongholds on the border or in the Irish territory, such as the Purcells at Ballynahow and Loughmoe (west and north of Thurles, respectively).

It is hard to determine how many settlers were actually introduced by Ormond. When he later received a seignory as part of the Munster plantation (with its centre at Swiffin, west of Tipperary town), the grant favourably mentioned his 'transplanting and planting English people' in Munster, although the precise location remains obscure. Thus, the position of the Butler territories in Kilkenny and Tipperary was strengthened, control over ancestral lands was re-established, castles were built, and the infrastructure improved, judging from lease conditions to repair or build corn mills.[90]

1560–80: continuity and change

The 1560s and 1570s saw both continuity and a dramatic change in colonial settlements. Although further border castles were built along the Pale frontier, they gradually assumed more the shape and comfort of fortified houses. A parallel development took place along the border of the Wexford Pale. Sir Peter Carew's attempts, supported by the government, to exploit ancient deeds to prove that properties in both the Gaelic and Old English spheres of influence belonged to the crown rather than to the occupants of the land, opened up a Pandora's box of possible challenges to estates across the country. As in the preceding period, Dublin courts paved the way for future challenges of concealments, indicating again how opportune it was for the Elizabethan New English to follow English law. In this period, the final shape of the Laois and Offaly plantations hardened, and the two central forts were turned into borough towns. The repeated assaults by displaced inhabitants attempting to recover their lands, however, showed how unprotected and isolated these settlements were in reality. Their location prevented them from absorption into the Dublin Pale, although there were sufficient strongholds on the supply route from Dublin.

The situation of two enclaves in Ulster was different. The newly founded settlement at Newry was within easy reach of the Pale, and it benefitted from a strong leadership and a substantial income derived from the large estate there, which helped to finance and strengthen the plantation. It constituted the first practical

---

89 Collins, *Letters of state*, i, pp 20, 239; Curtis (ed.), *Ormond deeds*, iv, pp 47, 54, 187, 222, 268–9; v, pp 105, 218; vi, pp 19, 29ff, 54. Cairns, *Towerhouses*, provided a thorough survey of Tipperary towerhouses but he did not map the distribution patterns of datable castles.   90 Lodge, *Peerage of Ireland*, iv, p. 37; M. MacCarthy-Morrogh, *The Munster plantation* (Oxford, 1986), p. 289; Curtis (ed.), *Ormond deeds*, v, pp 90, 98, 293.

demonstration in Ireland that a private individual, without much government help, could found a town as a centre of a large estate, which once in existence could become self-supporting. The other much older enclave at Carrickfergus struggled for its existence, while gradually improving its defensibility. Sidney's policy was to prevent towns from faltering and for good reason. He wrote to the Queen in 1567:

> These towns [in Ireland] are your highness's forts and garrisons and yet they cost you nothing in the keeping of them but rather render unto you service and rent. They are in effect the only monument of obedience and nurseries of civility in this country. [With the exception of Waterford, however, the towns were] greatly impaired and in the highway of utter ruin if your majesty do not prevent it … It shall therefore behove your majesty to take care for the conservation of these towns for the loss of them would be the loss of this your country.[91]

Preservation and expansion were to go hand in hand, however. In the north, huge tracts were granted to Englishmen if they could win the land for the crown. Significantly perhaps, neither New English nor Old English were invited into or volunteered for these dismal campaigns, although it is not clear whether this was based on foresight or on financial capacity. By the late 1570s, the lesson had been learned that it was a poor policy to initiate planting by conquering the land. Even though Sir Nicholas Malby was a failed projector in east Ulster, it is significant that he subsequently was highly successful in Connacht, where his office as Lord President conferred both the power and the income to pursue his colonial goals. In other respects, this was the age of private initiative both in Munster, and in Tipperary and Kilkenny, where Old English lords realised that colonial development would, and perhaps should, take place. The difference, however, between Ormond and Desmond was instructive: Ormond relied only on the Old English, while Desmond and his son were drawn into schemes with the New English. In a short time, however, it was the Old English (Fitzmaurice in 1579, Viscount Baltinglass in 1580) and several Gaelic groups in Munster and Leinster who took up arms. Their hostility was partially aroused by the new settlers, but more of it concerned religious convictions. The revolts' focus in the field, however, centred on the settlers' control over properties.

THE 1580s

Leinster

The tide was now turning against the New English, with major revolts erupting first in Munster, then in Leinster (Figure 2.2d). In the winter of 1580–1, a fresh government offensive took place resulting in a girdle of garrisons around the O'Byrnes of Wicklow and the Kavanaghs in north Wexford, necessitated by the humiliating defeat of a government force in Glenmalure in the O'Byrne country.

---

91 V. Treadwell, 'The Irish parliament of 1569–71', *PRIA*, lxv C:4 (1966), pp 55–89 at p. 60.

Garrisons were also established in the coastal towns of Wicklow and Arklow, and further south in Wexford at the inland site of Ferns, and at Clonmore. The western flank consisted of garrisons at Castledermot and Ballymore Eustace (both in Kildare). Lord deputy Grey, during his campaign in the enclosed area, decided to build two fortifications, one at Castlekevin, the other at Castle Comin (Wicklow). Their purpose was 'to sever the Cavenaughes and the Birnes' and 'to plant in places of most comoditye for their annoyance ... that could offende the Birnes'. These forts were situated within reach of the garrisons at Wicklow and Arklow. After the cessation of hostilities, the lands of the rebel Viscount Baltinglass, mostly located on the periphery of the Pale, were confiscated. No attempt was made by the government to plant his lands; instead, they were put up for sale on condition that the purchasers would be, at the very least, Old English of the Pale. It is unclear whether this group benefitted from the spoils: some New English certainly did. Baltinglass Abbey, situated on the western border of Wicklow, was occupied by Sir Henry Harrington's soldiers in 1583; he built or rebuilt a towerhouse at this location in 1587, situated within a bawn with corner turrets.[92]

The need for dwellings along the southern border of the Dublin Pale to retain defensive features remained strong. A few castles were built along its perimeter, such as at Athgoe (south Dublin) in 1579. In south Dublin, more opulent buildings arose, such as a small Elizabethan manor house at Donnybrook and, a little further west, the still surviving large fortified house at Rathfarnham (1583) of Adam Loftus, archbishop of Dublin, built on lands forfeited by the rebellion of Viscount Baltinglass. The castle, with its plan of 23m x 16m, was twice the size of the average new plantation castle elsewhere. Rathfarnham Castle also had four large spear-shaped towers for defence. A novel feature for Ireland was that individuals firing from any tower could cover the outsides of two other towers. This design reflected the freestanding nature of the structure; its owner, the archbishop and chancellor Loftus, probably had no intention of farming here, and the original building never needed an extensive cattle bawn, which would have impeded this mode of defence.

In this period, another novel colonial strategy emerged to resolve the problem of the repeated risings in the plantation of Laois and Offaly. In 1594, Ralph Lane, a soldier (and subsequently a planter in Virginia), with Lord deputy Perrot's approval, communicated a proposal to the Queen to transplant all of the O'Moores to some uninhabited part of Munster. The plan, originated by one of the O'Moores themselves, extolled its advantages for the planters and its more humane consequences for the O'Moores.[93] Why the O'Connors were not included is unclear. The transplantation was not implemented until the early seventeenth century.

Inhabitants of Laois experienced their own tensions from other quarters. On the Kilkenny border, the Mac Giolla Phádraig of Upper Ossory were engaged in a long-standing feud with Ormond and his followers. In 1563, the earl received a grant in

---

92 MacCarthy-Morrogh, *Munster plantation*, p. 22; Hore, *Wexford*, iv, p. 402; Stalley, *Cistercian monasteries*, p. 174; A. Vicars, 'Notes on Grange Con', *JKAS*, iii (1899–1902), p. 383.   93 Dunlop, *Leix and Offaly*, pp 86–7.

this border area of the abbey at Leix (Abbeyleix, Laois). He also planned several castles, as, for example, at Ballylehane, and required tenants to enclose the fields. A lease to the principal tenant of Dunmore (north of Kilkenny town) contained the clause that the 'farmers of the villages' would 'trench and enclose round about their principal farm houses and dwellings'. In the same area, a lease of Jenkinstown stipulated that the tenant should vertically extend the castle at this site, cover it with oak timber and slates, and build a bawn within four years. Ormond did not import New English; instead, his borders were reinforced with Old English and Gaelic tenants. As a result of the systematic settlement policy of the Butlers and embedded Old English traditions of farming in south Kilkenny, its highly evolved landscape (notably its extensive enclosures) was dramatically different from most other Irish counties at that time. In 1598, the county had 'the most show of civility of any other of the border counties, in respect of the fayre seats of houses, the number of castles and the Inglysh manner of inclosure of their grounds'.[94]

Expansion of English settlements in Wexford   Since the Middle Ages, English control in Wexford had been strongest in the southern baronies of Forth and Bargy. This area was described in 1578 as follows:

> The south part, as the most civil part, is contayned within a river called Pill [now the rivers Corock and Taghmon flowing into Bannow Bay at Wellington Bridge], where the auncyenest gentlemen, descended of the first conquerers, do inhabite; the other also, without [outside] the river, is inhabited by the original Irishe and the Cavanaghes, Moroghes [Murphys], and Kinselighes [Kinsellas], who possesse the wooddy part of the country, and yet are dailie more and more scattered by our Englishe gentlemen, who incroche upon them and plant castles and piles within them.[95]

Expansion took place in two directions: westward beyond the Corock into the barony of Shelburne, and northward into the area called the Duffry (part of the barony of Scarawalsh, west of the Slaney, and around Enniscorthy). The western expansion was facilitated by the confiscation of the extensive monastic properties of Tintern and Dunbrody, in what was considered a frontier area. Tintern Abbey, burnt during a minor rebellion about 1562, became the property of Anthony Colclough 'on his undertaking to fortify and maintain it'. A soldier, he executed martial law in the area in 1576. The adjacent abbey of Dunbrody was probably occupied by its grantees, the Itchinghams, judging from the adaptation of the structure for domestic purposes: it is unclear from documentary sources whether they actually settled there at the time.[96]

---

94 Curtis (ed.), *Ormond deeds*, v, p. 151; vi, pp 21–2, 134; Gwynn & Hadcock, *Medieval religious houses*, p. 125; Nolan, *Fassadinin*, p. 51; R. Butlin, 'Land and people *c.*1600', *NHI*, iii, p. 149.   95 Cited in J. O'Callaghan, 'Fortified houses of the sixteenth century in south Wexford', *Old Wexford Soc. Jn.*, viii (1980–1), p. 41.   96 Colfer, 'Anglo-Norman settlement', p. 88, Map 3.9; Hore, *Wexford*, iii, pp 133–4, ff 141; *Cal. pat. rolls, Henry VIII*, i, p. 497; *Fiants Eliz.*, 1259; *Anal. Hib.*, xx (1958), p. 6; White, 'Tudor plantations', p. 25; Goff, 'English conquest', p. 131.

Figure 2.8 Fethard Castle, County Wexford, by Francis Grose, 1791. This early fifteenth-century fortified house on the episcopal estate incorporated the gatehouse, drawbridge and other fabric from an earlier castle. The structure fuses two independent elements to form an L-shaped structure with a vaulted ground floor to guard against fire. The hall was on the first floor of the long wing. The round tower at the angle of the L-shape served as a belfry, while adding a dash of architectural panache. In the 1630s, the manor and castle passed into the acquisitive hands of the Protestant Loftus family.

Besides the secularised abbeys, a novel type of oblong castle was introduced, replacing the traditional square towerhouses with attached halls. Later scholars conferred the name 'hall-type fortified house' on these buildings and they consisted of an oblong two-and-a-half-storeyed structure incorporating a tower on one side. Examples at Fethard (Figure 2.8), measuring 6m x 12m, Dungulph (9m x 20m) and other locations (mostly in Shelburne barony) were similar. These houses were all built by local Wexford families in the late sixteenth century.[97] The structures were castellated and defensible, but were mostly built horizontally rather than vertically.

The westward expansion in this area was strengthened by the building of two forts, one at Duncannon (1587) to thwart a feared landing of the Spanish, the other at Coolyhune near St Mullins (1581) (Figure 2.9). The latter was situated on a pass between Wexford and Carlow, and commanded the Barrow to protect the trade of New Ross and its hinterland from the Kavanaghs. The innovative shape of the fort, a pentagon with five bastions, was erected as a 'gift' by Sir Henry Wallop, the principal settler at Enniscorthy. Its first constable, Anthony Colclough of Tintern, had a direct interest in defending this border, because these lands had once belonged to the abbey of Tintern.[98]

97 O'Callaghan, 'Fortified houses'.   **98** J. Gilbert (ed.), *History of the Irish confederacy* (Dublin, 1882–91), iv, pp xxvii, 366; Hore, *Wexford*, i, pp 260, 266.

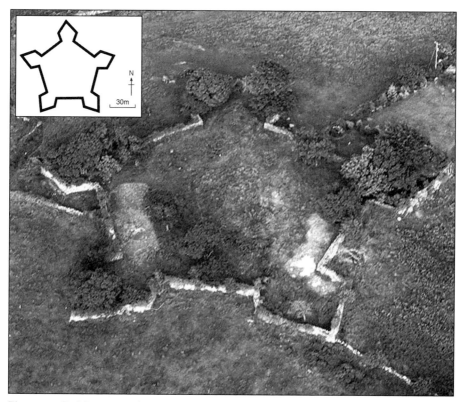

Figure 2.9 Coolyhune, a regular pentagonal fort of unmortared stone, near St Mullins, County Carlow. In 1581, a warrant was issued to raise £350 from the counties of Wexford, Kilkenny and Carlow and the cities of Kilkenny and Waterford to build a fort at St Mullins to defend the Pass of Poulmonty, to command the Barrow crossing at St Mullins and to protect the trade of New Ross against incursions by the Kavanaghs. In 1582, Anthony Colclough of Tintern Abbey was appointed captain of the new fort, which he was commissioned to erect, fit for 'a government garrison for the defense and quiet of those borders'.

North of the Wexford Pale lay another frontier with the Kavanaghs. Here the Franciscan friary of Enniscorthy was purchased in 1585–6 by Sir Henry Wallop, vice-treasurer of Ireland, who also obtained a lease of the King's castle at this location. He subsequently rebuilt the castle, equipped it with guns and requested a ward for its protection, characterising his estate as the 'key of that broken border'. He made the Slaney navigable and founded a timber industry in the extensive woods along the river, producing pipe staves for export mostly to France. He also attracted English artisans who were planted within a twelve mile (19km) area 'everie way' around Enniscorthy, as he claimed. The settlement was described as 'well inhabited and peopled' in 1587. Wallop had been one of the commissioners for the Munster plantation, where he had been refused a grant. His experience in establishing the vast Munster plantation must have benefitted his plantations at Enniscorthy.

Adjacent to Wallop, another Munster official, Lodowick Bryskett, settled at the priory of St John, where he described his life as a 'borderer' in 1592 as 'perillous'. Penetration of the adjoining Duffry area took place slowly in the late sixteenth century with settlements by the Browne family from Mulrankin. The same family was responsible for building two other border castles, each called Browncastle. Other settlements were at Duffry Hall, founded by a scion of the Colclough family from Tintern Abbey. All these settlements were established south of the Slaney: only Clohamon, a large estate, lay on its northern bank. It had been granted in 1581 to Sir Thomas Masterson, the soldier and constable of Ferns Castle, who was characterised as a 'very good borderer'.[99]

Ulster

The process of shiring west Ulster (Cavan, Donegal, Fermanagh, Monaghan, Tyrone) proceeded gradually between the late 1570s and early 1590s. Overall, few settlements took place. A possible exception was the ancient crown manor of the barony of Farney (Monaghan), which had been granted to the earl of Essex in 1576 in recompense for relinquishing his right to colonise parts of Ulster. The grant of Farney, which included baronial rights of law, stipulated that Essex would repair and rebuild castles and fortresses and place arms and garrisons therein. Essex died in that year; neither he nor his son ever resided on the estate. It was repeatedly threatened by the sons of Eibhear Rua MacColey MacMahon, former captain of Farney. For that reason, the government agreed to provide twenty soldiers for its defence to Essex's farmer John Talbot, himself undoubtedly of Old English stock, and originally from Castlering (Louth). Talbot resided at Farney Castle (probably Carrickmacross) that was eventually attacked and burned by the MacMahons. Little is known about the introduction of settlers on the estate. One of the few remaining fortified houses was built by an Elizabethan soldier named Hadsell at Magheranacloy. Possibly dating from the late sixteenth century, it had an oblong plan, 5.2m x 19.5m with two square towers, similar in plan to Bagenal's Newry castle, but not as tall.[100] Its ruins are spectacularly situated on a ridge and, given the rarity of surviving Elizabethan castles, are in dire need of preservation.

The daring but ultimately futile attempts at private conquest in Ulster in the preceding decade were not repeated. A less ambitious undertaking took place in 1584 when Christopher Carleill, stepson of the statesman Sir Francis Walsingham, set out from England on a naval expedition toward Maine or Nova Scotia in the New World. He ventured, however, no further than Ireland, where he established a small fort and settlement at Coleraine, on the north-eastern border of the Uí Neill territory. This may have been among the factors that provoked O'Neill to build his own fort on the opposite side of the Bann, but more upstream, in the following year. The Blackwater soon became the central focus of an English-Irish struggle for control. In 1587, Lord deputy Burgh built a second fort on the Blackwater, called Fort Burroghes (Figure 2.10). A contemporary drawing shows a fortified bridge crossing the river with a tower at either end; the tower adjoining the fort was

99 Hore, *Wexford*, iv, pp 408ff; O'Callaghan, 'Fortified houses', pp 8, 49; Collins, *Letters of state*, i, p. 282.   **100** *Cal. pat. rolls, Eliz. I, 1575–1578*, vii, p. 185; Butler, *Confiscation*, p. 35; Perrot, *Chronicle*, p. 81; M Byrne (ed.), *Ireland under Elizabeth … by Don Philip O'Sullivan Beare* (Dublin, 1903), p. 78: Shirley, *Monaghan*, p. 93; A. Brindley, *Archaeological survey* of *County Monaghan* (Dublin, 1986), p. 91.

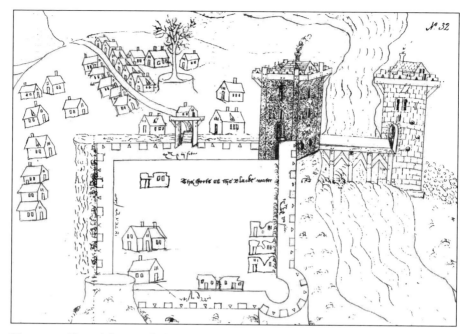

Figure 2.10 View of the second Blackwater fort, County Tyrone, designed to defend the vital river crossing in 1587 (National Archives, London: MPF 99).

constructed of timber and it served to protect the small fort as well. Even more than Coleraine, Fort Burroghes constituted a direct threat to Ó Néill whose principal residence at Dungannon Castle was only 10km away. Ó Néill soon attacked and reduced both Fort Burroghes and Essex Fort.[101]

As to the confrontations with the Scots in east Ulster, the Dublin government recognised its inability to drive them out. In 1586, the two major leaders Angus MacDonnell and Somhairle Buí (Sorley Boy) were granted the Glens and half of the Route respectively. After the latter's death in 1590, the Scots continued to expand their territory, with the government unwilling or impotent to intervene.[102]

Connacht

In the 1580s, the existing settlements in Roscommon flourished. However, English penetration beyond this county into Galway was minimal; the few instances were limited to the eastern periphery of that county. John Lawrence built a conventional keep at Ballymore close to the Shannon in 1585. Fifty years later, Lord deputy Wentworth and other commissioners for the Connacht plantation complained that Clanricard, the principal landowner in Galway, although making

101 Quinn, *Elizabethans*, p. 113; R. Lloyd, *Elizabethan adventurer: a life of Captain Christopher Carleill* (London, 1974), pp 95ff; Curtis (ed.), *Ormond deeds*, vi, p. 43. Carleill later had an interest in Island Magee, which he sold in 1590; Kerrigan, 'Irish castles: part 2', p. 278: Hayes-McCoy, *Ulster maps*, p. 14; PRO, MPF 99; P. Ó Conluain, 'Some O'Neill country maps 1575–1602', *Dúiche Néill*, i (1987), pp 13–24 at p. 15.   **102** Perceval-Maxwell, *Scottish migration*, p. 7.

some improvements, had 'not brought in one Englishman to plant amongst them (except some builders), so the county of Gallway in a manner consists of natives, and those altogether papists'. A 1574 report that listed the castles and towns built by the English during the Middle Ages illustrated how little was recovered by the government until that year.[103] This situation remained unchanged for many decades.

Even some walled towns in the county, depopulated during the wars, could not be occupied permanently. In 1567, Sidney commented that Athenry formerly had 300 householders, but that this had now been reduced to four. The town was attacked by the Irish five years later and was severely damaged. In 1575, Sidney ordered the rebuilding of half the town, for which taxation was levied on the inhabitants of Clanricard land. As in Calais, Sidney proposed to 'cut the towne almost into two equal partes, it being before full as bigge, with a faier high wall'. Soon after Sidney left, however, the Irish again attacked, set the new gates on fire and 'beat away' the masons and labourers. The inhabitants petitioned the Queen's council in England in 1584 to bring over English artisans and tradesmen, but nothing came of this, although several buildings were erected and numerous improvements were made. The shaky existence of Athenry was paralleled by the contemporaneous decline of the municipal organisation of Loughrea, another town founded by the Anglo-Normans in the same county.[104]

A decisive move by the government came in 1585 when it successfully negotiated that traditional Gaelic exactions and military cess were to be replaced by a composition rent collected by government officials. It was thought that the composition rent would stabilise Irish/English relationships, and it was therefore regarded as an alternative to colonisation through confiscation. Instead, the composition rent facilitated transfer of lands through purchase, but reports from Englishmen bewailed the difficulties of acquiring tenants to work the land. Moreover, composition rent would not be levied on wasteland, reducing the possibility of settlements there.[105]

In Mayo, John Browne described himself as 'the first Englishman in the memory of man that hath settled himself to dwell in the county of Mayo', where he arrived in the 1580s. He acquired an estate at the Neale in the south of the county, and elaborated grandiose and unsuccessful plans for developing the local economy. In the process, however, he was the first to prepare several maps of areas in Connacht, showing, for example, improvements in the defences of Galway and Athenry. Sir Richard Bingham undertook military campaigns in Mayo and took care to protect his own interests and those of his brother John, to whom he assigned the castle and

103 *Echoes* (Ballinasloe, 1988), p. 6; W. Knowler (ed.), *Letters and dispatches of the earl of Strafford* (London, 1739), i, p. 45; *Cal. Carew MSS 1601–1603*, p. 475.   **104** PRO, MPF 130 plan of Athenry, 1583; Collins, *Letters of state*, i, pp 28, 106, 119; *AFM*, v, p. 1661; D. Quinn (ed.), 'Calendar of the Irish council book 1581 to 1586', *Anal. Hib.*, xxiv (1967), p. 144; *Topog. dict. Ire.*, i, p. 83; Hogan & McNeill O'Farrell (eds), *Walsingham letter-book*, p. 91; Nicholls, *Gaelic society*, p. 423.   **105** B. Cunningham, 'The composition of Connacht in the lordships of Clanricard and Thomond 1577–1641', *IHS*, xxiv (1984), pp 5–6, 9.

estate of Castlebar in 1589.[106] Further north, a garrison had been established in Sligo in 1588, but no defensive features are now recognisable.[107]

The Old English   The opening up of the western frontiers attracted several Old English, both those from the intermediate border areas and from the Dublin Pale. Several possibilities existed for them. They could invest in properties through purchase or mortgages. George Cusack, undoubtedly from the Dublin Pale, was granted property 'for the better encouragement to inhabit the waste lands by him purchased' in Connacht. A 1592 report observed that 'the country came to be much better inhabited and especially the counties of Galway and Roscommon, for divers came from the English pale to dwell there', presumably mostly Catholics. In addition, Galway merchants were frequent purchasers of mortgages and lands in its hinterland.[108]

Among the most successful Old English investors was Theobald Dillon, collector of the composition rent in Connacht. In the 1580s, he acquired the entire barony of Costello by dubious legal means from the MacCostellos, formerly the Nangles of Anglo-Norman stock. He held further extensive lands in Roscommon and Westmeath.[109] Others built castles, which brought them into conflict with government officials in Dublin and with private colonial ventures. Sir Patrick Barnewall, seated at Turvey (north Dublin), and one of the most vocal critics of the Dublin government in the early seventeenth century, built 'a fair and strong fort and house' some time before 1611 at Ballyleague (now Lanesborough), one of the principal passages across the Shannon, between Longford and Roscommon. To the irritation of government officials, Barnewall's castle dominated the former Anglo-Norman fort 'over against it', which had been refurbished by the government prior to 1611; because of Barnewall's stronghold, the government fort was deserted a few years later.[110]

The Munster Plantation

Fitzmaurice returned to Ireland in 1579 where he landed near Dingle (Kerry), and made a fortification at Smerwick for his Irish and foreign troops. He was soon killed, but the leadership of the revolt was taken over by Sir John of Desmond. The earl of Desmond also joined the revolt in that year which petered out when he was killed

---

106 R. Gillespie, 'Lords and commons in seventeenth-century Mayo' in R. Gillespie & G. Moran (eds), *A various country: essays in Mayo history 1500–1900* (Westport, 1987), p. 47; J.H. Andrews, *Plantation acres* (Belfast, 1985), p. 45; PRO, MPF 71, 233; M. O'Sullivan, 'The fortification of Galway in the sixteenth and early seventeenth centuries', *JGAHS*, xvi (1934), opposite p. 10; B. Mac Giolla Choille (ed.), *Books of survey and distribution: vol. iii, County Galway* (Dublin, 1962), p. xxxviii; Cronin, 'Landlordism', pp 80, 88.   **107** *Cal. Carew MSS 1603–1624*, p. 295.   **108** Cunningham, 'Composition of Connacht', pp 5–6, 9; B. Ó Bric, 'Landholding by Galway townsmen in Connacht 1585–1641', *IESH*, ii (1975), pp 60–1.   **109** Gillespie, 'Lords and commons', p. 47; Cronin, 'Elizabethan colony', p. 114; *Cal. pat. rolls, James I*, pp 124–5. During the Nine Years War, the estate suffered greatly in Dillon's combat with the rebels when he lost 'my kinsmen, goods and houses and castles burnt and razed to the ground' (*Salisbury MSS*, xv, p. 148; *CSPI, 1603–1606*, p. 183).   **110** *CSPI, 1611–1614*, p. 51; *Cal. Carew MSS 1603–24*, p. 298; PRO, AO 1/290/1089. The government castle, called Oldcourt, was rebuilt before 1611.

near Tralee in 1583. English military campaigns had ravaged the countryside with the troops destroying the crops to make 'short wars'. The rebellion, however, had two results, a reduction in the population of Munster and the forfeiture of lands that had belonged to the rebels. The forfeitures hit the Old English hardest: 98 of 136 attainted individuals were Old English, while only 38 were Gaelic Irish. Their attainder was ratified by act of parliament in Dublin in 1585–6, which paved the way for what is now called the Munster plantation.

Of all the sixteenth-century Irish plantations, this one is best understood. The plantation eventually resulted in a massive infusion of Englishmen, who transformed the landownership, the landscape and the economy for centuries to come. The confiscation of the Desmond lands and those of his followers amounted to 231,000ha, or 97,000ha profitable and as much more as waste. After many preliminaries, and partial surveys of the lands, the first series of letters patent was issued in 1587, with others following until 1595. Pursuing the strategy pioneered in Ulster, planters were allowed to settle in companies as a way of preserving ties formed in England. Thus, for example, Sir Christopher Hatton and gentlemen of Cheshire and Lancashire were given lands together, while Sir Walter Raleigh and the gentlemen undertakers of Devonshire, Somersetshire and Dorsetshire were also allocated contiguous blocks of land.[111]

Since the Munster plantation was directed from London rather than from Dublin, it comes as no surprise that the majority of undertakers selected had no existing ties with Ireland, while a proportion had connections with the English court. Thus, the English administrators in Dublin were by-passed in the selection process for undertakers, and only a handful of officials from the Munster Presidency were included. The message may have been that as England had to foot the cost of the military campaigns to quell the revolt, England should also benefit most from the forfeited lands. Most importantly, the Old English and the Gaelic Irish were discarded as desirable candidates for government-sponsored colonial expansion.

The geographic extent of the plantation is only roughly known, since mapping of the townlands granted to the thirty-five undertakers has not yet been undertaken. Undertakers received one seignory, amounting to 12,000 acres, or decreasing proportions of 8,000, 6,000 and 4,000 acres (not including unprofitable land – 4,900ha, 3,200ha, 2,400ha, 1,600ha). Plantation conditions replicated those first applied to Laois and Offaly, and included clauses that the settlers were not to marry with the Irish, nor to lease to the 'mere Irish not descended of an English name and ancestor of any of the same lands'. Additionally, undertakers, their freeholders and copyholders must retain a specified number of horsemen and footmen in readiness for the defence of each plantation.[112] Most important of all were the new conditions that, for a full seignory, the undertaker had to settle ninety families, not counting his own, while tenants must live close to each other. A glaring omission in the leases

---

111 R. Dunlop, 'The plantation of Munster 1584–1589', *EHR*, iii (1888), pp 250–69; D. Quinn, 'The Munster plantation: problems and opportunities', *JCHAS*, lxxi (1966), pp 19–40; MacCarthy-Morrogh, *Munster plantation*. 112 BL, Sloane MS 1724, ff 6–ll; *CSPI, 1586–1588*, pp 84–9.

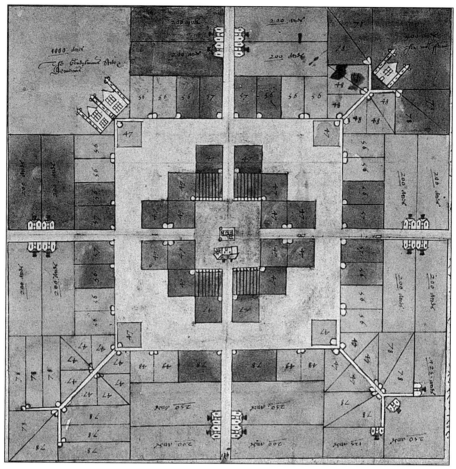

Figure 2.11 A model for laying out a plantation seignory (estate) in Munster in 1586. This plan
envisaged a square of 12,000 acres (4,900ha) with sides of four and a half miles (7.2km), serving
simultaneously as a manor and a parish. Its central feature was to be a Protestant church set in a village
green, with four roads radiating from it. Orderly paper landscapes of this type were never successfully
transferred intact to the intractable Irish landscape (National Archives, London).

was a clause requiring undertakers or their tenants to build defensive structures and
to enclose their lands.

Because the forfeited lands were so scattered across the whole of Munster (and
part of west Leinster), the plantation was fragmented and did not form a contiguous
area. Core settlements for each seignory were often far apart, and for that reason
they did not underpin a supporting network of strongholds. Moreover, roads were
not necessarily available to connect the core settlements. A contemporary concept of
a seignory of 12,000 acres (4,900ha) shows a square of four and a half miles (7.2km),
serving simultaneously as a manor and a parish (Figure 2.11). It included thirty-two
houses to be occupied by tradesmen, labourers and gardeners, close to the church
and mill. Surrounding farms were graded in six sizes from 78 acres to 1,000 acres
(32ha to 405ha), with the latter being the 'gentleman's demesne' and the manor

Figure 2.12 Mallow Castle, County Cork (Dúchas).

house. Nine such seignories would constitute a hundred or wapentake (an archaic historical subdivision of northern counties in England, corresponding to the hundred in other shires), in which the central village would be transformed into a market town with ninety-six families and more differentiated professions. The whole scheme exemplified Elizabethan concepts of the hierarchy of settlements and social order.[113]

In practice, the layout of seignories was considerably more haphazard than suggested by this elegant plan. There was a good supply of towerhouses and monastic buildings, which often were adapted by the new settlers. Prime sites for this purpose were Desmond's large castles at Newcastle, Askeaton and Lough Gur (Limerick), and Castleisland (Kerry). Sir William Herbert from Wales was assigned Castleisland, and he brought over a full complement of household goods and two cannons from England. He was among the first of the sixteenth-century English settlers in Ireland to create a formal garden with walks. Elsewhere, monastic estates were adapted to secular use. Sir Edward Denny built fifty houses for tenants at the abbey of Tralee, while Sir Richard Grenville rebuilt the abbey of Fermoy, purchased from Lord Roche, as well as Gill Abbey at Cork.[114]

113 J.H. Andrews, 'Geography and government in Elizabethan Ireland' in Stephens & Glasscock (eds), *Irish geographical studies*, pp 186–7.   114 MacCarthy-Morrogh, *Munster plantation*, p. 125; M. MacCarthy-Morrogh, 'The English presence in early seventeenth-century Munster' in C. Brady & R. Gillespie (eds), *Natives and newcomers: the making of Irish colonial society 1534–1641* (Dublin, 1986), p. 185; BL, Add. MS 4756, f. 93; G. Bushnell, *Sir Richard Grenville* (London, 1936), p. 225.

New buildings were constructed. Best known is the now ruinous Mallow Castle, Cork, built by Sir Thomas Norris *c.*1593 (Figure 2.12). It measured 10.4m x 26.8m, and had polygonal towers, an English Elizabethan feature also evident at some other planter houses (for example, Cullum's Castle near Ardagh, Limerick). With its many windows, Mallow Castle resembled a country house, although it was equipped with pistol loops. For defence, it relied on an extensive 37m square bawn, with walls that were 5.5m high. This, with other lower walled-in areas, covered 1.62ha, sufficient for a garrison of 600 soldiers. The whole layout cost £5,000, with another £1,000 for 'ordnance' (artillery) and 'other defensible furniture'. Norris initiated an ironworks in its neighbourhood. Further east in Waterford, Sir Christopher Hatton began building a house of a similar size on his seignory near Cappoquin, which remained unfinished in 1589. Less sumptuous towerhouses were erected at several locations – Dingle, Kerry, and Kilcolman, Cork – where the poet Edmund Spenser settled. Likewise, Henry Oughtred built 'a fair house' at Mayne (Limerick).[115]

Among the most studied plantation estates was that of Sir Walter Raleigh, who was in the exceptional position of receiving 42,000 acres (17,000ha) or a total of three-and-a-half seignories. His grant included an old deserted urban settlement at Tallow (Waterford), as well as at least eight castles and other structures.[116] A list of the principal tenants of his main estate showed thirty-four names, amongst whom were several merchants, thirteen gentlemen and four esquires. Some individuals may have been colonists with Raleigh at Roanoke in Virginia prior to settling in Munster. For those without an existing castle on their estate, the lease specified stipulations to build a 'mansion or dwelling house' within five years, but not necessarily a bawn; a clause was included, however, to enclose one hundred acres (41ha) with a hedge, ditch or quickset. Some planters doubled as soldiers on government pay, thus ensuring protection for the huge plantation.

Among the centres of the Raleigh estate was Inchiquin, where a towerhouse was inserted into a rectangular fort (as is evident on a contemporary plan and map). A more detailed map of the Mogeely estate, on the road between Youghal and Cork and leased to Raleigh by Henry Pyne, showed enclosures and mostly English field names, a sign of quickly changing times. The castle had a large enclosure and entrenchment, said to be able to lodge 300 men.[117] By 1589, 144 adult males had settled on the Raleigh estate, making a community of 300 to 400 persons, mostly New English, but also including some Old English and Irish tenants. With

115 *Salisbury MSS*, x, p. 447; A. Grosart (ed.), *Lismore papers* (London, 1886–8), series 2, i, p. 6; H. Leask, 'Mallow Castle, Co. Cork', *JCHAS*, ii (1944), pp 19–24; BL, Add. MS 4756, ff 96–96v; MacCarthy-Morrogh, *Munster plantation*, p. 127; Cuppage, *Dingle*, p. 380.   **116** D. Quinn, *Raleigh and the British empire* (New York, 1949); J. Pope Hennessy, *Sir Walter Raleigh in Ireland* (London, 1883); MacCarthy-Morrogh, *Munster plantation*, pp 42–3, 118, 121–2ff; W. Wallace, 'John White, Thomas Harriot and Walter Raleigh in Ireland', *The Durham Thomas Harriot Seminar*, Occasional Paper, no. 2 (1985), pp 3–24; D. Quinn acknowledged to me in 1990 that Wallace erred in placing Kilmore on the Raleigh estate; it was in Cuffe's seignory in north Cork; *Cal. pat. rolls, James I*, p. 38.   **117** BL, Titus, B xii, f. 538; J.H. Andrews, *Irish maps* (Dublin, 1978), Map 4; J. Healy, *The castles of County Cork* (Cork, 1988), p. 425. Andrews also published a drawing after a larger map of the area in 1589 (Andrews, *Plantation acres*, p. 37).

the help of a Dutch merchant, Pyne established a large-scale industry based on timber. Following the discovery of iron ore, iron-mills were also erected on the estate. These enterprises were emblematic of the Munster plantation, which had advocated the pursuit of profit since its public advertisement in 1585. Youghal became the principal commercial outlet for the products of this plantation. Raleigh was elected its mayor in 1588 and 1589; he may have built the still surviving gabled Tudor house in Youghal. By contrast with clannish Cork, Youghal was much more flexible in admitting New English as freemen and apprentices from outside the city.[118] The Munster plantation attracted 5,000 able-bodied Englishmen, according to a contemporary estimate of 1594; 4,000 is a more plausible estimate before the outbreak of revolt in 1598.[119]

Discovery of concealments

The most common outlet for government administrators and other New English to gain estates was through the discovery of concealments. Sir Peter Carew's assistants had ransacked ancient deeds for concealments to prove that current owners held their properties illegitimately. The search for concealments was pursued by private individuals rather than by the central government in Dublin. There were several reasons for this. There was no central registry of deeds; instead, most officials retained documents in their charge that helped to reveal concealments. Moreover, monastic properties were not all known or documented. Finally, as a result of revolts and warfare, the estates of numerous Gaelic Irish and Old English were forfeited to the crown.

After concealed properties had been identified, the crown's title was established through an inquisition. This paved the way for a grant of the lands either to the discoverer of the concealment or to someone patronised by him. One cannot overestimate how much uncertainty and dismay the question of concealments created for Irish landowners. The earl of Salisbury noted that 'there is nothing more sure than that [land] titles are obscure in Ireland'. The covetous pursuit of concealments by the New English and Old English during the sixteenth century has not been well documented. Initiated in the 1580s, they certainly accelerated during the 1590s and early 1600s when a multitude of properties of attainted individuals in the Gaelic and the Gaelicised parts of the country were forfeited.[120] Only a fraction of the discoveries of concealments resulted in settlements.

1570–90: a summary

The Munster plantation was paradoxical in several ways. It was an ambitious enterprise, promising a massive reformation of Munster. In reality, however, it

118 Lodge, *Peerage*, i, pp 57ff; C. McNeill (ed.), 'The Perrot papers', *Anal. Hib.*, 12 (1943), pp 23–4 at p. 39; A. Orme, 'Youghal, County Cork: growth, decay, resurgence', *Ir. Geog.*, v (1965–8), pp 121–49; Sheehan, 'Irish towns', pp 100–1; MacCarthy-Morrogh, *Munster plantation*, pp 241–3. 119 BL, Sloane MS 1472, f. 9; Quinn, 'Munster', p. 39; MacCarthy-Morrogh, *Munster plantation*, pp 108–19; A. Sheehan, 'The population of the plantation of Munster: Quinn reconsidered', *JCHAS*, lxxvii (1982–3), pp 107–17. 120 *Salisbury MSS*, xxi, p. 463; MacCarthy-Morrogh, *Munster plantation*, p. 14; Canny, *Reformation to Restoration*, p. 131.

was also unwieldy and difficult to survey. As a consequence, property rights were confused, creating acrimonious conflicts initially between former owners and settlers, and subsequently between the settlers themselves. A potentially positive feature of the Munster plantation was the scale of enterprise visualised, with the unit of a seignory of 12,000 acres (4,900ha). This was considerably smaller than the territories that Elizabeth had in mind as plantations in Ulster. The Munster lands were larger, though, than the average estate in the new plantations of Laois and Offaly. It proved hard to diagnose an optimal plantation size in this period, especially for undertakers who were expected to transport tenants and equipment from England.

Unlike in the Midlands, the government did not build advance forts or stimulate the building of new towns in Munster to provide additional protection for the settlers. Early in the 1580s, Lord deputy Sir James Perrot proposed to build seven walled towns, each 'a mile about', thereby creating significant space for the introduction of settlers. This scheme did not envisage the building of new towns, but proposed to wall existing settlements at Athlone, Sligo, Coleraine, Mayo, Dingle, Lifford and Newry. In addition, Perrot planned to build seven bridges and seven castles scattered all over the country.[121] The magical number of seven illustrates the possible biblical origin of this creative plan, which was not implemented.

During the 1570s and 1580s, the Dublin government dramatically revised its opinion of which groups should benefit from plantations. The position of the Gaelic Irish, already weak, never recovered. That of the Old English worsened, as the stain of disloyalty spread inexorably from their Catholicism. The accumulation of colonial intrusion, native reaction and the inevitable backlash contributed to a change of players. The Old English joined the Gaelic Irish as unsuitable groups for participation in the deepening of English control over Ireland. Ironically, most New English in Ireland, the soldiers and Dublin administration, who had helped to suppress revolts or who had aided in the exploration of the interior, were not invited to benefit from the spoils of confiscation. This did not deter several of them from eventually building up plantation estates through the discovery of concealments.

1590 TO 1603

County Monaghan

County Monaghan, situated between the Dublin Pale and the Tyrone lordship, served as a buffer between them (Figure 2.2e). In 1591, the Dublin government scored a major victory by achieving a division of that country, where, unusually, the government recognised the native freeholders' rights to their land. Sir George Carew expressed the hope that through the redistribution of land 'the Pale will be so much enlarged, that from henceforth Maguire's country [Fermanagh] and Tyrone are like to be the Irish border'. Confiscations in Monaghan were minimal, with the exception of termon (monastic) lands, granted to New English and Old English in 1591–2. The grants carried the condition of building a castle within five years,

---

121 McNeill, 'Perrot papers', p. 10.

but these grants were later revoked due to non-performance.[122] One of the more enduring settlements took place at the strategic location of the former abbey of Clones, granted first in 1588 to the soldier Sir Henry Duke, who was living there in 1594. This site, with its 'strong castle', protected a pass bordering on Fermanagh, thereby impeding incursions by the Irish into the Dublin Pale.[123]

Connacht before 1595

Sir Richard Bingham, who became governor of Connacht in 1584, was unable to claim either the English centres of Athlone or Roscommon for his own use. He was also concerned about expanding English control into north Roscommon and Mayo, which would strengthen that part of the frontier. This is why he sought to justify a grant of the abbey of Boyle in 1593:

> Boyle is the only thing to be planted with a town and a garrison in all these parts, bordering upon the frontiers of O'Rourke's country [Leitrim], and the only strait to keep out the traitor Maguire and these Ulster rebels from invading county Roscommon; besides it is the only passage and usual way over the mountain into county Sligo … if [Boyle] were inhabited and a town with a fort or castle planted there for a small garrison to reside in, Roscommon were wholly assured from any incursion of Maguire or any of the rest [from Fermanagh], and the next counties so much strengthened as in one year I would not doubt to see that desolation of so much scope of ground as well peopled with English as is about Athlone. [124]

Boyle, however, was not planted until the next decade. Instead, Lord deputy Russell assigned Ballymote (Sligo) to Sir Richard Bingham in 1585, 'with a whole hundred of a shire annexed to it, having been of the prince's possession these 300 years, wrongfully detained by the O'Connors of Sligo'. Subsequently, Ballymote was held by Sir William Taaffe, who was of Old English stock from the Pale, who had become sheriff of County Sligo and who was an ally of the Binghams in 1588–90.[125] The presence of Taaffe and his troops, however, did little to diminish the vulnerability of Roscommon and other parts of Connacht to incursions by the Ulster Irish.

Campaign forts (Figure. 2.13 a–c)

In 1595, Hugh O'Neill, earl of Tyrone, joined his kinsmen in a revolt against the crown. Hostilities had occurred earlier in Ulster, with Red Hugh O'Donnell expelling

---

122 A map of the division of County Monaghan is in PRO, MPF 79. The quotation is from Andrews, 'Geography', p. 182. For the settlement of Monaghan, see P. Duffy, 'Territorial organisation'; *CSPI, 1606–1608*, pp 185–7, 214–5; P. Ó Mórdha, 'The MacMahons of Monaghan 1603–1640', *Clogher Rec.*, ii:1 (1957), p. 150.   123 *Bath MSS*, v, p. 257; Gwynn & Hadcock, *Medieval religious houses*, p. 164; Folger Library, Add. MS 856, f. 85v; Shirley, *Monaghan*, pp 77, 83. Clones was granted in 1601 to Sir Francis Rush, Duke's son-in-law: the grant stipulated that Rush must maintain six 'able men of the English nation to defend and guard the house of Clonies at his own cost' (*Cal. pat. rolls, James I*, p. 11).   124 *Salisbury MSS*, iv, pp 338–9. Many inhabitants were not English but Gaelic Irish or Old English (Murtagh, 'Athlone', p. 85).   125 McNeill, 'Perrot papers', p. 29. Personal communication by Mary O'Dowd (1988).

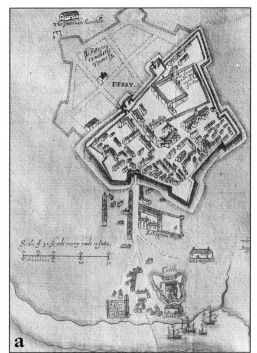
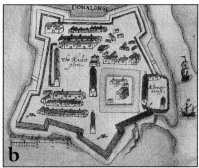
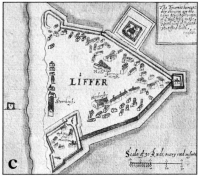

Figure 2.13 The Ulster forts of (a) Londonderry, (b) Dunalong, County Tyrone, and (c) Lifford, County Donegal, from the map 'A true description of the north part of Ireland' *c*.1600 (TCD MS 1209, f.14).

Captain Humphrey Willis (sheriff of Fermanagh) and his garrison from Donegal priory in 1592. Enniskillen (Fermanagh) was taken by a royal force two years later, further provoking the local chief Hugh Maguire. In 1595, Blackwater fort was burnt by Tyrone's brother. Lord deputy Russell began fortifications at Armagh in 1595, perhaps at the same site as the one started by Sidney twenty years earlier. Soon the revolt spread into Connacht. In 1596, one year prior to O'Donnell's invasion of the province, garrisons were positioned to better link Ballinasloe (Galway) with Galway city (indicating that the main road then ran from Kilconnell to Athenry and on to Galway). Two other garrisons were situated further south at Meelick on the Shannon and Mullaghmore, presumably on the road between Meelick and Athenry. Another more isolated garrison was placed at Cong in south Mayo. O'Donnell's advance was not stopped, however, and he proceeded to burn the suburbs of Galway in 1597.[126]

The Roscommon plantation, despite its density of settlement, was overrun by the Irish in the early 1590s, although some places (Boyle, Tulsk, Roscommon, Curraghboy) remained in English hands. In all, the settlers claimed to have lost forty-four castles, eight abbeys and nineteen earthen forts at this time. After the 1599 defeat of Sir Conyers Clifford, the chief commander in Connacht, a fort was

126 *Cal. Carew MSS 1598–1600*, p. 233; Hayes-McCoy, *Ulster maps*, p. 6. The Armagh garrison was abandoned a few years later (*Salisbury MSS*, vi, p. 544).

built at a pass in the Curlew mountains (Ballinafad, Sligo) where the road from Boyle (Roscommon) forks to Ballymote and Sligo. This castle with its square plan and four round towers still survives.[127]

Sir Ralph Lane, former governor of Roanoke in Virginia, offered his views on how to win the war in Ulster: instead of invading the land of the Great O'Neill, the English should 'infest him with sundry plantations in places fit for them, wherewith by their continual residence upon him in his fastness, he shall not only be wrought into, and as with a canker eaten into his bowels'. Mount Norris, one of the earliest forts built for this purpose in mid Armagh, was soon followed by Dunalong (Tyrone) (Figure 2.13b), and by Moyry (south Armagh), the latter protecting the road towards Newry. These forts, together with the fort and garrison at Armagh itself, were necessary to secure the transport of supplies and soldiers further north to the border with Tyrone. Here Lord deputy Mountjoy erected the third Blackwater fort (Mullen or New Fort) in 1601, across the river in Tyrone. The following year he supervised the building of Charlemont Fort (Armagh), further north, where a bridge was built across the same river.[128] At this time, another fort was erected under his guidance by a Dutch engineer further north in Tyrone, close to the shore of Lough Neagh, called Fort Mountjoy after the Lord deputy. Two other forts were established at Omagh and Augher in Tyrone in 1602, to protect the supply route from the Pale to Lifford and Derry (both *c*.1600). Thus, a network of equidistant garrisons was created. Virtually all these forts, constructed of ramparts and ditches on a polygonal plan with angular bastions, could only function as fortified camps capable of holding large garrisons.[129]

On the eastern flank of the advance, forts were built in Antrim in 1601 at Castle Toome and Massareene, both on the shores of Lough Neagh, to protect routes from Carrickfergus and Belfast eastward towards Derry, and also to make it possible for warships on Lough Neagh to be protected by northern harbours. The campaign forts built in 1601–2 consisted of an earthen enclosure without a keep; they needed to be manned by a larger number of soldiers than were necessary when a keep was present. At Sligo, a fort was erected in 1602 to protect the harbour from the landing of a foreign army by making the old abbey defensible, but it was badly situated according to a contemporary account. Inland, a fort was erected at Carrick-on-Shannon at a major ford across the Shannon between Roscommon and Leitrim (the only, if peripheral, infiltration of Leitrim until this date). Another fort was positioned at Ballyleague (now Lanesborough), at a passage across the Shannon between Longford and Roscommon.[130]

127 *Cal. Carew MSS 1575–1588*, pp 136–7. The date of Ballinafad is unclear but it has been ascribed to 1590 (Kerrigan, 'Fortifications', p. 147).   **128** *CSPI, 1600–1601*, p. 109; Kerrigan, 'Castles, Part 2', p. 279; NLI, MS 2656 (4); Jope, 'Fortification to architecture', Plate xiii.   **129** R. Loeber, 'Biographical dictionary of engineers in Ireland 1600–1730', *Ir. Sword*, xiii (1977–9); *CSPI, 1601–1603*, p. 463; *CSPI, 1603–1606*, p. 322; Andrews, 'Geography', p. 184: Gowen, 'Artillery forts', p. 241.   **130** *CSPI, 1600–1601*, pp 269, 448; Moryson, *Itinerary*, ii, p. 394; *CSPI, 1601–1603*, pp 419–20, 435. Carrick-on-Shannon was formerly called Carrick-Drumrusk (*Cal. pat. rolls, James I*, p. 189). The fort at Ballyleague was built prior to 1611 on the site of Old Court, an earlier Norman fort (PRO, A.O.1/290/1089; *Cal. Carew MSS 1603–1624*, p. 298).

The troubled times between the late 1590s and 1603 were unsuitable for colonial expansion. Nevertheless, isolated grants were issued, such as that to Sir Ralph Lane, who received Belfast Castle in 1598. Instead, he established 'a pale for an English colony' at Ringhaddy (Down) in 1602, where he proposed to settle a colony of 'men of trade of Manchester, Liverpool and Lancashire'. He had a remarkably broad view of how his settlement would serve to protect Strangford Lough against an invasion of the Spaniards. Here Lane applied a similar defensive strategy against the threat of a Spanish landing as he had done at Roanoke in Virginia in 1585, by suggesting the erection of fortifications equipped with ordnance as at the castle of Strangford. His death in 1603 terminated these plans and his colony.[131]

Leinster and Munster

The Dublin Pale remained highly exposed to incursions from the north. During hostilities in the late 1590s, Lord deputy Burgh in 1597 placed garrisons on its borders at Kells, Mullingar, Trim, Navan, and other places 'rather as a frontiers to defend theise partes'. In Wicklow, three forts were built during the military campaigns of 1595–7, including one at Rathdrum (immediately south of the existing fort at Castle Comin), another at Fort Russell (named after the then Lord deputy), and a third at Ballinacor (site of Fiach MacHugh's main residence), all on the road connecting Dublin to Ferns. Ballinacor, while inferior to the fort at Rathdrum, also protected the 'border' between the O'Tooles and the O'Byrnes.[132] It is unlikely that the building of the forts led to the introduction of settlers in these tumultuous times.

The revolt reached Munster in 1598, and took the plantations by surprise. Most settlers were incapable of defending themselves effectively, and within two weeks the settlements had been overrun and destroyed with only a few strongholds surviving. One commentator criticised the planters because they had 'so singled their dwellings that they lie open to the malefactor without ability of defence or mutual succour'. According to another account, two hundred 'defensible castles' were abandoned, which must have included ordinary houses, castles, bawns and reconstructed abbeys.[133] The *coup de grâce* was the landing of a Spanish army at Kinsale in 1601, a mortal threat to the English in the province. Eventually, Lord Mountjoy and his troops, after an arduous siege, forced the invaders to surrender in 1602. Soon after this event, plans were promoted to improve several fortifications in port towns to secure them from further invasions. Forts were built on the Cork peninsulas at Baltimore (1602) and Haulbowline (1602) near Cork city.[134] In the

131 Gillespie, *Colonial Ulster*, p. 44; *CSPI, 1601–1603*, pp 315, 319, 352, 503; *Arch. Sur. Down*, pp 248–9.   132 Wood (ed.), *Chronicle*, pp 91, 125, 142; Edwards (*Atlas of Irish history*, pp 94–5) incorrectly placed the border of the Pale in 1598 as far west as the Shannon and on the western boundary of Kilkenny. West Offaly was not effectively claimed by the government until early in the seventeenth century; *Cal. Carew MSS 1589–1600*, pp 16, 225–7, 250; Hore, *Wexford*, vi, pp 423–4, 437.   133 Butlin, 'Land and people', p. 152; MacCarthy-Morrogh, *Munster plantation*, p. 106; A. Sheehan, 'The overthrow of the plantation of Munster in October 1598', *Ir. Sword*, xv (1982), p. 17.   134 Loeber, 'Engineers'.

north, the rebels also eventually laid down their arms when Hugh O'Neill submitted to Mountjoy in 1603, terminating the Nine Years War.

The period from 1590 to 1603 produced an immense destruction of settlements; yet, because of an English victory, it ultimately laid the foundation of their later revival and further advanced English expansion. Although many garrisons were deserted after the war, some continued in the hands of the Dublin government; several formed nuclei for the next generation of plantations. Widespread confiscation of properties across the country further facilitated transfer of land into English hands. The country was not fully conquered, however. Hugh O'Neill (Aodh Ó Néill) and Rory O'Donnell (Ruaidhrí Ó Domhnaill), now earl of Tyrconnell, still retained their Ulster territories, despite their role in the war.

1603 TO 1609

Leinster

The English, as always after winning a war in Ireland, gained war booty in the form of the lands of those who had lost (Figure 2.2 f). Although the plantations in Laois and Offaly and then in Munster had suffered heavily, enough survived to allow them to respawn themselves. In addition, east Ulster was finally available for extensive plantations by Scots and English.

Following the cessation of hostilities, the four decades-old plantation in Laois and Offaly exhibited sufficient resilience to recover, despite the ravages of war. A visitor in 1610 noted that 'prettye castles & howses may be seene' between Philipstown and Maryborough, including 'som[e] that weare newly built, and som[e] old wal[l]es repayred & in some places in the fields English people making harvest, but not so aboundantly as wo[u]ld be looked for'. Plantation estates remained with the descendants of the original settlers. In the early 1600s, however, the native inhabitants were still restive. To resolve this situation, Sir Piers Crosby offered, in return for a grant of the 4,000-acre (1,600ha) Tarbert estate in Kerry, to transport the troublesome 'seven septs of Leix' to this remote location on the west coast. The transplantation proved a disaster and disgruntled members filtered back to Laois and Offaly over the subsequent decades.[135]

Another, even stranger, transplantation project took place during this period. On the borders between England and Scotland, the Grahams, originally a clan of Scottish border reivers (sixteenth-century raiders along the Anglo-Scottish border) had caused endless hassle to the English government and local inhabitants. Finally, to create a more peaceful situation, the government transplanted the Grahams, including their leaders. Eventually, a large group of them was sent to Roscommon to settle on the Malby estate. They arrived in six ships at Dublin in 1606, and

---

135 *4th Report*, p. 566; BL, Add. MS 4756, f. 81; A. Clarke, 'Sir Piers Crosby, 1590-1646: Wentworth's "tawney ribbon"', *IHS*, xxvi (1988), pp 142–60 at p. 149; *Strafford letters*, i, p. 69; R. Steele, *A bibliography of royal proclamations* (Oxford, 1910), ii, p. 30.

were quickly moved on to Roscommon. The company consisted of 114 Grahams, including two knights of that name, and 45 horses. Like the transplantation of the Laois and Offaly septs, many Grahams subsequently fled from their assigned lands.[136] This policy of selective transplantation of troublesome families was not to be employed again until Cromwell's time.

After the war, the government encouraged plantations in Leinster. In 1609, the lordship of Shillelagh in south Wicklow was granted to Sir Henry Harrington. His grant stipulated that he should build 'a castle or stone fortress, with a portcullis, for the defense of the said country' within five years. He probably rebuilt Grangecon, not far from Baltinglass, judging from the date stones of 1610 and 1622 in the castle there. In Westmeath, Sir Oliver Lambert, an officer who had fought in the Nine Years War, re-established a plantation at the former monastic estate of Kilbeggan, close to the Offaly border, which had been granted to him in 1606. In 1610, he was highly recommended as being as 'good' a planter as 'any man of our nation, having, at his own charge, voluntarily made a singular good plantation in the wild and most dangerous places in Leinster, more for the commonwealth than for his own profit', where he built a 'fair and strong building'.[137]

Ulster

In 1605, Lord deputy Chichester called for the settlement of Monaghan, Cavan, Fermanagh and Antrim, all on the outer perimeter of Ulster, without striking at the heartland of the O'Neill. Chichester justified his plans:

> These are the works of peace, intended in war, but never yet brought to any good perfection. As soon as there is a taste of quiet, the erection of citadels, castles, forts, planting of towns and corporations are presently thought a superfluous and needless charge; but without these this kingdom is as open to new rebellion, as it was before the last troubles.[138]

Areas around the former campaign forts, still manned by garrisons, provided natural opportunities for settlement. The governor of the fort at Moyry (Armagh) attracted English families to settle as farmers on the surrounding estate. At Derry, Sir Henry Docwra (the governor of Lough Foyle) already planned a 'plantation' (a fort in this instance) in 1600–1 and he employed forty masons and carpenters at the site. The fortifications consisted of half a pentagon, probably to be doubled as the town grew. After the war, Docwra was granted the area immediately surrounding the fort, which included the lucrative fishery of Lough Foyle. At Derry, he built a 'new' house for himself, a timber church, and buildings for his tenants: judging from a later fire, these were also mostly made of timber. In 1604, Docwra extolled the success of his 'colony' of English there, which had a 'good' number of inhabitants, and requested

136 *10th report*, app. iv, MSS, pp 229ff; *Salisbury MSS*, xix, pp 29ff; *CSPI, 1603–1606*, pp 551–8, 577–8; *CSPI, 1606–1608*, pp 50ff; *CSPI, 1611–1614*, p. 185.   **137** *Cal. pat. rolls, James I*, pp 87, 127; W. FitzGerald, 'Baltinglass Abbey', *JKAS*, v (1906–8), pp 401–2; G. Chalmers (ed.), J. Davies, *Historical tracts* (London, 1786), p. 292; *CSPI, 1609–1610*, p. 527.   **138** *CSPI, 1603–1606*, p. 342.

the incorporation of the settlement with such rights as 'may be least offensive to the Irish borderers thereabouts'. The Lord deputy and council, however, remarked in 1605 that, although they had found 'many good buildings' there, the settlement needed 'replenishment with merchants, tradesmen, and artificers from England and Scotland'. Docwra sold out in 1606. The 'poor infant city of Derry' was overrun and burnt down in the revolt of O'Doherty two years later. At that time, Chichester deplored the fact that no land had been assigned to the town, which was already decaying.[139] Only under the London Companies was the town's settlement more firmly established and its walls erected for protection.

Another small colony was founded by Sir Thomas Phillips at the abbey of Coleraine, where the initial settlement around the 1584 fort had not fared well. Phillips purchased the property, including the fishery at the Salmon Leap, in 1604–5. In his own words, 'there I began a plantation of my own endeavour, where I set up 30 thatched houses'. He also built a mill and adapted part of the old abbey for his dwelling. He attracted settlers by allowing them four years 'freedom' from paying rent; they were undoubtedly Protestants as they formed a good congregation to hear divine service on Sundays. When the Lord deputy and council visited in 1605, they recommended a plantation of English and Scottish settlers. Four years later, Phillips claimed that he had spent £1,000 in improvements, an additional £400 on fortifications and £150 on a water mill. Coleraine had obviously become a commercial centre, because he valued its market at £50 per annum. He also obtained a ten-year lease from the earl of Tyrone of fourteen square miles (36 square kilometres) of woodland along the Bann, where he felled timber for export to Scotland and England. He was given charge of one hundred foot soldiers, the government's way of supporting the settlers. Another small plantation was founded in this period at Lifford (Donegal) by another soldier, Sir Richard Hansard.[140]

Other privately sponsored infiltrations by the Old English into the Ulster periphery occurred prior to 1608 in Cavan; this area had seen virtually no new settlements until then.[141] Sometime before 1606, three Palesmen (including two officers) purchased lands from native inhabitants. Captain Gerald Fleming built a castle, or 'fort' as he called it, 'of great importance for the defence of the Pale, and annoyance of the evil disposed borders'. It was most likely situated at Cabra, just across the border from Meath and close to Monaghan. This castle, and probably Walter Talbot's site further west at Ballyconnell (Cavan), was called 'a civill plantation' by Chichester in 1608. At Ballyconnell, Talbot built and resided

---

139 *Cal. Carew MSS 1603–1624*, p. 226; *CSPI, 1601–1603*, p. 46; *Hastings MSS*, iv, p. 18; C. Milligan, *The walls of Derry* (Londonderry, 1948), pp 7ff; *CSPI, 1603–1606*, p. 321; T.W. Moody (ed.), 'Ulster plantation papers 1608–13', *Anal. Hib.*, viii (1938), p. 284.   **140** BL, Cotton MS Titus BX, ff 285–6; D. Chart (ed.), *Londonderry and the London Companies 1609–1629* (Belfast, 1928), p. 26; *Salisbury MSS*, xxi, p. 181; T.W. Moody, 'Sir Thomas Phillips of Limavady servitor', *IHS*, i (1930), pp 251–72; T. Mullin, *Coleraine* (Belfast, 1976), pp 28–9; Curl, *Londonderry plantation*, p. 431; Moody, 'Ulster plantation papers', p. 283.   **141** Walter Brady, a Drogheda merchant, and others of his name built a castle in the town of Cavan before 1596 (O. Davies, 'The castles of Cavan: part II', *UJA*, xi (1948), pp 81–126 at p. 101).

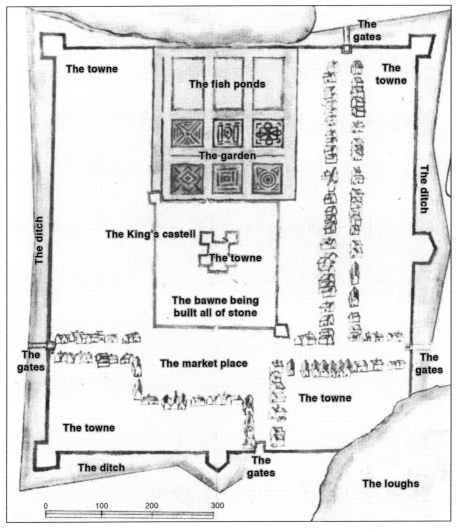

Figure 2.14 A projected layout of Monaghan town and its castle, begun in 1605. The plan envisaged sophisticated parterres and knots within a strongly formal layout, expressed, for example, in the three symmetrically disposed fishponds (TCD MS 1209/32 B).

at a strong castle of three storeys with a fortified bawn at a strategic site close to the Fermanagh border. Talbot, his family and his Old English and Irish tenants were all Catholic. The third Palesman, Captain Richard Tyrrell, proved to be popular locally in Cavan, and he was therefore considered as a threat to the Ulster plantation. Chichester wished that he could be 'dislodged' on some 'fair pretext', and exiled to England.[142] Chichester, endorsed by the English privy council, decided to build some castles on church lands 'to which the natives seldom laid

142 *CSPI, 1603–1606*, p. 565; *CSPI, 1606–1608*, pp 79–80; Moody, 'Ulster plantation papers', p. 282; *Salisbury MSS*, xx, p. 113; BL, Lansdowne MS 156; Davies, 'Cavan castles', pp 93–6; G. Hill,

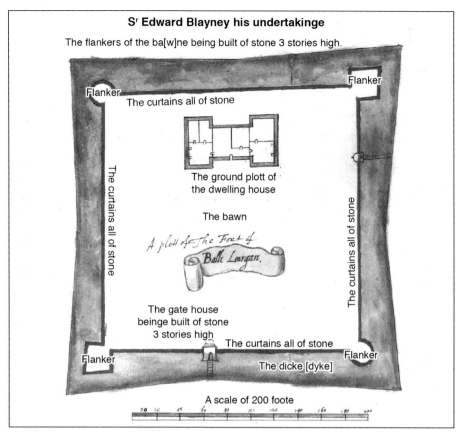

Sʳ Edward Blayney his undertakinge

The flankers of the ba[w]ne being built of stone 3 stories high.

Flanker

Flanker

The curtains all of stone

The ground plott of the dwelling house

The bawn

A plott of the Fort of Balle Loergan.

The curtains all of stone

The curtains all of stone

The gate house beinge built of stone 3 stories high

The curtains all of stone

Flanker

Flanker

The dicke [dyke]

A scale of 200 foote

Figure 2.15 'A plott of the fort of Balle Loergan', County Monaghan, 1607. Sir Edward Blayney built a symmetrical layout of house and bawn at Baile na Lorgan. Baile na Lorgan later became Castleblayney (TCD, MS 1209, f. 32A).

claim', and on lands forfeited by those MacMahons who had gone into rebellion. This resulted in two settlements.

In 1607, Sir John Davies observed that the decommissioned soldiers of the garrison in the shire town of Monaghan were living in scattered cabins, which did not deserve the name of a village. A small star-shaped earthen fort, built in 1602, was held by its governor Sir Edward Blayney, while a new castle in the middle of the village, begun in 1605, remained unfinished. A contemporary plan shows the triple defensive nature of the planned layout of the town of Monaghan: the centre was a small castle with four rectangular towers (similar to Mountjoy Fort), situated within a bawn of 87 yards (80m) square (Figure 2.14). Behind the castle were the gardens and fishponds, among the very earliest depictions of a settler's formal garden in the early seventeenth century. Both castle and garden were situated within a walled

An historical account of the plantation in Ulster (Belfast, 1877), pp 460, 473; BL Add. MS 4756, f. 104; *CSPI, 1608–1610*, p. 436; Tyrrell was styled as of Drumlaghan (Cavan) but elsewhere as of Kilteefany (Cavan) (*Egmont MSS*, i, p. 3; *CSPI, 1608–1610*, p. 115).

fortified town of 250 yards (229m) square. The whole layout was wedged between two lakes, thus effectively blocking the thoroughfare between Clones and Armagh. In Chichester's words, the main purpose of this garrison was to 'secure the English Pale from all northern incursions'.[143]

Since Monaghan was difficult to supply from Newry, an intermediate site at Ballynalurgan was granted to Sir Edward Blayney in 1607 (later called Castleblayney). The grant stipulated that Blayney build a strong and defensible castle or strong house, surrounded by a bawn, and that he should plant six to eight English tenants within four years. Here he built a large square bawn of lime and stone, eighteen feet high (5.5m), well flanked by 'bullwarks'. A contemporary plan and description showed an enclosure of seventy yards (64m) square, four three-storey flankers; and a small manor house within the bawn on (for Ireland) an unusual H-plan (Figure 2.15).[144]

Chichester's plantation

Among the most intensive colonisers in Ulster prior to 1609 was Lord deputy Chichester. He obtained vast estates, partly through devious means when the territory of Con O'Neill was dissolved.[145] In 1603, Chichester received a vast swathe of properties in Antrim, augmented by other grants in subsequent years. His plans were to settle Upper Clandeboy with captains who had served in the wars, who, according to Chichester, 'will adventure most of their fortunes in the settlement thereof, and this will be a good inducement to peace and civility in that barbarous land, where the people know not God, nor care not for man'. One grant, dated 1608, but not issued in his name, carried plantation conditions that were to typify the later colonisation of Ulster. It stipulated that the grantee was to build within eight years four castles or houses of stone or brick, at least 30 x 20 feet (9.1m x 6.1m), 'with a strong defensible court or bawne about the same', with a penalty of £300 for each place not built. Chichester's lands included the ruined castle of Belfast and its surrounding lands, which in his words stood on 'a straight passage, being the thoroughfare from one country to another, and the highway from those parts of the north to Dublin'. A 1611 survey of the Belfast plantation showed that Chichester had settled it with people from England, Scotland and Man, who built 'good tymber houses w[i]th chimneys after the fashion of the English palle'. While the castle was being built, Chichester constructed a deer park, three miles in compass (4.8km), close to the town, the first of its kind made by a New English settler in Ireland at that time.[146]

143 Davies, *Historical tracts*, pp 240, 252; *CSPI, 1603–1606*, p. 559; *CSPI, 1606–1608*, pp 23–4; TCD, MS 1209, f. 32(a), published in Kerrigan, 'Fortifications', opposite p. 145; PRO, SP 64/3/4; PRO, MPF 117.   **144** *Cal. pat. rolls, James I*, p. 103; *CSPI, 1603–1606*, p. 559; E.P. Shirley, *Some account of the territory or dominion of Farney* (London, 1845), p. 122; TCD, MS 1209, f. 32 (b).   **145** D. Chart, 'The break-up of the estate of Con O'Neill, Castlereagh, Co. Down, temp. James I', *PRIA*, xlviii:3, C (1942), pp 119–51; P. Roebuck, 'The making of an Ulster great estate: the Chichesters, barons of Belfast and viscounts of Carrickfergus 1599–1648', *PRIA*, lxxix:1, C (1979), pp 1–12.   **146** *Salisbury MSS*, xv, pp 196–7; *Cal. pat. rolls, James I*, p. 122; G. Benn, *A history of the town of Belfast* (London, 1877), pp 86–7.

Chichester's second settlement was in and around Carrickfergus, where he had become the governor of the castle in 1603. Five years later, he informed the townspeople that the King had assigned one hundred soldiers to assist in walling the town, which had been vulnerable to attack. The erection of walls began in 1609 and finished by 1615, enclosing an area twice the size of the medieval town. Chichester attracted immigrants from his native Devon to the town itself, who settled there between 1602 and 1612. New buildings soon arose, while leases stipulated that these should be built in the English manner of 'brick and lime, or stone and lime, or of cage-work, well tiled or slated, with handsome lights well glazed'. Within the town walls, Chichester started building his mansion Joymount in 1610: this became one of the grandest townhouses of that period.[147] Another potential area for settlement at Carrickfergus was the extensive commons, which had been divided among the town notables, including its New English members, in several waves of leases (1595–1606). Whether this induced settlement is unclear.

Apart from these leases, former strongholds of the bailiwick of Carrickfergus were assigned by Chichester to military officers. In 1606, considering the uncertainty of the soldiering profession during peacetime, he advised soldiers to settle themselves 'in part of the wast[e] lands of the north, w[i]thin my government of Knockfergus, wher[e] they shall have some scope of grounde to worke on'. Chichester presumably asserted the town's rights to its surrounding country on which he planted at least six settlers, mostly veterans from the wars, who started building their castles and residences some time prior to 1611. The lands of Marshallstown were leased to Baptist Jones, a former commissioner of the army, who had built 'a good English house' by 1611, including a garden and lawn trenched with a deep ditch and a strong 'pale' (wooden fence); his lands were enclosed with ditches and set with willows. At least one government grant, dated 1608, stipulated that John Dalway was to build within seven years a 'castle or house of stone or brick, 30 x 20 feet (9.1m x 6.1m) at least, with a court or bawne about the same'; by 1611, he had erected a bawn fifteen foot (4.6m) high, with flankers, and in it 'a pritie [pretty] house of tymber after the English manner'. Dalway, in turn, imposed building conditions on his tenants, stipulating in one case that the tenant must build a mansion of 'lyme and stone covered with slate, which shall cost in the building £300 sterl[ing]', a considerable sum at that time.[148]

Chichester and his officers revitalised Carrickfergus and its surrounding land. There was some hope that after the war the Lord Presidency of Ulster would be established at this location. Chichester's appointment as Lord deputy obviated the need for this because he remained centrally involved in the Ulster plantation that followed after 1609.

---

147 M'Skimmin, *Carrickfergus*, pp 110, 119; Robinson, *Carrickfergus*, p. 4; G. Camlin, *The town in Ulster* (Belfast, 1951), p. 34.   148 Robinson, *Carrickfergus*, pp 3–4; W. Trevelyan & C. Trevelyan (eds), 'Trevelyan papers part III', *Camden Soc.*, cv (1872), p. 87; R. Hunter, 'Carew's survey of Ulster 1611', *UJA*, xxxviii (1975), pp 81–2: Benn, *Belfast*, p. 676; *Cal. pat. rolls, James I*, p. 125. Dalway's Bawn still survives but in an altered form (M'Skimmin, *Carrickfergus*, p. 317).

The Scots

When the expulsion of the Scots from north Antrim had demonstrably failed, King James I, himself a Scot, legitimised their status in 1604. Sir Randall MacDonnell received a grant of north Antrim from Larne to Portrush, comprising well over 300,000 acres (121,000ha), one of the last grants of a fiefdom in Ulster. He set out to improve his lands, leasing to native Irish and to Scottish, and promoting modern agricultural practices on his estate. He restored the castle at Dunluce, which had suffered greatly under Perrot's siege in the 1580s, and he 'erected a good house of stone w[i]th many lodgings and other roomes'. The adjoining town in 1611 had 'many ten[e]ments after the fashion of the palle [Pale] peopled for the most part w[i]th Scotishmen'. Sir Randall's letters patent conferred the power to divide his vast estate into several precincts to be made into manors, and 'to build a castle or mansion house upon each within seven years'. It is not known whether he promoted such settlements (although, some other MacDonnell castles along the coast are known to have been improved as well).[149]

A major infiltration of Scots occurred in east Ulster after 1605 through the manipulations of the Scots Sir James Hamilton and Sir Hugh Montgomery, resulting in large grants in north Down. Their lands were also fiefdoms, where government officers such as sheriffs and justices could not exercise their privileges. One Hamilton grant contained the clause that he should 'inhabit the said territory and lands with English and Scotchmen'. A steady stream of immigrants from Scotland to Ireland was noted as early as 1605 and the flow was well established by the following year. In 1607, the King granted charters for the towns of Bangor, Coleraine, and Belfast 'for the better settling and incouraging of the new colonies of English and Scotish who do daylie indeavor to make civill plantacion within our counties of Downe and Antryme'.[150]

The results of the Scottish settlements in the first decade of the seventeenth century were impressive, with successful towns springing up at Holywood, Bangor and Newtownards. At Bangor, Hamilton built a 'fayre stone house' of 60 x 22 feet (18.3m x 6.7m), while the town consisted of eighty new houses in 1611, inhabited by Scots and Englishmen.[151]

The earl of Thomond's plantations in County Clare

The greatest advance in the west of Ireland was made on the sprawling O'Brien estate of the earl of Thomond in Clare, which under Queen Elizabeth was temporarily part of Connacht. By 1613, this Protestant was described:

> as good an undertaker & planter as any (nay above any of hys degree or meanes) in this kingdome: having always in [readiness] … above 500 armed

149 Gillespie, *Colonial Ulster*, p. 75; Benn, *Belfast*, p. 677; McNeill, 'Castles of Antrim'. **150** Gillespie, *Colonial Ulster*, pp 49–50. A 1606 grant stipulated that building conditions were also included but as he conveyed many of these lands to others it is unlikely that Hamilton considered himself personally bound to this condition (*Cal. pat. rolls, James I*, p. 78). See also Perceval-Maxwell, *Scottish migration*, pp 56–7.   **151** Benn, *Belfast*, p. 677.

men of hys owne tenants … besydes his strong castles buylt by himself & at hys sole chargde for ye security of those parte of Munster … Hee hath also settled many artifycers [craftsmen] of all sorte, to the great comfort & civillyzing of ye co[u]ntry.

He had developed plans for the reintroduction of tenants as early as 1602; four years later, he made improvements in the large area under his control and he had built at least one bridge. He introduced English and Dutch tenants, to whom he leased sizeable holdings. Members of this group also became the first burgesses of Ennis in 1612. His settlements expanded greatly in the following decade.[152]

Munster
The province had suffered greatly during the war; when it ended, most undertakers were no longer resident. As for the population, those 'that escaped the sword', wrote the Bishop of Cork, Cloyne and Ross in 1607, 'died through the famine; and out of these parts of his dioceses by credible report, 4,000 or 5,000 are departed, some for France, some for Spain; so that the country is without inhabitants especially from Cork to the west, as far as Berehaven. The inhabitants are mainly from Cork to Youghal'. Because the former proprietors of lands near Berehaven, Baltimore and Castlehaven, all ports of great consequence for the crown, had left for Spain, their lands could be settled with 'some gentlemen of worth and trust'. An influx of settlers was reported in 1607. Four years earlier, one of the undertakers approached the Dutch congregation in London, writing to them that Munster was so depopulated that the area around Crookhaven and Schoolhaven – at least 8,000 acres (3,200ha), including many 'fair' castles – could be settled by them. Even the promise of leases for one hundred years without charge could not entice the canny congregation.[153]

Sir Richard Boyle A large portion of the influx of settlers elsewhere in Munster was encouraged by the entrepreneur Sir Richard Boyle.[154] In 1613, he was characterised as 'a good planter', who had five hundred armed tenants under him, thus rivalling the earl of Thomond in Clare. Boyle was a shrewd man, with a cunning instinct for opportunities, a willingness to invest in industries, and a sharp nose for how, when and where to acquire estates. He was not among the original undertakers in the province; instead, he had served in a minor administrative capacity in Munster up to 1596, a role in which he mastered how to 'discover' lands concealed from the crown.

---

152 Grosart, *Lismore papers*, series 2, i, p. 154; *CSPI, 1601–1603*, pp 532–3; *1603–1606*, p. 573; *1611–1614*, p. 293. For the settlers in 1641, see P. Dwyer, *The diocese of Killaloe* (Dublin, 1878), p. 206. Since the dates of the large leaseholds are for the most part unknown, the settlement sites are not listed in the appendix.   153 *CSPI, 1606–1609*, pp 108, 132, 191, 379; J. Hessels (ed.), *Epistulae ecclesiae Londino-Batavae* (Cambridge, 1880), pp 924–31.   154 Grosart, *Lismore papers*, series 2, p. 154; The following has been drawn primarily from T. Ranger, 'The career of Richard Boyle, first earl of Cork' (DPhil, Oxford, 1959) and N. Canny, *The upstart earl* (Cambridge, 1982).

A second lucrative avenue of land acquisitions developed after the Nine Years War as prices plummeted, creating a buyers' market for those with ready cash. In 1602, Boyle purchased the large Raleigh estate, believing that the lands would soar in value once peace arrived. Soon after, he added other properties, so that he had made his fortune by 1614, which he largely ploughed back to further his investments. He was highly active in developing his properties, and founded ironworks in 1607. Boyle attracted tenants on a large scale, and granted twenty-one year leases to them on sufficiently favourable terms that they could improve their land, build houses, make field boundaries, expand their herds, or establish commercial and industrial enterprises. His building schemes in Munster dramatically changed the landscape, especially after 1609. His acquisitions of further seignories established a coherent block of estates, forming a defensive perimeter around Waterford and Cork, behind the natural barrier of the Blackwater river.

The ports
The memory and prospects of foreign invasions of Ireland remained potent. English control over the major coastal towns, however, was far from complete. In Carrickfergus, and to a lesser extent in Dublin, that control had grown considerably during the late sixteenth century. Other towns, notably Cork and Galway, remained largely independent from government control. One report in 1609 called for the building of a citadel or castle at every coastal town to be financed by the inhabitants. This would increase the customs due to the crown, which the towns were unwilling to yield, 'except they be overmastered with strong garrisons'. Plans for fortifications at Galway had been ruminated for several decades, especially to protect the city against a foreign attack as had been feared at the time of the Spanish Armada. Such a citadel, situated just outside the jurisdiction of the corporation, was constructed between 1602 and 1610. It was more than just a fortification, because its governor exerted considerable influence over the town.

At Cork, another citadel, Elizabeth Fort, was started in 1603. It was attacked by townsmen attempting to demolish it in the same year, as they refused to acknowledge King James. Corkonians alleged that its real function was to overawe the town, under the pretext of defending it against a foreign attack. Likewise, a fine imposed in 1601 on the mayor of Limerick was used to repair the royal castle in the city, 'to bridle the insolence' of the townsfolk. After the defeat of the Spaniards in 1601, the inhabitants of Kinsale (Cork) were forced to contribute to the building of a new fort at Castle Park (1604). Thus, the government increased control over coastal towns by locating garrisons at adjacent fortifications, rather than through the systematic intrusion of settlers. In Dublin city, no citadel was planned or considered necessary; instead, Dublin Castle exercised a long-term but more insidious influence on the city's governing body, leading to a gradual displacement of Catholic councillors by Protestant Irishmen and Englishmen considered loyal to the crown.[155]

---

155 BL, Lansdowne MS 156, f. 213v; O'Sullivan, 'Galway', pp 26–7; M. Mulcahy, 'Elizabeth Fort, Cork', *Ir. Sword*, iv (1959–60), pp 127–34; Sheehan, 'Irish towns', p. 109; Lennon, *Lords of Dublin*.

1603–9: a summary

From the end of the war in 1603 to 1609, there were no major government sponsored plantations, although extensive contiguous areas could have been confiscated to serve that purpose. Instead, this was the heyday of private entrepreneurship, with plantations being founded by purchase or by discovery of concealments. Settlements emerged in Antrim especially. By contrast, settlements in Armagh, Cavan, Fermanagh, Donegal and Longford were scarce. Two major strategies of colonial settlement emerged side by side. The first approach consisted of the wholesale transfer of large tracts of land such as occurred in east Ulster with the introduction of settlers from Scotland and England. The second approach left the bulk of the lands in Irish hands and encouraged concentrated settlements at selected sites with a fort as nucleus.[156] In both cases, the governments in Dublin and London set limited settlement rules, but relied on private initiatives to turn the ventures into success. In Munster, government intervention was limited to the founding of citadels and forts at major coastal towns. In contrast to Ulster, government regulations were not issued for new ventures in this province, where Sir Richard Boyle built up his estate and where the earl of Thomond started a large-scale settlement. Ireland was touted as conquered, but large areas still remained under the control of the Lords of Tyrone and Tyrconnell, with virtually no English infiltration into Fermanagh, Donegal, Tyrone and Leitrim. All this changed with the Flight the earls in 1607 and after Sir Cahir O'Doherty revolted in 1608. The floodgate was now opened for the Ulster plantation, which in turn was followed by smaller government-sponsored plantations across Leinster.

THE GEOGRAPHY AND PRACTICE OF SETTLEMENTS

The English strategy of 'little and little to stretch the Pale further', initiated in the 1530s, had succeeded by the first decade of the seventeenth century.[157] What can we glean from studying colonisation efforts by the English over the preceding eight decades? The main question concerns the geography and practice of English settlements and their geographic expansion in Ireland. A first opportunity for settlement occurred when the dissolved monasteries around the Dublin and Wexford Pales were assigned to New English officers. A further strengthening of the Pale was accomplished when the government subsidised building of castles, although the extent of this programme remains unclear. A third method, the creation of fortified outposts, was initially undertaken in Laois and Offaly, and later in Wicklow. At the same time, the corridor along the Barrow connecting the two Pales was strengthened, which also served as a double frontier towards Carlow to the east and Laois to the west. Beginning with Lord deputy St Leger, the government's policy in Wicklow (in contrast to that for the Midlands) was not to colonise it but to set aside limited monastic lands for plantations. This policy was later associated

156 Perceval-Maxwell, *Scottish migration*, p. 67.   157 Cited in Ellis, *Tudor Ireland*, p. 274.

with the greater tractability of the Kavanaghs, compared with the O'Moores and the O'Connors in Laois and Offaly.[158]

Several grants were issued to New English to encourage them to conquer large territories in east Ulster. None of these projects resulted in permanent settlements. Elsewhere, some privately sponsored plantations by the New English fared reasonably well, in Westmeath, Roscommon, Carlow, south Cork, and on the borders of the Wexford Pale. Ormond successfully reclaimed ancestral lands and stimulated settlements in the border areas of Kilkenny and Tipperary. Scottish settlements in north Antrim expanded quickly once the Scots there had been recognised by the government in Dublin. English incursions and advance during the reign of Elizabeth have also been documented, especially in Ulster, by means of the geographic patterns of coin-hoards.[159]

Several government-sponsored initiatives were also successful. A redivision of land in Monaghan, which included native freeholders, fostered stable conditions. The government also seized the opportunity offered by the confiscation of the lands of the O'Connors and the O'Moores to establish a comprehensive plantation programme in the eastern parts of Laois and Offaly. This set the template for the Munster plantation, once the lands of Desmond and his followers were confiscated. The later plantation resulted in a greater influx of settlers from England than had taken place in Laois and Offaly. Yet in both cases, plantations were founded so thinly that they were all too easily overrun by the Irish. One commentator concluded in the late sixteenth century that 'Ireland will never be quiet until a number of English are planted there sufficient to put down any sudden rising'.[160]

In Ulster, the government repeated the initial stage of the Laois/Offaly approach – infiltrating Irish territory through the building of forts. The difference was that an entire network of fortifications was laid out, necessitated by longer supply routes. Although government officials identified an urgent need to protect the coast from foreign invasions from Spain, France or Scotland, the success of policies to strengthen the coast through the introduction of settlers was dismal. Likewise, the building of forts to protect harbours proved insufficient to prevent the landing of foreign armies in 1579 and 1601.

Virtually every English settlement suffered from incursions by the Irish, some being overrun several times in the late sixteenth century. Urban centres occupied by the New English, which were either not walled or poorly walled, were burnt frequently during raids by the Irish as, for example, in Connacht at Athenry (1576); in Leinster at Leighlinbridge (1569, 1577), Carlow (1577), Naas (1576), Athlone (1573), Ballymore Eustace (1578) and Wicklow (1580); in Munster at Youghal (1579) and Kilmallock (1583); and in Ulster at Carrickfergus (1573). Widespread destruction of settlements also took place during the Nine Years War. The ability of the inhabitants or their successors to revive their former settlement sites is remarkable. Few if any settlements founded during the sixteenth century were permanently deserted afterwards.

158 Ellis, *Tudor Ireland*, p. 203.   159 M. Dolley, 'The pattern of Elizabethan coin-hoards from Ireland', *UJA*, xxxiii (1970), pp 77–87.   160 *CSPI, 1601–1603*, pp 250, 252–3.

In east Ulster, at the end of the Nine Years War and prior to 1609, a massive surge of immigrants from England and Scotland took place. Some privately sponsored plantations emerged around government forts. At the same time, the plantations in Munster assumed a new shape and were considerably strengthened by successful private initiatives.

Territorial expansion proceeded in regional spurts, reflecting the fragmented approach towards the Irish problem adopted by successive Lord deputies and privy councils in England. The relationship between seneschalships and settlements is unclear. The sixteenth-century colonial expansion was confined to areas of recently suppressed rebellions, for some plausible pretext or legal fig leaf was required before dispossessing an existing landowner. Thus, settlements often emerged piecemeal and spasmodically as a result of local rebellions rather than as part of a coherent national plan. This compartmentalised approach was also reflected in contemporary cartography, which rarely showed Ireland in its entirety. Only at the end of Elizabeth's reign did a synthetic cartography finally emerge.[161] Although counties were created all over Ireland, government sponsorship of shire towns occurred only in some counties (positive instances are Mullingar, Monaghan, Philipstown and Maryborough). The cash-strapped Dublin government rarely subsidised the necessary walling of otherwise indefensible towns. Besides the two new boroughs in Laois and Offaly, the Dublin government failed to found new towns. It did, however, extend its control over existing urban centres, dominated mostly by the Old Irish, as at Dublin, Carrickfergus, Cork, Youghal and Galway. English efforts to reassert control were undoubtedly shot through with ambivalence.

The extent of regional variations in that control is still unclear. Initial attempts to re-establish the network of administrative areas outside of the Dublin Pale, lost during the Middle Ages, often incited rebellions, and thus failed to increase English control directly through peaceful means. Instead, English policy faded into a military preoccupation with forts and garrisons, and the launching of punitive raids. Military campaigns were oppressively expensive so governments loved the idea of financially self-sufficient colonies. The pendulum oscillated continuously and episodically between military and plantation solutions, with no inherited institutional learning from facts on the ground. Three topics were inextricably concatenated: local government reform, linked to new towns, and civil-plantations protected by soldiers. In reality, however, this sequencing was never fully appreciated by government officials.[162] English colonial expansion, whether through military campaigns, settlements, or the discovery of concealments, fuelled further rebellions. The relentlessly self-serving New English saw these revolts as a great advantage because they instigated more confiscations and further settlements. Chichester remarked after the revolt by Sir Cahir O'Doherty that it forced 'the forfeiture of his country' while 'the extirpation of the ungrateful inhabitants will recompense all their harms'.[163]

161 Andrews, 'Geography', pp 181, 185.   162 Ibid., p. 182.   163 Ranger, 'Boyle', p. 19; Hayes–McCoy, 'Protestant Reformation', p. 89; B. Bradshaw, 'Sword, word and strategy in the Reformation of Ireland', *Historical Jn.*, xxi (1978), p. 484; *CSPI, 1606–1608*, p. 480.

The frontiers in Ireland between English and Irish dominated areas had their counterparts in the border area between England and Scotland. Each border area was defended by royal strongholds and privately built castles. The changing warfare after the introduction of cannon affected the defences added to structures, but possibly more so at the Scottish border than in Ireland. The building of a major system of defensive ditches was considered on each side of the Irish Sea. Further links between the two frontier areas may surface in terms of personnel used, common elements among fortifications and the formulation of strategic moves to advance frontiers.[164]

In Ireland, the composition and other rents levied by the new landlords required cash instead of the traditional food and services. This dash for cash was not serviced by the government, which was reluctant to reform the Irish coinage and to reintroduce a mint into the country. As a consequence, a shortage of coin marked the period. The widespread mortgaging of estates by the Gaelic Irish was likely accelerated by the forced march towards a cash economy. This interpretation is reinforced by a Munster document from 1587, which argued that 'those Irish lords are in great poverty and want', and that settlers 'by that policy [taking mortgages] win still upon them without force'.[165]

The ousting of the Old English

Alongside the Gaelic Irish losing ground, the most important shift in power during the late sixteenth century was the struggle of the Old English to maintain their role in colonial settlements. In the initial building up of the defences of the Pales, the Old English were still recognised, but they gradually suffered setbacks. First, revolts originated within this group, such as those leading to the fall of the House of Kildare, the risings under the Butlers and Viscount Baltinglass, and eventually the Desmond rebellion. Second, they resolutely refused as a group to comply with the Reformation. Their alliance with the forces of the Counter-Reformation and their continental connections inevitably disturbed the suspicious minds of constantly anxious government officials, who feared a Spanish or French invasion of Ireland. The polarisation between the Old English and New English was hastened by religion, with the Lord deputy denouncing the Palesmen as 'arrant papists' in the 1570s, at a time when the Old English increasingly turned away from England as a choice for the education of their children and pivoted instead towards elite Catholic universities on the continent.

It is unsurprising, therefore, that the Dublin and London governments drew increasingly fewer Old English into government-sponsored plantations. At the same time, however, the excluded Old English, often under protest, were forced to contribute to the defence of the English Pale, to military incursions by the Lord deputies and their armies beyond the Pale, and to support new plantations in Laois

---

164 H. Colvin, J. Summerson, J. Hale & M. Merriman, *The history of the King's works, vol. iv, 1485–1660 (part II)* (London, 1982), pp 606–13, Plate 49; D. Tough, *The last years of a frontier* (Oxford, 1928), p. 196.   **165** MacCarthy-Morrogh, *Munster plantation*, p. 81.

and Offaly.[166] Whenever the Old English undertook privately organised settlements, as in Roscommon and Cavan, these were perceived by government officials as anomalous irritants, even when they constituted spearheads into Gaelic territories. Inexorably, the Old English lost their favoured status and were lumped together with the Gaelic Irish as a joint threat to the English Protestant project. The enthusiastic pursuit of concealments by the New English, and the willingness of courts to accept the flimsiest of pretexts, became a powerful weapon aimed at wresting lands from the Old Irish but increasingly it was trained on the newly vulnerable Old English as well.[167]

Dutch influence

A less obvious influence on Irish plantations emanated from the Low Countries, where some eventual settlers had served in the English army helping the Dutch in the struggle against the Spaniards. During the second half of the sixteenth century, several commanders with territorial control in Ireland served in the northern Netherlands, such as Sir John Norris and Sir Richard Bingham, respectively Lord Presidents of Munster and Connacht. Some lesser officers who became planters after 1603 also had experience in the Low Countries, as with Sir Henry Docwra (who settled at Derry), Sir Edward Blayney (at Monaghan and Castleblayney, both Monaghan) and Sir Oliver Lambert (former governor of Duisburg in the Low Countries, who settled at Kilbeggan in Westmeath). Although their experience in the Netherlands centred on winning the war there, they witnessed the amazing growth of the Dutch economy and its innovative industry.

Interchange and transmission of colonial practices

One perspective is of a succession of expansions occurring in different locales. The same individuals occupied a leading role in different locations (Figure 2.16). Briefly, the movements of individual planters generally took place from east to west, the general direction of colonial expansion. Others, however, moved along a south/north axis. Such movements indicated the general traffic in men, ideas and actions that existed between plantations, although their precise nature needs to be elucidated. Such traffic extended far beyond Ireland. Several individuals were involved in North American colonisation, either prior to or subsequent to their labours in Ireland.

Architecture

This survey described the contribution of colonial settlements to architectural changes. Assertions that the sixteenth century witnessed no notable architectural developments are unfounded. Consideration of buildings and documentary sources allows us to draw tentative conclusions. The sixteenth century was the last period in which subsidised castle building took place, by which the border of the Dublin

166 *Cal. Carew MSS 1515–1574*, p. 341; *Cal. Carew MSS 1575–1588*, pp 87–101.
167 Bottigheimer, *Kingdom and colony*, p. 50; Canny, *Old English elite.*

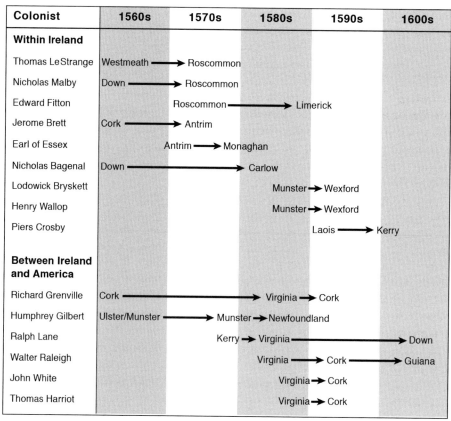

Colonist	1560s	1570s	1580s	1590s	1600s
Within Ireland					
Thomas LeStrange	Westmeath ⟶ Roscommon				
Nicholas Malby	Down ⟶ Roscommon				
Edward Fitton		Roscommon ⟶ Limerick			
Jerome Brett	Cork ⟶ Antrim				
Earl of Essex		Antrim ⟶ Monaghan			
Nicholas Bagenal	Down ⟶ Carlow				
Lodowick Bryskett				Munster → Wexford	
Henry Wallop				Munster → Wexford	
Piers Crosby				Laois ⟶ Kerry	
Between Ireland and America					
Richard Grenville	Cork ⟶ Virginia → Cork				
Humphrey Gilbert	Ulster/Munster ⟶ Munster → Newfoundland				
Ralph Lane			Kerry → Virginia ⟶ Down		
Walter Raleigh			Virginia ⟶ Cork ⟶ Guiana		
John White			Virginia → Cork		
Thomas Harriot			Virginia → Cork		

Figure 2.16 Interchange of colonists within Ireland and between Ireland and America.

Pale was reinforced. Virtually all known settler sites were built of stone rather than of timber. The introduction of settlers stimulated, if it did not indeed initiate, the brick-making industry in Munster in 1584.[168] The new architecture, especially in Munster, was clearly based on English precedents. However, many references to new buildings in Ulster draw attention to their resemblance to the architecture of the Pale. Even in 1608, on the eve of the Ulster plantation, Chichester advocated that the natives be 'inforced to build houses like those of the Pale'.[169] Some sixteenth-century architecture in Ulster elicited comments on its Pale characteristics, and it may well have been constructed by craftsmen from there. Colonial buildings modelled on the Pale reflected the general tendency, expressed by Stanihurst, to eulogise the anglicised Pale as the exemplary model of law, apparel and language for the reform of Gaelic Ireland. In Tipperary, Kilkenny and parts of Cork, however, some sixteenth- and early seventeenth-century architecture adhered to distinct local traditions not found elsewhere in Ireland. The mansion at Burncourt (Tipperary),

168 Craig, *Architecture of Ireland*, p. 122. Bricks were in use in Dublin as early as 1560. The castle in Mountjoy Fort (Tyrone) was among the earliest completely brick-clad buildings.   **169** Moody, 'Ulster plantation papers', p. 285.

built in the early seventeenth century, had poorly defensible square rather than spear-shaped bastions, and a timber gallery at roof level supported by a stone machicolation, facilitating vertical forms of defence.

As to interiors, comfort increased even in the smallest towers with the introduction of chimney flues and the insertion of fireplaces, replacing the open fires on the top floors. This rendered redundant the stone vault in the upper storey, which had previously set a limit on the width of buildings. At several sites, fireplaces were decorated in (for Ireland) novel Renaissance mouldings or designs.[170] To preserve the defensive capacity of buildings, however, chimneystacks were not initially allowed to project outside at ground level, but were built so that they were corbelled above the ground floor, as at Athclare (Louth), Odder (Meath), Magheranacloy (Monaghan), Newry (Down) and in various hall-type houses in Wexford. Whether corbelling was also applied to living quarters above the ground floor remains to be investigated.

The nature of warfare changed dramatically during the sixteenth century; inevitably, this impacted on defences around buildings. For the first half of the sixteenth century, English garrisons in Ireland employed more archers than arquebus men, but the archers were gradually phased out, while after mid century the arquebus was replaced by the heavier musket. The musket's range of 180m allowed the building of structures with widely spaced bastions and wider outworks.[171] Cannon were increasingly used not only by government and New English forces to defend their outposts, but also by Gaelic lords, who were now able to batter down formerly impregnable towerhouses and castles. A major impediment to cannon was their transportation across the boggy countryside. The increased availability of guns in private strongholds – pistol, arquebus, musket, cannon – produced a change from vertical defences (firing from the parapet) to horizontal defences (with gun holes to cover the flanks). Although some castles were equipped with cannon-ports, the actual construction of the buildings themselves was not adjusted to meet the new realities of warfare where field guns could pierce structures, and where tall towerhouses were particularly vulnerable. From the 1550s, some towerhouses in Tipperary (but also elsewhere, as along the Barrow) were provided with large mullioned windows, while the wall walks become narrower or sometimes disappeared altogether when gables were built flush with the outer walls. Decreased defensibility of the main house, however, may have been accompanied by improved defences of the bawns, but these are little studied.[172]

Several fortified bridges were built, either with a tower at each end or with a central tower, as was proposed for a bridge at Enniscorthy (Wexford) in 1581, and for one which was actually built at Castlemaine in Kerry. In either case, the towers were battlemented and equipped with 'murdering holes'.[173]

Alongside the building of traditional towerhouses, residences emerged on a rectangular plan with more commodious rooms. In some houses, the conventional

170 As at the earl of Ormond's house at Carrick-on-Suir (Tipperary).   **171** Kerrigan, 'Irish castles: part 1', p. 202; 'Irish castles: part 2', p. 276.   **172** Cairns, *Towerhouses*, p. 13.   **173** Hore, *Wexford*, vi, pp 406–7; *Pacata Hibernica*, ed. S. O'Grady (London, 1896), i, opposite p. 111.

vaults were altogether omitted. In a few instances, Elizabethan mansions echoing English examples were erected safely within town walls, such as Ormond's house in Carrick-on-Suir and Chichester's at Joymount in Carrickfergus, but sometimes outside of towns, as in the case of Ussher's house at Donnybrook (south of Dublin) and Norris's Mallow Castle (Cork). Another break with tradition was embellishment of façades by symmetrical fenestration. The impetus for symmetrically designed exteriors found expression in Loftus's Rathfarnham Castle and also in the much earlier rebuilding of Malby's Roscommon Castle. The need for defence remained paramount, however, but even here innovations took place, as with spear-shaped rather than rectangular flankers at Rathfarnham Castle. It is unclear whether these new styles of buildings were built by English artisans only, or if Irish masons and carpenters were also employed.

Implications of English expansion

Although examination of the introduction of agricultural techniques by the English is still wanting, the English certainly stimulated the search for iron ore in Ireland in the sixteenth century, and used the extensive woods to operate iron mills. Immigrants must have imported numerous new tools and techniques to Ireland. Another massive influence was the resurgence of the English language in Ireland.[174]

Alongside the introduction of English lifestyles, the central government increasingly discouraged Irishmen from acting or dressing in their traditional ways. This did not reflect just a rejection of Irish customs, but a bias against native inhabitants, eventually growing into a government-approved policy of separating the Irish from the English. Thus, separate Irish towns emerged at New English centres such as Newry, as shown in a late sixteenth-century view of the town.[175] The frontier formed a cultural as much as a physical divide.[176] The disappearance of the frontiers in Ireland, and King James I's adoption of Irishmen as citizens with access to the law equal to that of the New English or the Old English, did not banish the internalised frontiers separating people. A self-aggrandising English Protestant minority controlled the future of the Irish Catholic majority. At the same time, settlers, unlike officials, often had less fear of the native inhabitants, and did not regard themselves as an endangered minority needing protection. Settlers soon married into Gaelic Irish or Old English families, and participated in the traditional fostering of children.[177] Whereas most New English settlers remained Protestant, some turned Catholic, although it is unclear under what circumstances.

---

174 D. Fischer, *Albion's seed* (New York, 1989), explores the influence of various regions of England on the plantations in North America. See also N. Canny, 'The Irish background to Penn's experiment' in R. Dunn & M. Dunn (eds), *The world of William Penn* (Philadelphia, 1986), pp 139–56.   **175** Andrews, 'Plantation Ireland', p. 7.   **176** Lydon, 'Problem of the frontier', p. 17; Leerssen, *Mere Irish*, pp 51–3.   **177** N. Canny, 'Dominant minorities: English settlers in Ireland and Virginia 1550–1650' in A. Hepburn (ed.), *Minorities in history* (London, 1978), pp 51–69; Canny, 'Permissive frontier', pp 24, 31–2; M'Skimmin, *Carrickfergus*, pp 316–17. Sir Thomas LeStrange, Robert Hartpole and John Briscoe are other examples of settlers marrying outside their English circle.

Geography of settlements

This chapter illustrates how documents and field evidence highlight the choice of settlement sites and the location of strategic passes in the country. Reference has been made to the siting of fortifications and to the roads, passes, bridges, or supply routes that they protected. This survey lacks the necessary precision to link field and documentary evidence together in a reconstruction of the sixteenth-century countryside, taking cognisance of natural barriers such as bogs and woods. The information provided here can serve as a stimulus to re-examine the countryside to understand why certain settlements happened at certain locations and to interpret the nature of the historic landscape. Further exploration of documentary and field sources is necessary to create a more comprehensive picture.

Sequel

Conquest was usually seen as a prerequisite for colonisation and plantation. King James I, however, turned the order around by saying that the easiest way of achieving a complete conquest was to implement plantations. In his own honeyed words, 'no kynd of conquest can be more easie and innocent than that which doth proceede from plantationes'.[178] This also applied to early seventeenth-century Ireland. A costly lesson had been learned in the sixteenth century that fire and sword were counterproductive to colonisation, although a conquest produced rebels and traitors, whose reactions then provided a handy legal pretext for the confiscation of their properties. This instigated extensive colonisation in west Ulster in the early seventeenth century.

Another method, brought to perfection in the sixteenth century and preferred in the first decades of the next century, was the more insidious one of 'discovering' ancient titles and concealments from the crown. This non-violent chicanery also freed land for plantations. However, conquests and discoveries without inhabiting territories proved useless. In Sir Anthony St Leger's words, unless the country 'be peopled with others than be there already, and also certain fortresses there builded and warded, if it be gotten the one day, it is lost the next'.[179] The sixteenth-century experience of plantation was of great use for the formulation of the next generation of plantations.[180] Thus, a path was paved for a tiny minority to exert more effective control over the Irish people and their land. This time, however, the path chosen by the Dublin and London governments was no longer available to the Old English and the Gaelic Irish, and the effect was more insidious and less direct. Four reasonably peaceful decades followed the end of the war in 1603 but the further conquest of Ireland through plantations spawned the next revolt of 1641 with a grim inevitability.

---

178 D. Laign (ed.), *Royal letters, charters and tracts relating to the colonisation of New Scotland* (Edinburgh, 1867), p. 12.   **179** Dunlop, 'Leix and Offaly', p. 61.   **180** F. Jones, *Mountjoy 1563–1606* (Dublin, 1958), pp 191–2.

Appendix 2.1: Colonisation 1536–1607

Dating of structures   Sites mentioned in the text refer to their location in a modern county. The dates have been derived from contemporary documents or from date stones in buildings. The former mostly refer to the year when letters patent had been issued by the crown granting the property to a settler, or when habitation at a site occurred. Date stones can have several meanings: they can refer to the start of building, to rebuilding or to the completion, which may have been several years apart. Dates should be interpreted as approximations rather than the exact year of settlement. In many cases, buildings have survived without documentary evidence as to their date; in those instances, its architectural features help assign it to a particular period (this is indicated by the absence of a date for a structure). This method, however, has been used sparingly because the chronology of architectural styles for the period is underdeveloped. In the case of garrisons, the date refers to the earliest occupation of the site. Several garrisons, however, were temporary and never functioned as permanent strongholds. A minus sign means before that date. A plus sign means after that date.

Date	Place	County	Type	Date	Place	County	Type
1536	Alenscourt	Kildare	Settlement	1557	Carlow	Carlow	Town, garrison
1536	Powerscourt	Wicklow	Settlement	1557	Tintern	Wexford	Settlement
1536	Woodstock	Kildare	Settlement	1558	Ferns	Wexford	Settlement
1542	Kilteel	Kildare	Settlement	1558	Ballybrittan	Offaly	Settlement
1542, 1584	Coleraine	L'derry	Fort	−1560	Blackford	Laois	Fort
1545	Hollywood	Wicklow	Settlement	1560	Narrowwater	Down	Settlement
1546	Ballyadams	Laois	Garrison	1561	Tristernagh	Westmeath	Settlement
1547	Athlone	Westmeath	Town, garrison	1561	Durrow	Offaly	Settlement
1547	Portlester	Meath	Settlement	+1561	Killyleagh	Down	Settlement
1547	Castlekevin	Wicklow	Settlement	1562	Carbury	Kildare	Settlement
1547	Nenagh	Tipperary	Garrison	1562	Abington	Limerick	Settlement
1547	Brittas	Tipperary	Settlement	−1563	Dingle	Kerry	Settlement
1548	Maryborough	Laois	Fort	1563	Corbetstown	Offaly	Settlement
1548	Clonmullen	Carlow	Settlement	1563	Clonmore	Offaly	Settlement
1549	Listerlin	Kilkenny	Settlement	1563	Cloghan	Offaly	Settlement
1549	Killabban	Laois	Settlement	1563	Barnan	Offaly	Settlement
1549	Monasterevan	Kildare	Settlement	1563	Clonearl	Offaly	Settlement
−1550	Monkstown	Dublin	Settlement	1563	Barnaboy	Offaly	Settlement
1550	Kilbeggan	Westmeath	Settlement	1563	Clonbulloge	Offaly	Settlement
1550	Ballyburley	Offaly	Settlement	1563	Tinnakill	Laois	Settlement
+1550	Newry	Down	Town	1563	Clonreher	Laois	Settlement
−1551	Kilbane	Antrim	Settlement	1563	Ballymaddock	Laois	Settlement
1552	Greencastle	Down	Garrison	1563	Loughteeog	Laois	Settlement
1552	Killeagh	Offaly	Settlement	1563	Abbeyleix	Laois	Settlement
1552	Belan	Laois	Settlement	1563	Raheen	Laois	Settlement
1552	Ballyknockan	Laois	Settlement	1563	Killeshin	Laois	Settlement
1553	Dungarvan	Waterford	Fort	−1564	Trusk	Roscommon	Settlement
1553	Castlerickard	Meath	Settlement	1564	Cullenagh	Laois	Settlement
+1553	Ticroghan	Meath	Settlement	1564	Ballymore	Westmeath	Settlement
+1553	Killyncrosse	Meath	Settlement	1566	Newcastle	Wicklow	Settlement
1555	Enniscorthy	Wexford	Settlement	1566	Roscommon	Roscommon	Town, garrison
1556	Monasteroris	Offaly	Settlement	1566	Boyle	Roscommon	Garrison
−1556	Ballyleakin	Offaly	Settlement	1566, 1583, 1601	Londonderry	L'derry	Fort
1556	Stradbally	Laois	Settlement				
1557	Kilclonfert	Offaly	Settlement	1567	Kilmainham Beg	Meath	Settlement
−1557	Bracklin	Offaly	Settlement				
−1557	Kinnafad	Kildare	Settlement	1567	Haggardstown	Louth	Settlement
−1557	Kishawanny	Kildare	Settlement	1567	Glenarm	Antrim	Garrison
−1557	Ballinure	Kildare	Settlement	+1567	Lismoyny	Offaly	Settlement

Date	Place	County	Type	Date	Place	County	Type
1568	Timogue	Laois	Settlement	-1585	Galey	Roscommon	Settlement
1568	Passage	Waterford	Fort	-1585	Rahara	Roscommon	Settlement
+1568	Tracton	Cork	Settlement	1585	Ballymote	Sligo	Settlement
+1568	Carrigaline	Cork	Settlement	-1586	Ballymurray	Roscommon	Settlement
-1569	Ballina	Kildare	Settlement	1587	Duncannon	Wexford	Fort
1569	Philipstown (Daingean)	Offaly	Fort	+1587	Corgrid	Limerick	Settlement
				+1587	Dunammon	Limerick	Settlement
1569	Geashill	Offaly	Settlement	+1587	Ballygrennan	Limerick	Settlement
1569	Shaen	Laois	Settlement	+1587	Kilmore	Cork	Settlement
1569	Ballyroan	Laois	Settlement	+1587	Tralee	Kerry	Settlement, town
1569	Older Fleet	Antrim	Settlement	+1587	Ballyderown	Cork	Settlement
1570	Dowdstown	Louth	Settlement	-1588	Turrock	Roscommon	Settlement
1571	Tankardstown	Laois	Settlement	1588	Monksgrange	Laois	Settlement
1571	Corkbeg	Cork	Fort	1588, 1602	Sligo	Sligo	Garrison, fort
1573	Kilkea	Kildare	Settlement	1588	Donegal	Donegal	Garrison
1573	Skegoniell	Antrim	Fort	+1588	Clones	Monaghan	Settlement
1573	Essex Fort	Armagh	Fort	+1588	Fedamore	Limerick	Settlement
1574	Edmundstown	Louth	Settlement	+1588	Glenogra	Limerick	Settlement
1575	Ballinasloe	Galway	Settlement	+1588	Loughgur	Limerick	Settlement
1575	Bruce's Castle (Rathlin)	Antrim	Garrison	+1588	Kilfinny	Limerick	Settlement
				+1588	Hospital	Limerick	Settlement
1575	Dunluce	Antrim	Garrison	+1588	Molahiffe	Kerry	Settlement
1575	Armagh	Armagh	Fort	+1588	Mallow	Cork	Settlement
1576	Shrule	Laois	Settlement	+1588	Kinalmeaky	Cork	Settlement
1576	Loughrea	Galway	Town, garrison	+1588	Castlemahon	Cork	Settlement
1576	Claregalway	Galway	Garrison	1589	Castlebar	Mayo	Settlement
+1576	Carrickmacross	Monaghan	Settlement	+1589	Rathurde	Limerick	Settlement
1577	St Catherines	Dublin	Settlement	+1589	Castleisland	Kerry	Settlement
1579	Athgoe	Dublin	Settlement	+1589	Currans	Kerry	Settlement
1579	Castlemaine	Kerry	Garrison	+1589	Ballymacdonell	Kerry	Settlement
1580	Ballynakill	Tipperary	Settlement	+1589	Carriglemerly	Cork	Settlement
1580	Ballymore Eustace	Kildare	Garrison	+1589	Carrignedy	Cork	Settlement
				+1589	Knocknamona	Waterford	Settlement
+1580	Kilcolman	Cork	Settlement	+1589	Ballynatray	Waterford	Settlement
+1580	The Neale	Mayo	Settlement	1590	Waterford	Waterford	Town, fort
-1581	Clonagh	Kildare	Settlement	+1590	Askeaton	Limerick	Settlement
1581	Three Castles	Wicklow	Garrison	1591	Poulnalong	Cork	Settlement
1581	Wicklow	Wicklow	Town, garrison	1591	Youghal	Cork	Town
1581	Castle Comin	Wicklow	Fort	+1591	Swiffin	Tipperary	Settlement
1581	Arklow	Wicklow	Town	+1591	Newcastle West	Limerick	Settlement
1581	Cloggrennan	Carlow	Settlement	+1591	Fermoy	Cork	Settlement
1581	Clonmore (near Gorey)	Wexford	Settlement	+1591	Mogeely	Cork	Settlement
				+1591	Inchquin	Cork	Settlement
1581	Clohamon	Wexford	Settlement	1592	Killorglin	Kerry	Settlement
1581	St Johns	Wexford	Settlement	1592	Castletown	Limerick	Settlement
1581	Coolyhune (near St Mullins)	Carlow	Settlement	+1592	Mocollop	Waterford	Settlement
				+1592	Cappoquin	Waterford	Settlement
-1583	Castlemartin	Kildare	Settlement	+1592	Lismore	Waterford	Settlement
1583	Rathfarnham	Dublin	Settlement	+1593	Beauly	Limerick	Settlement
1583	Castlerheban	Kildare	Settlement	1594	Enniskillen	Fermanagh	Garrison
1583	Ballymore	Galway	Settlement	1594	Craigue	Tipperary	Settlement
1583	Baltinglass	Wicklow	Settlement	1595	Kill of Grange	Dublin	Settlement
-1584	Castleward	Down	Settlement	1595	Fort Russell	Wicklow	Fort
-1584	Ballymacgirraght	Roscommon	Settlement	+1595	Ardagh	Limerick	Settlement
-1584	Coolteige	Roscommon	Settlement	-1596	Killeenboy	Roscommon	Settlement
-1584	Carrowroe	Roscommon	Settlement	-1596	Fuerty	Roscommon	Settlement
1584	Jenkinstown	Kilkenny	Settlement	-1596	Curraghboy	Roscommon	Settlement

Date	Place	County	Type	Date	Place	County	Type
-1596	Killegan	Roscommon	Settlement	1604	Red Bay	Antrim	Settlement
-1596	Dundonnell	Roscommon	Settlement	+1605	Downpatrick	Down	Settlement
-1596	Cavan	Cavan	Settlement	+1605	Dundrum	Down	Settlement
1596	Dundalk	Louth	Town, garrison	1606	Lisgoole	Fermanagh	Garrison
1596	Carlingford	Louth	Town, garrison	1607	Finnea	Westmeath	Garrison
1596	Drogheda	Louth	Town, garrison	+1607	Castleblayney	Monaghan	Settlement
1596	Ardee	Louth	Town	-1608	Castle Chichester	Antrim	Settlement
1596	Kells	Meath	Town, garrison	1608	Newtownards	Down	Settlement
1596	Longford	Longford	Garrison	1608	Ballyconnell	Cavan	Settlement
1596	Kilconnell	Galway	Garrison	1608	Cabragh	Cavan	Settlement
1596	Naas	Kildare	Town, garrison	1609	Ballycastle	Antrim	Settlement
1596	Tully	Kildare	Garrison	1611	Dungiven	L'derry	Fort
1596	Rathdrum	Wicklow	Fort	1611	Hollywood	Down	Town
1596	Ballinacor	Wicklow	Fort	-1611	Dalway's Bawn	Antrim	Settlement
1596	Castledermot	Kildare	Garrison	-1611	Castle Dobbs	Antrim	Settlement
1596	New Ross	Wexford	Town, garrison	-1611	Kilroot	Antrim	Settlement
1596	Meelick	Galway	Garrison	-1611	Marshallstown	Antrim	Settlement
1596	Athleague	Roscommon	Garrison	-1611	Muckamore	Antrim	Settlement
1596	Cong	Mayo	Garrison	-1611	Castle Upton	Antrim	Settlement
1596	Athenry	Galway	Town, garrison	-1611	Bangor	Down	Settlement
1596	Mullaghmore	Galway	Garrison	-1611	Castlereagh	Down	Settlement
1597	Tulsk	Roscommon	Garrison	-1611	Hillsborough	Down	Fort
1597	Castle Jordan	Meath	Settlement	-1611	Dromore	Down	Fort
1597	Buroghes	Tyrone	Fort	-1611	Ballyleague	Roscommon	Settlement
+1597	Dunganstown	Wicklow	Settlement	-1611	Carrick-on-Shannon	Leitrim	Fort
-1598	Tarbert	Kerry	Settlement				
-1598	Ballybeg	Cork	Settlement	Undated	Burt	Donegal	Garrison
+1599	Ballinafad	Sligo	Fort	Undated	Chatterton	Armagh	Fort
-1600	Bellanagargy	Cavan	Garrison	Undated	Magheracloone	Monaghan	Settlement
-1600	Ballymascanlan	Louth	Settlement	Undated	Edenderry	Offaly	Settlement
1600	Togher	Laois	Garrison	Undated	Lea	Laois	Settlement
1600	Culmore	Donegal	Fort	Undated	Moret	Laois	Settlement
1600	Lifford	Donegal	Fort	Undated	Dysart	Laois	Settlement
1600	Mountnorris	Armagh	Fort	Undated	Rathleague	Laois	Settlement
+1600	Dunalong	Tyrone	Fort	Undated	Timahoe	Laois	Settlement
1601	Killilea	Tipperary	Settlement	Undated	Ballyloughan	Carlow	Settlement
1601	Galway	Galway	Fort, town	Undated	Graiguenamanagh	Kilkenny	Settlement
1601	Cloghoughter	Cavan	Garrison	Undated	Duffry Hall	Wexford	Settlement
1601	Rathmullan	Donegal	Garrison	Undated	Monart	Wexford	Settlement
1601	Toome	Antrim	Fort	Undated	Brownscastle (near Enniscorthy)	Wexford	Settlement
1601	Massareene	Antrim	Fort				
1601	Ballyshannon	Donegal	Fort	Undated	Brownscastle (near Taghmon)	Wexford	Settlement
1601	Mullin	Tyrone	Fort				
1601	Kilclief	Down	Settlement	Undated	Rathumney	Wexford	Settlement
1601	Moyry	Armagh	Fort	Undated	Dungulph	Wexford	Settlement
-1602	Ringhaddy	Down	Settlement	Undated	Fethard	Wexford	Settlement
1602	Omagh	Tyrone	Fort	Undated	Redmonds Hall (Loftus Hall)	Wexford	Settlement
1602	Mountjoy	Tyrone	Fort				
1602	Monaghan	Monaghan	Fort	Undated	Slade	Wexford	Settlement
1602	Augher	Tyrone	Fort	Undated	Kilcloggan	Wexford	Settlement
1602	Baltimore	Cork	Fort	Undated	Dunbrody	Wexford	Settlement
1602	Cork	Cork	Fort, town	Undated	Ballylehane	Kilkenny	Settlement
1602	Haulbowline	Cork	Fort	Undated	Ballyragget	Kilkenny	Settlement
+1602	Inishloughan	Antrim	Fort	Undated	Maynooth	Kildare	Settlement
+1602	Charlemont	Armagh	Fort	Undated	Donnybrook	Dublin	Settlement
1603	Knockgraffon	Tipperary	Settlement	Undated	Tallaght	Dublin	Settlement
1604	Castlepark	Cork	Fort				

Date	Place	County	Type	Date	Place	County	Type
Undated	Clane	Kildare	Town	Undated	Franstown	Limerick	Settlement
Undated	Rathangan	Kildare	Settlement	Undated	Lisfinny	Waterford	Settlement
Undated	Loughlinstown	Dublin	Settlement	Undated	Tallow	Waterford	Town
Undated	Dromineer	Tipperary	Settlement	Undated	Poulacurry	Cork	Settlement
Undated	Ballymackey	Tipperary	Settlement	Undated	Kinsale	Cork	Town
Undated	Loughmore	Tipperary	Settlement	Undated	Robertstown	Meath	Settlement
Undated	Ballynahow	Tipperary	Settlement	Undated	Abbeylara	Longford	Settlement
Undated	Farneybridge	Tipperary	Settlement	Undated	Odder	Meath	Settlement
Undated	Ballyseedy	Tipperary	Settlement	Undated	Abbeyshrule	Longford	Settlement
Undated	Adare	Limerick	Settlement	Undated	Bective	Meath	Settlement
Undated	Castlematrix	Limerick	Settlement	Undated	Tyrellspass	Westmeath	Settlement

CHAPTER THREE

The architectural impact of the plantations in Ireland: Ulster and the Midlands

INTRODUCTION

THE ULSTER PLANTATION, INITIATED IN 1608 during the reign of James I, followed the largest confiscation ever of lands from Irish lords. These confiscations facilitated grants to settlers, massive immigration from England and Scotland, and displacement of the native landowners. By 1659, the six confiscated counties in Ulster had attracted 26,000 English and Scottish settlers.[1] An even larger influx, however, occurred outside of Ulster: between 1603 and 1641, as many as 100,000 British settlers migrated to Ireland.[2] Over the following decades, the Ulster plantation of the 1610s was mirrored by others in several smaller lordships in the Midlands. The Ulster and Midlands plantations adopted a geographically coherent approach to the challenge of imposing government control over the Gaelic lordships and to breaking the enduring power of the Gaelic lords.[3]

Whereas the Ulster plantation sought to secure the northern third of the island, the Midlands plantations addressed two corridors: the Shannon, which had facilitated the link between the Ulster and the Munster Irish during the Nine Years War, and that between the Pale and south Wexford – with its significant Old English presence. Land confiscation was followed by government-imposed building schemes that created a massive construction boom especially in Ulster. Irish architecture of the late sixteenth- and early seventeenth-century period has received much less attention than its English and Scottish equivalents.[4] Irish developments are significant, however, because they represent immigration patterns and transformations in material culture, as well as local and national economic patterns, thereby advancing our understanding of how British architecture took root in Ireland, how it was re-interpreted and adapted there, and how it impacted on indigenous Irish architecture.

---

1 Robinson, *Plantation of Ulster*, p. 105.   2 W.J. Smyth, *Map-making, landscapes and memory: a geography of colonial and early modern Ireland c.1530–1750* (Cork, 2006), p. 100.   3 B. Mac Cuarta, 'The plantation of Leitrim 1620–41', *IHS*, 32 (2001), pp 299–300.   4 M. Airs, *The Tudor and Jacobean country house: a building history* (Godalming, 1998); N. Cooper, *English manor houses* (London, 1990); A. Gomme & A. Maguire, *Design and plan in the country house* (New Haven, 2008); M. Girouard, *Robert Smythson and the Elizabethan country house* (New Haven, 1983); M. Girouard, *Elizabethan architecture: its rise and fall 1540–1640* (New Haven, 2009); P. Henderson, *The Tudor house and garden: architecture and landscape in the sixteenth and early seventeenth century* (New Haven, 2005).

There is a major gap in the literature on appraising how the new structures of the Ulster plantation compared with earlier Gaelic architecture. Equally lacking is a comparison of Ulster plantation architecture with that in the Midlands, an understanding of the architecture occupied by Gaelic grantees under the plantations, and a comparison of plantation architecture with what was already present in the rest of Ireland and Britain. The plantation period undoubtedly contributed to major changes in architecture.

Historical context

The confiscation of Irish land was the prerequisite for the Ulster plantation: it covered six adjacent counties (the modern counties of Donegal, Cavan, Fermanagh, Tyrone, Londonderry and Armagh) comprising over 1.5 million hectares, which was seven times larger than the area confiscated in Munster in the late sixteenth century.[5] While the Ulster plantation started in the early 1610s, it matured in the 1620s and the 1630s. By contrast, the plantations across the Midlands were more scattered geographically and took place gradually during the late 1610s and the 1620s. The Midlands plantations concerned Leinster counties, in chronological order, Wexford, Longford, Offaly, Laois, Wicklow and Kilkenny, and the only Connacht county Leitrim.

During the Ulster plantation, the indigenous Irish lost control of all their lands and only a small minority received compensatory grants. The indigenous Irish in the Midlands lost 25% to 75% of their land. In both areas, the land granted to the indigenous Irish was of poor quality.[6] Government officials entertained the fallacious idea that granting properties directly to the indigenous Irish would wean them away from the powerful control exercised by their Irish lords. In Ulster, the indigenous Irish were assigned lands in locations away from their former estates. By contrast, grants to the indigenous Irish in the Midlands were in locations that they had already long owned. The impact of confiscation and redistribution was accordingly felt more severely in Ulster.

The study of early seventeenth-century Irish architecture has advanced in recent decades through archaeology, systematic surveys and the publication of contemporary surveys and maps.[7] A major limitation to studying plantation architecture is that so little survives; archaeology and contemporary documentation are therefore indispensable. This is equally the case for Ulster and the Midlands plantations, although Ulster is much better served by excavation.[8] It is difficult to match surviving structures to what we know of the plantation conditions from

5 Robinson, *Plantation of Ulster*, p. 86. **6** Mac Cuarta, 'Plantation of Leitrim', p. 313. **7** C. Donnelly, 'The archaeology of the Ulster plantation' in A. Horning, E. Ó Baoill, C. Donnelly & P. Logue (eds), *The post-medieval archaeology of Ireland 1550–1850* (Dublin, 2007), pp 37–50. **8** W. Roulston, 'The Scots in plantation Cavan 1610–42' in B. Scott (ed.), *Culture and society in early modern Breifne/Cavan* (Dublin, 2009), p. 127; P. O'Donovan, *Archaeological inventory of County Cavan* (Dublin, 1995); M. Moore, *Archaeological inventory of County Leitrim* (Dublin, 2003); B. Lacey, *Archaeological survey of County Donegal* (Lifford, 1983); M. Moore, *Archaeological inventory of County Wexford* (Dublin, 1996); C. O'Brien & P.D. Sweetman, *Archaeological inventory of County Offaly* (Dublin, 1997); P.D. Sweetman, O. Alcock & B. Moran, *Archaeological inventory of County Laois* (Dublin, 1995); *Arch. Sur. Down* (Belfast, 1966).

documentary and archaeological evidence, and no known surviving structure adheres exactly to plantation specifications. Nevertheless, some observations and deductions can be made on the basis of the available material. This chapter concentrates on the main residences of the substantive landowners rather than on those of tenants, and it does not address the architecture of towns and villages.

Building types and terminology

The evolution of different forms of architecture inside and outside the plantations areas during the early seventeenth century is remarkable. This is evident from a variety of sources: the 1611 and 1619 government surveys of all the plantations, the 1622 record for the Midland plantation, later inquisitions, modern archaeological surveys and surviving fabric. During the late sixteenth and early seventeenth centuries, the building of traditional towerhouses persisted but more so in Ulster than in the Midlands.[9]

A notable development is that towerhouses on a square plan were gradually replaced by novel structures on a rectangular plan. These new structures fell into two categories – fortified houses and strong houses – that formed intermediate stages linking towerhouses with the later Big Houses.[10] By the second half of the seventeenth century, these formal houses had jettisoned the defensive features of towerhouses, strong houses and fortified houses. Extant records do not clearly distinguish among castles, fortified houses and unfortified houses. 'Fortified house' is a modern term, and it was not used in the seventeenth century. A fortified house had fewer defensive features than castles, including the towerhouses (also a modern term), and they can be defined as dwellings with one or more defensive features, either structural or in terms of siting.[11] The fortified houses retained several defensive features from the towerhouse era, notably bartizans on the wall angles and machicolations over doorways, while strategically placed gun loops facilitated flanking fire from angle towers and bartizans to protect vulnerable walls and doors. Their defensive properties, however, rested principally on the presence of an outer bawn wall with gatehouses, mural towers and copious gun loops.[12]

'Strong house' was the term often used at the time and it encompassed both 'fortified houses' and 'strong houses' as specified in plantation surveys: it refers to residences that were smaller than fortified houses, two storey high with the ground floor pierced by narrow slit openings, while the less vulnerable first floor had larger

---

9 Craig, *Architecture of Ireland*, pp 111–36; T. Reeves-Smyth, 'Community to privacy: late Tudor and Jacobean manorial architecture in Ireland 1560–1640' in Horning et al. (eds), *Post-medieval archaeology*, pp 289–326; Donnelly, 'Archaeology of the Ulster plantation'; S. Weadick, 'How popular were fortified houses in Irish castle building history?: a look at their numbers in the archaeological record and distribution pattern' in J. Lyttleton & C. Rynne (eds), *Plantation Ireland: settlement and material culture 1550–1700* (Dublin, 2006), pp 61–85; H. Leask, 'Early seventeenth-century houses in Ireland' in E. Jope (ed.), *Studies in building history* (London, 1961), pp 243–50; D. Sweetman, *The medieval castles of Ireland* (Cork, 1999); D. Waterman, 'Some Irish seventeenth-century houses and their architectural ancestry' in Jope (ed.), *Building history*, pp 251–74.   10 Loeber, 'Irish houses and castles 1660–90', this volume, pp 164–211.   11 Weadick, 'Fortified houses in Irish castle building', pp 64–5.   12 Sweetman, *Medieval castles*, pp 175–6.   13 Sweetman, *Medieval castles*, pp 175–6.

windows.[13] Bartizans, machicolations and crenellations were usually absent, although most strong houses likely had outer defensive works in the form of a bawn or the outer circuit of a ringfort. Contemporaries referred to castles, whereas surviving remains clearly indicate fortified houses.[14] Modern distinctions concerning defensive structures map only imperfectly onto early seventeenth-century terminology.

Contemporary documents also refer to timber structures, for example, cagework (framed) 'houses after the English manner' that presumably can be identified with the timber houses depicted in the drawings of the London Companies. These show houses that were completed, and others in a timber-framed form prior to the wall planes being filled with brick or clay and rendered in lime-plaster finishes.[15] Not all English-like houses, however, were timbered. 'English-like' houses on the Kilclaghan estate (Cavan) had stone and clay walls, thatched roofs and stone chimneys.[16] The term 'Irish house' in contemporary documents refers to a single-storey house, built with wattles (woven hazelwork) rather than of lime and stone, with two to three rooms, a thatched roof and a chimney at one end.[17] The term 'Irish house' did not include cabins with clay walls. Plantation surveys also refer to 'coupled timber houses', presumably cruck constructions, consisting of a single-storey house with an attic in which the timber uprights took the form of an A-frame, made of bent tree trunks connected with wooden pins at the apex.

Confiscation of Ulster lordships

The dramatic confiscation of the Ulster lordships occurred in the aftermath of several earlier confiscations of large territories and their subsequent plantations in the late sixteenth century. Among the earliest were plantations of parts of Counties Offaly and Laois, followed by the much larger plantation of Munster (over 100,000 useable hectares) in the wake of the Desmond rebellion between 1569 and 1583 (Figure 3.1).[18] The Ulster plantation was initiated by the English and Irish governments after the flight of the O'Neills and the O'Donnells in 1607 and the O'Doherty rebellion in 1608.[19] Unlike the Desmond rebellion in Munster, where the subsequent confiscation

14 Curl, *Londonderry plantation*, Plate 82, plan of castle at Moneymore (Londonderry). The largely non-defensible Castle Caulfield (Tyrone) was called a 'castle' in 1622 (Robinson, *Plantation of Ulster*, p. 133).   15 Robinson, *Plantation of Ulster*, p. 136.   16 V. Treadwell, *The Irish commission of 1622: an investigation of the Irish administration 1615–22 and its consequences 1623–24* (Dublin, 2006), p. 511.   17 Davies, 'Castles of County Cavan', pp 106, 110–11, 117–20; G. Hill, *An historical account of the plantation in Ulster at the commencement of the seventeenth century 1608–1620* (Belfast, 1877), pp 459–60. While plantation documents often speak of English houses, there should be no presumption that such houses were necessarily sophisticated.   18 Loeber, 'Geography and practice' and its listing of settlements 1534–1609, this volume, pp 40–1. For the Munster plantation, see C. Breen, *An archaeology of south-west Ireland 1570–1670* (Dublin, 2007); M. MacCarthy-Morrogh, 'The English presence in early seventeenth-century Munster' in Brady & Gillespie (eds), *Natives and newcomers*, pp 171–90; MacCarthy-Morrogh, *Munster plantation*, p. 289; E. Klingerhofer, *Castles and colonists: an archaeology of Elizabethan Ireland* (Manchester, 2010); D. Power, 'The archaeology of the Munster plantation' in Horning et al. (eds), *Post-medieval archaeology*, pp 23–36.   19 A. Clarke, 'Pacification, plantation and the Catholic question 1602–23' in *NHI*, iii, p. 193.

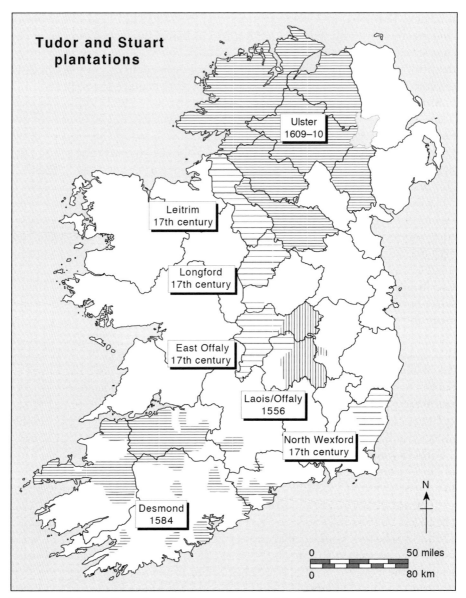

Figure 3.1 Tudor and Stuart plantations by county (map by Matthew Stout).

consisted of scattered lands, the government gained control of a unified block of six Ulster counties (Donegal, Cavan, Fermanagh, Tyrone, Londonderry, Armagh), but counties Antrim and Down were excluded (Figure 3.1).

Confiscation in these counties was followed by a government-directed settlement scheme based on the biblical narrative of the coming of the Jews to Canaan,[20] a

20 Robinson, *Plantation of Ulster*, pp 89–90; R. Loeber, '"Certyn notes": biblical and foreign signposts to the Ulster plantation' in Lyttleton & Rynne (eds), *Plantation Ireland*, pp 23–42.

precedent recounted in Ulster plantation papers. Plantation sites were selected, land grants were issued, and the principal settlers within each barony were generally awarded an ancient Irish land measure called baile biataigh (anglicised ballybetagh) that had been in the personal possession of the Irish lord. Thus, new settler lords displaced the old Gaelic lords. The settlers included the following categories: 'undertakers' (English and Scottish settlers), 'servitors' (former soldiers, several native Irish) and 'natives' (Gaelic Irish, but with a smattering of Old English). Each category was assigned different amounts of land. Most land was granted to the undertakers, followed by the indigenous Irish, while the least went to the servitors, who as military veterans were sited in strategically vulnerable locations. Lands were also granted to the Irish Society and its twelve constituent London Companies.[21] The Old English, because of their suspected disloyalty on sectarian grounds, were excluded from receiving grants in the new plantations in Ulster and the Midlands.[22] Although most undertakers were Protestant, a tiny minority were Catholic, for example, Lords Audley and Abercorn.

Confiscations of Midlands lordships

Unlike in Ulster, confiscation of Gaelic lands in the Midlands proceeded in the absence of revolts: it was based on legal chicanery purporting to show that several Gaelic lords lived on lands lacking clear title according to English law, or on lands that Gaelic lords allegedly usurped in the past from English grantees. This formed the pretext for the dispossession of Gaelic lords and their dependents. The main families so affected were the Kinsellas, MacDavymores and O'Morchoes in north-east Wexford, the MacCoghlans, O'Carrolls, Molloys and Foxes in west Offaly, the O'Dunnes and FitzPatricks in north Laois, the O'Rourkes in Leitrim, the O'Ferralls in Longford, the MacLoughlins in west Westmeath, the O'Brennans in Kilkenny, and the Byrnes in south Wicklow (Figure 3.1). Inquisitions to provide a legal pretext for further confiscations of large areas in Connacht were underway during the 1630s, but the 1641 rebellion terminated plantation plans for that province.

The distinction between civilian undertakers and military servitors in the Ulster plantation as the basis for assignment of different types of land was abandoned in the Midlands schemes. Midland plantations (notably Wexford and Longford) included very few grantees from England or Scotland. Several Scots, however, were allocated lands in the Leitrim and Longford plantations, for example, at Manorhamilton (Leitrim) and Castle Forbes (Longford). The Midlands confiscations also affected some Old English and New English landowners, whose acquisition of properties predated the confiscation. The new grantees were often courtiers, royal servants and government officials from Dublin, but they also included many army officers, who generally lacked sufficient resources to develop their estates.[23]

---

21 Lands were also set aside for towns, churches and Trinity College, Dublin. See Map 5 in Clarke, *NHI*, iii, p. 198; N. Canny, *Making Ireland British 1580–1650* (Oxford, 2001), pp 209, 257. 22 A. Clarke, *The Old English in Ireland 1625–1642* (London, 1966), pp 16–17. 23 Mac Cuarta, 'Plantation of Leitrim', p. 307.

PRE-PLANTATION ARCHITECTURE OF GAELIC LORDSHIPS

Ulster
The architecture in Gaelic areas in Ulster and the Midlands prior to the
1610s can be assessed to gauge the extent to which plantation buildings were
qualitatively different from preceding architecture.[24] Unlike other provinces in
Ireland, west Ulster saw few Anglo-Norman settlements. During the fourteenth
and fifteenth centuries, Anglo-Norman settlements weakened over the entire
island, including east Ulster, and the expulsion of English settlers by resurgent
Gaelic forces was more complete in Connacht and Ulster than elsewhere in
Ireland. Until the seventeenth century, towns were uncommon, although some
(Cavan, Armagh) flourished.

Power in Ulster was concentrated in a system of large Gaelic lordships, notably
the O'Neills and the O'Donnells, operating a hierarchical system of overlordships
and underlordships (including the O'Reillys and O'Cahans). Several Gaelic lords in
Ulster built stone towerhouses, usually on a square plan.[25] Leitrim Castle was built
by Brian Ó Ruairc (O'Rourke) in 1540 as a defence against the 'wars' waged against
him.[26] Bodley's 1609 survey of Fermanagh, a county dominated by the Maguires,
showed only three ruined stone castles (Enniskillen, Lisnaskea, Iniskeen), probably
of recent construction. Enniskillen Castle, chief seat of the Maguires, was the largest
stone castle in that area (Figure 3.2).[27] Bodley's survey of Tyrone showed ten castles,
all occupied by the ruling O'Neills. Dungannon Castle, the principal seat of Aodh
Ó Néill (Hugh O'Neill), was ruined in 1602 (Figure 3.3). Clusters of castles were
sprinkled across the lands of the O'Donnells, especially on the coast, but also along
the borders with Tír Eoghan, the Úi Néill lordship.

Irish lords were not the only ones to build stone castles; several prominent
gallowglasses (a mercenary class of elite warriors), physicians, poets and judges
(breitheamh, anglicised brehons) lived in castles. The castle at Drom Brochas (later
Castle Coole) in Fermanagh, for example, formerly belonged to the O'Cassidys,
hereditary physicians to the Maguires of Fermanagh. Several gallowglass leaders
lived in stone castles on the north coast of Donegal: Rahan Castle was built by the
McSwineys, who were professional swordsmen.[28]

24 Loeber, 'Gaelic castles and settlements', this volume, pp 1–34; see also T. McNeill, 'The
archaeology of Gaelic lordship east and west of the Foyle', pp 346–56, C. Donnelly, 'Towerhouses
and late medieval secular settlements in County Limerick', pp 315–28; O'Conor, 'Gaelic lordly
sites in North Connacht' in Duffy, Edwards & FitzPatrick (eds), *Gaelic Ireland*, pp 329–45: A.
Horning, 'Dwelling houses in the old barbarous manner: archaeological evidence for Gaelic
architecture in an Ulster plantation village' in Duffy, Edwards & FitzPatrick (eds), *Gaelic Ireland*,
pp 375–96; Robinson, *Plantation of Ulster*, pp 26–30; O'Conor, *Archaeology of medieval rural
settlement*, pp 102–4. 25 Rowan, *North-west Ulster*, pp 27–8; [H. Bagnall], 'The description and
present state of Ulster', *UJA*, 2 (1854), pp 145–60. 26 Loeber, 'Gaelic castles and settlements',
p. 30. 27 *Maps of the escheated counties of Ireland in 1609* (Southampton, 1861). The castle was
17.1m high and measured 17.1m (east/west) x 11.6m (north/south). The walls were 2.4m thick.
The barbican wall was 4.3m high and stood 13.7m from the castle. At the bridge, the moat was 11m
wide. 28 Hill, *Plantation in Ulster*, p. 480; Rowan, *North-west Ulster*, p. 27.

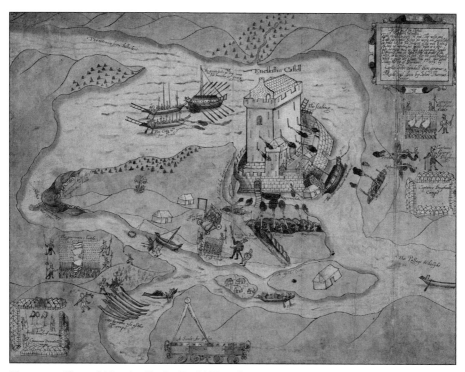

Figure 3.2 Siege of Maguire Castle, Enniskillen, County Fermanagh in 1594: 'The measure of the Castell of Eneyskillen as foloeth: First the castell in height 56 foott. The weste and easte sid[e]s in bredth 56 foot the northe and southe sides in breath 38 foott. The thicknes of the wall 8 foott. It hath no windo[w]es but spicike holles [spike holes] as is here. The barbegan [barbican] wall in h[e]ith 14 foote and standes distannte from the castell 45 foott. The bre[a]dth of the Ditch at the bridge 36 foott. ffor the land the scall [scale] which is passes [paces] at 5 foot the pase. [T]his castell taken the 17 of ffebruare 1594 by Capttn John [D]owdall then governor and d[raw]nn by John Thomas sold[i]er (British Library, Cotton Augustus I. ii. 39) (National Archives, London: MPF 1-80).

Structurally, Fermanagh castles were similar to towerhouses in Down and Tipperary.[29] The same is true of Gaelic towerhouses in Tyrone, Cavan and Donegal. The stronghold of Cormac Ó Néill at Augher Castle, with its two corner wall bartizans halfway up the elevation, closely resembles the O'Flaherty keep of Aughnanure Castle (Galway).

In comparison to Leinster and Munster, south-central Ulster (Cavan, Fermanagh, Monaghan) exhibited a low density of towerhouses (Figure 1.2). Principal dwellings here were presumably composed of timber, with bawns made of sods (confirmed by structures built by the indigenous Irish under the Ulster plantation). Prominent members of less dominant septs living under the O'Neills resided in timber or wattle structures inside earthen enclosures. O'Donnelly, a powerful sept leader, occupied a ringfort later known as Fort O'Donnalie (and which later again was called Castle Caulfield in the Ulster plantation), depicted on an early seventeenth-century map.[30]

---

29 J. Johnston, 'The plantation of County Fermanagh 1610–1642' (MA, QUB, 1976), p. 105. **30** Loeber, 'Gaelic castles and settlements', this volume, p. 16.

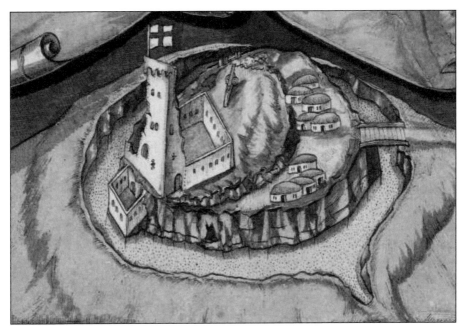

Figure 3.3 Richard Bartlett's 1602 drawing of O'Neill's ruined castle in Dungannon, County Tyrone. This is an unusual example of a Gaelic castle inside a wet moat (NLI, MS 2656).

Since the archaeology of timber structures is in its infancy, much remains to be gleaned about the nature of these buildings. An image of a timber castle owned or built by a Gaelic lord has not been identified. However, a timber towerhouse (Figure 3.4), built by the English government in 1587 to face a stone tower on the other side of a bridge across the Blackwater, could have been constructed by Ulster-Irish carpenters: it offers insight into the timber castles of the Gaelic lords. [31]

The other major pre-plantation settlement type in Ulster was the crannóg. [32] The main residence on a crannóg was mostly of timber, but sometimes of stone (Cloughoughter, Cavan, Augher, Tyrone), [33] and enclosed by defensive palisades built of timber or wattle. [34] Some strongholds were situated on an island in a river (Enniskillen Castle, Fermanagh, Figure 3.2). Houses on crannógs were not necessarily archaic. An early seventeenth-century Monaghan map by Richard Bartlett showed a crannóg with a cruciform house, probably constructed of timber and comparing closely to late sixteenth-century English examples (Figure 3.5). [35] Irish lords often used both a towerhouse and one or more crannógs, which offered a retreat if their towerhouse was besieged. An island castle at Lough Scur (Leitrim) was erected in

---

31 Ibid., pp 1–34. The drawing suggests that the castle had four large upright corner beams attached by wooden corbels to a projecting machicolation at roof level. 32 A. O'Sullivan, *The archaeology of lake settlement in Ireland* (Dublin, 1998); A. O'Sullivan, 'Crannógs in late medieval Gaelic Ireland *c*.1350–*c*.1650' in Duffy, Edwards & FitzPatrick (eds), *Gaelic Ireland*, pp 397–417. 33 For Augher crannóg and castle, see Hayes-McCoy (ed.), *Ulster maps*, Plate x. 34 A. O'Sullivan, *Crannógs: lake dwellings of early Ireland* (Dublin, 2000). 35 Hayes-McCoy (ed.), *Ulster maps*, Plate xi.

Figure 3.4 Irish-constructed timber towerhouse (to the left) inside the fort at Blackwater, County Tyrone (National Archives, London).

1570 by Seán Mac Raghnaill (John Reynolds) probably for security reasons.[36] An auxiliary tower on the lakeshore defended the causeway access to the crannóg.[37]

Midlands

The incidence of towerhouses in the Midland plantation areas differed from that in Ulster. Heavily wooded north Wexford and south Wicklow had comparatively few stone castles, and Irish lords and their tenants there most likely lived in timber structures. Compared to Ulster, stone towerhouses were more common in west Offaly and Longford. The Ely O'Carroll territory in Offaly contained at least forty-five castles in the early seventeenth century.[38] Most were in the hands of the ruling O'Carrolls and a small group of families subordinate to them. The largest example (Leap Castle) was the chiefry castle, while the rest were much smaller towerhouses.[39] Some towerhouses had stone or mud halls attached. A few were courtyard castles, of which Birr Castle was the largest. In the MacCoghlan lordship, also in Offaly, the settler Mathew De Renzy counted twenty-eight castles in the early seventeenth century. As can be gleaned from their Latin inscriptions, these castles dated primarily

---

36 Loeber, 'Gaelic castles and settlements', this volume, pp 30, 34.   37 The Down Survey shows a towerhouse at this site, close to the early seventeenth-century house of the Reynolds family, later known as Castle John.   38 Loeber, 'Gaelic castles and settlements', this volume, pp 15–16.   39 R. Loeber, 'The changing borders of a Gaelic lordship: conflict and diplomacy' in Nolan & O'Neill (eds), *Offaly*, pp 287–318.

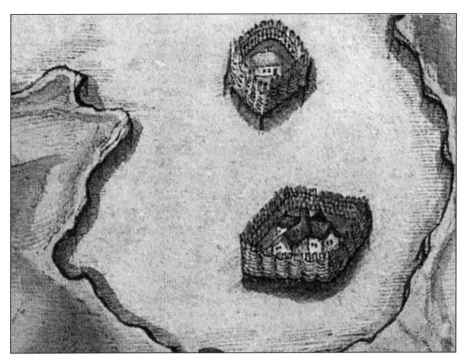

Figure 3.5 Richard Bartlett's 1602 drawing shows a crannóg containing a sophisticated cross-plan house (NLI, MS 2656).

from the sixteenth century.[40] Pre-plantation maps of the 1620s showed fifty-one towerhouses in Longford. According to a contemporary description, 'manie of the principall natives have good ancient castles, and most have bawnes about them, but they are somewhat ruinous'.[41] Crannógs were surprisingly rare in the lake-studded Midlands, although a handful are known in west Offaly and in Leitrim.

There were several distinct features of the architecture of the Gaelic Irish before the plantations. This architecture was originally under the control of the chiefs of each lordship and its dependents, but this changed abruptly when the Irish and English government, after confiscating the Gaelic territories, imposed novel building conditions on settlers and indigenous Irish alike. The pre-plantation architecture of Gaelic Ulster and the Midlands shared many features, such as towerhouses occupied by the Gaelic lords and their dependents, which were remarkably uniform in appearance. Timber houses occupied by the Gaelic lords, as yet invisible in the archaeological record, were common in Ulster and in the areas that suffered the Wicklow, Wexford and Leitrim plantations. Gaelic lords also sought refuge in crannógs, common in Leitrim, Cavan and Fermanagh, unusual in the Midlands and entirely absent in south Leinster.

40 R. Loeber, 'Civilisation through plantation: the projects of Sir Mathew De Renzi' in Murtagh (ed.), *Irish Midland studies*, pp 121–35; B. Mac Cuarta, 'Mathew De Renzy's letters on Irish affairs 1613–1620', *Anal. Hib.*, 34 (1987), pp 128, 136, 139, 157, 176–7.   **41** BL, Cotton, I Aug., i (14–48), ii (25, 26, 28); BL, Add. MS 4756, f. 127v.

PLANTATION BUILDING CONDITIONS

Government-sponsored settlements could have emulated the strengths and advantages of native architecture or they could choose to promote new and stronger forms of buildings. Government regulations shed light on official aspirations for settler architecture, notably the emphasis on defensible dwellings and bawns. These documents alert architectural historians and archaeologists as to what to seek on the ground.

The Ulster plantation was not the first in Ireland for which building conditions were imposed. Such regulation in Ireland started in the Pale in 1430 when a statute promoting border castles provided a subsidy of £10 for the construction of castles of 20 x 16 feet (6.1m x 4.9m) and 40 feet (12.2m) in height. A similar subsidy to build border castles around the Pale was offered by the Irish government in the mid sixteenth century. Remarkably, no building conditions were stipulated for the planters in the Offaly/Laois plantations, while conditions for the massive Munster plantation during the late sixteenth century offered only vague exhortations, such as building a 'principal residence' by the grantee and his main farmers, without specifying size, defensibility or materials.[42]

Most new strongholds in the Offaly/Laois and Munster plantations were destroyed during subsequent rebellions by the Irish in the late sixteenth century. Government officials in the early seventeenth century concluded that two changes were needed. First, it would be insufficient simply to reinforce borders by constructing strategically placed strings of castles. Instead, a close network of castles should be established to cover all the newly confiscated lands, which would allow settlers to succour each other in case of attack. Second, detailed building specifications were needed, such as minimum standards for the sizes and materials of houses and bawns. These conditions could vary by the size of estates on a sliding scale, with smaller structures for smaller estates and larger structures for larger estates (Appendix 3.1). The building conditions also specified the extent to which the main residence and the bawn should be made defensible.

Building conditions for planters varied between Ulster and the Midlands. In contrast to the Midland conditions, the Ulster regulations did not stipulate minimum sizes but instead spoke of 'castles' and 'houses'. Furthermore, the Ulster conditions required a 'strong court or bawn', whereas the Midland plantations demanded a bawn of brick or stone, or one with a 300-foot (91m) compass (equivalent to a bawn of 23m square).

While only one set of instructions for Ulster has survived, several variants exist for plantation structures in the Midlands (Appendix 3.1).[43] The Midlands versions

---

42 Loeber, 'Geography and practice', this volume, pp 79–83; Treadwell, *Irish commission of 1622*, p. 477. The settlement of Monaghan in 1591–2 stipulated that castles had to be built. The castles at Monaghan and Ballylurgan were built shortly afterwards.   43 Appendix 3.1 does not list conditions for the twelve London Companies, because such conditions have not survived. However, each company built a main residence and settlements (Curl, *Londonderry plantation*; Chart, *Londonderry and the London companies*; Moody, *Londonderry plantation*).

encompassed a wider range of estate sizes (six categories from 200 to 2,000 acres, 81ha to 809ha), whereas those in Ulster ranged from 1,000 to 2,000 acres (405ha to 809ha); these sizes all proved to be major underestimates.[44] The conditions for both plantations specified that the main residence and the bawn must be built of stone or brick held together with lime. The only exceptions were the two smallest categories in the Midlands, which required the building of a 'house of framed timber after the English manner', with a chimney of brick or stone made with lime, and a 'defensible bawn of earth'.

Remarkably, the specified size of the main residence in the Midlands plantation was similar across the three largest estate categories (1,000, 1,500 and 2,000 acres; 405ha, 607ha and 809ha): this amounted to a minimum ground surface of 20 x 30 feet (6.1m x 9.1m), and a height of 20–5 feet (6.1m–7.6m) (another version stipulated 35 feet (10.7m) in height). Compared to the border castles of 1430, the planned Midlands castles were only 2.7m longer, but much lower at 6.1m to 7.6m high rather than 12.2m.

The Ulster and Midland conditions did not require planters of 1,000 acres (405ha) to render their houses defensible by means of vaults, battlements, bartizans, pistol loops, etc. Many fortified houses had minimal defences, and some were entirely non-defensible houses (Castle Caulfield and Castle Curlews, both in Tyrone, and several main residences built by the London Companies). Other structures, particularly those built by undertakers from Scotland, were more defensible.

The strictest building regulations were reserved for bawns rather than dwellings.[45] Bawns were regarded as the main line of defence for the planters, their tenants and their villagers. In the specifications for the different plantations (Appendix 3.1), the bawn was to be strongly built of stone or brick bound with lime. Only in the smallest plantation estates in the Midlands did the minimum regulations permit a 'defensible bawn' of earth or a strong ditch. The bawn regulations never required a defensible gate, gatehouse or flankers, battlements or a boardwalk inside the bawn walls, all vital features to make a bawn properly defensible.

Building regulations also applied to native grantees. The documents, however, lack specific details: native settlers were to occupy similar residences 'as the former undertakers'. The impression given is that native grantees were not held as strictly to building requirements as the foreign settlers. The plantation documents did not prohibit living on crannógs, a tradition that persisted into the 1650s, and which demonstrated their military capacity in that it later proved very difficult to dislodge incumbents from them.[46]

Building conditions for the plantations in Ulster and the Midlands were much more specific than earlier ones and sought to establish a network of supportive strongholds across the entire plantation areas. The guidelines focused on

---

44 R. Hunter, 'The English undertakers in the plantation of Ulster 1610–41', *Breifne*, 4 (1974), p. 476.   45 Both the 1619 and 1622 surveys list bawns first and then the residences for each parcel.   46 R. Loeber & G. Parker, 'The military revolution in seventeenth-century Ireland' in J. Ohlmeyer (ed.), *From independence to occupation: Ireland 1641–1660* (Cambridge, 1995), p. 83.

new structures and ignored the rebuilding or re-use of Gaelic forms such as stone towerhouses, timber dwellings, crannógs, ringforts or other earth works. The preferred building materials were stone and brick with lime, rather than dwellings and bawns made of wattle, sods or clay, which tended to decay faster and needed constant maintenance. Only the smallest estates in the Midland plantations were allowed houses of framed timber 'after the English manner' but the unexpressed underlying concept was that settlers should shun native forms of architecture.

Scope of plantation buildings

The Ulster plantation generated a much larger building programme than in the Midland plantations.[47] In 1619, Nicholas Pynnar, director general of fortifications and buildings, claimed that 107 castles (of which 19 lacked a bawn) had been built in the Ulster plantation counties, as well as 42 bawns without castles or houses, and 1,897 dwelling houses of 'stone and timber after the English manner'. However, a comparison of Pynnar's statistics with the 1622 survey showed that his 'castles' actually included houses of every type – defensive, unfortified, large, small, formal, traditional, etc.[48] Many settlers were absentees, who delayed or never executed their building projects, and sold their properties on. Of 164 plantation estates in the surveys, 38 lacked a principal dwelling.[49] The number of main residences fell well short of what had been originally envisioned. The Midland plantations generated notably fewer new castles and bawns than in Ulster, explained by the smaller territories involved but also by a remarkable degree of non-compliance. The Leitrim

---

47 The following text draws on the ensuing sources: Rowan, *North-west Ulster*, pp 33–5; T. McNeill, *Castles in Ireland: feudal power in a Gaelic world* (London, 1997), pp 163–4; R. Hunter, 'Plantation in Donegal' in W. Nolan, L. Ronayne & M. Dunleavy (eds), *Donegal: history and society* (Dublin, 1995), pp 283–324; Roulston, 'Scots in plantation Cavan', pp 121–46; Johnston, 'Plantation of County Fermanagh'; J. Lyttleton, 'Rathcline Castle: an archaeology of plantation in County Longford' in M. Morris & F. O'Ferrall (eds), *Longford: history and society* (Dublin, 2010), pp 135–59; Hunter, 'English undertakers', pp 471–500; Fennelly, 'Towerhouses in Co. Offaly'; M. D'Alton, 'The architecture of the Leix and Offaly plantations *c.*1540–1600' (MLitt, TCD, 2009); W. Roulston, 'Seventeenth-century manors in the barony of Strabane' in J. Lyttleton & T. O'Keeffe (eds), *The manor in medieval and early modern Ireland* (Dublin, 2005), pp 160–87; Klingerhofer, *Castles and colonists*; P. Kerrigan, *Castles and fortifications in Ireland* (Cork, 1995); W. Kelly & J. Young (eds), *Scotland and the Ulster plantations* (Dublin, 2009); Sweetman, *Medieval castles*, pp 175–98; Perceval-Maxwell, *Scottish migration*; J. Mallory & T. McNeill, *The archaeology of Ulster from colonization to plantation* (Belfast, 1991); Robinson, *Plantation of Ulster*; Curl, *Londonderry plantation*; B. Wilsdon, *Plantation castles on the Erne* (Dublin, 2010); B. Scott, *Cavan 1609–53: plantation, war and religion* (Dublin, 2007); M. Salter, *Castles and strong houses of Ireland* (Malvern, 1993); Davies, 'Castles of County Cavan', pp 73–100; Mac Cuarta, 'Plantation of Leitrim', pp 297–320; J. Johnston, 'Settlement and architecture in County Fermanagh 1610–41', *UJA*, 43 (1980), pp 79–89; Nolan, *Fassadinin*; V. Treadwell, *Buckingham and Ireland 1616–1628: a study in Anglo-Irish politics* (Dublin, 1998); J. Lyttleton, 'Native and newcomer in post-medieval Ireland, changing cultural identities in County Offaly: an archaeological perspective' (PhD, UCC, 2006, 3v).   **48** Robinson, *Plantation of Ulster*, p. 132.   **49** Ibid., p. 129, p. 132; Perceval-Maxwell, *Scottish migration*, pp 166, 169–70.

plantation in 1622 lacked evidence of any new buildings:[50] eventually a handful of residences were built at Dromahair, Manorhamilton and Aughry.[51] Longford and Wexford gained only a modest number of residences. Specifications for the Midland plantations stipulated sizes for buildings. The actual scale of construction was on a larger scale than specified. This must reflect settlers' perceptions of what was acceptable as adequate living quarters for their family or their agent – more extensive than the government's.

Documents, extant buildings and archaeology make it possible to assess the extent to which towerhouses and other earlier building types persisted in the plantation period. It is also possible to ascertain the extent to which new forms of architecture emerged in these plantations and to evaluate whether this architecture was distinctive compared to contemporary equivalents in Ireland outside the plantation areas.

A key issue in assessing the new plantation architecture is to know how many main residences were made defensible against attacks and theft of property and cattle. The government surveys indicate a greater interest in standards of defence for incoming settlers rather than for any natives who had received land grants. In the early stages of the plantations, the necessity for physical defences against the indigenous Irish was clear. Contemporary reports refer to widespread dissatisfaction among the Irish and their willingness to use violence to seek redress. Reports from the 1620s mention 'daily robberies' of settlers in the Ulster plantation,[52] and plots to overthrow the plantation by burning settlements.[53] This was also the case elsewhere: in 1620, Maurice MacEdward Kavanagh and his followers surprised the plantations of Sir James Carroll and William Marwood at Ballycarney in north Wexford, 'murdered their servants, [and] burned their towns'.[54] Thus, defence was clearly a pressing issue for the new planters.

The widespread building programmes in each plantation area was informed by the destruction of settler residences in the sixteenth-century Offaly/Laois and Munster plantations and by the knowledge that defensible housing stock was urgently needed. It was prudent policy to emphasise the protection of the resident owner, his family and his servants against understandably aggrieved locals who had lost land, power and prestige as a result of the plantations.

Persistence of older building traditions

Irish landowners of every background were familiar with the effectiveness of towerhouses and adjoining bawns against intrusions. For that reason alone, it would be logical to assume that settlers would prefer to build towerhouses rather than less defensible if more comfortable structures. However, only a minority of buildings

50 Mac Cuarta, 'Plantation of Leitrim', p. 309; Treadwell, *Irish commission of 1622*, p. 679.   **51** For the less well-known Aughry Castle, see R. Stalley (ed.), *Daniel Grose (c.1766–1838): the antiquities of Ireland* (Dublin, 1991), Plates 65–6.   **52** Chart (ed.), *Londonderry and the London companies*, pp 151, 153; BL, Add. MS 4756, f. 119v; Hill, *Plantation in Ulster*, p. 441.   **53** Mac Cuarta, 'Plantation of Leitrim', p. 311; Johnston, 'Plantation of County Fermanagh', p. 82.   **54** Goff, 'English conquest of an Irish barony', p. 139.

erected during the Ulster plantation continued in the tradition of towerhouses on a square plan with thick walls, often reinforced by vaults.[55] There were certainly some examples: several vaulted castles on a square plan, with a thatched roof, were built in the Cavan plantation.[56] Likewise, in Armagh, Lord Grandison's castle at Tanderagee measured 32 to 33 feet (9.8m–10.1m) square and was 39 feet (11.9m) high.[57] In Fermanagh, at least two castles were built, one at Termon Magrath, measuring 25 x 29 feet (7.6m x 8.8m), and another at Drumbochus (Donegal) of the same size (24 x 30 feet, 7.3m x 9.1m).[58] Although towerhouses continued to be built in the Ulster plantation, they proved to be the exception rather than the rule.

The building of towerhouses prior to 1641 was not a phenomenon unique to Ulster. In adjoining County Down, castle building on a square plan also continued: Castle Ward was built in 1610 (probably by Irish masons) and Kirkistown Castle in 1622.[59] In the Midland plantations, towerhouses went out of fashion and no more were built during the early seventeenth century.

In Ulster, the uprooting and resettlement of native landowners was much more widespread and severe than in the Midlands. Gaelic landowners were forced out of their former strongholds by the settlers and they accordingly needed to erect new dwellings, often at a considerable distance from their former habitation. Unlike in the Midlands, the stone castles of the native landowners were occupied by new settlers in Ulster. Examples include Dungannon, Strabane and Augher (Tyrone), Limavady (Londonderry), Donegal and Burt (Donegal) and Enniskillen (Fermanagh). Several castles were refurbished by settlers to match contemporary living expectations. The keep of Donegal Castle received triangular gables and an oriel window, while triangular gables also topped the new wing, a common feature in both the south of Ireland and in England.

Gaelic Irish in the plantations

The plantation surveys show that only a minority of Irish freeholders were allowed to apply for letters patent for plantation lands, as a special reward for their service and loyalty to the English crown. The number of native freeholders within the plantations was curtailed, thereby reducing multitudes of freeholders to the lower status of tenants.[60] This drained the financial liquidity for the leading families, who could no longer borrow against their estate for financing improvements, such as new buildings, and who also suffered a catastrophic loss of income by becoming tenants. In the entire Ulster plantation, only 26 Irishmen were granted estates of over 1,000 acres (405ha).[61] Settlements by the Gaelic Irish in the plantation areas are difficult to trace in documents because many eventually mortgaged, conveyed or sold

---

55 Many older towerhouses were not exactly square but slightly oblong with the proportion of length to breadth being 1:0.75–1:0.8.   **56** Treadwell, *Irish commission of 1622*, p. 512.   **57** Ibid., p. 551. Significantly, however, an addition on a rectangular plan was constructed, which presumably housed the domestic quarters.   **58** Johnston, 'Plantation of County Fermanagh', p. 110. Thomas Flowerdew, a British settler in Fermanagh, built a stone castle (Treadwell, *Irish commission of 1622*, p. 526).   **59** Salter, *Castles and strong houses*, p. 141.   **60** Mac Cuarta, 'Plantation of Leitrim', p. 310.   **61** Robinson, *Plantation of Ulster*, pp 199–200.

their lands. This presumably meant that their residences were abandoned as they downsized to less expensive houses when reduced to tenant status. In the Wexford plantation, the proportion of lands owned by the Gaelic Irish was dramatically reduced in this manner between 1615 and 1641.[62]

Some native grantees succeeded in establishing enduring residences. Maol Muire Óg Ó Raghallaigh (Mulmorie Oge O'Relie), a grantee of 3,000 acres (1,214ha), occupied 'an old castle' set within a bawn of sods at Bellanagargy in Cavan.[63] In 1651, this building was known as 'the strongest fort of the enemy' in County Cavan.[64] Other native planters in Cavan included Seán Mac Pilíb Ó Raghallaigh (Shane McPhillip O'Reilly), Maol Muire Mac Pilíb Ó Raghallaigh (Mullmorie McPhillip O'Reyley), and Muiris Mac Theallaigh Ó Raghallaigh (Maurice McTelligh). Their buildings were characterised in 1619 as 'Irish houses', situated within a flankerless sod bawn (one with a moat as well), which represents native architecture of an older vintage.

In Ulster, the Gaelic Irish grantees did not build large fortified houses or new towerhouses and probably continued a tradition of building wattle or timber residences. Captain Turloch Ó Néill (Turloe O'Neale), a former officer in the English army in Ireland, was assigned 4,000 acres (1,600ha) in Tyrone: here he built a bawn of lime and stone with two flankers, inside which was 'a fair coupled timber house'.[65] Similarly, some native settlers in Fermanagh built timber houses. Brian Maguire and Conchubhair Shéain Ó Néill (Conn Shane O Neill) in Fermanagh built 'great copelled [coupled] houses' set in a bawn made of earth and sods.[66] These structures were probably temporary dwellings, because eight years later these grantees were living in buildings of lime and stone.[67] In 1635, an English visitor to the wooded area west of the Wexford plantation described a timber residence near the Slaney as a 'handsome Irish hall'.[68] However, in the absence of drawings, it is difficult to envisage what these structures actually looked like.

In contrast to the native planters in Cavan, their counterparts in Donegal lived in houses of lime and stone with bawns made of the same materials.[69] There is no evidence that flankers were built for the bawns owned by native planters, suggesting that flankers were absent in indigenous architecture. This may reflect an absence of the muskets necessary to defend the length of bawn walls.[70] Whether sod bawns were

---

62 R. Loeber & M. Stouthamer-Loeber, 'The lost architecture of the Wexford plantation' in Whelan (ed.), *Wexford*, pp 173–200; Goff, 'English conquest of an Irish barony', p. 139. See also Johnston, 'Plantation of County Fermanagh', p. 81 for the process leading to a reduced proportion of native landowners after the plantation in Fermanagh.   63 Hill, *Plantation in Ulster*, p. 460; Treadwell, *Irish commission of 1622*, p. 514.   64 C. Firth, *The memoirs of Edmund Ludlow* (Oxford, 1894), p. 491.   65 Treadwell, *Irish commission of 1622*, p. 587; Hill, *Plantation in Ulster*, pp 316–17.   66 Johnston, 'Plantation of County Fermanagh', pp 27, 100, 173. The fact that there were masons preparing and hewing stone indicates that additional stone structures were also planned.   67 Hill, *Plantation in Ulster*, pp 492–3; Treadwell, *Irish commission of 1622*, p. 514.   68 Loeber & Stouthamer-Loeber, 'Wexford plantation', p. 185. It is unclear whether this structure was a recent one.   69 Hill, *Plantation in Ulster*, pp 492–3, 526–7; Treadwell, *Irish commission of 1622*, p. 532.   70 In a rare instance, a British settler occupied a dwelling inside a bawn constructed of sods (Treadwell, *Irish commission of 1622*, p. 578).

on a rectangular or round plan remains unclear, but older sites, were often reused. Bawns around the main residence of Gaelic grantees may have been round rather than rectangular, replicating the shape of a ringfort.[71] There were two traditional materials for building bawns. The first was sods; the second was clay and stone, which were 'rough cast over with lime', presumably weather-proofing them, as rain wreaked havoc on exposed clay walls. Several of these bawns were built in Fermanagh, and even more in Donegal.[72]

In the Midland plantations, prominent Gaelic landowners remained resident at their former towerhouses. Examples include the MacCoghlans at Garrycastle and Cloghan Castle (Offaly), the O'Carrolls at Leap Castle (Offaly), the O'Ferralls at Mornin (Longford), and the Mageoghegans at Donore (Westmeath). Strategically situated castles, notably those along the Shannon, were confiscated and granted to settlers. Examples include Banagher and Raghra (Offaly), Rathcline (Longford) and Dromahair (Leitrim).

Only a few major Gaelic grantees in the Midland plantations erected a new structure on a large scale. The MacCoghlans built Jacobean-style country houses at Kilcolgan and probably Kincora (both Offaly).[73] Some Irish grantees added stone houses to their stone keeps, for example, Leap Castle and Clonlyon Castle (both Offaly). Some chose crow-stepped gables (said to be characteristic of Irish architecture) for their new structures, for example, additions to the castles at Ballymooney and Leap, and the gables at Cloghan Castle (all in Offaly).[74] Crow-step gables were also common, however, in Scotland and they can be found on the buildings of some Scottish settlers, for example, Newtownstewart (Tyrone) built by Sir William Stewart of Galloway. Outside the plantation areas, large stone residences were built by the principal Gaelic families, often the successors to the Irish lordships: examples include Portumna Castle (Galway) by the earl of Clanrickard and the O'Callaghan residence at Dromaneen (Cork).

Several native settlers in the plantations followed traditional methods of building wattle houses within sod-bawns. Both inside and outside the plantation areas, the construction of towerhouses was uncommon in the first half of the seventeenth century. Hardly any Gaelic grantees in the plantation areas built a towerhouse between 1610 and 1641. One of the last towerhouses (on a rectangular plan and without a vault) was built in 1643 at Derryhivenny (Galway) by a Gaelic chief of the Madden family, during a cessation in the hostilities of the 1641 rebellion.[75] Defensible towerhouses erected in Ulster prior to 1641 were all built by English and Scottish settlers. The lack of enthusiasm for building towerhouses by Gaelic grantees may have represented

---

71 Thomas Flowerdew, a British settler in Fermanagh, built a stone bawn over a ringfort, presumably made of sods (Treadwell, *Irish commission of 1622*, p. 526).   72 Hill, *Plantation in Ulster*, pp 477, 516, 523.   73 J. Lyttleton, 'Faith of our fathers: the Gaelic aristocracy in Co. Offaly and the Counter-Reformation' in Lyttleton & Rynne (eds), *Plantation Ireland*, p. 199.   74 Wilsdon, *Plantation castles on the Erne*, p. 226. Another plantation house, Castle Cuffe (Laois), built by Sir Charles Coote, also had step-gables.   75 A tower at Castle French (Roscommon) has a date stone of 1682 but it may have belonged to an earlier gate building.

restricted finances, or acculturation in adopting more modish English forms of architecture. Under the Gaelic system, castles were built at the charge of the lordship in general and no personal investment was therefore necessary.[76] With the transition to plantations, Gaelic lords lost power over their tenants and could no longer force them to build or finance their castles. In these circumstances, native grantees possibly regarded English-style buildings as an acceptable alternative.

Towerhouses evidently did not fall into absolute disfavour because native and English grantees alike continued to live in them, sometimes with the addition of commodious extensions. The phasing-out of new towerhouses occurred later in Ulster than in the Midlands. All over Ireland, starting in the late sixteenth century, novel forms of hybrid towerhouses and fortified houses on a variety of plans emerged. They had a smattering of defensive features (machicolations, bartizans), and also placed a novel emphasis on the domestic comforts of greater space, more windows and additional fireplaces.

Finally, a new style of building – a low rectangular strong house with a long vaulted basement – originated in the late sixteenth century in the Pale, as, for example, at Robertstown and Riverstown (both Meath). This style was adopted in the Ulster plantation. Among the Scottish settlers, William Baylie had built a 'strong castle' in County Cavan by 1618 that was 30 feet x 20 feet (9.1m x 6.1m), of two storeys with a vaulted ground floor, and covered by a thatched roof. It may have resembled the slightly longer 'strong house' occupied by Maol Muire Mac Aodh Ó Raghallaigh (Mullmory McHugh O'Reilley) in the same county.[77]

NEW ARCHITECTURAL FORMS

Architectural innovations during the late sixteenth and early seventeenth centuries can now be considered, to assess whether there were variations in innovations between the Ulster and Midland plantations, and whether a similar variation marked areas inside and outside planted areas. In a larger context, British and continental influences on the innovations can be addressed, and the extent to which uniquely Irish features persisted. Also considered is how defensive features of the houses performed during the 1641 rebellion. Our understanding of early seventeenth-century architecture, however, is necessarily selective as it depends on the patchy survival of structures and documentation. Because fortified houses of the early seventeenth century had thinner walls than the earlier towerhouses, fewer of the former compared to the latter have survived.

Development of novel architectural forms and details in late sixteenth and early seventeenth-century Ireland had practically nothing to do with stipulated building conditions in the plantation areas. Compared to the earlier towerhouses, the most significant architectural innovation in the plantations (and elsewhere in Ireland) was

76 Mac Cuarta, 'De Renzy', p. 123.   77 Hill, *Plantation in Ulster*, pp 456, 468; Treadwell, *Irish commission of 1622*, pp 511–12.

the variety of plans, elevations, defences, decoration and interiors that emerged during the early seventeenth century (Appendix 3.2). While existing studies focused on the external stylistic origins of the buildings in England, Scotland and elsewhere, this chapter considers additional internal influences from the Pale and other parts of Ireland.

Stylistic origins

Scholars of seventeenth-century Irish architecture have observed that Scottish planters introduced a distinct Scottish style of castle and architectural elements into the Ulster plantation.[78] This is unsurprising because the tradition of building defensible castles, of paramount importance for plantation architecture, persisted in the Scottish border regions longer than in England. In Ulster, the Scots brought with them the use of tall profiled towers, the L-plan, crow-stepped gables, projecting turrets on decorative corbel courses, and a rectangular plan with towers at diagonally opposite corners to achieve the greatest fire-cover (sometimes called a Z-plan), such as Enniskillen Castle (Fermanagh) and Burt Castle (Donegal). Within the Ulster plantation, Scottish-style castles were built, of which prime examples are Derrywoone and Mountcastle (both Tyrone), Castle Balfour (Figure 3.6) and Monea (both Fermanagh) and Mongavlin (Donegal). Scottish features in buildings before 1600 were not unique to the Ulster plantation, but were also present elsewhere in the north of the country. Dunluce Castle (Antrim) is an example while Castle Blayney (Monaghan) and Killyleagh (Down) – before its rebuilding – also had characteristic Scottish corbelled turrets. Scottish-style castles were uncommon in the Midland plantations.[79] Scottish settlers shuttled between their Scottish and Irish estates, and imported craftsmen to build in Ireland in the process.

English settlers are said to have introduced several non-defensive architectural elements into Ulster plantation houses. Examples are bay windows, porches and other features (Appendix 3.2).[80] Although these features are evident in the Ulster plantation, their putative English provenance is far from definite because they also occurred in Ireland in many locations outside the plantations. Thus, bay windows were built at Dunluce Castle (Antrim), Joymount (Sir Arthur Chichester's townhouse at Carrickfergus in Antrim), and Sir Toby Caulfield's house inside Charlemont Fort (Armagh). Oriel windows (a bay window usually situated on an upper storey housing the principal living rooms) were introduced into Ireland in the late sixteenth century – Ormond Castle in Carrick-on-Suir (Tipperary) – and remained rare in the plantation areas (Donegal Castle, Donegal; Castle Curlews, Tyrone) and elsewhere during the early seventeenth century (Athlumney in Meath, Figure 3.7a–b; Lismore Castle in Waterford, Figure 3.8).

78 Johnston, 'Plantation of County Fermanagh', pp 107, 112; E. Jope, 'Scottish style castles in the north of Ireland', *UJA*, 14 (1951), pp 31–47; E. Jope, 'Castleraw near Loughgall, Co. Armagh', *UJA*, xvi (1953), pp 63–7; E. Jope, 'Mongavlin Castle, Co. Donegal' *UJA*, xvii (1954), pp 169–72; Waterman, 'Irish seventeenth-century houses', pp 261–4. The sixteenth-century origin of the Watergate at Enniskillen Castle is disputed (Wilsdon, *Plantation castles on the Erne*, p. 91). **79** An exception was Aughry Castle (Leitrim). **80** Waterman, 'Irish seventeenth-century houses', pp 258–65.

Figure 3.6 Castle Balfour, County Fermanagh. This Scottish-style plantation castle has a typical L-shaped plan and corbelled projections.

Regional studies connecting Irish plantation structures to the home of English settlers – notably Devon or Suffolk – only partly explain the migration of variations in English stylistic features to Ireland.[81] The national, regional or cultural origins of settlers provided no guarantee that they would build in their home style. Thus, several Scottish settlers did not build in a Scottish manner. For example, two Scottish undertakers in Fermanagh built English-style houses (Derrygonelly and Tullykelter).[82] Several English settlers adopted an Irish style of building. John Sedborough's house in rural Fermanagh was described as 'an Irish house' divided into 'three rooms' and with a 'wattled chimney in it', set in a round bawn of sods that must have resembled a ringfort.[83] Likewise, the planter Sir John Fish built a large round bawn on top of a ringfort at Dromany (Cavan) with a circumference of 415 feet (127m).[84] Sometimes, a building combined Irish and English features: the house at Thomas Blenerhasset's settlement in Fermanagh was characterised

---

81 Hunter, 'English undertakers', p. 478.   82 Johnston, 'Plantation of County Fermanagh', p. 113.   83 Hill, *Plantation in Ulster*, pp 481–2.   84 Treadwell, *Irish commission of 1622*, p. 516. The bawn around the Clothworkers' residence was round (Chart, *Londonderry and the London companies*, opposite p. 81).

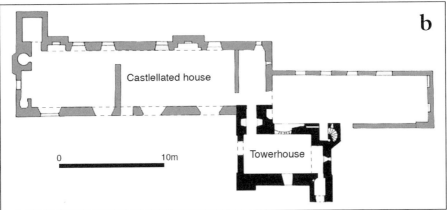

Figure 3.7a–b Illustration of 1794 (Francis Grose) and plan of Athlumney Castle, County Meath.

as 'a fair large Irish house', with 'windows and rooms after the English manner', suggesting that different cultural allusions could be employed simultaneously.[85]

One should not discount influences on plantation architecture originating from other areas in Ireland. Several Ulster plantation grantees also owned estates outside the plantation areas. For example, Sir James Hamilton held a plantation estate in Cavan, where he built 'a very large strong castle' called Castle Aubigny, and he also owned the lands and castle of Killyleagh (Down).[86] Sir Thomas Dutton was a planter in counties Cavan, Leitrim and Longford, while Lord Lambert, who held a large estate at Kilbeggan (Westmeath), became a planter in Cavan.[87] There are numerous

85 Hill, *Plantation in Ulster*, p. 489.   86 Hill, *Plantation in Ulster*, p. 452.   87 Roulston, 'Scots in plantation Cavan', p. 125; Lyttleton, 'Rathcline Castle', p. 138; for Lord Lambert, see Treadwell, *Irish commission of 1622*, p. 519.

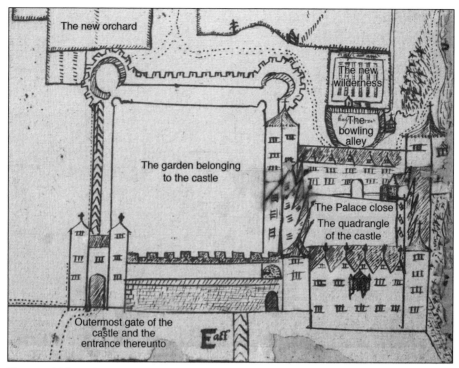

The new orchard

The new wilderness

The bowling alley

The garden belonging to the castle

The Palace close
The quadrangle of the castle

Outermost gate of the castle and the entrance thereunto

Eaſt

Figure 3.8 Plan of Lismore Castle, County Waterford, showing Richard Boyle's fortifications and gardens in the early seventeenth century. Note the oriel window providing a view over the river Blackwater (Chatsworth Archive).

other examples of individuals building both inside and outside the plantation areas.[88] In these instances, craftsmen of one Irish estate were likely employed on other Irish estates, ensuring that the distinction between architecture inside and outside plantation areas was necessarily blurred.

The transmission of shared architectural elements between structures in widely dispersed locations remains a puzzle for architectural historians. Commonly accepted modes of transmission included pattern books, craftsmen and architects working on different sites, and the desire by patrons to repeat the design of a successful building at another location. There is limited documentation about the use of pattern books in Ireland in the late sixteenth and early seventeenth centuries. Richard Boyle, first earl of Cork (1566–1643), possessed a booklet with hand-drawn designs of funerary monuments in perspective, and Viscount Conway (1594–1655), a planter at Lisburn (Antrim), owned architectural pattern books: however, there is little evidence for any direct impact exerted by such works on contemporary building projects.[89]

Craftsmen were often the vectors of stylistic innovations across areas. Craftsmen imported from England and Scotland worked in the plantation areas, but (with a

88 Mac Cuarta, 'Plantation of Leitrim', pp 316–17; Loeber, 'Geography and practice', this volume, p. 74.   89 Loeber, 'Early Classicism in Ireland', this volume, p. 215.

few exceptions) their links to specific surviving main residences remain tenuous.[90] Exceptions are the London bricklayer Peter Benson, who was recommended to build the London Ironmonger's Company settlement at Lizard (Londonderry) in 1615. He also built for himself a planter's house with two asymmetrical 'returns' and a bawn at Shragmiclar (Donegal). The builder William Parrott (or Parrat) is another example: he contracted for the construction of St Columb's Cathedral in Londonderry in 1627 in a late Gothic style. He probably executed work for the earl of Antrim at Dunluce (Antrim), and he also surfaced in the building accounts of the Merchant Taylors' Company estate at Macosquin (Londonderry). The main dwelling at this site was an unusual hybrid of a non-defensible English squire's house with bay windows and defensive bartizans at roof level.[91]

Many buildings in the Ulster plantation were presumably built by a small number of skilled and mobile craftsmen, some of whom could also design structures. Precise documentation for the design for one building being copied from another building is lacking. In the south, however, designs for building at the vast estate of the first earl of Cork were recycled in several instances. In 1636, the earl sent craftsmen to Doneraile (north Cork) to take 'a module' (model) of the Lord President's new house in order to build a similar structure for his son Francis Boyle at Carrigaline (probably the later Shannon Park).

Although several great builders of this period owned estates on both sides of the Irish channel, it did not necessarily follow that designs for the owner's Irish estate were slavishly copied from an English house. The earl of Clanricarde's English seat of Somerhill (Kent, 1613) was inspired by a plan copied from the design book *I quattro libri dell' architettura* published in Venice in 1570 by the ground-breaking Italian architect Andrea Palladio (1508–80), yet no such inspiration was expressed at his Portumna Castle (Galway), built just a few years later.[92]

The demand for craftsmen and builders in the Ulster plantation must have been substantial, especially during the 1610s and early 1620s. Some craftsmen were probably paid by being awarded tenancies on the plantation land. The Irish carpenter Henry Quincy was a tenant on the Aghieduff estate owned by an English undertaker in Cavan.[93] Gaelic talent was employed at numerous building sites in the Ulster plantation, as is evident from permission granted to undertakers to hire Irish masons and other labourers, and a government undertaking not to expel native building workers from the plantation area. Some names of Irish craftsmen are known from contemporary records, such as the mason Francis FitzSymons of Fermanagh, and the carpenter Séamus Buí Mac Craith (James Boy McGrath) of Termon Magrath (possibly related to the notorious Archbishop Miler McGrath (Maolmhuire Mac Craith), builder of Termon Magrath Castle in Donegal). Sir Thomas Ridgeway used an unnamed 'Irish

90 Moody, *Londonderry plantation*, p. 322; *Downshire*, ii, p. 486; *Cal. state papers Carew*, pp 75–9, 94–5, 220, 323, 225–7, 231; Moody, 'Ulster plantation papers', pp 253–4; Canny, *Making Ireland British*, p. 218; Curl, *Londonderry plantation*, p. 182.   91 R. Loeber, *A biographical dictionary of architects in Ireland* (London, 1981), pp 20–1, 40, 83–4; B. Blades, '"In the manner of England": tenant housing in the Londonderry plantation', *Ulster Folklife*, 27 (1981), p. 46. George Costerdyne was supervisor to the Company's building works (Curl, *Londonderry plantation*, pp 305, 308).   92 Loeber, *Biographical dictionary*, pp 13, 110.   93 Girouard, *Elizabethan architecture*, p. 89.

Figure 3.9 'The Skinners bvildinge at Dvngevin' (Dungiven, County Londonderry) as drawn by Thomas Raven in 1622. Raven employed a distinctive zig-zag motif to denote water. The plantation house has been fused with a pre-existing church. 'Six resident freeholders, and twelve British men present in this proporcon. It is necessary there was a stronge plantacon upon this proporcon, in a [fit] place at the foote of the mountaines ent[e]ring into the woode of Glanconkeyne for the safetie of those parts which withe so good a purpose to answeare the test of the said plantacons of Londonderrie' (Drapers' Company, London).

Figure 3.10 Charlemont Fort, County Armagh, offers a sophisticated design for the early seventeenth century (William Lawrence photograph, NLI).

house carpenter' at his residence in Cavan, but he imported ten carpenters from London and his native Devonshire, and he had ten masons, possibly also imported, working on his unique building at Augher (Tyrone).[94] Given the tradition of building timber houses and the scarcity of stone castles owned by the Gaelic Irish in Ulster, it is likely that masons, whose skills were in such high demand in the Ulster plantation area, were recruited from Britain or the Pale. Native craftsmen were also employed by Sir Lawrence Parsons to transform Birr Castle into an 'English' house, and by the first earl of Cork at his numerous building sites in Munster.[95]

Only in rare instances do contemporary records mention that craftsmen from the Pale were employed in the government-ordered plantations.[96] The Dublin bricklayer Peter Harrison was employed in building a house in Killabegs in the Wexford plantation.[97] It is far from clear, however, to what extent building traditions from the Pale influenced plantation architecture in Ulster or in the Midlands.

The survival of architectural designs for buildings of the period is very rare, and architectural drawings can be linked to actual structures in only a few instances. Craftsmen imported by the London Companies, in contrast to those introduced from

94 Hill, *Plantation in Ulster*, p. 461.   **95** *CSPI, 1615–25*, p. 323; *Cal. state papers Carew*, pp, 143, 202, 220, 231; *CSPI, 1611–14*, p. 137; Hill, *Plantation in Ulster*, p. 538.   **96** J. Fenlon, 'Some early seventeenth-century building accounts in Ireland', *Ir. Arch. & Dec. Studies*, 1 (1998), pp 84–99; Loeber, *Biographical dictionary*.   **97** The Cavan plantation records refer to tenants from the adjoining Pale, but it is unclear to what extent the tenants included craftsmen (Treadwell, *Irish commission of 1622*, pp 512, 522–3).

the English or Scottish countryside, brought more up-to-date building styles, hailing as they did from the metropolitan centre, but evidence remains tentative (the Skinners' Company domestic buildings at Dungiven (Londonderry) incorporated an older church – Figure. 3.9). An innovation generated in the Ulster plantation was English-inspired buildings with bay windows, of two to three storeys tall, which appear non-defensible.[98] Compared to other plantation houses, these houses provided better-lit interiors at each floor including the ground level. The bay-window houses were most common among the principal residences of the London Companies in rural Derry and they were more typical of freestanding houses within a bawn rather than those built against a bawn wall. Out of the twelve main company houses, three (Fishmongers, Haberdashers, Merchant Taylors) were of this type.[99] The remaining residences of the London Companies showed a mishmash of styles, plans and elevations. The most elegant of the bay-window houses was the one inside Charlemont Fort (Figure 3.10). Built by Sir Tobias Caulfield (who also built Castle Caulfield, Tyrone), this four-sided symmetrical gem possessed two three-storey bay windows on each of its four façades, making a total of eight bays. Composite chimneystacks rose elegantly from each of the four corners.[100]

Building influences from the Pale can be gauged from stylistic comparisons. The 1619 survey mentioned that 'good co[u]pled' houses in Donegal town were built 'in the manner of the Pale'.[101] In architectural interiors, the surviving classically-inspired spindle chimney piece at the plantation castle of Dromahair (Leitrim) resembles a chimney piece in the early seventeenth-century addition to Athclare Castle (Louth): even though the two counties are not adjacent, both chimney pieces may have emanated from the same workshop.[102] Another example is chimneystacks 'springing' from the first floor walls, thereby avoiding the possibility that attackers could shelter behind a ground-floor chimneystack. The castle at Newry (Down) built in 1578 had four such stacks. This feature was characteristic of the Pale, where it is still visible at Odder Castle and Athcarne Castle (both in Meath)[103] and adjoining counties (for example, at Maghernacloy in Monaghan).[104] It can also be seen further afield at Ballycowan (Offaly), several castles in Wexford (notably Ballyhealy) and Carnew (Wicklow).

Stylistic features from Scotland, England and the Pale were incorporated into plantation buildings. Especially in the case of the English features, it is possible that they were transmitted through both external English and internal Irish channels. The migration of styles was partly aided by craftsmen from Scotland, England and within Ireland working in the Ulster plantation. There is no evidence, however, that British craftsmen were employed in the Midland plantations, where architectural influences from within Ireland carried much greater weight.

98 Loeber & Stouthamer-Loeber, 'Wexford plantation', p. 199.   **99** Judging from Sir Thomas Phillips' critical comments (Moody, *Londonderry plantations*, pp 202–3).   **100** Chart (ed.), *Londonderry and the London companies*, plates opposite pp 49, 69, 101.   **101** A contemporary drawing, probably less reliable, of the house and fort shows more windows in each bay than are shown in an early twentieth-century photograph. The plan of the house at Charlemont Fort resembles the plan for Sir William Rigden's 1603 house in Lincolnshire (Gomme & Maguire, *Design and plan*, plan 70).   **102** Hill, *Plantation in Ulster*, p. 514.   **103** Waterman, 'Irish seventeenth-century houses', p. 252.   **104** Loeber, 'Geography and practice', this volume, p. 53.

Innovations in plans and elevations

During the sixteenth century, at least three versions of more spacious strong houses appeared, each on a rectangular plan with a length to breadth proportion of two to one. In comparison to towerhouses, these 'strong houses' had more internal space, better lighting from larger windows and improved heating from greater numbers of fireplaces.[105] Strong houses of two storeys with a defensive ground floor appeared but with more commodious rooms and windows on the first floor. These structures were most common in the Midlands and absent from the south-east (Carlow, Wicklow), south and south-west (Cork, Kerry, Limerick) and Cavan.[106]

A second type of strong house has been termed a 'hall-type fortified house', usually attached to a smallish tower. This form of strong house emerged in south Wexford during the late sixteenth century and it was mostly of two storeys with the main living quarters on the first floor over a defensible basement (Coolhull, Dungulph). These castles, shorter than those at Newry and Carnew, still employed a length to breadth proportion of two to one.[107]

A third type of strong house emerged primarily in the Pale, possibly also during the late sixteenth century. This form was of two storeys but differed from the Wexford strong house because the Pale examples inserted a long vault at ground-floor level. Examples are Darver Castle (Louth) and Robertstown Castle (Meath). There is no evidence that semi-fortified houses of either the Wexford or Pale types were built in the Ulster plantation.

Appendix 3.3 summarises examples of buildings laid out on novel plans that emerged during the late sixteenth and early seventeenth centuries, as well as specifying examples of each category of building in the plantation areas of Ulster, the Midlands and elsewhere in Ireland. The most defensible plans were the rectangular residences with four corner towers, followed by residences with two diagonally placed corner towers. Next were residences on a Z- or Y-plan, followed by the T-plan. Less defensible houses were those on a U- or H-plan, while the cross-plan houses with four wings proved the least defensible. The plan outlines were crucial because they restricted the layout of rooms and dictated the placement of chimneys and other interior features.

A rectangular plan was the most common form among the main plantation residences. Without corner towers, these buildings were not very defensible, but they were usually sited along one side of a bawn and the bawn-side elevation was rarely pierced by any windows. Only a few new castles in the Ulster plantation were built on a rectangular plan with four flankers.[108] The variants in plan with round or square towers

---

105 C. Manning, 'Maghernacloy Castle and the Hadsors' in C. Manning (ed.), *From ringforts to fortified houses: studies on castles and other monuments in honour of David Sweetman* (Bray, 2007), pp 209–16.   106 The transition between a square and a rectangular towerhouse of a 2:1 proportion of length to breadth during the sixteenth and seventeenth centuries can be seen as a revival of hall houses, said to date from the thirteenth and early fourteenth centuries, which also employed a 2:1 proportion (for hall houses, see McNeill, *Castles in Ireland*, pp 148–55; Sweetman, *Medieval castles*, pp 89–104; D. Sweetman, 'The hall house in Ireland' in J. Kenyon & K. O'Conor (eds), *The medieval castle in Ireland and Wales* (Dublin, 2003), pp 121–32). However, hall houses differed from later rectangular towerhouses because they tended to have an external entrance to first floor, their walls were thicker and their distribution was mostly in the west of Ireland.   107 Sweetman, *Medieval castles*, p. 193.   108 Loeber, 'Geography and practice', this volume, p. 94.

harked back to medieval times (for example, Carlow Castle with its round towers, and Bunratty Castle in Clare, with its square towers). Houses with acute angle flankers were a novelty in Ireland from the late sixteenth century onwards, and only one settler in the Midland plantations – at Manorhamilton (Leitrim) – chose such a plan. This plan was more popular outside the Midlands, as, for example, at Ballynalurgan (later Castleblayney, Monaghan).

In the Midland plantations and in Down, a unique type of structure emerged on a rectangular plan with a single large round corner tower. The rectangular castle with a unique massive round angle tower was normal in Scotland at this period.[109] Irish examples are Castle Forbes (built by a Scottish settler), Castle Wilder and probably Longford Castle (demolished), all three in Longford, as well as Garrycastle and probably Franckfort Castle (both Offaly) and Killyleagh Castle (Down). The single round tower presumably housed the stairs and it must also have facilitated flanking fire along two sides of the façades.[110] It leaves open the question as to how the other two sides were defended, and whether this was facilitated by now vanished bawns.

The second most common plan was the T-plan, where the projection, usually in the rear, had the dual purpose of serving as a flanker and housing a timber staircase. T-plan forms were characteristic of vernacular houses in south-west England,[111] but they also became common in the Midland plantations, outside of the plantation areas, and in the regenerated areas of the Munster plantation.

Compared to the T-plan, the Z-plan with its diagonally placed towers proved more defensible. The same applied to the Y-plan: it basically consisted of a U-plan with one more projection to the rear, often housing a staircase. A sophisticated Y-plan was used at Birr Castle (Offaly) where the main block was connected to two wings set on an angle (Figure 3.11). This lacked Irish precedents and it may have been inspired by Warmwell Manor in Dorset.[112] Another unusual structure was Sir Thomas Ridgeway's castle of Spur Royal (Tyrone), built on the plan of an eight-pointed star, resembling the spur-royal shown on a fifteen-shilling coin current in James I's reign and giving the castle its distinctive name.[113]

Less common and less defensible were L-plans, although these were once said to have been particularly used by Scottish undertakers.[114] Houses on an L-shaped plan, however, were also found inside and outside the Midland plantations, built by owners with no Scottish background – for example, Tinnahinch Castle (Carlow). The Ulster plantations had several residences built on a cross-plan with four wings. The cross-plan was much less common in the Midland plantations but it was more evident in Munster.

Among the least defensible plans were houses built on a U- or H-plan. Houses built on a U-plan (sometimes called a half H-plan) tended to be larger than those built on a rectangular plan, and offered a wider range of rooms (a H-plan house at Castle Cuffe (Laois) is shown in Figure 3.12). U-plans were uncommon in the

109 Kerrigan, *Castles and fortifications*, p. 64; Treadwell, *Irish commission of 1622*, p. 510.   **110** Jope, 'Scottish style castles', p. 45.   **111** The remaining two façades faced the inside of a bawn and were likely protected in another manner.   **112** Robinson, *Plantation of Ulster*, p. 134.   **113** Gomme & Maguire, *Design and plan*, Figure 52.   **114** Rowan, *North-west Ulster*, p. 34.

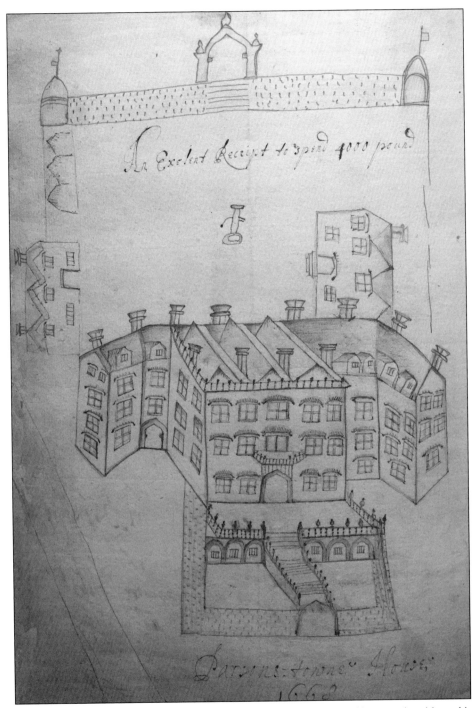

Figure 3.11 'Parsonstowne House, 1668' (Birr Castle). Dorothy Parsons adds a punning title to this drawing of her house, as it appears in her recipe book: 'An exc'lent receipt to spend 4000 pound'. The unusual structure carefully shown in the rear courtyard appears to be a water pump (Recipe book of Dorothy Parsons, Rosse Papers, A/17, Birr Castle Archives).

Figure 3.12 Castle Cuffe, County Laois, a house without defences (reconstruction drawing by Mairtín D'Alton).

Ulster plantation. An exceptional U-plan was Castle Curlews (Tyrone), now in a ruinous and fragmentary condition, whose remains consist of the side wing of a much larger layout.[115] Castle Curlews was an unusually elaborate house for that time and place, well lighted and devoid of any discernible concern for defence (Figure 3.13a–b).[116] U-plan structures were present both inside and outside the Midland plantations. In all these instances, the purpose of the rooms in the arms of the U remains unclear, but it is possible that they were closets, which are known in U-plan Irish country houses of a later period. Finally, there are no known H-plan houses from either the Ulster or Midlands plantations, although the plan form is evident elsewhere (Appendix 3.3).

In summary, the late sixteenth and early seventeenth centuries saw a multiplication of new plans for main residences in Ireland that resembled the proliferation of domestic architectural plans in Britain. The temporal priority of these developments in the two countries is nearly impossible to establish. Ingenious plans with symbolic meanings, however, found in theory and practice in England,[117] were exceedingly rare in Ireland. An exception was Castle Dollard, the triangular hunting lodge built by the first earl of Cork (1566–1643), which survives in the Comeragh Mountains between Waterford and Cork (Figure 3.14).[118]

115 Waterman, 'Irish seventeenth-century houses', p. 261.   116 R. Loeber & T. Reeves-Smyth, 'Lord Audley's grandiose building schemes in the Ulster plantation' in B. Mac Cuarta (ed.), *Reshaping Ireland 1570–1700: colonisation and its consequences* (Dublin, 2011), pp 82–100.   117 D. Waterman, 'Sir John Davies and his Ulster buildings: Castlederg and Castle Curlews, Co. Tyrone', *UJA*, 23 (1960), p. 95.   118 Girouard, *Robert Smythson*, pp 24–8.

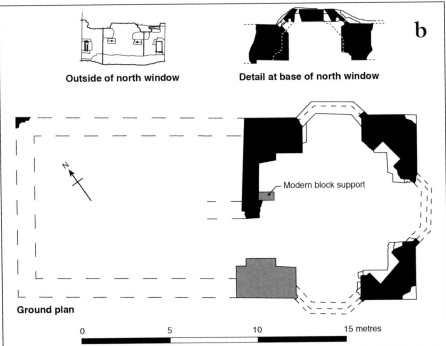

Figure 3.13 Castle Curlews, County Tyrone: photograph (a) and plan (b). This castle was built by the Quixotic English Catholic George Touchet (1551–1617), first Baron Audley. The surviving three-storey wing with its canted bay windows may form part of a U-shaped plan. The house is well lighted and well warmed with fireplaces, but undefended.

Figure 3.14 Castle Dollard Hunting Lodge, County Waterford, was built by Richard Boyle in the early seventeenth century. The tower walls rose 21 feet high (NLI, AD 3594/12).

House size

A remarkable transformation during the early seventeenth century was the increase in living area in fortified houses compared to medieval towerhouses. The characteristic small late medieval towerhouse at Clara (Kilkenny) measured 10.7m x 10.7m on the outside, and 19.5m high to the walkway of the battlements, giving a useable living area of 134 square metres. Dunsoghly Castle (Dublin), much larger at 45 square metres per floor, enjoyed 181 square metres of living space.[119]

How do these sizes compare with fortified houses inside and outside the plantation areas? The minimum prescribed external surface size of the main residence in the Midland plantations was 20 feet x 30 feet (6.1m x 9.1m). Once the thickness of walls (0.5m) is excluded, 43 square metres are left per floor (this may have been less for the ground floor where walls often were thicker than 0.5m). Assuming four to five floors, the minimal interior living space in the plantation castle with a height of 10.7m was 171 to 213 square metres. Thus, the prescribed minimum size of plantation castles for undertakers of 1,000 acres (405ha) in the Midlands was shorter and smaller externally than a small towerhouse, but larger by almost one-half in terms of living space.

The provision of more extensive living space is also suggested when towerhouses are compared to other seventeenth-century buildings. Even without considering additional floor space supplied by flankers, Raphoe Castle (Donegal) and Burncourt (Tipperary) each had 153 square metres living space per floor, compared to 242 square metres in Kanturk Castle (Cork), and 424 square metres for Portumna Castle (Galway).[120] Given that these houses had three to four floors over a basement, their total living space ranged from 613 to 1,694 square metres, three to nine times larger than the floor space in a characteristic towerhouse.

---

119 A storey and a wing have been added later, but for its original elevation and plan, see NLI, AD 3594/12. The building is much less decorative than the triangular lodge built at Rushton (Northamptonshire) by Sir Thomas Gresham (*ob.* 1605).   **120** Maurice Craig, pers. comm.

Double- and triple-pile plans

Size was related to roof construction. Most plantation houses and most large buildings outside of the plantation areas (for example, Burncourt in Tipperary, and Buttevant Castle in Cork) were built on a single-pile plan and were one room deep (unless internally divided by light timber walls). The depth of single-pile plan houses was dictated by the maximum length of timber beams capable of spanning the space between parallel walls. A major innovation was the emergence of the double-pile and triple-pile plans in the early seventeenth century: these consisted of two to three ranges placed on either side of a corridor (or back-to-back with a spinal wall) and topped by two to three roof ridges with an intervening roof valley.[121] The advantages of a double-pile house included enhanced space, a parallel sequence of rooms, and the possibility of more complex house plans. A disadvantage was the need for costly lead to clad the roof valley and the necessity to add rain-pipes to protect the house from rainwater.

The spacious double-pile plan remained uncommon in the Ulster plantation. Among the exceptions were Newtownstewart (Tyrone), probably Raphoe Palace (Donegal), Ballykelly and Killowen, the main residences on the Fishmongers' and Clothworkers' estates, and the planned house for the Drapers' Company (all in Londonderry).[122] Double-pile plans were also exceptional outside the plantation areas: Galgorm, Glenarm, Joymount (all in Antrim), Brazeel (north Dublin), and Jigginstown and Ballyshannon (both Kildare). The more spectacular triple-pile plan was used in the early seventeenth century at only a few major buildings: Portumna Castle (Galway), Birr Castle (Offaly), and two structures built by Sir Arthur Chichester (1563–1625): Chichester House (Dublin city, demolished) and Belfast Castle (Antrim, demolished).[123]

Elevations and symmetry

Among the most drastic late sixteenth and early seventeenth centuries changes was the design and construction of symmetrical buildings in terms of elevations and ground plans. Symmetry was the hallmark of the new architecture based on classically inspired buildings in Italy, France and the Low Countries. Symmetry could be expressed in the massing of parts of a building, including projections, roof structures and bawns, or in terms of components of façades, including windows, door openings and clusters of chimneystacks.

In Ireland, the earliest symmetrical façades date from the second half of the sixteenth century. Notable examples are Lord Ormond's house at Carrick-on-Suir (Tipperary, 1565), the rebuilding of Roscommon Castle in the 1580s, the grand Rathfarnham Castle (Dublin, 1583) and the recently rediscovered Newry Castle (Down, 1578), previously known only from contemporary drawings.[124] Rathfarnham

---

121 Ibid.   122 T. Reeves-Smyth, 'Community to privacy: late Tudor and Jacobean manorial architecture in Ireland 1560–1640' in Horning et al. (eds), *Post-medieval archaeology*, p. 307.   123 Hill, *Plantation in Ulster*, p. 579; Curl, *Londonderry plantation*, Plate 82.   124 In Birr Castle, three parallel roof ridges ran perpendicular to the façade, an unusual configuration. This was necessitated by the presence of two spinal walls running in the same direction

has some similarities with the published design of Sebastian Serlio's Poggio Reale (commissioned 1487) in Naples.[125]

Symmetrical façades proved inherently difficult for L-plan structures, but much more viable for houses on a rectangular, T-, Y-, U-, H-, E-plan, or a cross-plan with four wings. Judging from examples where either the façade or a drawing survives, symmetrical façades were rare in plantation structures. The imposing Castle Caulfield and Newtownstewart (both Tyrone) had irregular window openings. Asymmetrical elevations were commonplace outside the plantation areas, for example, at Loughmoe Castle (Tipperary), Lemeneagh Castle (Clare) and the spectacular Jigginstown House (Kildare). The adoption of symmetry proved uneven and the less-than-symmetrical house prevailed during the early seventeenth century, as indicated by Ardmayle Castle (Tipperary), additions to Athlumney Castle (Meath) and Brazeel (Dublin).

Symmetry was more likely to be employed in the design of the façade of larger rather than smaller buildings and its presence may indicate the hand of an architect. This is illustrated by several of the houses of the new settlers: Rathfarnham Castle, built in 1583 by the Irish Lord Chancellor Sir Adam Loftus, who hailed from Yorkshire, and two houses of the 'new' clergy from Britain, including Raphoe Castle (Donegal) and Oldbawn (both in Dublin). Several large houses built by British military officers (for example, Monaghan Castle, Monaghan, demolished) and the house inside Charlemont Fort (Armagh, demolished) had symmetrical façades. With the exception of Birr Castle (Offaly), hardly any known planters' residences were symmetrical in their elevations.

Symmetry in architecture was not, however, the exclusive privilege of new settlers. Several grand houses of the Old English approximated to symmetry, such as Burncourt (Tipperary) and Clogrennan (Carlow).[126] Symmetrical aspects were also found in the houses of the descendants of the Gaelic chieftains, such as Kanturk Castle (Cork) and Portumna Castle (Galway).[127] Among the more stunning symmetrical buildings is Glinsk Castle (Galway), seat of the Gaelic Mac Burkes, that exhibits symmetrically arranged window openings on all four façades.[128] Whether external symmetry was mirrored by internal symmetry is difficult to prove in the absence of surviving interiors, but it is probable.

Examples of 'new' bawns laid out in a symmetrical fashion in the Ulster plantation include Tully (Fermanagh), Castlederg (Tyrone) and Faugher (Donegal). In these instances, however, the main residence was placed asymmetrically inside the bawn. A similar partly symmetrical arrangement can be seen outside the plantations at Moygara Castle (Sligo) and Ballyduff Castle (Waterford).

A superior level of symmetry emerged in the early seventeenth century, embracing the relationship between the main residence and the bawn. A rare

---

as the roofs on each side of the former castle gatehouse that was incorporated into the later residence. **125** *Arch. sur. Down*, Plates 69–70. Sebastiano Serlio (1475–1554) was an Italian mannerist architect. His *Five bookes of architecture* were published in English in London in 1611. **126** Gomme & Maguire, *Design and plan*, plan 222. **127** For Clogrennan, see NLI, MS 392, f. 81. **128** Two windows in the rear façade are not fully symmetrical, but perhaps they are a later alteration.

instance of a documented symmetrical layout of house and bawn was the Merchant Taylors' main residence at Macosquin (Londonderry), where the principal house was situated in the centre of a large bawn of 46m x 40m.[129]

Outside the plantations, among the earliest symmetrical layouts of house, bawn and walled garden was Monaghan Castle, begun in 1605 by Sir Edward Blayney (1570–1629), who had served as an officer in Spain and the Low Countries. There the bawn was 19 square metres, while the adjoining garden enclosure was 23 square metres. The complex of fortified residence and enclosures was arranged in a sequence of increasingly large spaces.[130] While this complex does not survive, the double courtyard type is still extant at Portumna Castle (Galway) where both the courts and the entrance to them are situated on an axis with the front of the building, and each angle tower is answered by another angle tower.[131] Other good examples of the symmetrical layout of house and bawn were Ightermurragh Castle and Coppingers Court (both in Cork) and the plantation castles at Limerick and Prospect (both in north Wexford).[132] These two sites each had two enclosures, one of which may also have served as an enclosed garden.[133] Similarly, the former gardens at Lismore Castle (Waterford) were situated on an axis with the main house.[134]

Burncourt (Tipperary) has an exceptional arrangement of three rectangular enclosures, one probably consisting of a garden. Completed in 1641, they were laid out to form a long sequence with the house, aligned along a south-west to north-east axis.[135] Sequential courtyards occurred at several sites in the early seventeenth century, but these did not set the stage for the integrated development of house, courtyards, avenues and estate village, which emerged only in the second half of the seventeenth century and then became prevalent during the eighteenth century.[136]

Decoration

There were few buildings with classical or mannerist[137] decoration on doorways, window surrounds or walls in the domestic architecture of the Ulster plantation. Among rare surviving examples are the doorway and magnificent mannerist

---

129 The building is a smaller version of Borthwick Castle (Midlothian, 1430) but more symmetrical: for Borthwick Castle, see Gomme & Maguire, *Design and plan*, Plate 42. **130** Curl, *Londonderry plantation*, p. 308. **131** Loeber, 'Geography and practice', this volume. **132** Another example was at Limerick in north Wexford, where the bawn was 66 feet (20m) square surrounded by a wall 18 feet (5.5m) high; the garden enclosure was slightly larger at 76 feet (23m) square with 12 feet (3.7m) high walls (Exeter College, Cambridge, MS 95). The courts were probably situated in an adjoining position rather than on each side of the castle (contrary to the reconstruction in Loeber & Stouthamer-Loeber, 'Wexford plantation', p. 191). **133** The garden at Ightermurragh (Cork) is said to have been located in the far court (T. O'Keefe & S. Quirke, 'A house in the birth of modernity: Ightermurragh Castle in context' in Lyttleton & Rynne (eds), *Plantation Ireland*, p. 97). **134** Exeter College, Cambridge, MS 95. **135** Visible on an early seventeenth-century drawing (I owe this information to Peter Murray). **136** The late seventeenth-century plan of Birr Castle (Lyttleton, 'Native and newcomer in post-medieval Ireland', Figure 9.14) shows two adjoining garden enclosures towards the town, while the bawn with its service buildings was on the opposite side of the residence. **137** Mannerist means a rich, decorative, late Renaissance style.

Figure 3.15 A Baroque chimney piece at Donegal Castle, depicted by Anne Deane in 1849. It is now much weathered. In 1566, Sir Henry Sidney described Donegal Castle, built in 1474 on a bend in the River Eske, as 'the largest and strongest fortress in all Ireland': 'it is the greatest I ever saw in an Irishman's hands: and would appear to be in good keeping; one of the fairest situated in good soil and so nigh a portable water a boat of ten tonnes could come within ten yards of it' (NLI AD 3588/14).

chimney piece at Donegal Castle (Figure 3.15).[138] In contrast, Classicism appeared more widely outside the plantations in Ulster and the Midlands, both on the outside of buildings, for example, Portumna (Galway), and the castles of Kanturk and Dromaneen (both Cork), and inside residences in the form of stone or wooden

---

138 However, see evidence of a probably planned but now vanished village at Termon Magrath (Donegal) based on an aerial photograph (Lacey, *Archaeological survey of Donegal*, Plate 68).

chimney pieces, as at Loughmoe (Tipperary) and at Myrtle Grove (near Youghal, Cork) where some wooden chimney pieces of the period survive.[139] The presence of tomb carvers working in a mannerist style in Leinster and Connacht may have greatly facilitated the spread of classical and mannerist features in buildings outside Ulster.

The early seventeenth century also saw buildings highlighted by the deliberate contrast of rough-cast wall surfaces with finer-treated plaster quoins (also called a block-and-start) – for example at Castle Cuffe in Laois – and in rustication patterns around windows – for example, at Burncourt (Tipperary) and Brazeel (Dublin, demolished). Occasionally, the framing of whitish surfaces became even more accentuated when corner quoins were executed in plaster mixed with charcoal, providing a starker contrast between whitewashed walls and the darker quoins (for example at Portumna Castle, Galway). The plantation house at Ballyduff (Waterford) had similar quoins but these ended in a diamond shape.[140]

Overall, most plantation buildings were utilitarian in form and elevation and lacked decorative stonework. Thus, the carved, rounded crenellations without a clear defensive purpose that could be seen in the south of Ireland, both inside and outside plantation areas – for example, Kilcolgan More Castle (Offaly), Menlough Castle and Portumna Castle (both Galway); Loughmoe Castle (Tipperary), Clogrennan (Carlow, demolished), Drimnagh Castle (Dublin), Dunganstown (Wicklow) – was rare in Ulster, although present at Galgorm Castle (Antrim).

Innovations in building materials

Mapping plantation sites in terms of building materials revealed a concentration of timber-framed structures in a circular area in central Ulster, which is unsurprising given that the area had extensive woods.[141] This area also had few towerhouses of the Gaelic period, which may suggest continuity of timber-framed buildings from the Gaelic into the plantation era.

Some Gaelic landowners lived in 'Irish' houses – in all likelihood, houses made of clay and straw with a roof of thatch. There is no documentation of the Irish using brick as a building material for whole buildings prior to the plantations. In contrast, the conditions for the Ulster plantation (Appendix 3.1) repeatedly stipulated that the principal residences of undertakers and servitors must be constructed from stone or brick bound by lime. Thus, the incidence of brick in the plantation areas indicated the novel introduction of that building material. Newly built rectangular brick houses occasionally appeared in the plantation in Ulster, particularly in Armagh.[142]

---

139 A fragment of an Ionic pilaster survives at Manorhamilton Castle (Leitrim) (Waterman, 'Irish seventeenth-century houses', p. 124). **140** Loeber, *Biographical dictionary*, pp 49–63. **141** R. Loeber, 'Sculptured memorials to the dead in early seventeenth-century Ireland: a survey from *Monumenta Eblanae* and other sources', *PRIA*, lxxxi:11, C (1981), pp 267–93; C. Tait, *Death, burial and commemoration in Ireland 1550–1650* (London, 2002); P. Cockerham & A. Harris, 'Kilkenny funeral monuments 1500–1600: a statistical and analytical account', *PRIA*, ci:5, C (2001), pp 135–88. **142** Robinson, *Plantation of Ulster*, Map 11.

The other prominent 'new' building material was glass. Glass had been used in churches since the Middle Ages, but there is no evidence that the Gaelic Irish manufactured glass during the early seventeenth century. The widespread increase in the size of transom-and-mullion windows during the early seventeenth century, however, must have been supported by a growing industry of window-glass making. Window glass was manufactured at Salterstown (Londonderry) and several other locations in Ireland during the early seventeenth century.[143] The panes, however, tended to be small and of a diamond shape, and were held together with lead strips, which by this time had become distinctly old-fashioned in elite houses in England.

Interiors

In the historiography of early seventeenth-century Irish architecture, one of the least-studied aspects is the interior of plantation buildings.[144] This is because of the lack of surviving complete interiors, the scarcity of documents and drawings, and the use of easily removed timber partitions and wooden wainscoting. Some light can still be shed on the interiors of the main plantation residences.

The 1619 and the 1622 surveys of the Ulster plantation provide details primarily of the main external features of buildings, and show very little interest in interiors. Some details are supplied for the three-storey dwelling of Sir Archibald Achenson in Armagh, which contained a hall of 36 feet x 18 feet (11m x 5.5m), and a parlour of 18 feet (5.5m) square. Although their height is unknown, the proportions of these two spaces approximate those common in Renaissance architecture in England and Italy as disseminated by architectural treatises. The upper storey contained two 'chambers' and three studies. The third storey contained a chamber and a gallery 'within the roof'.[145]

A plan of the plantation 'castle' at Moneymore (Londonderry) showed a rectangular building with three main spaces: hall and kitchen (with buttery) at either end of a central corridor, and a parlour to the other. Access to the house was through two entrances on either side of the corridor.[146] A wooden timber partition with two doors served as a screen to the hall (18 feet x 16 feet, 5.5m x 4.9m). The arrangement of the hall with its two entrances recalls the medieval arrangement of surviving dining halls at some Oxford and Cambridge colleges. This arrangement was also known from the rebuilding of the refectory at Mellifont Abbey (Louth) as a dwelling house in the late sixteenth century, and from the main hall at Portumna Castle (Galway).[147]

Surviving fabric of plantation castles and houses reveal the presence of plaster work, but usually bereft of decoration. Exceptions are the plaster frieze at what is now the muniment room in Birr Castle (Offaly), decorated with foliage and grapes on each side of a bearded face. A surviving sketch of the elaborately carved stone chimney piece formerly at Kilcolgan More Castle (Offaly) shows a central arrangement of carved Jacobean-Renaissance strap work over a broad architrave,

143 Hill, *Plantation in Ulster*, pp 466, 563, 571; Robinson, *Plantation of Ulster*, Map 11.   **144** N. Roche, 'The manufacture and use of glass in post-medieval Ireland' in Horning et al. (eds), *Post-medieval archaeology*, pp 405–20.   **145** But see Waterman, 'Irish seventeenth-century houses', p. 256.   **146** NLI, MS 8014, f. ix.   **147** Curl, *Londonderry plantation*, Plate 82.

flanked by two obelisks. The strap work is reminiscent of the Fox tomb at Rathreagh (Longford, 1636).

A 1615 plan by the English mason Anthony Lipsett of a compact, non-defensible house for the London Drapers' Company depicted a hall next to a parlour. Remarkably, the elevation shows classical pedimented windows on the first storey, a highly uncommon feature at this time (we do not know whether this house was ever actually built).[148] A hall adjoining a parlour is also visible on a plan of the castle at Agivey by William Brock in 1614 for the Ironmongers' Company estate (Londonderry).[149]

Since bawn walls were often high, views from the ground floor of the main building were restricted, and the wider landscape could only be appreciated from the upper storeys.[150] It is therefore unsurprising that some plantation buildings positioned their main rooms on the first storey, for example, Castle Balfour and Tully (both Fermanagh), Castle Caulfield (Tyrone) and Donegal Castle (Donegal). This is confirmed by the presence of one or more large transom-and-mullion windows on the first floor, for example, of Donegal Castle (Donegal), Rathcline Castle (Longford) and Kilcolgan More Castle (Offaly, demolished). At Rathcline, the large first-floor window had four mullions and two transoms, providing fifteen lights through which to view the garden and the landscape beyond – a number otherwise unparalleled in Ireland.[151] The tradition of placing the main room, including a gallery, on the first floor did not originate with plantation architecture; it occurred (and can still be seen) at Ormond's house at Carrick-on-Suir (Tipperary, 1565). The placement of the main rooms on the first floor in late sixteenth- and early seventeenth-century houses was a major departure from traditional towerhouses, which located their main hall on the top floor.

Bawns

Irrespective of the plan of the main house, bawns were ubiquitous. In Ulster, bawns were square or rectangular in plan, and varied from 18.3 to 30.5 metres in length and breadth. Where flankers were built, the distance between them had to be sufficiently close to facilitate firing a musket which were accurate within 46 to 64 metres. Plantation surveys only occasionally mentioned battlements on bawn walls, as at the Drapers' and the Vintners' plantations (Londonderry).[152] Most bawns had outworks such as flankers. If the main residence shared the outside wall of a bawn, then two flankers commonly defended the main residence. An alternative to a flanker was a bartizan high up on a corner of the building, for example, at Monkstown (Cork), but

---

148 Sketch plan in the Burgage collection, Irish Architectural Archive; RIA, MS 3D4, plans and elevations of Portumna (Galway). 149 Curl, *Londonderry plantation*, p. 184, Plates 80 & 87. 150 Sometimes, as at Ightermurragh (Cork), a house was built on a semi-basement, which improved the view from the ground-floor. Another large window on an early seventeenth-century structure is still visible at the second storey of the north-west façade of Loughmoe Castle (Tipperary): it has three mullions and two transoms, making twelve lights. 151 See photograph in Lyttleton, 'Rathcline Castle', Plate 7.5. 152 Hill, *Plantation in Ulster*, p. 587; Chart (ed.), *Londonderry and the London companies*, opposite p. 152.

the disadvantage of a bartizan was that its main line of defence was vertical. Only
when a bartizan had a platform and gun loops could it contribute to a horizontal
form of defence. In contrast, the exclusive defensive line of flankers was horizontal.
The defence created by corner corbels characteristic of Scottish buildings was also
horizontal rather than vertical because they were not constructed as machicolations.
Corbel defences in Ireland are principally found in Ulster and were used only rarely
in the Midland plantations.

In many instances, bawns were built larger than required by the plantation
building specifications. The height of their walls varied greatly from 2.4m to 4.3m,
with the tallest bawns providing the best deterrent against intruders scaling the
walls with ladders. When a bawn doubled as a garrison, the walls tended to be even
higher. The bawn walls around Mallow Castle (Cork) and Ballynalurgan Castle
(Castleblayney, Monaghan) were 5.5m high (by comparison, the walled garden
enclosure at Mallow Castle was 3.7m high).[153] Many bawns had round flankers
which were far from ideal for defence by means of flanking fire when compared to
flankers with an acute-angle plan, but which performed more effectively as a defence
against undermining.[154]

Very few Ulster plantation houses had gun platforms for cannon. An example
is Limavady Castle (Londonderry) but its gun ports may date from earlier when
the castle was an O'Cahan stronghold prior to 1609.[155] Another example is Lord
Grandison's Castle at Tanderagee (Armagh) where 'one falcon and two falconets
[light cannon] of brass' were mounted on carriages to defend the bawn.[156] With
the exception of Birr Castle (Offaly), evidence is lacking for earthwork defences
and cannon in private houses in the Midland plantations.[157] However, magnates
elsewhere in Ireland equipped their houses with cannons, which was the case at
Ormond's Castle (Carrick-on-Suir, Tipperary), Kilkenny Castle (Kilkenny) and
probably Lismore Castle (Waterford), where the bawn next to the castle formerly
possessed substantial round flankers viable for cannons.

Several private structures outside of the plantations were set within a fort
and had earthen outworks with flankers, suitable for defence with and against
cannon. An early example, noted in 1611, was at Glaslough (Monaghan), where
Sir Thomas Ridgeway built a fort of 160 feet x 212 feet (48.8m x 64.6m) with 'a
rampier [rampart] or footpace of earth round about with 4 bulwarks' and 'a ditch or
trench 18 foot broade and 10 feet deepe' (5.5m, 3.1m).[158] Ridgeway had also fortified
Augher. His interest in cannon was enduring: he established a cannon foundry on

153 BL, Add. MS 4756, ii, ff 96r–96v; R. Hunter, 'Carew's survey of Ulster 1611: the voluntary
works', *UJA*, 38 (1975), p. 81.   154 The exception was when stone spurs were added to round
towers, but that was rarely done (see Carrickmacross Castle, Monaghan, demolished).   155 Sir
James Craig's bawn at his house in the proportion called Drumshed and Killagh (Cavan) had
a timber walk strong enough for 'small [field] pieces' (Treadwell, *Irish commission of 1622*, p.
521).   156 Treadwell, *Irish commission of 1622*, p. 551. Another example is Sir James Craig's
settlement in Cavan (Hill, *Plantation in Ulster*, p. 471); Loeber & Parker, 'Military revolution',
p. 67.   157 An exception is the earthworks formerly at Birr Castle (Offaly), but these could
equally be from the late seventeenth century (M. Salter, *The castles of Leinster* (Malvern, n.d.), p.
129).   158 Hunter, 'Carew's survey of Ulster 1611', p. 81.

his estate of Ballinakill (Laois) in the 1630s. Few residences in Ireland prior to 1641 were surrounded by earthen fortifications: an exception was Lord Strafford's timber hunting lodge at Fairwood (Wicklow) in the 1630s.[159]

The Midland plantation houses almost invariably had bawns with flankers similar to those in Ulster. One of the most remarkable large bawns (69.5m x 77.1m) survives at Kilcolgan More Castle (Offaly), built by one of the MacCoghlans in 1649 (according to a date stone formerly on the entrance gate) during a lull in the hostilities following the 1641 rebellion. Uniquely, the four tall flankers had curved projections, elegant in shape, but creating dead space for defence. This feature is known only from the Midlands (Castle Ireton, Tipperary and Longford Castle, Longford, demolished). The bawn formerly at Mosstown (Longford, demolished) literally stood out because of its immense height.

Servitors, as former army officers, had technical knowledge and a stronger desire to build fortified houses and bawns. The Ulster plantation surveys of 1619 and 1622 do not clearly indicate this, possibly connected with the meagre financial resources of the officers. Some servitors, however, did build larger bawns than other settlers.[160] Several servitors also constructed very strong residences. Sir Frederick Hamilton built a highly defensible castle at Manorhamilton (Leitrim) in the 1630s, on his return from the Thirty Years War in Germany. The house had four flankers with acute salient angles, and it was set in a spacious bawn with a further four acute salient flankers (Figure 3.16). Acute salient angles of flankers were not exclusively a feature of buildings constructed by military men: they were also employed at the bishop's palace at Raphoe (Donegal).

The architecture of the Midland plantations has been less intensively studied than that of Ulster.[161] The main residences in the Midland plantations have long disappeared, but contemporary surveys shed some light on these structures. Among these surveys, that of the plantation houses in north Wexford in 1622 is the most detailed, describing plans and other details. Six of the sixteen main plantation sites were small, with bawns measuring 40 feet square (12.2m) and within them a house of two-and-a-half storeys high on a rectangular plan of 40 feet x 24 feet (12.2 x 7.3m).[162] There were some larger houses in this plantation, such as Sir Lawrence Esmond's residence at Limerick, near Gorey.[163]

A comparison of the plans of plantation houses in north Wexford and Ulster shows that they were very similar. An insight into the differences between them as perceived by contemporaries, however, is offered by Sir Francis Blundell, one of

159 For Fairwood, see Loeber & Stouthamer-Loeber, 'Wexford plantation', pp 173–200; R. Loeber, 'Settlers' utilisation of natural resources in the seventeenth century' in K. Hannigan (ed.), *Wicklow: history and society* (Dublin, 1994), p. 273. The earthworks at Ballyshannon (Kildare) and Ticroghan (Meath) may relate to military events in 1641.   **160** Treadwell, *Irish commission of 1622*, p. 519. See also Mallow Castle (Cork) and its enclosures (Treadwell, *Irish commission of 1622*, p. 499).   **161** Loeber & Stouthamer-Loeber, 'Wexford plantation', pp 173–200; Loeber, 'Settlers' utilisation of natural resources', pp 267–304; Lyttleton, 'Rathcline Castle', pp 135–59; Lyttleton, 'Native and newcomer in post-medieval Ireland'; P. Kerrigan, 'Castles and fortifications of County Offaly *c.*1500–1815' in Nolan & O'Neill (eds), *Offaly*, pp 393–438.   **162** Exeter College, Cambridge, MS 95.   **163** Loeber & Stouthamer-Loeber, 'Wexford plantation', pp 182–98.

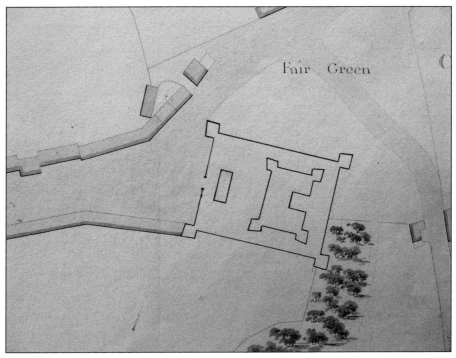

Figure 3.16 Plan of the fortified house and bawn at Manorhamilton, County Leitrim (NLI).

the Wexford grantees, and himself a government official, a plantation planner and a planter.[164] In 1622, he compared the defensiveness of the Ulster plantation buildings with those of County Wexford: 'undertakers [in Ulster] are not able to defend themselves against their owne [Irish] tenants if they should rebel much less against a more potent enemy'. In contrast, the planters in north Wexford built castles that made that part of the country 'strong and defensible against an Irish enimie'.[165]

PLANTATION ARCHITECTURE: A SUMMARY

Inherently, conclusions about the features of the new plantation architecture, its origins and its regional differences are hampered by the loss of the buildings known from contemporary surveys. For that reason, the following conclusions are necessarily tentative. The preceding discussion may make it appear that the plantations were full of interesting and solid buildings. However, this impression is misleading as only the strongest buildings have survived. One traveller, writing from Enniskillen (Fermanagh) in 1620, commented that 'the residences of the gentry were, as a rule, extremely mean in appearance' and that 'most of them were thatched'.[166] The plantation buildings in Ulster and the Midlands were similar in

164 Mac Cuarta, 'Plantation of Leitrim', pp 300, 307–9.   165 BL, Harl. MS 3292, ff 40–5.
166 Johnston, 'Plantation of County Fermanagh', p. 116.

many respects, and showed a major increase in the variety of plans employed in comparison to traditional forms of castle building. These plans were shared to some degree between the plantations and they were also circulated outside the plantation areas. The distribution of the novel ground plans and elevations of early seventeenth-century houses was widespread across Ireland. Plantation architecture, even given the influence of incoming English and Scots settlers in Ulster, was not determined by changes in the architecture outside of the plantation areas. Although dating structures remains problematic, architectural innovations in plans and elevations took place more or less simultaneously across the country.

The architectural innovations were adopted among culturally diverse groups: New English and Scottish settlers, English officials working in Ireland, Old English and Gaelic Irish. Only a modest amount is known about the designers of the new architecture and their backgrounds,[167] and this lack of knowledge is even more acute for buildings erected by the Old English and the Gaelic Irish, largely owing to widespread destruction of their estate records. Innovations included a replacement of the vertical layout of rooms (as was common in towerhouses) by a more horizontal layout over two to four storeys. This promoted a distinct break from situating the most important rooms on the top floor (as in earlier towerhouses) to placing them on the first floor. A desire to create views into the enclosed gardens that gradually emerged next to the bawn may have inspired this development, but there could also be other reasons in play, for example, the need to locate service rooms (kitchens, buttery, storage rooms) on the ground floor level.

Sir Richard Boyle, first earl of Cork, was responsible for the largest private building programme in the new style of building, not in Ulster or the Midland plantations, but in Munster and Leinster. His town residences included houses in Dublin and Youghal. He favoured courtyard castles and he extensively rebuilt the ranges at Lismore Castle (Waterford) for himself in the English style with triangular gables, rows of transom-and-mullion windows and an oriel window overlooking the Blackwater. He also paid for the rebuilding of the courtyard castles of Castlelyons (Cork) and Maynooth (Kildare) for two of his son-in-laws. Boyle employed a small army of masons, carpenters, architects and engineers to build his towns of Bandon (Cork) and Tallow (Waterford), as well as churches, almshouses, schools and bridges, and he commissioned sculptors to create flashy funerary monuments. Boyle also commissioned the mannerist polychrome marble decoration for the outer gate to his house at the College of Youghal.[168]

Although there is no evidence that the new classical architecture championed by Inigo Jones (1573–1652) in England ever reached Ireland during the early seventeenth century, the mannerist style of continental Europe emerged in the details of chimney pieces, door cases and roofline embellishments.[169] In several parts of Ireland, symmetrical plans and elevations in main residences, bawns and gardens did emerge, which surely set the stage for a more explicitly neo-classical architecture in the second half of the seventeenth century.

---

167 Loeber, *Biographical dictionary*. **168** Loeber, *Biographical dictionary*, pp 13, 43–4, 52, 57–8, 66, 68, 70, 77–8, 98, 103, 108, 110,112, 115. **169** Loeber, 'Early Classicism', this volume, pp 212–45.

Against the backdrop of such innovation, traditional forms of architecture persisted during the early seventeenth century, particularly the building of conventional towerhouses. Although considerations of defence influenced the choice of building towerhouses, the number of newly built towerhouses dwindled in comparison to those built in the sixteenth century or earlier. Defences continued to influence most but not all of the newly built fortified and semi-fortified houses of the early seventeenth century.

Regional differences emerged among innovative houses of the early seventeenth century. In Tipperary and Cork, for example, fortified houses uniquely retained projecting wooden wall walks supported by stone corbels. Similarly, carvings in a style characteristic of the preceding century continued sporadically in the centre of the country (both can be observed at Burncourt, Tipperary). New-built houses on a square plan with four small defensible square towers attached to each corner were more common in the centre of the country than in the Pale or in the Ulster plantations, where bastion-type towers, borrowed from continental books on fortifications, were built on an acute salient angle plan providing superior defences. Likewise, the replacement of angular crenellations by repeated curvilinear, non-defensible gables and crenellations was more common in the centre of Ireland than in Ulster. In many areas, particularly the Ulster plantation counties, the architecture of the Gaelic Irish languished. Only in the centre of the country did major Gaelic Irish landowners embrace the new architecture and abandon their traditional towerhouses.

English, Scottish or Irish architecture?

Once the stylistic similarities of buildings in the Ulster and Midlands plantations and elsewhere in Ireland have been compared with the architecture of Scotland, England and the continent, further questions arise: did British architecture establish roots in Ireland, how was it interpreted and adapted there, and to what extent was there an indigenous Irish architecture?

English styles of architecture were widespread in Ireland during the early seventeenth century inside and outside the plantation areas. Many Irish principal residences would have been unremarkable if found in Somerset, Suffolk or Dorset. The same is true of Scottish-style residences in Ulster; they would not have stood out if they had been built in various parts of Scotland.

However, there were remarkable differences in the architecture of the two islands, and there was substantial room for the development of an indigenous Irish architecture with its own distinctive idiom. Ireland had many more towerhouses in the early seventeenth century than England. Fortified residences continued to be built in Ireland much longer than in England, Scotland and Wales. Thus, although they might have superficially looked British from a distance, many defensive features of Irish residences were retained in the first half of the seventeenth century. Second, plantation architecture constituted the early stages of architectural evolution under harsh economic conditions. Planters in Ulster or the Midlands as a rule simply lacked the sustained income over many years that would allow them to expand their houses or to transform their initial buildings into sprawling and commodious country houses. Those transformations in Ulster took place a century or more later when massive new residences – like Castle Coole (Fermanagh) and Baronscourt (Tyrone) – started to replace the plantation buildings. Thus, it is not an accident that the largest early seventeenth-century residences (Portumna Castle, Galway; Loughmoe, Tipperary; Lismore, Waterford) lay outside the plantation areas and were the results of stability, peace and sustainable increases in income.

When comparing early seventeenth-century architecture in Ireland and England, difference can be assigned to variations in the developmental phases of creating estates and their buildings, with Ireland being in an earlier phase. There were many more large Jacobean country houses in Britain built during the late sixteenth and early seventeenth centuries that lacked an Irish counterpart for this same reason.

Finally, continental classical influences on Irish architecture operated during the early seventeenth century. Mannerist classical decoration, including strap work, banded pillars and heavy mouldings, was part of a stylistic movement that extended from France to Sweden, and from the Netherlands to Britain and Poland. In Ireland, mannerist Classicism became a favoured decoration not only for funeral monuments but also for details on building, including doorcases (Dromaneen Castle and Kanturk Castle, both Cork; Menlough Castle and Portumna Castle, both Galway; Killyleagh Castle, Down; Antrim Castle, Antrim), gateways – Rathcline Castle, Longford; Portumna Castle, Galway; Newtownards Priory, Down; Dungiven, Londonderry – and chimney pieces (Donegal Castle, Donegal; Kilcolgan More, Offaly). The widespread dissemination of mannerist Classicism can best be explained by the publication of pattern books, for example, Jan Vredeman de Fries's *Architectura* (Antwerp, 1563) and the migration of architects and craftsmen.

The façades of Irish plantation buildings may also have been influenced by mannerist façades in the Netherlands. For example, the combination of step-gables and voussoirs (wedge-shaped stones used to build an arch) around the windows at the ruined Castle Cuffe (Laois, 1621; Figure 3.12) are remarkably similar to Dutch buildings of the period, including the town hall of Hoorn in the Netherlands (1613).

EPILOGUE

The Ulster (and to a lesser extent the Midland) plantations areas generated the largest architectural enterprise ever undertaken up to that time (and for several centuries to come) in Ireland. Compliance with the building regulations of the plantations, however, was hugely uneven: many undertakers and servitors in Ulster and the Midlands evaded the government-imposed plantation specifications, either in terms of residence, exclusion of native Irish tenants or in building. The government ordered an investigation into the City of London's adherence to the plantation conditions, which alleged that they failed to replace the native population with British settlers. A trial in the Star Chamber in London in 1635 led to the confiscation of 40,000 acres (16,000ha) and a heavy fine.[170] However, many of the

---

170 Mac Cuarta, 'Plantation of Leitrim', p. 309; J.H. Ohlmeyer, 'Strafford, the "Londonderry business" and the "New British History"' in J. Merritt (ed.), *The politics of Thomas Wentworth, earl*

new residences and bawns built by the City Companies and by other Ulster planters were larger than those stipulated in the building regulations. Minimum building regulations were perceived as too small for comfort and settlers were prepared to make more of an investment than was strictly required.

How did the new structures of the Ulster plantation compare with Gaelic architecture prior to the plantation? Although Gaelic architecture of the sixteenth century is poorly documented, the plantations precipitated a massive transformation in building appearance, plans and construction methods. Another question is how the architecture employed by English and Scottish settlers in the Ulster plantation compared with buildings in the Midland plantations. In stylistic terms, the two areas shared many architectural features, with the only exception being that Ulster, both inside and outside the plantation areas, imported more Scottish influences than did the Midland plantations. It is clearly inadequate to assign architectural styles to the geographic origin of settlers. Ulster plantation architecture is an amalgamation of English, Scottish and Gaelic influences. The influences from the Pale and other areas in Ireland should not be discounted, especially because many settlers also had estates and main residences in other parts of the country. Thus, the history of stylistic influences defies simplification. That said, architectural innovations flourished across the country, including in the plantation areas.

The sternest test of the adequacy of the government-imposed building conditions and the wherewithal of the planters to build strong defensive structures was the degree to which plantation settlements could withstand an assault by the indigenous Irish. The rebellion of 1641 provided a litmus test for the defensive capabilities of plantation buildings. Although a militia of settlers and tenants had operated in Ulster during the 1630s, Lord deputy Strafford was singularly unimpressed by the military preparedness of the muster: he dismissed the Ulster colony as 'a company of naked [unarmed] men'.[171] The plantation condition requiring settlers to remove Irish tenants from their estates and replace them with British tenants to increase security was widely flouted.[172]

In Ulster during the 1641 rebellion, Irish forces initially used small arms (artillery became available to them later) and quickly overran the plantations in counties Tyrone and Armagh. The majority of the main plantation residences fell or surrendered and the settlers and their families were expelled.[173] One of the first castles seized by Sir Phelim O'Neill was Dungannon (Tyrone), formerly the main seat of the O'Neill chiefs. His second target was Charlemont Castle and fort (Armagh), where the earl of Tyrone's son had been held prisoner for a long time. The choice of targets shows how deeply Sir Phelim O'Neill's feelings ran of having being wronged by the plantation in Ulster.

A detailed map of the large numbers of plantation sites overrun in 1641 and subsequently[174] demonstrates that only the strongest castles – Croghan and Keelagh

of Strafford 1621–1641 (Cambridge, 1996), pp 209–29; A. Clarke, 'The government of Wentworth 1632–40' in *NHI*, iii, p. 265.   **171** Cited by Hunter, 'English undertakers', p. 488; see also Loeber & Parker, 'Military revolution', p. 75.   **172** Canny, *Making Ireland British*, pp 210, 248–9. **173** Wilsdon, *Plantation castles on the Erne*, pp 43–8, 80–2.   **174** M. Perceval-Maxwell, *The outbreak of the Irish rebellion of 1641* (Montreal, 1994), p. 215; J. Hogan (ed.), *Letters and papers relating to the Irish rebellion between 1642–46* (Dublin, 1936), pp 182–4.

(Cavan), Enniskillen (Fermanagh), Ballycastle and Limavady (both Londonderry), Manorhamilton (Leitrim) – provided a secure refuge for the settlers, their families and tenants.[175] Of these six locations, four were new plantation building sites, and two were renovations of Gaelic Irish castles (Enniskillen, Limavady). It remains unclear to what degree the defensibility of sites made a major difference in resisting the Irish forces, even if the site contained a vaulted towerhouse. Some castles, including Crom Castle (Fermanagh), were seized, repaired and occupied by the Irish.[176] The rebellion soon spread to the plantation areas outside Ulster, and affected counties Wicklow, Wexford, Longford and Leitrim.[177] The 1641 depositions chronicle the losses incurred by the settlers in terms of their houses, goods and chattels.[178]

In subsequent military campaigns that included the artillery trains of the New Model Army under Cromwell and his officers, castles and houses owned by the Gaelic Irish and Old English landowners could not withstand the enhanced firepower of cannons. The castle of Termon Magrath (Donegal) was bombarded by Cromwellian soldiers, destroying the north wall of this towerhouse.[179] Most landowners were simply not in a position to withstand attack by cannons, as they lived in less defensible residences built in the recent decades. As one Kerry gentleman lamented in 1641, 'My house I built for peace, having more windows than walls'.[180]

Several Gaelic Irish landowners, having been defeated, retreated back to their trusted crannógs. In 1650, after the taking of Charlemont Fort, its governor, Sir Phelim O'Neill, retired to the island of Kinard (Caledon, Tyrone) and in 1652 he moved to the island in the Loch of Ruchan (Tyrone) on which stood a house, but 'no kind of work to defend them'.[181]

Only in the wake of the devastating Cromwellian conquest and the subsequent expropriations and land settlement did an uneasy peace descend, encouraging new and old waves of settlers to build and rebuild selected plantation sites. This resurgence came at a crushing cost to the Gaelic Irish and the Old English, who saw more of their lands transferred to old and new settlers under the Cromwellian settlement. The upheavals marked the end of an era and a decisive turning point in architecture. Starting in the Commonwealth period and accelerating after the 1660s, the characteristic features of early seventeenth-century architecture were largely abandoned, and neo-classical architecture became more widespread.[182]

175 Roulston, 'Scots in plantation Cavan', pp 141–5; K. McKenny, *The Laggan army in Ireland 1640–1685* (Dublin, 2005), pp 36, 49.   **176** Johnston, 'Plantation of County Fermanagh', p. 157.   **177** Perceval-Maxwell, *Irish rebellion of 1641*, p. 225.   **178** The 1641 depositions can be found at 1641.tcd.ie/.   **179** Lacey, *Archaeological survey of Donegal*, p, 351.   **180** Loeber & Parker, 'Military revolution', p. 73; R. Gillespie, 'Destabilising Ulster 1641–2' in B. Mac Cuarta (ed.), *Ulster in 1641* (Belfast, 1993), p. 111.   **181** E. Hogan (ed.), *The history of the war of Ireland from 1641 to 1653 by a British officer of the regiment of Sir John Clottworthy* (Dublin, 1873), pp 133, 144–6. See also Loeber & Parker, 'Military revolution', p. 83.   **182** Loeber, 'Irish country houses and castles', this volume.; W. Roulston, 'Domestic architecture in Ireland 1640–1740' in Horning et al. (eds), *Post-medieval archaeology*, pp 327–44.

Appendix 3.1: Building conditions for main plantation residences

ULSTER						
Main residence		**Undertakers**				**Natives**
2,000 acres	1,500 acres	>1,000 acres	>600 acres	<600 acres	200 acres	—
castle	house; stone or brick					'as the former undertakers'
Bawn		**Undertakers**				**Natives**
2,000 acres	1,500 acres	>1,000 acres	>600 acres	<600 acres	200 acres	—
'strong court or bawne'	'strong court or bawne'	'strong court or bawne'				'as the former undertakers'

MIDLANDS						
Main residence		**Undertakers**				**Natives**
2,000 acres	1,500 acres	>1,000 acres	>600 acres	<600 acres	200 acres	—
'castle' (30 x 20 x 25 feet high; exclusive of roof & battlements)	'castle' (30 x 20 x 25 feet high; exclusive of roof & battlements)	'stone or brick house' of 30 x 20 x 20 feet high (from 800 to 1000 acres)		'house of framed timber after the English manner' (chimney of stone or brick & lime: from 400–500 acres)	'house of framed timber'	'castle' (30 x 20 x 25 feet high; exclusive of roof & battlements)
Bawn		**Undertakers**				**Natives**
2,000 acres	1,500 acres	>1,000 acres	>600 acres	<600 acres	200 acres	—
'bawn' (stone, brick or lime)	'bawn' (stone, brick or lime)		'defensible bawn' (earth)			

WEXFORD						
Main residence		**Undertakers**				**Natives**
2,000 acres	1,500 acres	>1,000 acres	>600 acres	<600 acres	200 acres	—
	defensible castle or house 'stone & brick', 24 feet x 50 feet	defensible house of stone or brick', 24 feet x 24 feet	defensible tower (at 500 acres)			
Bawn		**Undertakers**				**Natives**
2,000 acres	1,500 acres	>1,000 acres	>600 acres	<600 acres	200 acres	—
					strong ditch planted with quicksets (at 120 acres)	

LONGFORD & ELY O'CARROLL (OFFALY)						
Main residence		Undertakers				Natives
2,000 acres	1,500 acres	>1,000 acres	>600 acres	<600 acres	200 acres	—
		20 x 30 x 35 feet high of stone or brick & lime	'strong house'; stone or brick & lime	'good house' stone or brick & lime		'left to themselves'
Bawn		Undertakers				Natives
2,000 acres	1,500 acres	>1,000 acres	>600 acres	<600 acres	200 acres	—
		(dimensions not given) stone or brick & lime	200 feet in compass	200 feet in compass		

LEITRIM, O'DOYNE'S COUNTRY (LAOIS), MOLLOY'S, MACCOGHLAN'S & FOX'S COUNTRIES (OFFALY), MACLOUGHLIN'S COUNTRY (WESTMEATH)						
Main residence		Undertakers				Natives
2,000 acres	1,500 acres	>1,000 acres	>600 acres	<600 acres	200 acres	—
		20 x 30 x 25 feet high of stone or brick & lime	'strong house'	'house' of stone, brick or lime		'as the former undertakers'
Bawn		Undertakers				Natives
2,000 acres	1,500 acres	>1,000 acres	>600 acres	<600 acres	200 acres	—
		300 feet compass & 14 feet high (stone or brick & lime)	200 feet compass (stone or brick & lime)	200 feet in compass		'as the former undertakers'

Appendix 3.2: Comparison between towerhouses, fortified and unfortified houses

(Sources: Weadick, 'Fortified houses', Table 4.1; Waterman, 'Irish seventeenth-century houses', p. 256.)

Towerhouses	Fortified & unfortified houses
Defences	**Defences**
Defensible battlements	Gradual disappearance of battlements, sometimes replaced by non-defensible curvilinear crenellations
Defence of main entrance through loop-holes & overhead machicolation. Doors secured by draw-bars & iron grille	Projecting towers or wings with loop-holes for flanking fire; disappearance of overhead machicolation as defence for main entrance: loop-holes in adjacent wall.
Round corner towers, an effective defence against sapping	Occasional round corner towers sometimes, but rectangular flankers more common in Ulster plantation.
Flankers at bawn corners	Flankers attached to the house
	Emergence of rectangular-plan houses without flankers; only occasional use of bartizans for protection of corners
Batter very common	Batter rarely used
Elevation and plan	**Elevation and plan**
Vertical layout of rooms	Mostly horizontal layout
One major space per storey	Major space divided by timber partitions into several rooms
Modest size of living areas	Larger living areas
Standard square plan, but change to rectangular plan	Increased variety of plans (e.g., L-, U-, H-, Y-plans)
Asymmetrical elevations & window openings	Improved symmetry in plan, elevation & window openings
Few small windows; largest windows on top floor	Many larger (transom & mullion) windows; occasional presence of bay windows; largest windows usually at the first floor but often at higher floors as well.
Stone window surrounds	Stone window surrounds remain common, but wooden window frames introduced
	Hood mouldings over windows (also on late towerhouses)
No string-courses	String courses to prevent rain dripping into window openings
Two gables at most	Multiple gables
Interior	**Interior**
Few fireplaces; few chimney stacks	Multiple fireplaces & chimney stacks, with decorative mouldings
Mural stone stairs in round or elongated spaces	Larger timber stairs in square spaces
Thick walls	Thinner walls
Stone vaults below & wooden floors higher up	Wooden floors only
Main hall on top floor, sometimes on first floor	Gradual appearance of main hall on first floor; long gallery on first or higher floor
Few types of rooms	Increased types and functions of rooms
Garderobe (latrine or privy) with external chute	Disappearance of external chute
	Decorative plaster work, inside & outside
	Emergence of woodworking (interior walls, staircases, chimney pieces, panelling)
	Increased classical detailing in interior & exterior decoration including chimney pieces & doorcases

Appendix 3.3: Innovative house plans, late sixteenth and early seventeenth centuries

(Sources: Partly based on field work, Reeves-Smyth, 'Community to privacy', pp 303–8; Hill, *Plantation in Ulster*, pp 82–7; *CSPI, 1611–14*, pp 492–4; Treadwell, *Irish commission*, pp 643, 651, 671–2; Lambeth Palace, Carew MS 625, f. 14)

ULSTER PLANTATION	MIDLAND PLANTATIONS	ELSEWHERE
Rectangular with four angular, square or round towers		
Raphoe Palace (Donegal)		Castleblayney (Monaghan)
Mountjoy Castle (Tyrone)		Rathfarnham (Dublin)
Roughan Castle (Tyrone)		Lambay (Dublin)
Clonyn (Cavan)[183]		Killenure (Tipperary)
Castle Aubigny (Cavan)[184]		Burncourt (Tipperary)
		Mountfin (Wexford)
		Kanturk Castle (Cork)
		Monkstown (Cork)
		Mountlong (Cork)
		Aghadown House (Cork)
		Portumna Castle (Galway)
T-plan		
Tully Castle (Fermanagh)	Cloncourse (Offaly)	Cregg (Sligo)
Castle Archdale (Fermanagh)	Broughal (Offaly)	Fennor (Meath)
Castle Balfour (Fermanagh)		Graney (Kildare)
		Derrin (Laois)
		Huntington (Carlow)
		Ballintemple (Cork)
		Kincor (Waterford)
		Reenadisert (Kerry)
Y-plan		
Tullykelter (Fermanagh)		Birr (Offaly)
		Dunganstown (Wicklow)
		Coppinger's Court (Cork)
L-plan		
Derrywoone Castle (Tyrone)	Ballycowan Castle (Offaly)	Castle Baldwin (Sligo)
		Ballygally (Antrim)
		Castleblayney (Monaghan)
		Maghernacloy (Monaghan)
		Killincarrig (Wicklow)
		Ballea Castle (Cork)
		Dromaneen (Cork)
		Baggotstown (Limerick)
		Menlough (Galway)
Cross-plan with four wings		
Ballynahatty (Tyrone)		Ightermurragh (Cork)
Castleraw (Armagh)		Kilmaclenine (Cork)
Manor Chichester (Donegal)[185]		Ballyduff (Waterford)
U-plan		
Castle Caulfield (Tyrone)	Dromahair Castle (Leitrim)	Glinsk (Roscommon)
Goldsmiths (Londonderry, dem.)	Kilcolgan More Castle (Offaly, dem.)	Gort (Roscommon)
Manorhamilton (Leitrim)	Ballinamore (Longford)	Athleague (Roscommon)
		Dunbrody (Wexford)
H-plan		
		Castleblayney (Monaghan).
		Cappoge (Louth, dem.)
		Oldbawn (Dublin, dem.)
		Drynam (Dublin, dem.)
		Castle Cuffe (Laois)
E-plan		
		Carrickmacross (Monaghan, dem.)

---

183 Hill, *plantation of Ulster*, p. 470.   **184** Treadwell, *Irish commission of 1622*, p. 510   **185** Also known as Kincor.

CHAPTER FOUR

Irish houses and castles 1660–90

'he would caligulate by multiplicables the alltitude and malltitude until he seesaw by
neatlight of the liquor wheretwin 'twas born, his roundhead staple of other days to
rise in undress maisonry upstanded (joygrantit!), a waalworth of a skyerscape of most
eyeful hoyth entowerly, erigenating from next to nothing and celescalating the himals
and all, hierarchitectitiptitoploftical, with a burning bush abob off its baubletop and
with larrons o'toolers clittering up and tombles a'buckets clottering down'.

James Joyce, Finnegans Wake, *Chapter One.*[1]

INTRODUCTION

AN EARLIER GENERATION OF ARCHITECTURAL HISTORIANS believed that the second
half of the seventeenth century in Ireland was 'architecturally speaking, a
featureless gap',[2] arguing that the times were too eventful to permit the building of
Big Houses, and claiming that no unfortified residences were erected prior to 1690.[3]
Even in the extensive English literature on architecture between 1640 and 1690,
virtually no mention is made of contemporary Irish seats.[4] Whereas building activity

---

1 Tim Finnegan, the builder in the ballad 'Finnegan's Wake', is being discussed. 'Tim Finnegan
lived in Watling Street, / A gentleman Irishman mighty odd / He had a brogue both rich and
sweet / An' to rise in the world he carried a hod'. A paraphrase of Joyce's passage about 'this
man of hod, cement and edifices' might go as follows: He would calculate by multiplication the
altitude of his walls, using a spirit level (neat whiskey) until he saw his round tower of undressed
(wondrous) masonry (maison/masonry) rise gigantic, a veritable Woolworth's of a skyscraper,
to a most awful (eyeful/Eiffel tower) Himalayan (himals) height (Howth) entirely, an eyeful
originating (Johannes Scotus Eriugena John born in Ireland, erigo Latin for erect) from next to
nothing, his architectural masterpiece with a bush stuck on the top of it (an indication that it was
a pub), and with (Dublin) men (Laurence O'Toolers: French larrons = thiefs) with tools hurrying
up the ladders and men with buckets (Thomas á Becketts) scurrying down them.   2 Leask,
Irish castles and castellated houses, p. 150. See T.C. Croker, *Researches in the south of Ireland*
(London, 1824), p. 267; J. Ide, *Some examples of Irish country houses of the Georgian period* (New
York, 1959), p. 3. P. Harbison, *Guide to the national monuments of Ireland* (Dublin, 1970) lists
nothing in this field.   3 C. Maxwell, *Country and town under the Georges* (Dundalk, 1949), pp
68–70; *The Georgian Society Records of eighteenth-century domestic architecture and decoration in
Ireland* (London, 1913), v. However, a few books (such as the *Georgian Society Records*, v, and
Georgian mansions in Ireland) provide good leads to late seventeenth-century country houses,
although the latter of these misleadingly emphasises that big house building was not promoted
from 1641–90 (T. Sadlier & P. Dickinson, *Georgian mansions in Ireland, with some account of
Georgian architecture and decoration* (Dublin, 1915), p. 4).   4 O. Hill & J. Cornforth, *English
country houses: Caroline 1625–1685* (London, 1966) has a useful bibliography. R. Dutton, *The age
of Wren* (London, 1951) cites a single Irish example – Beaulieu (Louth).

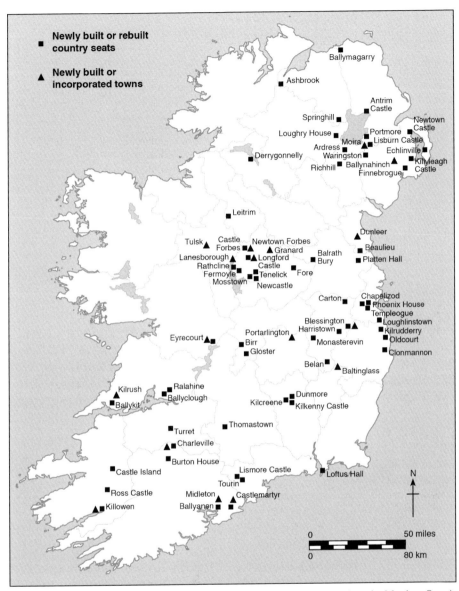

Figure 4.1 Newly built or re-established country houses and towns 1660–90 (map by Matthew Stout).

in seventeenth-century Ireland prior to the rebellion in 1641 is documented to some degree,[5] this chapter covers the neglected period from 1660 to 1690.[6] The seventeenth century in Ireland elicited a succession of building styles, which followed each other with unusual rapidity. Still focused on castle building at the beginning of the century,

5 Leask, *Irish castles and castellated houses.*   **6** Waterman, 'Irish seventeenth-century houses'; E. Jope, 'Moyry, Charlemont, Castleraw and Richhill: fortification to architecture in the north of Ireland', *UJA*, xxiii (1960), pp 97–123.

Ireland attained the complete acceptance of the country seat before 1690. This turning point in Irish history is the main focus of this chapter (Figure 4.1).

Cromwellian architecture

The rebellion of 1641 and the subsequent military campaigns caused devastation on a previously unparalleled scale. 'There hath scarce been a house left undemolished', wrote the Commissioners for Ireland in 1654, 'fitt for an Englishman to dwell in' nor much timber left 'undestroyed'.[7] Hundreds of castles, semi-fortified houses and churches had been ruined; the unrest undoubtedly impeded building activity for many years. The Cromwellian settlement was followed by massive confiscations, transplanting the old landholders beyond the Shannon, or forcing them to emigrate. The subsequent depopulation was so extensive that whole districts became uninhabited.[8] Confiscated estates were allotted to English adventurers and soldiers, of whom many settled in Ireland. Clarendon characterised the Cromwellian settlement by stating that 'Ireland was the great capital out of which all debts were paid, all services rewarded, and all acts of bounty performed'.[9] Ireland during the Protectorate was probably a more agreeable residence than England for those whose property was confirmed by the settlement.[10] The recovery of Ireland after these turbulent times allowed for a subsequent increase in building.[11]

The aggressive Cromwellian settlement necessitated the widespread erection of fortifications to defend the settlers from the hostile Irish. Although settlement accelerated only until 1654–5, an undetermined number of fortifications and dwellings were built before that date. By 1650, Hillsborough Fort (Down) had already been erected, a combination of private residence and fort, certainly not the last of its kind in Ireland.[12] Colonel Richard Le Hunte spent £1,000 on fortifications near Cashel[13] and a stone citadel was started at Clonmel (also in Tipperary) in 1652.[14] Similarly, a fortification was erected at Rosscarbery (Cork) by Captain Robert Gookin, 'ten miles [16km] nearer the enemy than any other garrison thereabout'.[15] West of it, however, a new fort at Bantry (Cork) with its four bastions was 'capable to be very considerable' (Figure 4.2).[16] County Cork gained other new fortifications, such as Bryan's Fort at Castletownshend in 1650.[17] Furthermore, Orrery erected a

---

7 C. Fleetwood, M. Corbett & J. Jones to Secretary Thurloe, 27 June 1654 in [J. Thurloe], *A collection of state papers of John Thurloe*, ii, p. 404.   8 R. Bagwell, *Ireland under the Stuarts* (London, 1909), ii, p. 333.   9 G. Twentyman (ed.), *Macaulay's essay on Sir William Temple* (London, 1905), p. 23.   10 Bagwell, *Ireland under the Stuarts*, ii, p. 309.   11 Ibid., ii, p. 338.   12 Jope, 'Moyry, Charlemont', p. 98. For Hillsborough Fort, see *Arch. sur. Down*, pp 409–11.   13 *CSPI, 1647–60*, p. 675.   14 Thurloe, *State papers*, ii, p. 430. The citadel was pulled down in 1673 (*Ormond*, n.s., iii, p. 331).   15 *CSPI, 1647–60*, p. 623. See also pp 624–5, 803, 815–16. This is an exaggeration: Bryan's Fort near Castletownsend was erected in west Cork in 1650 and a fort was built at Bantry even further west under the Protectorate.   16 S. Johnson & T. Lunham, 'On a manuscript description of the city and county of Cork by Sir Richard Cox', *JRSAI*, cxxxii (1902), p. 360. See also *CSPI, 1660–2*, p. 283.   17 Lord Killanin & M. Duignan, *The Shell guide to Ireland*, second ed. (London, 1967), p. 158. The fort, consisting of a bawn, an internal house and spear-shaped flankers, was erected by Colonel Richard Townsend (*JCHAS*, cxliii (1938), p. 55).

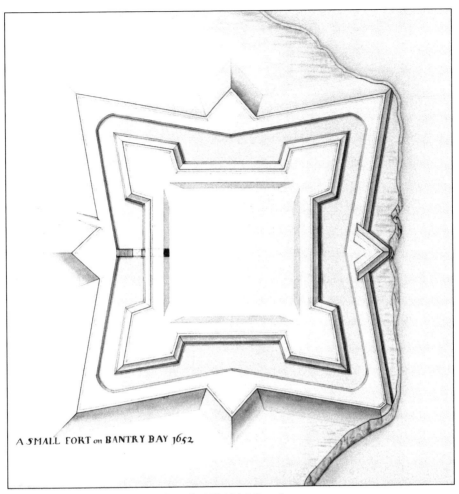

A SMALL FORT on BANTRY BAY 1652

Figure 4.2 'A small fort on Bantry Bay 1652' (British Library).

fort at Dunboy in Castletown Berehaven:[18] he wrote in 1666 that it was demolished by 'the usurpers'; at Newmarket in the same county a strong fort was erected, while the market town near it was rebuilt subsequently.[19]

Vincent Gookin, brother of Robert Gookin, in a pamphlet directed against the transplantation of the Irish, highlighted the contemporary building trade: there were five or six carpenters and masons among every hundred Irishmen, who 'were more handy and ready in building ordinary houses and much [more] prudent in applying the defects of instruments and materials than English artificers'.[20] Gookin's positive experience with Irish craftsmen during the building of his house in County Cork in 1653–4 was not replicated by Daniel Thomas a few years later.

18 Orrery to Lord lieutenant, 18 April 1666, *CSPI, 1666–9*, p. 92.   19 Richard Aldworth to Ormond, 13 April 1683, *Ormond*, n.s., vii, p. 12. See also *CSPI, 1666–9*, p. 635.   20 V. Gookin, *The great case of transplantation discussed* (London, 1655).

Thomas was employed by Henry Cromwell, probably to restore Portumna Castle, (Galway),[21] ancient seat of the earls of Clanricarde, which had been reserved for the Lord deputy, Henry Cromwell, along with 6,000 acres (2,400ha). Thomas was an experienced architect who had built numerous houses in London.[22] At Portumna, he proposed a bridge across the Shannon, for which he needed 'sa[w]yers, especially English, [who] both in Dublin and all ye nation over are very rare and scarce to bee hadd'. His supply of labour was curtailed by the oath of abjuration for 'ye Irish workmen are runn away from mee, for since the oath of abjuration is come amoungst them, they had rather doe any man's worke then build places of strength wh[ich] may subdue & keepe them in obedience and have skattered themselves some ten, some twenty, some forty myles from mee'.[23] Henry Cromwell also built in Dublin, where Randolph Beckett and John Mills added a wing to Phoenix House, the royal residence, for him.[24] Remarkably, no illustrations of this house are known to exist.

John Perceval, a large landowner, rebuilt Castlewarden (Kildare) early in 1655: he was so busy building that a friend was afraid that he was 'infected with the Spanish curse, which is the spirit of building'.[25] In 1659, Perceval moved to Ballymacow (Cork), later called Egmont, where the building of his 'small nest' preoccupied him.[26] Another landlord, Sir William Temple (later a famous diplomat), moved to Ireland in May 1656, where he built a residence at Staplestown (Carlow).[27] Building activity under the Commonwealth was certainly not confined to the south of Ireland. Already in 1651, two Big Houses were built in County Down,[28] at Kilwarlin and Moira (made of brick).[29] In adjacent Antrim, the second Viscount Conway began additions to Lisburn Castle in 1654.

These were not isolated examples: many more seats were undoubtedly erected in Ireland before the Protectorate ended. Practically nothing is known about the physical appearance of these examples of Cromwellian architecture. Whether they were based on contemporary English examples remains to be seen. The sparse references almost all show the fortified nature of these residences. Similarly, there is a dearth of information concerning the buildings of the transplanted Irish. Did divided Ireland develop two distinct styles of architecture? Or did the transplanted Irish collapse completely into utter poverty?

21 Portumna was besieged by General Ludlow in 1651 when it may have been damaged. Daniel Thomas speaks of sawyers and slaters, possibly working on the castle (R. Ramsey, *Henry Cromwell* (London, 1933), p. 226). The bawn gate at Portumna resembles the classical gate at Rathcline (Longford).   22 Thomas listed 'all ye buildinge of ye Inn of Chancery called Furnifall's inn, Holborne, Southhampton house behinde Gray's inn, the Lord Grey of Warcke in ye Charterhouse yard, the Charter house itsealfe ... and severall other good buildings, of my owne undertaking and p[er]forminge': Ramsey, *Henry Cromwell*, pp 227–8.   23 Ibid., pp 226–7.   24 E. MacLysaght (ed.), 'Commonwealth state accounts: Ireland 1650–56', *Anal. Hib.*, 15 (1944), pp 292–4.   25 William Dobbyns to John Perceval, Feb. 1655–6, *Egmont*, i, p. 575.   26 John Perceval to Robert Southwell, 29 Nov. 1659, *Egmont*, i, p. 610.   27 H. Woodbridge, *Sir William Temple, the man and his work* (New York, 1940), pp 51–2.   28 George Rawdon to Lord Conway, 20 Nov. 1651, *CSPI, 1647–60*, p. 383.   29 Major Edward Burgh to Colonel Edward Conway, 20 Jan. 1652, *CSPI, 1647–60*, p. 386.

Historical context

The restoration of King Charles II in 1660 renewed uncertainty for many landlords about their estates. The Act of Settlement, followed by the Act of Explanation, brought relief to some, and misery to multitudes. Ireland was treated as a cake that could be handed out three times over. The forfeitures, forced upon many loyal subjects, were in sharp contrast to the permissive attitude toward Cromwellian landowners such as the newly created earl of Orrery, Viscount Conway, Sir John Perceval, Lord Herbert of Cherbury and others.[30] Some years later, Orrery characterised Ireland as 'a body sick of many diseases, and, if you cure but one, it will die of the rest'.[31] Ireland proved to be far healthier than he diagnosed. The peaceful decades after the Restoration expanded the economy, and stimulated considerable prosperity, shown in part by an extensive increase in building activity over much of Ireland.[32]

Whereas a traveller in 1670 reported that there were very few houses in the countryside from the Curragh to Limerick,[33] Lord lieutenant Clarendon wrote that 'there were many buildings raised for beauty, as well as use, orderly and regular plantations of trees and fences, and enclosures throughout the kingdom'.[34] Basic to the history of architecture at that time was the settlement of Ireland, or, as Orrery expressed it, the 'planting of a wild and dangerous country with industrious and faithful English'.[35] Many new towns were founded, and old ones expanded. Saw mills were erected under a special patent for cheaper rebuilding after the 'trouble and injury of the late times'.[36] Craftsmen from England were imported to assist in the reconstruction.

Renewed affluence increased rents and decreased interest rates.[37] Petty in his *Political arithmetike* estimated that Ireland in the latter half of the seventeenth century had 16,000 houses with more than one chimney, and 160,000 houses lacking a chimney.[38] Ireland was considerably less wealthy than England (Petty estimated its wealth as one-sixth that of England's),[39] and had many inhabitants living in the most wretched of circumstances. Travellers passed haughty comments on their condition, as in these comments in 1662: 'I must complain of the bad inhabitants of this good country. A generation of people scarce one removed from savages, if not in the same form of brutality, their houses are like hog-styes, … and they themselves swine like in all things but shape … their homes are not to be gone but groped into, they make their doors as low and little as they can, and their ceilings thatch as low as a man's head'.[40] Ireland's wealth was depleted by large sums transferred to England.

---

30 Dorothy Rawdon to Edward Conway, 13 Nov. 1654, *CSPI, 1647–60*, p. 542.   **31** Orrery to Conway, 25 April 1673, *CSPD, 1673*, p. 173.   **32** Petty estimated that improvements in Ireland quadrupled from 1652 to 1673 (C. Hull (ed.), *The economic writings of Sir William Petty* (Cambridge, 1899), i, p. 197).   **33** Philip Froude to Joseph Williamson, 6 Aug. 1670, *CSPI, 1669–70*, p. 210.   **34** Twentyman (ed.), *William Temple*, p. 23.   **35** Orrery to Ormond, 8 July 1663, *Ormond*, n.s., iii, p. 59.   **36** Patent for Sir Hugh Midleton, *CSPI, 1666–69*, 8 May 1667; renewed 8 March 1669.   **37** Simms, *Jacobite Ireland*, p. 14.   **38** Hull, *Petty*, i, pp 214–15. In a document of 1679, hostile to the Catholics, the figures are 225,000 families, of which 15,000 lived in houses with one or more chimney. Of these families, 8,000 were Protestant (*CSPD, 1679–80*, p. 353).   **39** *CSPD, 1686–7*, pp 91–3: W. Petty, *Political arithmetike …* (London, 1687).   **40** Colonel Edward Cooke to Lord Bruce, 12 Nov. 1662, *Fifteenth Report*, app. vii, p. 169.

For example, £20,000 was sent over from the Irish Revenue to rebuild Windsor Castle in 1672.[41] What might Ireland's appearance have been like had these sums been applied to building in the country itself, rather than to enhancing English architecture? Non-resident landlords such as Lord Conway regularly dispatched their Irish rents to England.[42] Notwithstanding these financial drawbacks, much was still expended on Big Houses in Ireland.

DUBLIN BUILDINGS 1660–90

The growth of Dublin after 1660 was so rapid that Lord lieutenant Essex reported in 1673 that the city was almost twice as large as at the Restoration[43] and its architectural development was impressive.[44] Soon after the Restoration, it became inevitable that regulations would be imposed on building activity in the city. A 1665 statute prohibited brick burning within half a mile (0.8km) of the gates of Dublin, to preserve the health of the inhabitants.[45] Other measures taken by the Dublin Assembly were directed at fire prevention, such as the 1660 ban on thatched houses within the city and suburbs.[46] Four years after the Great Fire in London (1666), the Privy Council issued a similar proclamation, modelled on building regulations devised in London. It prohibited 'jutting out windows or any overhanging works whatsoever, balconies excepted', and required that thatch be replaced by slate or tiles.[47] There was an apparent lack of adherence to these rules; until the beginning of the eighteenth century, houses with overhanging eaves continued to be built.

The growth of Dublin consisted primarily in the expansion of residential areas. Lord Longford and Lord Conway erected considerable houses, while Sir Maurice Eustace, then Lord Chancellor of Ireland, built 'a great house' in Dame Street shortly after the Restoration:[48] this was apparently coveted by many, since after his death disputes broke out between parties who sought to occupy it. Although no parliaments were held between 1666 and 1690, many landowners maintained townhouses in Dublin, possibly serving as retreats from the tedium and danger of life down the country.

The city was embellished by public buildings such as Smock Alley theatre, built for £2,000, of which most was spent on the interior; the English bookseller John Dunton spoke highly of it as the equal of London theatres.[49] Most new buildings in Dublin were in the artisan mannerist style,[50] a very loose interpretation of the

---

41 King to Lord lieutenant, 15 Jan. 1676, *CSPD, 1675–6*, p. 515.   42 Petty estimated that the owners of one-quarter of the real and personal estate in Ireland lived in England in 1672 (Hull, *Petty*, i, p. 185).   43 Essex to Arlington, 22 July 1673 in O. Airy (ed.), *Essex papers 1672–5* (London, 1890), p. 103.   44 M. Craig, *Dublin 1660–1860* (Dublin, 1969). 45 26 July 1665, Steele, *Royal proclamations*, ii, p. 92.   46 *CARD*, iv, pp 197–9. 47 *CSPI, 1669–70*, pp 248–9.   48 E. Tickell, 'The Eustace family and their land in Co. Kildare', *JKAS*, xiii (1958), p. 319.   49 E. MacLysaght, *Irish life in the seventeenth century*, second ed. (Cork, 1950), pp 214–51.   50 J. Summerson, *Architecture in Britain 1530 to 1830* (London, 1970), describes English examples of this style.

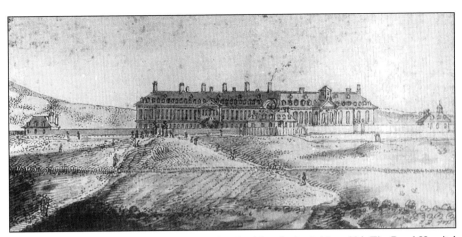

Figure 4.3 'The soldiers hospitall at Dublin the n[orth] and w[est] sides of it'. The Royal Hospital Kilmainham drawn by Francis Place in 1698 (Rhode Island School of Design, Providence).

classical style. The Blue Coat School, begun in 1669, charming in its details, was quite asymmetrical,[51] and the city Tholsel was an eccentric structure with an accumulation of pilasters, not strictly classical, which took seven years to complete.[52] On the second floor, it housed the Exchange, which had increased in importance as trade expanded. At the same time, street trading became so obstructive that the Ormond Market was erected in 1682–3, patronised, if not designed, by Sir Francis Brewster,[53] who also presented designs for a palace to replace Dublin Castle in 1682.[54] The market must have been a striking building, with its central rotunda; it survived until 1890.[55]

Far more classical in outlook was the Royal Hospital in Kilmainham designed by Surveyor-General William Robinson, the only unaltered building of this period still existing in Dublin (Figure 4.3). As early as 1677, plans existed at Whitehall to build a hospital for soldiers, as appears from a letter to the Marquis de Louvois in which he was requested to send 'the plan of the Hotel des Invalides drawn with all the fronts'.[56] Robinson may have seen these drawings, as he went to London in 1678 to obtain approval for his designs for Charles Fort near Kinsale.[57] By 1680, the hospital was already started, and it became Dublin's largest building, preceding Wren's Chelsea Hospital in London by some years.

In 1683, the front of Trinity College was started.[58] The building is vaguely reminiscent of Rainham Hall (Norfolk) but its middle projection was likely copied

---

51 Craig, *Dublin*, pp 22–3, and *CARD*, iv, pp 459–60, 485, 542 (there are building accounts on p. 495). 52 *CARD*, v: see drawing in [T. Dineley], 'Observations made on his tour in Ireland and France 1675–1680', NLI, MS 392. It was of modest dimensions (64 feet x 64 feet), while its tower was 100 feet high (19.5m x 19.5m x 30.5m). 53 *Ormond*, n.s., iv, pp 412, 514, 530. 54 *Ormond*, n.s., iv, pp 398, 421, 514. He later wanted to use the Royal Hospital, Kilmainham for Trinity College, Dublin, and to transfer the old soldiers to Trinity College. 55 Craig, *Dublin*, p. 26. 56 Monmouth to M. de Louvois, 29 Nov. 1677, *CSPD, 1677–8*, p. 476. 57 Longford to Ormond, 8 Oct. 1678, *Ormond*, n.s., ii, p. 212. 58 *CARD*, v, pp 274 and 285.

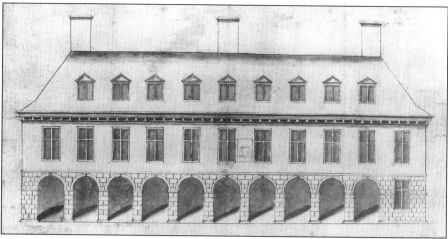

Figure 4.4 Elevation of the 'Great new building on piers and arches' for the south–east range of Dublin Castle *c.*1684. This arched façade is most likely the work of William Robinson (British Library).

from the centre building of Hotel des Invalides, suggesting that Robinson was its architect.[59] It shows an unusually high-pitched roof, behind a pediment extending the entire length of the projection. Here, the pavilions have remarkable Holborn gables (curvilinear pedimented gables of the type traditionally called 'Dutch billies' in Dublin). After 1682, Trinity College saw the erection of a hall and a chapel. The latter was described in 1775 as being 'as mean a structure as you can conceive; destitute of monumental decoration within, it is no better than a Welsh church without'.[60] This offered a sharp contrast to the elegant carvings by James Tabary and the fine plaster work in the chapel in the Royal Hospital Kilmainham (1687). The newly erected Hall of Trinity College emerges only vaguely from the bills of plasterers and carpenters preserved in the College.[61] Little trace remains of seventeenth-century buildings there.

As well as building new churches, old churches in Dublin were repaired, such as St Patrick's and Christ Church.[62] For the choir of Christ Church, King Charles II allocated a meagre £100 in 1679.[63] His successor James II was equally closefisted; while expending thousands of pounds on his chapel in Whitehall and commissioning the most expensive Sir Christopher Wren as architect, Grinling Gibbons as wood carver and Arnold Quellin as sculptor, he spent a mere £789 on the Royal Chapel in Dublin Castle. More significantly, among the craftsmen employed there was

59 Robinson likely had access to the newly published Lejeune de Boullencourt, *Description générale de l'Hostel royal des invalides, établi par Louis le Grand dans la plaine de Grenelle près Paris: avec les plans, profils & élévations de ses faces, coupes et appartemens* (Paris, 1683).   **60** Quoted in C. Maxwell, *History of Trinity College* (Dublin, 1946), p. 101, from Campbell's *Philosophical survey*, 1775.   **61** TCD, shelf B4, Flat Box 9, Drawer 91, which contains bills from 1684–6, mentioning the plaster work of James Smith and carpentry by Thomas Lawson. As late as 1688–9, work was done by John Whinrey at the College.   **62** Craig, *Dublin*; H. Wheeler & M. Craig, *The Dublin city churches of the Church of Ireland* (Dublin, 1948).   **63** King to Lord lieutenant, 17 June 1679, *CSPD 1678–80*, p. 182.

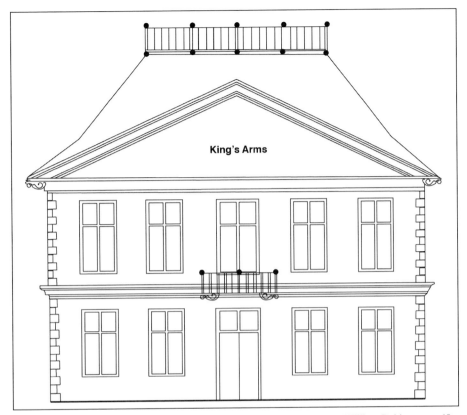

Figure 4.5 Elevation of the grand entrance, Dublin Castle, most likely by William Robinson, c.1684: redrawn by Matthew Stout (British Library).

Frances Quellin (wife of Arnold), who had also been working at James' chapel in Whitehall:[64] might Wren, Gibbins or Quellin also have been involved at the chapel in Dublin Castle? The vicissitudes of this building were obviously related to the political climate. In 1684, William Robinson started plans for rebuilding Dublin Castle,[65] on which he worked day and night to be able to send them to England for approval.[66] His designs for the Castle survive (Figures 4.4–4.5).[67] The proposed buildings excel in their simplicity, stripped of the usual clutter of the artisan mannerist style, such as pilasters and decorated window surrounds. Robinson did not see the completion of his Irish buildings; he decamped to England on the arrival of the Jacobite Richard Talbot as Lord deputy in 1687, while his fellow Surveyor-

64 J.Y. Akerman (ed.), 'Moneys received and paid for secret services of Charles II and James II from 30 March 1679 to 25 Dec., 1688', *Camden Society*, clii (London, 1851), pp 155, 160. The craftsmen were John Coquns (silverwork), Rene Cousin (gilding), Francis Duddell and John Heysenbuttell (joinery) and Francis Quellin ('holland and laces, and making several things').   **65** 15 May 1684, *Ormond*, n.s., vii, p. 227; see also pp 253, 257.   **66** Arran to Ormond, 16 July 1684, *Ormond*, n.s., vii, p. 258.   **67** J. Cornforth, 'Dublin Castle, I', *Country Life*, 30 July 1970.   **68** [C. Molyneux], *An account of the family and descendants of Sir Thomas Molyneux* (Evesham, 1820), p. 63.

General William Molyneux stayed on and built, as he himself explains, 'the great new building on piers and arches' (Figure 4.4).[68] Phoenix House and Chapelizod House (the other royal residences) were repaired, expanded and embellished.

BUILDING ACTIVITY IN EXISTING AND NEWLY BUILT TOWNS

In Munster, and probably elsewhere, the towns, having forfeited their charters by the Rebellion of 1641, were granted new charters after 1660, modified so as to force the Corporations to rebuild their official buildings and to improve their towns.[69] However, forfeited houses in towns like Athlone, Limerick and New Ross were allotted to the "49 officers', delaying the rebuilding process considerably, due to conflicting claims. Uncertainty about property rights caused a general deterioration of existing conditions, reflected in the observation of Sir John Perceval in 1664 that 'the towns daily decay beyond imagination, no man going to the charge of laying one slate on his house'.[70] It was a decade after the Restoration before plans were made to rebuild Athlone and rescue it from utter ruin.[71] Most towns suffered horribly under the Rebellion: Antrim town had been destroyed, but it had been 'in a good measure re-edified' before 1665.[72]

After 1670, the rebuilding of towns accelerated. In that year, the Duchess of Ormond approved the replacement of thatched cabins by brick houses in Kilkenny, decreasing the 'mischief' of fires.[73] In 1684, Kilkenny gained an Exchange and a Court House. Although the town had an annual income of £500, according to the correspondent, 'I see no works of grandeur either in building, charity or hospitality proceeded from them'.[74] The reluctance of towns to spend money on official buildings is indicated by the fact that another Exchange was erected in Limerick in 1673 at the sole expense of its mayor, William Yorke.[75] A 1681 drawing showed that it was in the same artisan mannerist style as the Tholsel in Dublin.[76] The first floor was an open arcade, supporting with pillars a six-bayed second storey, covered by a sprocketed roof with turret. The whole was crowned by two lions as finials, while a statue topped the turret.

A Custom House was built in Belfast,[77] while another was repaired in Limerick.[78] A session house for the assizes and a gaol had already been erected in Omagh, even

---

69 King to Lord justices, 9 April 1661, *CSPI, 1660–62*, p. 30. See also *CSPI, 1666–9*, p. 172.   **70** John Perceval to Robert Southwell, 23 March 1663–4, *Egmont*, ii, p. 8. See also *CSPI, 1663–5*, p. 21, for the decay in Galway.   **71** Lord lieutenant to Arlington, 23 Aug. 1669, *CSPI, 1669–70*, p. 241. For New Ross, see *CSPI, 1664–5*, p. 525.   **72** King to Lord lieutenant, 28 June 1665, *CSPI, 1663–5*, p. 599.   **73** Duchess of Ormond to Captain George Mathew, 21 Jan. 1670–1, *Ormond*, n.s., ii, p. 446.   **74** Samuel Gorges to Captain George Mathew, 4 May 1684, *Ormond*, n.s., vii, p. 231.   **75** Francis Foulke to Orrery, *Orrery papers*, p. 122.   **76** R. Herbert, 'Antiquity of the Corporation of Limerick', *NMAJ*, iv (1945), pp 85–130, Plate iv. Its rusticated window surrounds are reminiscent of those at Eyrecourt (Galway).   **77** G. Hill (ed.), *Montgomery MSS* (Belfast, 1869), n. 109.   **78** Bill of Joseph Grey, tailor, 1 Aug. 1678, *Orrery papers*, NLI, MS 13,777. The Custom House at Limerick was formerly called the Bear.

before it was certain that the Tyrone county assizes would be kept there.[79] Another 'commodious' session house was built at Naas (Kildare), 'most of it new and advan't upon pillars which yet are soe disproporcend and dwarfish that a mean artist might judge them set up in the darkest time of barbarizme and before propocon or scimitry [symmetry] was thought on'.[80] The same correspondent remarked on County Kildare in 1682 that 'these towns seem to be totally neglected, the revenewe being never applied to any publique use or generall good of the Corporacon or improvement of the towne noe [other] buildgens are here to be found'. However, some towns underwent considerable renovations. Clonmel (Tipperary), where Ormond had founded the woollen manufacture, and where his Palatine Court resided, saw the erection of the Main Guard in 1674,[81] as well as plans by William Robinson for its prison,[82] and the strengthening of the fortifications.[83]

In some towns, development was promoted through building covenants in leases. Sometimes, as in Dingle (Kerry), this did not work out because of the anxiety of the people about a Turkish attack.[84] Many Irish towns must have looked like Dingle at that time, with only a handful of slated houses, and dense huddles of thatched cabins. The larger centres, such as Cork and Limerick, also expanded beyond their walls.

Government policy sought to extend its control over the whole of Ireland and this resulted in the promotion of new plantations and towns (Figure 4.1). The numerous grants for manors after 1660 almost all referred to 'the encouragement of all persons as shall settle themselves' on the lands,[85] or 'the better planting of the manor'.[86] Some of the plethora of manors that were created, sporting such imaginative names as Gethinsgrott and Donovan's Leap,[87] probably never materialised. On the other hand, many manors proved viable, mainly because of strenuous efforts by their owners to build villages, attract industries and promote tillage.

There was often a direct relationship between the building of a Big House and the rise of an estate town. Orrery's castle at Charleville (Cork), started in 1661, was shortly followed by the development of the town of Charleville (modern Rathluirc), where Orrery built a school as well as a church.[88] At Newtown Forbes (Longford), a new village was founded near the renovated seat of the earl of Granard,[89] where he also built 'a fair and large church sumptuously adorned within'.[90] Primate Michael

---

79 30 Jan. 1687, *CSPD, 1686–7*.   **80** Co. Kildare in 1682, TCD, MS 1.1.3.   **81** William Robinson probably designed it: M. Craig & Knight of Glin, *Ireland observed* (Cork, 1970). It is one of the few surviving late seventeenth-century buildings in an Irish town. Its arcade has been filled in.   **82** George Mathew to Ormond, 25 Sept. 1677, *Ormond*, n.s., iv, p. 44.   **83** Rev. Samuel Ladyman to Ormond, 12 Sept. 1679, *Ormond*, n.s., v, p. 203. Ormond also planned the improvement of Nenagh (Tipperary) in 1681 (*Ormond*, n.s., vi, p. 171, 30 Sept. 1681, Ormond to Colonel John Fitzpatrick).   **84** Francis Brewster to Captain Mathew, 30 June 1673, *Ormond*, n.s., ii, pp 328–9; *Ormond*, n.s., v, p. 184.   **85** Grant of manor of Bettramon [Ballytrammon?] Co. Wexford, to Duke of Albemarle, 16 April 1668, *CSPI 1660–69*, p. 595.   **86** Grant of manor of Blessington to Primate Micheal Boyle, 3 May 1669, *CSPI, 1660–69*, p. 722.   **87** *CSPI, 1666–69*, p. 770; *CSPD, 1671*, pp 168–9.   **88** Castlemartyr (Cork) was developed after Orrery settled at the castle there in 1672.   **89** [Granard], *Memoirs of the earls of Granard* (London, 1868), p. 72.   **90** Co. Longford in 1682, TCD, MS 1.1.3.

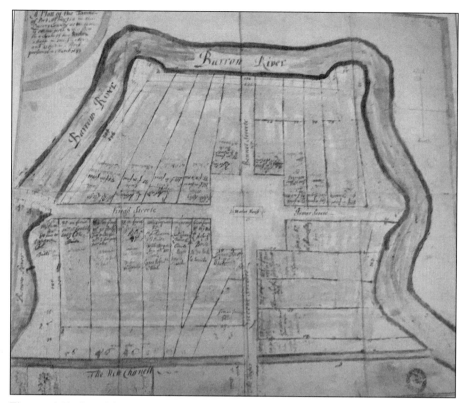

Figure 4.6 'A plott of the town of Portarlington in the Queens County', drawn to a scale of two and a half perches to inch (1:630), March 1678 (NLI 21.F.55 (1)).

Boyle erected his palatial house at Blessington under the Wicklow Mountains, founded the town of the same name, and built a church at the end of the vista leading from his house. The church was consecrated in 1683, and had a steeple containing 'a ring of six bells', imported by Boyle from England.[91] Similarly, Sir George Lane (later Lord Lanesborough) enlarged his seat at Rathcline (Longford), and promoted the building of stone houses at Lanesborough, as well as a 'very fair church stately beautified within and with a tall steeple'.[92] John Eyre founded the town of Eyrecourt (Galway) near his newly built seat, and erected a chapel there in 1677. The high craftsmanship of its interior stimulates speculation about the decoration of this small, now ruined, church.

By far the most enthusiastic developer was the third Viscount Conway, and his indefatigable agent George Rawdon. They literally recreated Lisburn (Antrim) after its destruction in 1641, while improving Lisburn Castle and building the seat and demesne at Portmore. Some houses in Lisburn compared favourably with townhouses in England, such as that built by the carpenter John Darley in 1677, described as 'very fine work, set out to the street with medallions and cornice'.[93] It

91 *CSPD, 1682*, p. 230: and *CTP, 1681–5*, vii, part 1, p. 503.   92 Co. Longford in 1682, TCD, MS 1.1.3.   93 R. Millmay to Lord Conway, 4 July 1677, *CSPD, 1677–8*, p. 228.

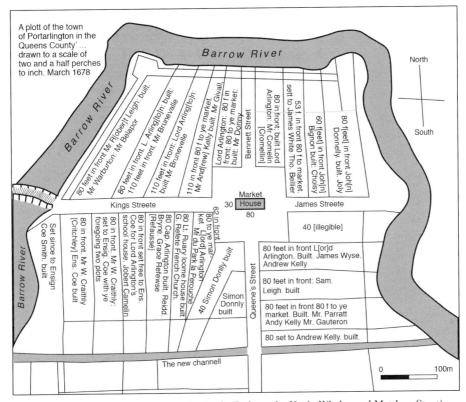

Figure 4.7 'Plott of … Portarlington', Co. Laois (Redrawn by Kevin Whelan and Matthew Stout).

would be supernumerary to list all Conway's improvements at Lisburn.[94] Rawdon also made many improvements on his own estate, building the market towns of Moira and Ballynahinch (Down).[95] On Conway's estate, several churches were built, such as the one near his Portmore mansion at Ballinderry (1666–8, recently restored),[96] and at Aghalee,[97] both in Antrim. Furthermore, the church at Lisburn was raised to cathedral status, and subsequently a gallery was added.[98]

In isolated instances, a town was erected away from the neighbourhood of a new seat. Portarlington (Laois) was laid out in 1667 by Sir George Rawdon for the earl of Arlington, an absentee landlord.[99] A 1678 plan (Figures 4.6–4.7) shows its grid-outlay, with a market house in the centre, the whole enclosed by fortifications.[100] A printed memorandum from 1666, drawn up to attract settlers to the town, stated that timber for building could be had 'above a musket shot from the town'.[101] Stringent regulations advised new settlers that their houses in the town must 'be made of good lime and stone', roofed with shingles, tiles or slates, and have dormer windows facing the streets.

94 *CSPI* and *CSPDom* for 1642 to 1683.   **95** Lodge, *Peerage of Ireland*, iii, p. 104.   **96** *Shell guide*, p. 85.   **97** George Rawdon to Conway, 17 Feb. 1677, *CSPD, 1676–7*, p. 5.   **98** Rawdon to Conway, 29 March 1670, *CSPI, 1669–70*, p. 93.   **99** Rawdon to Conway, 16 March 1667, *CSPI, 1666–69*, p. 318. Arlington also built Euston Hall in Suffolk at this time (A. Oswald, 'Euston Hall, Suffolk, I', *Country Life*, 10 Jan. 1957).   **100** NLI, 21 F. E. 55 (1).   **101** *CSPI, 1666–69*, pp 59–61. For building at the earl of Leicester's Cork estate in 1667, see *De L'Isle*, vi, p. 528.

Sometimes, a landowner of the old stock ordered the laying out of a town. In 1672, the earl of Thomond granted a lease to Colonel John Blount, including a covenant to lay out Kilrush (Clare) 'and settle therein ten English families, or in want of them, ten tradesmen, and to build no houses but with brick or stone and lime, to be slated'.[102]

Other landlords made minor improvements to towns on their estates, such as Lord Herbert, who had a market house built at Castleisland (Kerry)[103] and Sir John Perceval, who rebuilt Burton House, then started a church at Churchtown (Cork),[104] and planned an inn: 'But in ye mean time I think it will answere the charge if I run up a stable of cabins in the towne with a sign to show strangers there is room for their horses tho' there is none for themselves'.[105] Perceval's guardian and relative, Sir Robert Southwell, brought improvements not only to his own estate near Kinsale,[106] where he, among other things, raised almshouses in 1682,[107] but he also built a church in Killeshandra (Cavan).[108] Among the landowners whose estates were furthest west was Sir William Petty. He built his house and settlement at Killowen at the head of Kenmare Bay in Kerry, where he developed fisheries, ironworks, lead mines and marble quarries, and designed an ingenious chariot with a single wheel to reach his dwelling along the poor Kerry roads.[109]

Obviously, these buildings were executed by a multitude of workmen. Most remain anonymous. Only in rare cases do contemporary records shed light on their lives, as when the traveller Dineley depicted Staplestown village (Carlow), naming both the local mason (Hugh Brookshaw) and the local carpenter (Nicholas Langford), as well as drawing their cottages.[110]

CHURCH BUILDING

From 1660 until 1669, Catholic priests enjoyed comparative freedom in Ireland, a relief after the intense Cromwellian repression. About 1666, the Franciscan Friars of Bonamargy (Antrim) enlarged their vault and added a chapel, likely not an isolated case.[111] The Catholic position became less tenable after the Popish plot of 1678. Orrery, a hater of Papists, reported on his return to his castle at Charleville (Cork) in 1670 that 'many convents have in my absence been erected. I am now pulling them down'.[112] Catholic ability to circumvent restrictive measures was evident in the building of four Catholic chapels in Kilkenny, right beside Ormond's

102 E. Shirley & J. Graves (eds), 'Extracts from the journal of Thomas Dineley, giving an account of his visit to Ireland in the reign of Charles II', *JRSAI*, 16 (1867), p. 190.   103 Edward Kenney to Lord Herbert, 18 July 1683, W. Smith (ed.), *Herbert correspondence* (Dublin, 1963), p. 280.   104 Sir John Perceval to Thomas Smith, 25 Feb. 1681, BL, Egmont papers, Add. MS 46958c.   105 Sir John Perceval to Sir Robert Southwell, 19 May 1683, *Egmont*, ii, pp 131–2.   106 King to Lord lieutenant, 2 April 1675, *CSPD, 1675–6*, pp 50–1.   107 *Egmont*, ii, p. 91.   108 *Shell guide*, p. 334.   109 *Fifteenth report*, app. ii, pp 175–6.   110 Dineley, 'Observations 1675–1680'.   111 D. Chart, E. Evans & H. Lawlor, *Preliminary survey of the ancient monuments of Northern Ireland* (Belfast, 1940), p. 11.   112 Orrery to Conway, 20 Sept. 1670, *CSPI, 1669–70*, p. 267.   113 Ormond to Arran, 2 Oct. 1683, *Ormond*, n.s., vii, p. 139.   114 Dudley Pearce to Francis Marsh, 22 Dec. 1684, *Ormond*, n.s., vii, p. 312.

castle,[113] and the 'hopeful progress of repair' of Kilnalehine abbey and Kilconnell monastery (Galway) occurred as late as 1684.[114] At the 1685 accession of James II, the prospects of Catholic Ireland temporarily brightened. During Tyrconnell's time, the religious orders once more appeared in public in clerical garb, and rebuilt their churches: a Benedictine foundation was erected in 1688 in close proximity to Dublin.[115] In another case, Viscount Gormanston, a Catholic landlord of the Pale, erected a domestic chapel adjoining his castle in 1687.[116]

After the English Revolution, many ancient churches that had been lost at the Reformation were reclaimed by the Catholics, flaunting James II's specific prohibition.[117] The ensuing Williamite War curtailed Catholic supremacy, reducing them to enforced submission, and thwarted their scope for public church building.

Under the Commonwealth, the Puritans frequently repaired parish churches, renaming them as 'meeting houses'. In 1653, orders were issued to repair the church at Carlow, which was effected two years later. Similarly, meeting places in Jamestown (Leitrim), Swords (Dublin) and Waterford were restored during this period;[118] in 1654, a Presbyterian meeting house was erected at Urney near Strabane (Tyrone).[119] Residences for ministers and their families were also newly built or modified.[120]

In 1672, a scandalised Bishop of Derry reported that 'a separate congregation' had built a large meeting house within the walls of the city, 'within two to three doors of the Bishop's mansion house'.[121] Dissenters, concentrated in the north, became so 'confident' that they built 'oratoryes for themselves in almost every parish' near Lisburn (Antrim).[122] They finally planned to build a meeting house in Lisburn itself in 1681: an infuriated Rawdon noted that 'it is near 50 years we have lived here in peace and I shall not willingly admit any such interruption in my days'.[123] Conway exhibited sharp dislike of Anabaptist and Quaker tenants, 'whose design is only to turn out the landlords';[124] he did later employ the Quaker carpenter John Darley. Conway's wife became a Quaker, without softening Conway's attitude, as he directed his agent Rawdon 'to prosecute vigorously' any Dissenters who intruded on his lands to preach.[125] In Dublin, the Dissenters erected a meeting house close to Dublin Castle in 1681, but it was quickly repressed.[126]

Many landlords, while improving their estates, built Protestant churches as part of their plans for newly created towns. Other churches were erected in the countryside.

---

115 T. King Moylan, 'The district of Grangegorman III', *Dublin Historical Record*, 18 (1945), pp 1–15. The Franciscans returned to Nenagh (north Tipperary); their friary bell still carries an inscription dated 1687: D. Gleeson, *The last lords of Ormond* (London, 1938), p. 216. 116 *Shell guide*, p. 80. 117 Simms, *Jacobite Ireland*, p. 88. 118 St John D. Seymour, *The Puritans in Ireland 1647–1661* (Oxford, 1921), p. 45. 119 Rebuilt 1695: *Shell guide*, p. 430. 120 St J.D. Seymour, *Puritans in Ireland*, p. 49. 121 Robert Mossom to Lord lieutenant [1672], *CSPD, 1672*, p. 517. 122 George Rawdon to Lord lieutenant, 27 March 1669, *CSPI, 1666–69*, p. 703. 123 George Rawdon to Conway, 2 March 1681, *CSPI, 1680–1*, p. 193. 124 Edward Conway to George Rawdon, 5 July 1659, J. Bramhall (ed.), *The Rawdon papers* (London, 1819), p. 199. 125 George Rawdon to Granard, 2 June 1681, *CSPD, 1680–1*, p. 323. 126 Lord lieutenant to secretary Jenkins, 18 April 1681, p. 235; Lord lieutenant to secretary Jenkins, 21 May 1681, *CSPD, 1680–1*, p. 291. Protestant Dissenters were hardly persecuted in the first years of James II's reign (J.C. Beckett, *Protestant dissent in Ireland 1687–1780* (London, 1948), p. 22).

Richard Nugent, earl of Westmeath, retired to the former Benedictine priory at Fore (Westmeath), granted to his ancestors at the Dissolution of the monasteries, and rebuilt his castle and chapel there before 1680.[127] Sir Robert Colville bought the manor of Newtownards (Down) in 1675, and converted the old church there into his private chapel. Judging from an eighteenth-century description, it was the neatest church in Ulster: 'The pulpit is finely carved and gilded, and so are two large seats of the Colvilles ... the compass ceiling divided into nine panels, and curiously adorned with stucco work in plaister of Paris, well executed in various wreaths, foliages and the figures of angels. The communion table is raised and wainscotted, and encompassed with twisted pillars carved and gilded'.[128]

If classical precedents were followed, these were loosely interpreted, as in the Protestant parish church in Castlecaulfield (Tyrone, 1685).[129] Its seventeenth-century doorway shows attached pillars of crude form, above which two cherubs hold a bible.[130] Bolton described the interior of a contemporary church:

> The Royal arms are either above the chancel door or in the centre of the western gallery ... The wide central passage is paved perhaps with black and white marble; the walls are wainscoted; the windows with cases and mullions of wood or stone and glazed with sheet glass; ... the roof of Irish oak is either uncovered, revealing finely carved hammer beams, or plastered and sometimes richly decorated with stucco work, and from it are suspended the branches in the centre and in the transept.[131]

These churches were laid out in simple cruciform or rectangular plans, lacking aisles:[132] among other interior features, they sometimes contained a finely carved bishop's throne, pulpit and reading desks, a chancel screen, and a Corinthian altarpiece.[133]

The upsurge in church building was promoted by Commissioners appointed for this purpose under the Act of Settlement. Not all bishops favoured this tendency: Primate Boyle argued that 'this is not an age to build cathedrals, since it is so hard a matter to get one removed'.[134] Notwithstanding, many cathedrals were restored, such as Armagh,[135] Lismore[136] and Kilkenny (where brass guns were melted down to cast six bells in 1674–5).[137] Bells for St Patrick's cathedral in Dublin were cast by the Perdue brothers in 1670.[138] A new cathedral was built by Bishop Jeremy Taylor at Dromore,[139] while the cathedral at Kildare received a classical choir in 1686.[140] Cork

127 Lodge, *Peerage of Ireland*, i, p. 243.   **128** Quoted in Hill (ed.), *Montgomery MSS*, p. 122.   **129** *Shell guide*, p. 263.   **130** R. Oram & P. Rankin, *Historic buildings in and near Dungannon and Cookstown* (Belfast, 1971), p. 46.   **131** F.R. Bolton, *The Caroline tradition of the Church of Ireland, with particular reference to Bishop Jeremy Taylor* (London, 1958), pp 213–14.   **132** Bolton, *Church of Ireland*, p. 207. Hillsborough Church (Down, 1663) had a plain cruciform plan. The churches at Middle Ballinderry (Antrim, 1664) and Eyrecourt (Galway, 1677) were rectangular in plan.   **133** Ibid., pp 214–35.   **134** Major Rawdon to Viscount Conway, 20 Dec. 1664, *CSPI, 1663–5*, p. 548.   **135** Restored 1663: Jackson, *Cathedrals of the Church of Ireland*, p. 73.   **136** Restored in 1682–3: Jackson, *Cathedrals of the Church of Ireland*, p. 7.   **137** *CSPD, 1663–5*, p. 536: *Ormond*, n.s., iii, pp 354–5.   **138** Jackson, *Cathedrals of the Church of Ireland*, p. 60.   **139** Shortly after 1661: *Shell guide*, p. 207.   **140** *Shell guide*, p. 318.

gained at least two steeples at this time: in 1671, James Chatterton, John Seawell and 'the best masons of Munster'[141] built the steeple of St Finbarre cathedral, while the spire of St Peter's church soared up in 1683.[142] Undoubtedly, the list of renovated or newly built churches was in actuality much longer.[143]

BRIDGES

Communications in Ireland at the end of the seventeenth century were impeded by unpaved roads, often winding through treacherous bogs. Contemporary sources mention frequent repairs, for example, those in Ulster undertaken by Sir George Rawdon ahead of a visit from the Lord lieutenant.[144] Rawdon was dubbed the 'best highwayman' in the north because of his improvement of roads. Closely related with these improvements was bridge building. Acts were passed for this purpose,[145] or collections held, as in the case for a bridge in Galway.[146] At Chapelizod (Dublin), a bridge was built in 1668 costing £195.[147]

James Archer built a bridge at Carrick-on-Suir (Tipperary) in 1668 for the Duke of Ormond, half of which was finished within ten weeks.[148] Two years earlier, attempts to finish the bridge failed because of threats from the tories.[149] Fear of the Irish torpedoed some plans for bridges: one over the Bann was abandoned, because the river was considered as 'a great security hitherto from the Irish in Tyrone, Londonderry and the adjacent counties'.[150]

The 1677 bridge at Lanesborough (Longford) was 'in length and breadth the largest in this Kingdom'.[151] Another twelve-arched bridge, still in progress in 1689, was erected over the Lagan at Belfast, where it acquired the local name the 'great bridge'.[152] Dublin added three new bridges over the Liffey,[153] an expression of the increased profile of engineering as a more prominent contributor to shaping the Irish landscape. Bridges exerted a major impact on communications and they also impacted military planning. As the engineer Thomas Phillips remarked, new bridges instantly rendered obsolete the old passes through bogs and woods, formerly of crucial strategic importance.[154] This in turn necessitated the development of new

---

141 Thomas Herbert to Lord Herbert, 1671, Smith (ed.), *Herbert correspondence*, pp 198–9.   142 T. Lunham, 'Some historical notices of Cork in the seventeenth and eighteenth centuries', *JRSAI*, 14 (1904), p. 65.   143 Leask's valuable survey *Irish churches and monastic buildings* (1960) reached only as far as the dissolution of the monasteries.   144 George Rawdon to Conway, 22 June 1678, *CSPD, 1678*, p. 239.   145 The different acts in 1663 concerned the following bridges: over the Liffey at Ballymore-Eustace; over the Bray between Dublin and Wicklow; over the Blackwater at Cappoquin (Waterford) and over the Erne between Fermanagh and Donegal (*CSPI, 1663–5*, pp 81–2). A little later, an act was transmitted to build a bridge at Ballyleague over the Shannon, between Longford and Roscommon (*CSPI, 1663–5*, p. 228).   146 *Tenth report*, app. v, p. 39.   147 *Ormond*, n.s., iii, p. 291.   148 James Archer to Ormond, 1 Dec. 1668, *Ormond*, n.s., iii, p. 291.   149 Lord Le Poer to Ormond, 3 April 1666, *Ormond*, n.s., iii, p. 291.   150 George Rawdon to Conway, 10 Feb. 1677, *CSPD, 1676–7*, pp 548–9.   151 Co. Longford in 1682, TCD, MS 1.1.3.   152 Hill (ed.), *Montgomery MSS*, p. 425.   153 Craig, *Dublin*.   154 *Ormond*, ii, p. 312.

defensive techniques, careful consideration of how to protect bridge infrastructure and rethinking of where best to locate barracks.

FORTIFICATIONS IN THE COUNTRYSIDE

The post-Cromwellian period was characterised by frequent reports on fortifications, often by officers of the English Ordnance. These show the interdependent relationship between the Irish and the English military establishments. Although contemporary data on Irish fortifications are abundant, information on related architecture, such as buildings inside the forts and the gates, remains sparse.

In one of the earliest reports after the Restoration, it was stated optimistically that £5,000 was required for the repair of the 'King's castles, forts, citadels, bulwarks and platforms'.[155] This plan was necessary because of the imminent threat of French (and later Dutch) invasion, and by the intermittent but frequent disturbances by tories. The ruling class found itself caught between planning for the dangers of a foreign attack or thwarting the revenge of the disgruntled dispossessed. Recommendations for repairs of fortifications followed each other at intervals, for example in 1666, and again in 1672–3,[156] directing attention mainly to the coasts. Lord lieutenant Essex felt that the situation was so urgent in February 1673 that he contemplated recalling Parliament,[157] but the sorry state of the forts four years later was still 'no less shame than danger that it should be known, and concealed it cannot be'.[158] At the end of Charles II's reign, Thomas Phillips, an English Ordnance engineer, was commissioned to survey the garrisons; his full report has been preserved, illustrated with admirable watercolours.[159]

The continuous need for repair was met in incidental emergencies. One of the first newly erected forts was at Kinsale (later called Charles Fort) in 1682. The imminent threat of a Dutch attack in 1667 on the valuable fleet in Kinsale harbour resulted in expansion of the fortifications, some laid out by Prince Rupert in 1649. Supervision of the work was in the hands of the gentleman-architect, the earl of Orrery, then Lord President of Munster.[160] When fears of a Dutch attack subsided, work on the fort was stopped. It was resumed in 1672 under the pompous engineer-in-chief Paulus Storff, who thought himself indispensable for the progress of the work.[161] In the same year, he was already making maps and models of Munster towns and forts, and he stated that any place would fall in 48 hours, adding self-assertively that he could 'take presently' (immediately) the town and castle of Limerick.[162]

---

155 Memorandum to Sir Robert Byron (1665), *CSPI, 1663–5*, p. 705.   156 *Ormond*, n.s., iii, p. 227; Airy (ed.), *Essex papers 1672–5*, p. 59.   157 Essex to Arlington, 11 Feb. 1672; Airy (ed.), *Essex papers 1672–5*, p. 59.   158 Instructions to earl of Arran, 7 Jan. 1677, *Ormond*, n.s., iii, p. 85.   159 *Ormond*, ii, pp 312–33. See also his *Survey of Ireland* (NLI, MS 2557 and MS 3037).   160 *CSPI, 1666–9*, p. 390.   161 Captain Paulus Storff to Orrery, 19 Nov. 1672, *Orrery papers*, iii.   162 Francis Foulke to Countess of Orrery, 12 Aug. 1672, *Orrery papers*, iii, p. 105.

The building of Charles Fort resumed seriously in 1677, although now in accordance with the designs of the Surveyor-General William Robinson, assisted by Captain James Archer, with Orrery again playing a supervisory role. The designs were carried over by Robinson to the King in London to obtain royal approval.[163] Orrery, an enthusiastic promoter of Irish fortifications, had already erected three new citadels in the cities of Cork and Limerick.[164] Plans for the defence of Limerick castle were once again prepared in 1678 by Colonel Hervey.[165] The repair of Galway fort was undertaken in 1666,[166] necessitated again fourteen years later, when William Robinson made an estimate.[167] Sir William Armorer, governor of Duncannon Fort (Wexford), had his fort repaired in 1672.[168]

Little is known about the rebuilding of walls and gatehouses, whose architectural features offer a promising field for study. Dublin had outgrown its walls and consequently lacked any proper defence. In 1673, Essex, then Lord lieutenant, resurrected an older plan for the erection of a citadel, 'as ye towne grows more considerable, so ye reasons for it become still more pregnant (relevant)'.[169] He organised the arrival from England of Sir Bernard de Gomme, who made surveys of Dublin in 1673 and 1675,[170] designing a citadel so vast, and so prohibitively expensive, that it remained unbuilt, although hopes of its execution still lingered on in later years.[171]

The fortification of interior garrisons like Athlone and Charlemont attracted less attention from the authorities than the crucial coastline. However, periodic threats from tories intensified the focus on inland garrisons and forts. In 1666, a fort was erected at Belturbet (Cavan), costing £300.[172] An older fort at Charlemont (Armagh) saw variegated renovations after Viscount Conway became its governor in 1672. The work was supervised by the then inexperienced William Robinson,[173] and much of it collapsed the following year.[174] However, a decade later, Robinson was again requested to provide designs to fortify the place: once bitten, twice shy, he declined because the local soil would inevitably cause subsidence issues.[175]

163 Longford to Ormond, 8 Oct. 1678, *Ormond*, n.s., iii, p. 212. For Robinson's papers on Charles Fort, 1677–8, see BL, Add. MS 28,085. **164** Orrery to Essex, 4 June 1672; Airy (ed.), *Essex papers 1672–5*, p. 8. **165** William King to Ormond, 15 Nov. 1678, *Ormond*, n.s., iv, p. 235. **166** Robert Byron to Ormond, 3 Aug. 1666, *Ormond*, n.s., iii, p. 240. **167** Colonel Theodore Russell to Granard, 8 March 1680, *Ormond*, n.s., v, pp 600–1. **168** Essex to Arlington, 24 Dec. 1672, *CSPD, 1672–3*, p. 315. See also *CSPI, 1666–70*, pp 706–7. **169** Essex to Arlington, 8 July 1673, Airy (ed.), *Essex papers 1672–5*, p. 94. **170** H. Colvin, *A biographical dictionary of English architects 1660–1840* (London, 1954), p. 240; *CARD*, v, pp 566–73. **171** Arran to Ormond, 26 Jan. 1677, *Ormond*, n.s., iv, p. 95; Report by Thomas Phillips, *Ormond*, ii, p. 313. Petty also projected a plan to fortify Dublin in 1680, using wood for the defences (Marquis of Lansdowne (ed.), *The Petty papers* (1927), pp 62–70). **172** *CSPD, 1672*, p. 329, [July?] 1672. **173** William Robinson to Conway, 16 April 1673, *CSPD, 1673*, p. 148; William Robinson to Conway, 26 April, 1673, *CSPD, 1673*, p. 181. **174** Lord lieutenant to Conway, 21 Feb. 1674, *CSPD, 1673–5*, p. 175; J.J. Marshall, *History of Charlemont and Mountjoy Forts* (Dungannon, 1921); P. Tohall, 'Charlemont Fort, Co. Armagh', *Ir. Sword*, 3 (1957–8), pp 183–6. **175** Ormond to Arran, 9 Aug. 1683, *Ormond*, n.s., vii, p. 102; Ormond to Arran, 18 Aug. 1683, *Ormond*, n.s., vii, p. 108.

The periodic presence of foreign engineers like Storff and de Gomme in Ireland was notable. Their presence in Ireland becomes less remarkable once one realises that a similar situation prevailed in England.[176] Previous to the Irish rebellion, John Rosworme, a German, had worked in Ireland[177] and he was also active as a portrait painter.[178] A Danish engineer, very likely Captain Frederick Fieffe, arrived in December 1684.[179] An unidentified Italian engineer was working in Ireland in 1688.[180] Two English engineers crossed the Irish Channel in 1674. Andrew Yarranton surveyed ironworks, woods and lands and projected a citadel at Ringsend to protect Dublin harbour.[181] The better-known Sir Jonas Moore was one of many to make a model of the citadel of Dublin.[182] He also completed a survey of the Irish Ordnance stores, assisted by William Robinson.[183] During the Williamite War, many foreign engineers were employed; James II hired French engineers, while William III's army included a Dutch chief engineer, Meesters,[184] and numerous colleagues, mostly German and Danish.[185]

The layout of fortifications was influenced by existing design books. Information on their use in Ireland is scarce, but Ormond certainly had such works in his library.[186] Irish engineers went abroad to study fortifications. The Catholic James Archer, who supervised the work at Charles Fort, had been in the French service, and Ormond rated him as a more experienced engineer than William Robinson.[187] Robinson went to England several times, if not further afield, and he must have been familiar with foreign fortifications. In 1685, his fellow Surveyor-General, the scholar William Molyneux, was despatched by the Irish Government to take draughts of the most important fortifications in Flanders. During the greater part of his travels through Holland, Germany and France, he was accompanied by Lord Mountjoy,[188] then Master of the Ordnance in Ireland.

HOUSES AND CASTLES

The Irish poets and musicians, such as Dáibhí Ó Bruadair, Aogán Ó Rathaile and Turlough O'Carolan, visited mansions but they presented very few architectural

---

176 J.J. Murray, 'The cultural impact of the Flemish Low Countries on sixteenth and seventeenth-century England', *American Historical Review*, clxii (1957), pp 837–54, at p. 853. 177 *DNB*, xvii, pp 291–2; *CSPI, 1647–60*, p. 284; *CSPI, 1660–2*, p. 68. 178 William Montgomery of Rosemount had his portrait painted by Colonel Rosworm, 'an Hungarian': Hill (ed.), *Montgomery MSS*, p. 39. 179 Ormond to Dartmouth, 13 Sept. 1684, *11th Report* v, p. 121; King to Lord lieutenant, 6 Dec. 1684, *CSPD, 1684–5*, p. 238. 180 Philip Musgrave to Lord Dartmouth, 22 Nov. 1688, *CSPD, 1684–5*, p. 211. 181 *DNB*, xxi, pp 1199–1201; *CARD*, v, pp 573–6, for his 1674 report on Dublin Harbour. 182 *DNB*, xiii, pp 820–1. 183 RIA, MS H.iv.1 (May–July 1674). 184 N. Robb, *William of Orange 1674–1702* (London, 1966), ii, p. 317. 185 *DNB*, xvii, 184–5 on Wolfgang Romer; NLI, MS 2742, plan for Irish fortifications 1690 by Goubet; K. Danaher & J.G. Simms (eds), *The Danish force in Ireland 1690–1* (Dublin, 1962). 186 Ormond's library at Kilkenny Castle included a French work, *Perrot on fortifications* (J. Perrot, *Report on the state of Ireland*, 1581, BL, Stowe MS 159, f. 182) and *The King's works* [?] (*Ormond*, n.s., vii, pp 514–15). 187 Ormond to Orrery, 26 Jan. 1677, *6th Report*, 26 Jan. 1677, p. 731. 188 [Molyneux], *Sir Thomas Molyneux*, p. 30.

details.[189] Original drawings of the houses excel only in their rarity. Practically all known houses of this period were subsequently changed beyond recognition, ruined or simply erased from the landscape. Only in Beaulieu (Louth) does Ireland still possess a splendid survivor of a former abundance.

Fortunately, contemporary records show many details of these houses, and it is from these accounts that examples will be chiefly drawn. We should first imagine the contemporary landscape that served as a backdrop to these houses. The enclosed landscape of later centuries, with its myriad of fields, hedges and stonewalls, did not then exist. The landscape lay much more open and unenclosed, traversed by winding tracks and paths rather than roads.[190] Here the gentry erected their seats, developed demesnes and founded towns.[191]

The new houses were not concentrated in the Pale, but extended as far west as Kerry. Few lay in Connacht, and those few clustered close to the Shannon. Many midland counties (Limerick, Tipperary, Laois, Offaly, Westmeath, Cavan, Monaghan) contained remarkably few new seats. In Ulster, most houses were erected around Lough Neagh, together with a concentration in County Down. These counties had been allocated to the adventurers and soldiers during the Cromwellian settlement, while other counties (Dublin, Kildare, Carlow, Cork) were reserved for disposal by the government. Several houses were built in Dublin and Kildare, a fact that was not obvious to a contemporary writer.[192]

In occasional cases, the policy of settling and planting came in the form of a royal bounty, as when nobleman Sir Henry O'Neale was granted 600 oak trees to encourage him to build a house at Killyleagh.[193] O'Neale was among a handful of the old Gaelic stock restored to his estates; another was the soldier Daniel O'Neill, cousin of Eoghan Rua Ó Néill, who elected to use his substantial fortune to build Belsize House near London.[194] He was an exception; it was more usual that a wealthy Irish landowner owned both Irish and English seats. Ormond owned Moor Park (Hertfordshire) and possessed Marston Bigott (Somerset), while Viscount Conway had an English estate at Ragley (Warwickshire). These are only a few examples.[195] Especially in the case of Conway's Ragley estate in England, and his Irish estates at Lisburn and Portmore (Antrim), the same craftsmen were shuttled across the Irish

189 MacLysaght, *Irish life in the seventeenth century*, p. 100. 190 MacLysaght, *Irish life in the seventeenth century*, p. 8. 191 Petty (*Political anatomy of Ireland*, 1672) gives the following numbers and prices of houses: 2,500 houses with 7, 8 or 9 chimneys (cost £300); 700 houses with 10, 11 or 12 chimneys (cost £600); 400 houses with 13 to 20 chimneys (cost £1000); 20 houses with more than 20 chimneys total cost £78,000. In contrast, a common Irish cabin was worth five shillings or less (C. Hull (ed.), *The economic writings of Sir William Petty* (Cambridge, 1899), i, pp 142–3, 188). 192 [T. Monk], 'A descriptive account of the county of Kildare in 1682', *JKAS*, vi (1910), pp 339-46, at p. 343. 193 King to Lord lieutenant, 16 July 1666, *CSPI, 1666–9*, p. 156. 194 Evelyn visited and described Belsize House in 1676 (E. de Beer (ed.), *Diary of John Evelyn* (Oxford, 1955), iv, p. 92). 195 Other examples are: Lord Burlington who had Hugh May build Burlington House (Piccadilly, 1665); the Ranelaghs owned Chiswick (near London); Viscount Longford inherited East Clandon in Surrey; Sir Robert Southwell bought Kings Weston (near Bristol) in 1679; Lord Herbert of Cherbury owned two seats at Llyssyn and Lymore in Montgomeryshire, where he built after he had erected Castle Island (Kerry, 1671).

Channel. Not all landowners in Ireland, even if absentee, felt complete Englishmen. Conway exhibited a keen interest in Ireland and called it 'our country'.[196] Apart from their English country houses, many Irish noblemen retained townhouses in Dublin as well as in London.[197]

The 'improvement' of estates was widespread in the 1670s and 1680s. This is reflected in the money expended on improvements. Orrery reported in 1677 that he had laid out £20,000 'in building and parks and their improvement for the good of posterity'.[198] A wall surrounding the demesne at Hillsborough (Down) cost the considerable sum of £2,000. These amounts were outdone by the expense of building a wall around Phoenix Park, then a royal deerpark, for a whopping £7,890;[199] the wall was of such poor quality that immediate repairs were necessary to keep it standing.

Some landowners, notably Ormond and Thomond, held vast estates, leased to gentlemen upon 'fee-farm or quitrents and military tenures, by which they were obliged to follow their lord' into the field 'upon any occasion of hosting'.[200] These gentlemen often included building covenants in their leases, such as one to Donough O'Brien who had to enclose within seven years 'his parts of the outbounds with a double stone wall; to build a house of four couples [principal rafters] and two ends, with a double stone chimney'.[201] Ballyclough (Clare) was built by Henry Hickman on land leased from Viscount Clare in 1668 (Figure 4.8).[202] The new Irish landowners preferred English tenants, although experienced landowners such as Ormond considered that husbandry could not be carried out without the aid of 'very many Popish tenants'.[203] In many other ways, landowners were mainly oriented towards England and English manners. Orrery repaired his castle at Castlemartyr (Cork) to make it 'English-like',[204] while the earl of Barrymore, himself of Old Irish stock, called Conway's estate at Lisburn 'the best and most absolute English-like plantation in this kingdom'.[205] A lease for the building of a house in Belfast stipulated that it should be a 'good handsome English-like house'.[206] Leases included occasional statements that the tenant should plough in the English manner or 'preserve the underwood in the English manner'.[207] Irish names of places had English ones substituted. Orrery changed Rathgogan to Charleville, Conway's Lisnegarvey became Lisburn, and Perceval preferred Egmont to Ballymacow.

196 Conway to Rawdon, 29 Oct. 1667, Bramhall (ed.), *Rawdon papers*, p. 231.   **197** Ormond had a house at St James Square; Viscount Longford owned a mansion in the fashionable quarter of Whitefriars; Viscount Conway had a house built in Queen Street. His friend Viscount Ranelagh erected a house at Chelsea. Petty leased a house in Piccadilly in 1673.   **198** Rawdon to Conway, 4 April 1668, *CSPI, 1666–9*, p. 589.   **199** Account by earl of Anglesey, 1666, *CSPI, 1666–9*, p. 258.   **200** Carte, *Ormond*, iv, p. 212. The same was true for the gentleman-tenants of Viscount Conway.   **201** Lease by Murrough, earl of Inchiquin to Donough O'Brien, 28 April 1663 in J. Ainsworth (ed.), *Inchiquin manuscripts* (Dublin, 1961), p. 359. See also pp 364–5, 367, 387–8 for similar leases. Shirley & Graves, 'Dineley', p. 189.   **202** Ibid., p. 193.   **203** Ormond to Ossory, 23 April 1679, *Ormond*, n.s., v, p. 61.   **204** K. Lynch, *Roger Boyle, first earl of Orrery* (Knoxville, TN, 1965), p. 201.   **205** Barrymore to Ranelagh, 25 Oct. 1677, *CSPD, 1677–8*, p. 445.   **206** C. Brett, *Buildings of Belfast 1700–1914* (London, 1967).   **207** Ainsworth (ed.), *Inchiquin manuscripts*, pp 364, 387.

Figure 4.8 'Ballyclogh Castle', County Clare, drawn by Thomas Dineley in 1685. Note the high quality ironmongery on the exterior door, capped by an anti-intruder top, and the balcony casement above the main door. 'Ballynacloghy' Castle, near Sixmilebridge, was the property of Teige M'Glanshy in 1570. The Meic Fhlannchadha (McClancys) were hereditary lawyers to the O'Briens of Thomond. Ballyclough passed out of Clancy possession in the late sixteenth century. After a Cromwellian interlude, Sir Donat O'Brien reacquired Ballyclough, renamed it Stone Hall, and settled it on his sons by his second marriage. This family later removed to Blatherwyche Park in Northamptonshire (demolished in 1948), where a large stable building survives bearing the inscription 'DOB 1770' (Donatus O'Brien). Ballyclough Castle has now disappeared and only some ruins of the later dwelling-house are extant (NLI).

Defensive considerations

Big Houses often stood as isolated islands in a hostile sea of Irish inhabitants, especially when located far from English garrisons. Irish landowners, once their estates were forfeited, turned into tories, and started to rob houses. This became a grave threat to the landlords, as expressed by Lord lieutenant Essex in 1673: 'As for ye robberys committed, they doe dayly increase, and are, I confess, grown too such an height [that they] look almost like petit [small] rebellions, they going by 20 or 30 in a company, breaking open houses even in ye day time'.[208] Lord Herbert, who had built Castleisland (Kerry) in 1671, considered that he was living in 'a country wild and barbarous by reason of the ill ways to it and the dangerous inhabitants'.[209]

1673 marked a climax in robberies, as in the north many inhabitants fled their houses and flocked to the towns to escape the tories.[210] In the following years, reports again flooded in about robberies, only alleviated for short intervals due to individual and later organised campaigns that killed local tories.[211] One gentleman, describing his sporting amusements, noted casually that 'we have not had more success in any sport than Tory hunting'.[212] Tories were interested in valuable contents.[213] Some

208 Essex to Charles II, 1 Dec. 1673, Airy (ed.), *Essex papers 1672–5*, pp 147–8. **209** [Lord Herbert] to anon., 1673, Smith (ed.), *Herbert correspondence*, p. 214. **210** 17 Dec. 1673, *CSPD, 1673–5*, p. 62. **211** Rawdon to Conway, 12 Dec. 1676, *CSPD, 1676–7*, p. 451. The militia played a role in suppressing tories. **212** Sir William Stewart to Ormond, 17 March 1682, *Ormond*, n.s., vi, p. 544.

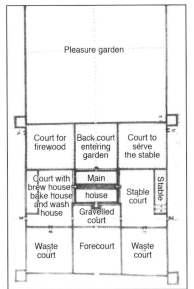
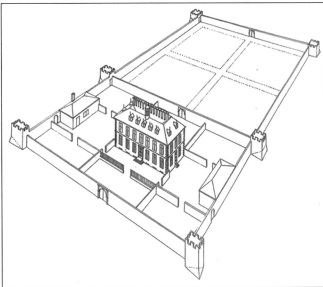

Figure 4.9 Proposed plan by Thomas Smith of Burton House and gardens, County Cork, 1671: redrawn by Matthew Stout (British Library) (left). Reconstructed isometric view of Burton House, County Cork in 1670 as devised from the original plan by Rolf Loeber in 1972 (right).

houses withstood their attacks, such as Lord Aungier's house at Longford, attacked by a band of tories, who burned the village.[214] Other seats were less fortunate, sometimes being forced to surrender. This happened to William Petty's Killowen House in distant west Kerry, which finally fell to the Irish in 1687.

Understandably, the tory threat impacted on the design of country mansions. While early seventeenth-century castles still sprouted pistol holes, corner turrets, corbelled galleries or machicolations, these disappeared in mid century. Instead, Big Houses were built which lacked defensive characteristics, except for their heavy doors with spyholes, iron bars on the windows of the first floor,[215] and the 'firelock musquets' of the inhabitants.[216] A notable fortified house was Charleville (Cork), designed by the gentleman-architect Orrery in 1661. It consisted of living quarters on one side of a walled court with flankers, defended by sixteen guns.

The lack of defensive capabilities was compensated for by the erection of curtain walls around or in front of the house (Figures 4.8–4.9).[217] The development of this arrangement from early seventeenth-century examples was the placement of a house in the artisan mannerist style within the enclosure.[218] The defensive purpose

213 Orrery to Ormond, 22 Nov. 1678, *Ormond*, n.s., iv, p. 21. Tories interfered with the building of the bridge at Carrick-on-Suir.   **214** *CSPI, 1666–9*, pp 158–9.   **215** As at Burton House (BL, Add. MS 46947 B-734C).   **216** Sir George Lane, then Lord Lanesborough, had twelve 'firelock musquets' at Rathcline (Longford) in 1684 (*Fourteenth report*, app. vii, p. 390).   **217** Siting an undefended house within the protective embrace of a bawn harked back to an older tradition of building (Jope, 'Moyry, Charlemont', pp 97–123).   **218** The projected enclosures for the pleasure garden at Burton (Cork) measured 216 feet x 248 feet (65.8m x 75.6m) and 248 feet x 248 feet (75.6m x 75.6m) (BL, Egmont papers, Add. MS, 46958c, 7 Feb. 1670–1, Proposed plan of Burton House by Thomas Smith).

Figure 4.10 Killyleagh Castle, County Down (NLI).

of these enclosures is unquestionable. The one at Killyleagh Castle (Down, 1666) still has merlons (the solid upright section of a battlement in medieval architecture or fortifications, sometimes pierced by narrow, vertical slits designed for observation and fire), each with a gun hole, behind which runs a narrow wall walk (Figure 4.10). Sometimes, as at Burton House (Cork, Figure 4.9) and Rathcline (Longford), the enclosures consisted of two square walled spaces,[219] one containing the house, the other the pleasure garden. This design required significant outlays; the two enclosures at Burton House measured 464 feet in length, with a breadth of 248 feet (141m x 76m).[220] In many cases, including Burton and Rathcline, both enclosures had turrets on each corner. Apart from external defences at Burton House, there was also internal ones: 'eyther of the four doors of the maine house may be defended from two turretts', in the case of a surprise attack.[221] To make this inward defence possible, the walls surrounding the different courts within the enclosure were intended to be only 7 feet high (2.1m), while the outer walls were designed to be 13 feet (4m) in height between the turrets (Figure 4.9). The defensive importance of

219 The thickness of the walls is not taken into account in these measurements.   **220** Burton House probably had turrets on the far side of the pleasure garden: the manuscript (BL, Egmont papers, Add. MS 46958c) is damaged here.   **221** Two more entrances were added later to the projected plan.

Figure 4.11 Shane's Castle, County Antrim, formerly called Edencarrickduff, is located near Randalstown, on the shores of Lough Neagh. This 1780 watercolour is by John Nixon (1750–1818). The ruins are used as a location in the TV series *Game of Thrones* (RIA/009/B).

these turrets cannot be underestimated, and this is also clear from the restoration of the turrets at Lisburn Castle (Antrim) in 1665.[222]

While only one entrance to the enclosure existed at some seats, like Ballyclough (Clare, Figure 4.7) and Killyleagh (Down, Figure 4.10),[223] some had more, which rendered the defensive aspect less pertinent. Rathcline had three entrances and Burton House at least four.[224] These entrances were occasionally adorned with classical surrounds.[225]

Building covenants for gentlemen tenants stipulated a 'double stone wall' around the house. In other cases, regulations were drawn up to 'enclose at least an acre (0.4ha) of ground with a good stone wall or a double ditch'.[226] Many country houses – Springhill (near Moneymore, Derry)[227] and Old Court (near Bray, Wicklow) – had walled enclosures.[228] These were not necessarily erected of stone: Beaulieu (Louth) was surrounded by a 12-foot (3.7m) hedge or palisade,[229] while Killowen (Kerry) was ensconced within a clay enclosure.[230] However, in a few houses, traces of enclosures have not yet been found, such as at Kilcreene (Kilkenny) and Eyrecourt (Galway).

---

222 George Rawdon to Conway, 2 Sept. 1665, *CSPI, 1663–5*, p. 636.   223 Killyleagh Castle had one of the largest bawns, measuring 100 x 50 yards (91m x 46m) (A.H. Rowan, 'Killyleagh Castle, Co. Down', *Country Life*, 19 & 26 March, 2 April & 9 April 1970).   224 BL, Egmont papers, Add. MS 46958c.   225 For example, at Rathcline (Longford, now incomplete).   226 Lease by Colonel Daniel O'Brien to Bryen Hanraghane, 1 May 1667 in Ainsworth (ed.), *Inchiquin manuscripts*, pp 364–5.   227 M. Bence-Jones, 'Springhill', *Irish Times*, 2 July 1963.   228 J. Burke, *A visitation of the seats of the noblemen and gentlemen of Great Britain and Ireland*, second series, 2 vols (London, 1853), ii, p. 166.   229 D. Guinness & W. Ryan, *Irish houses and castles* (London, 1971), pp 242–3.   230 Killowen House was encompassed by a clay wall 14 feet (4.3m) high and 12 feet (3.7m) thick, with flankers 'in the manner of an irregular pentagon': E. FitzMaurice, *The life of Sir William Petty 1623–1687* (London, 1895), p. 289.

The latter house in particular, lying far out in the west, across the Shannon, had remarkably flimsy defensive capabilities.

Some large houses, such as Blessington (Wicklow) and Portmore (Antrim), never had enclosures. Rather, their security was guaranteed through the quartering of soldiers in the direct neighbourhood,[231] or by having them sleep in the house.[232] These measures were not immediately necessary for inhabited older Irish seats, like Bunratty (Clare) and Carrigogunnel (Limerick), and numerous small keeps, which maintained their earlier defences. Besides the erection of new houses, old castles received additions, such as Ross Castle (Kerry), which was finished in 1688,[233] and Ballyclough (Clare, Figure 4.7). The rebuilding of Ballykit (Clare) comprised the incorporation of the old castle into the new house, whereas the ancient keep was retained at the rear at a new seat at Tourin (Waterford).[234] Ancient castles like Kilkenny, Lismore and Shane's Castle could be so completely renovated as to entirely lose their defensive characteristics (Figures 3.8, 4.11).[235] The Moore family lived in old abbeys at Mellifont (Louth) and Monasterevan (Kildare), restored as a dwelling house in 1661.[236]

House plans

The once popular rectangular plan of the early seventeenth century, with its flankers on the corners, as at Kanturk (Cork) and Portumna (Galway), declined in favour in the middle of the seventeenth century.[237] The same fate befell the Greek cross plan, on which houses such as Ichtermurragh (Cork) and Castle Raw (Armagh) were built.[238] Instead, the simple rectangular plan was preferred in the last half of the seventeenth century. As part of the rectangular plan, some houses had a projecting frontispiece, set in the centre of the front façade, as at Eyrecourt (Galway) and Carton (Kildare). At Beaulieu (Louth), two projecting frontispieces were employed, not in the centre but on the extremes of the house.[239] The older H-plan, as at Oldbawn (Dublin, 1635, Figure 4.12),[240] was little imitated, except at Boyle's seat at Blessington (Wicklow), and at the late seventeenth-century Finnebrogue (Down).[241] On the other hand, Loughlinstown (Dublin), Platten Hall

---

231 In the case of many houses with enclosures, garrisons were quartered in neighbouring towns.   232 Richard Mildmay to Conway, 31 Jan. 1683, *CSPD, 1683*, p. 36. Four soldiers were quartered in Portmore at that time.   233 E. MacLysaght (ed.), *The Kenmare manuscripts* (Dublin, 1942), p. 404. The wing had two storeys, each of four bays (NLI, MS map 16.H.8 (12)).   234 Additions were erected to the castle at Doneraile (Cork) before 1690, after the castle had been destroyed in 1641 (I am indebted for this information to Lady Doneraile).   235 Shane's Castle (Antrim) was possibly rebuilt in the same period. Lismore Castle (Waterford) was made habitable by the first earl of Burlington, after it had been destroyed in 1645 (M. Girouard, 'Lismore Castle, Co. Waterford, I', *Country Life*, 6 Aug. 1964, pp 336-40, at p. 340).   236 J. Tighe, *Moore Abbey* (n.p., n.d.), pp 1–3. Richard Nugent, earl of Westmeath, resided at the old priory at Fore (Westmeath).   237 A notable exception was Old Carton, where four towers were placed on both sides of the house rather than the corners.   238 Jope, 'Moyry, Charlemont'; Waterman, 'Irish seventeenth-century houses'; and Leask, 'early seventeenth-century houses'.   239 Burton House (Cork), Eyrecourt (Galway), Beaulieu (Louth) and Old Carton (Kildare).   240 Leask, 'early seventeenth-century houses', p. 250.   241 Dunmore (Kilkenny) had the plan of an incomplete H.

Figure 4.12 Oldbawn House, near Tallaght, County Dublin (Peter Walsh).

(Meath), Richhill (Armagh) and Kilcreene (Kilkenny) were all built on U-plans, although these differed in the length of the legs of the U.

The size of houses varied greatly and they can be differentiated into three groups. Blessington (eleven bays) and Dunmore (Kilkenny) were among the largest.[242] A group of smaller but still considerable country houses consisted of Old Carton (Kildare), Richhill (Armagh) (Figure 4.13) and Finnebrogue (Down).[243] A group of smaller houses was formed by Burton (Cork), Eyrecourt (Galway) and Beaulieu (Louth), each of seven bays.[244] Killowen (Kerry) was the smallest of all, measuring only 13.4m x 13.4m.

Elevations and roofs

Apart from their plans and sizes, the late seventeenth-century houses also differed considerably from earlier houses in their elevations. Whereas Jacobean houses had large windows, those built between 1660 and 1690 had smaller window openings. Furthermore, there was a distinct shift towards symmetry, and, most important of all, the use of classical details on the exteriors. For the first time in Ireland, a

---

242 The old house at Thomastown (Tipperary, 1670) was very large with its fifteen bays.   **243** Old Carton measured 95 feet x 55 feet (29.0m x 16.8m), Richhill 98 feet x 50 feet (29.9m x 15.2m), and Finnebrogue (with its nine bays) 88 feet x 58 feet (26.8m x 17.7m).   **244** Burton, as projected in 1670, measured 76 feet x 57 feet (23.2m x 17.4m) (*Egmont*, ii, p, 22). Eyrecourt measures 23.9m x 18.7m. The dimensions of Beaulieu are 20.7m x 16.1m.

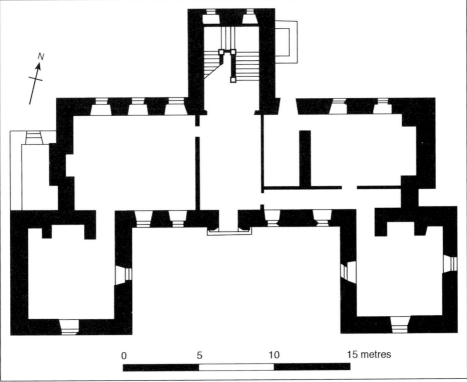

Figure 4.13 Richhill, County Armagh: photograph and plan.

pediment became a regular feature above the frontispiece, as at Eyrecourt and Carton (decorated with a coat of arms). The pediment was not applied everywhere, as one can judge from Beaulieu, Kilcreene and Blessington, although these houses still exemplified classical ideas. They share the regular placing of wall openings (windows, doors), always totalling to an odd number, so that the front door could be placed in the centre of the building. Moreover, these houses invariably had high-pitched roofs sprinkled with dormers, features that only faded from Ireland at the beginning of the Georgian era. A particular feature of the roof could be a lantern, which, in the case of Burton (Cork), had a copper ball on top of it, 3 feet (0.9m) in diameter.[245]

The roofs of country houses can be distinguished into three types. Hip-roofed houses (Figure 4.9) were often sprocketed (slightly curved at the base), giving the houses a frivolous elegance (Figures 4.4–4.5).[246] Projecting roof rims were supported by gracefully curved cantilevers.[247] The chimneystacks were usually executed in brick and frequently adorned with recessed panels.[248] The second roof type employed Holborn gables ('Dutch billies'), which embellished Echlinville (Down) and they are still extant at Waringstown (Down) and Richhill (Armagh). This style of gable was not used outside Ulster in the late seventeenth century. The third roof type was in gabled houses, relatively simple houses with two large gables at each end. Mosstown and Fermoyle (both Longford), Belan (Kildare) and Ballykit (Clare) were of this type.

Classical façades were based on architectural pattern books, published in Italy, France and Holland.[249] Although information on actual use of these books in Ireland is lacking, Ormond had in his library Rubens' *Palazzi di Genova* (1622). [250] Lady Anne Conway read Wotton's *The elements of architecture* and very likely also Vitruvius's *Dieci libri dell' architettura*.[251] Although she was not a regular visitor to Ireland, she advised on the building of one of her husband's seats there.[252] Her portrait by the Dutch painter Samuel van Hoogstraten showed her in a symbolic setting dominated by classical features, emphasising a highly sophisticated sense of contemporary architecture (Figure 4.14).

245 Thomas Smith to John Perceval, 31 Jan. 1681–2, BL, Add. MS 46946A, MS 13096.   **246** As at Eyrecourt (Galway) and Kilcreene (Kilkenny).   **247** At Eyrecourt, Beaulieu and Kilkenny Castle (removed in the nineteenth century).   **248** As at Richhill (Armagh), Kilcreene (Kilkenny) and Old Carton (Kildare). An early seventeenth-century example was Brazeel (earlier called Corduffe) House (near Swords in north Dublin, demolished 1978).   **249** S. Serlio, *Tutte l'opera d'architetura et prospetiva* (Venice, 1584); J.A. du Cerceau, *Les trois livres d'architecure*, 3 v. (Paris, 1559–82); P.P. Rubens, *Pallazzi di Genova* (Genoa, 1613) and P. Vingboons, *Af beeldsels der voornaamste gebouwen*, 2 v. (Amsterdam, 1648–74).   **250** Catalogue of the books of Ormond at Kilkenny Castle, 6 Jan. 1685, *Ormond*, n.s., vii, pp 514–15.   **251** Anne Conway to her father-in-law, [after Sept. 1651], M. Nicholson (ed.), *Conway letters* (London, 1930), p. 17. Henry Wotton, *The elements of architecture*, appeared in London in 1624. Vitruvius's book was published in Rome in 1567.   **252** Lady Conway to her husband, 15 April 1659 in Nicholson (ed.), *Conway letters*.

Figure 4.14 Oil painting of Lady Anne Conway by the Dutch painter Samuel van Hoogstraten. Lady Anne Conway (née Finch) (1631–79) married Edward, third Viscount Conway, in 1651. He was heir to estates in Warwickshire and County Antrim, but their only child died in infancy. The couple owned one of the finest private libraries of the period. A convert to Quakerism, she was among the tiny minority of seventeenth-century women who pursued an interest in philosophy. Her book *Principia philosophiae antiquissimae et recentissimae de Deo, Christo et creatura id est de materia et spiritu in genere* was published posthumously in Amsterdam in 1690 (Foundation Johan Maurits van Nassau, Den Haag, Nederlands).

English influence

Intensive relations with England exerted a more direct influence on Irish architecture. Many English craftsmen obtained letters of denization in Ireland, among them the bricklayer, Richard Mills,[253] who concluded a contract to erect Sir Jerome Alexander's building at Trinity College, Dublin in 1672.[254] He later became assistant to the master of the city works, in which capacity he was involved with several buildings in Dublin.[255] Mills was one of only four English bricklayers to obtain letters of denization. They were part of a larger group of twenty-three glaziers, carpenters, masons and plasterers who arrived from England between 1664 and 1673.[256] Not all the English craftsmen coming over to Ireland stayed permanently. William Hurlbut, who later built Ragley (Warwickshire) after the designs of Dr Robert Hooke, visited Ireland at least once with three workmen to work at the enormous stable at Portmore.[257] His patron, Lord Conway, was an amateur architect himself, and Hurlbut likely left his mark on his Irish houses.[258]

The scientist-architect Robert Hooke was employed by Sir Robert Southwell in England.[259] Although it is unlikely that Hooke ever actually set foot in Ireland, Southwell encouraged him to advise Sir John Perceval, who was then building Burton House (Cork).[260] Perceval made several recommendations, 'because upon inquiery here in London, I find ye fashion to have ye doores of roomes as much as may be in ye corners of ye roomes'.[261] At Kilkenny Castle, piers were constructed in 1681, probably for the water house, for which Hugh May was consulted, who in turn sought the opinion of Christopher Wren.[262] Wren may have been involved at the Royal Chapel of Dublin Castle, on which English craftsmen were employed. Irish architects, notably William Robinson, periodically visited England, where they presumably met their colleagues,[263] and visited new buildings in London and the country. Robinson's designs for the Royal Works were usually sent over to England for approval by the king, who undoubtedly was advised in these matters by leading

---

253 W. Shaw (ed.), *Letters of denization and Acts of naturalisation for aliens in England and Ireland 1603–1700* (Lymington, 1911), p. 344; letter of denization, 25 April 1671.   **254** TCD, V MUN lc, General Registry, vol. iii, f. 157.   **255** Craig, *Dublin*, pp 75, 78, 112, where his name appears in relation to the workhouse (1703), Molyneux House (1706) and the tower of the Royal Chapel of St Matthews (1713).   **256** Shaw (ed.), *Letters of denization*, listed thirteen carpenters: John Baily, Michael Banes, William Barloe, John Cook, Thomas Goughton, Edward Hopkins, Hugh Kender; James Levesley, William Longwood, Thomas Piggott, Solomon Sample, John Street and Thomas West; five bricklayers: Thomas Collins, Thomas Crane, John Hearne, Richard Mills and Jeoffrey Reeves; three glaziers: John Beard, George Colvert and Daniel Halgan; two masons: Anthony Drunton and William Johnson; three plasterers: Ralphe Bayly, Robert Mullenax (Molyneux) and Peter Nicholas; and one joiner: Eusebius Creeke.   **257** William Temple to Conway, 29 June 1671, *CSPD, 1671*, p. 349.   **258** Conway to Sir Edward Harley, 22 Nov. 1677, *14th Report*, app. ii, p. 357; Conway to Sir Edward Harley, 5 May 1683, *Fourteenth report*, app. ii, p. 374.   **259** M. Espinasse, *Robert Hooke* (London, 1956), p. 99.   **260** Robert Southwell to Robert Hooke, 4 March 1682, *Egmont*, ii, pp 108–9.   **261** John Perceval to anon., 25 Feb. 1682, BL, Add. MS 46946c, MS 13096.   **262** Longford to Ormond, 27 Dec. 1681, *Ormond*, n.s., vi, pp 282–3.   **263** In William Robinson's case, this is hard to substantiate. Although it is certain that he was in England several times, he does not appear in the diaries of John Evelyn, Robert Hooke and Samuel Pepys, nor is he mentioned in connection with Wren.

English architects, adding another source of foreign influence on Irish architecture. Only one Irishman reached the Surveyor General's office in England; this was the poet Sir John Denham, who lacked any technical architectural knowledge,[264] and to whom no building can be ascribed with certainty.

Windows and door surrounds

Among notable architectural features are window surrounds. These were sometimes executed simply as plaster rustication (a range of masonry techniques designed to furnish visible surfaces with a finish that contrasts in texture with the smoothly finished, squared-block masonry surfaces called ashlar),[265] or in delicately rubbed brick of very high quality as at Beaulieu,[266] together with string-courses that enclose the house firmly. At Beaulieu, the windows on the side façade are grouped, thus avoiding monotony. Windows in these houses were small as compared with their predecessors,[267] and built of wood rather than stone, as at Eyrecourt (Galway), where they were of the transom-and-mullion type, decorated externally with carvings.[268] Occasionally, very tall windows were projected, as at Burton (Cork), which were to be ten feet (3.1m) high.[269] Although pediments above windows did not occur at any known country house constructed between 1660 and 1690, they had been used earlier[270] and they were applied to crown two side doors at Beaulieu, supported by pilasters.

The surrounds of the front doors often exhibited mannerist details in their capitals,[271] deviating from strictly classical rules. Front doors were frequently surmounted by either a scroll[272] or a segmented pediment.[273] An exception was the classical surround of the front door at Killyleagh (Down), which was topped by heavy but elegant strap work, flanked by two lions (replaced in the nineteenth century).[274] As a general rule, front doors were taller than in later Georgian examples. Two features, recurrent in English country houses, have not yet been discovered: platforms on the roof 'for the pleasure of the prospect, [and] walk'[275] as the English gentleman-architect Sir Roger Pratt described it, were absent in Irish country houses.[276] Having a fine prospect was considered an asset when judging country houses. After passing Eyrecourt in 1691, the soldier John Stevens

264 Colvin, *Biographical dictionary of English architects*, pp 171–2.   **265** The plaster rustication at Eyrecourt is original. This type also appeared at Kilkenny Castle.   **266** The bricks are thinly pointed.   **267** The windows of Eyrecourt measure 2m x 1.6m.   **268** The remains of the wooden frames still show marks where the transom and mullions were attached, which were later replaced by sash windows. Kilkenny Castle also had transom and mullion windows. The carved decoration on the Eyrecourt windows is repeated on parts of its staircase (now in Detroit).   **269** William Kenn to John Perceval, 3 Aug. 1665, *Egmont*, ii, pp 14–5.   **270** The early seventeenth-century Killenure (Tipperary) had pedimented dormers (Waterman, 'Irish seventeenth-century houses', p. 256).   **271** See the front doors of Beaulieu and Eyrecourt.   **272** Kilkenny Castle and the stable of Ralahine (Clare).   **273** Beaulieu.   **274** I am indebted for this information to Lt.-Col. D.A. Rowan-Hamilton. Parts of the old surround are now incorporated in a garden wall at Killyleagh Castle.   **275** R. Gunther, *The architecture of Sir Roger Pratt* (Oxford, 1928), p. 253.   **276** A drawing of the grand entrance to Dublin Castle, probably by William Robinson, shows a balustraded platform on the roof (Figure 4.5, this volume, p. 173).

complained: 'the house large with a pleasant wood in the back of it; but no good prospect any way, nor any river near it'.[277]

Giant pilasters were not applied on the façades of Irish houses (they were first used at the Royal Hospital, Kilmainham). However, at Clonmannon (Wicklow), a small house can be found, possibly dating to the late seventeenth century,[278] where Doric pilasters were placed on the front, of much reduced proportions. These rest upon a rusticated ground floor, the whole executed in brick of a warm colour, a design more Palladian than Caroline, and among the first of its kind to appear in Ireland. The absence of giant pilasters and platforms, however, does not make late seventeenth-century Irish houses that much different from their English counterparts. Most Irish examples of the artisan mannerist style reflect the English tradition of building at the time, although they tended to be built somewhat later than in England.

Brick, shingles and glass

Brick was not often used as the main building material, except at Blessington. At Eyrecourt, local bricks were used for the inner walling, while rubble covered by plaster was employed for the exterior.[279] Late seventeenth-century Irish bricks usually measured 8.25 inches x 4 inches x 2 inches (210mm x 102mm x 51mm) but this could vary.[280] They were often fired near the site of the house. More commonly, houses were built of rubble, or hewn stone, from a quarry in the direct neighbourhood.[281] Similarly, although Ireland imported Norway timber for building construction, the timber for many houses was obtained from adjacent woods.[282] The condition of Irish woods steadily deteriorated during the seventeenth century, caused by extensive cutting for the ironworks and the scarring of live trees for tanning. Much timber was also destroyed for shingling,[283] then a regular roofing material. To reduce the use of shingling, the manufacture of pantiles was promoted by the issue of special patent in 1667.[284] Other roofing materials were slate and thatch: some gentry in counties Cork and Limerick lived in 'thatched houses'.[285] Thatching of larger houses was common in the planters' houses of the north. Waringstown (Down) and several other houses originally had thatched roofs.[286]

277 R. Murray (ed.), *The journal of John Stevens containing a brief account of the war in Ireland 1689–91* (Oxford, 1912), p. 203.   **278** Craig & Knight of Glin, *Ireland observed*, p. 32.   **279** Castleisland (Kerry) was also plastered on the outside.   **280** The irregularly shaped bricks of Eyrecourt measured 8.25 inches x inches 4 x 2 inches (210mm x 102mm x 51mm); those at Beaulieu, 8.25 inches x inches 4 x 1.5 inches (210mm x 102mm x 32mm) and those at Killyleagh Castle, 8 inches x 3.5 inches x 2 inches (203mm x 89mm x 51mm).   **281** Well-known quarries were located near the Phoenix House (Dublin), near Charleville (Cork), and near Lisburn Castle (Antrim).   **282** John Brodrick to Captain Kenn and Lieutenant Greene, 25 June 1662, *Orrery papers*, pp 22–3.   **283** George Rawdon to Conway, 8 May 1678, *CSPD, 1678*, p. 165.   **284** Patent to Sir John Stephens and others to make pantiles in 1667, *CSPI, 1666–69*, p. 285. A pantile is a clay-fired roof tile, S-shaped and single lap – the end of a tile laps only the course immediately below it (flat tiles normally lap two courses). A pantile-covered roof is notably lighter than its flat-tiled equivalent and it can be laid to a lower pitch.   **285** Barrymore to Ormond, 24 Sept. 1680, *Ormond*, n.s., v, p. 432.   **286** Ulster Architectural Heritage Society, *List of historic buildings in the area of Craigavon within the Moira Rural District* (Belfast, 1969), p. 6. In the same publication, see also Grange (1668) (p. 7), and Berwick Hall (*c.*1700) (p. 10).

Obviously, glass for windows could not easily be obtained in the countryside, and it had to be transported from bigger cities, such as Cork.[287] Already in 1656 and again in 1665, Sir George Rawdon considered establishing a glass manufacture at Lisburn for the production of bottles and window panes (mirror glass is not mentioned).[288] Five years later, a small glass works was established in Portarlington (Laois),[289] while Dublin counted several glassmakers by that time. In 1672, Sir George Rawdon could write that 'Gabriell is as good a glasier as can be had anywhere', and that 'glass may be gott as well in Ireland',[290] implying that the import of glass from England was frequent before that date.

Window frames were also sent over from Chester in 1653 for John Perceval's buildings.[291] The import of building materials from England covered a wide variety, from nails,[292] to 'linseed and colours' to elm planks.[293] After the pulling down of Conway Castle in Wales, Conway had thirty-three tons of its lead transported to Lisburn Castle for use there.[294] At Kilkenny Castle, Purbeck pavement was installed, similarly carried over from England.[295] The import of these building materials was to some extent reciprocated by the export of timber (and also marble) from Ireland to England after the great fire of London in 1666.[296]

Interiors

Except for plans of the interiors at Beaulieu and Kilcreene, little is known of the arrangement of rooms in late seventeenth-century houses. Both houses lack a double-pile arrangement of rooms. Beaulieu is characterised by its great hall in the centre, taking up two storeys; its staircases were set in the back of the building.[297] Kilcreene, on the other hand, had a one-storey hall, similar to that at Eyrecourt. Only at Kilcreene were the stairs placed in the centre of the house at the sides of the hall.[298] In most buildings, the living quarters were on the first floor, although there was a piano nobile at Eyrecourt, taking up the second floor.[299]

In some houses, inner walls were erected of wood, a practice more common for earlier Jacobean and Elizabethan buildings.[300] A carved staircase often formed the

---

287 Thomas Herbert to Lord Herbert, 22 Feb. 1659, Smith (ed.), *Herbert correspondence*, p. 157.   288 George Rawdon to Conway, 5 April 1656, *CSPI, 1647–60*, p. 602; Rawdon to Conway, 4 July 1665, *CSPI, 1663–5*, p. 602.   289 Robert Leigh to Arlington, 14 Nov. 1670, *CSPI, 1669–70*, pp 301–2.   290 George Rawdon to Conway, 5 June 1672, PRO, S.P. 63/331, 80.   291 Valentine Savage to John Perceval, 2 Dec. 1653, *Egmont*, i, p. 528. Probably for Castlewarden (Kildare). See also *Egmont*, ii, p. 15.   292 PRO, S.P. 63/331, p. 80.   293 William Kenn to John Perceval, 3 Aug. 1665, *Egmont*, ii, p. 15.   294 *CSPD, 1664–5*, pp 536 & 636; *CSPI, 1663–5*, p. 692.   295 Captain John Baxter to Captain George Mathew, 19 Aug. 1683, *Ormond*, n.s., vii, p. 110.   296 *CSPD*, 17 Oct. 1667.   297 One staircase was replaced, probably on the same site.   298 I am indebted for this information to Dr H.J. Roche. The late seventeenth-century Richhill (Armagh) has a projecting staircase at the rear of the house.   299 This can be concluded from the magnificent stairs leading up to it, in conjunction with the presence of the wainscot decoration on the second-floor landing, while the first floor hall is relatively bare. The doors coming out on the landing of the second floor were very tall double ones (2.7m x 1.5m, and 2.7m x 1.2m). Burton House, as originally planned, also had a *piano nobile*, later abandoned for a first-floor arrangement.   300 As at Burton (Cork) and probably at Eyrecourt (Galway).

Figure 4.15 Wooden chimney piece from Oldbawn House, County Dublin (National Museum).

main centrepiece. The one at Dunmore (Kilkenny) was 'so large that twenty men might walk abreast'.[301] Burton once had a smaller staircase of elmwood imported from Bristol, which was to be cut through in 'leaves and antics' following London examples.[302] One masterpiece of carving has survived, originally at Eyrecourt (Galway) but now crated at the Detroit Institute of Arts.[303] This massive staircase (Figure 4.16), delicately carved in oak, has two flights ascending commodiously to a common landing, where it united to form one flight leading up to the second floor. While ascending the stairs, one had ample opportunity to rest upon any of the three landings in between, and to enjoy the curling wave of leaves of the balustrades, flaming down from two long-nosed masks upstairs. The staircase is adorned with an exuberance of masks, some hidden among the acanthus leaves and strap work. They carry ferocious expressions, glaring at the powerless spectator, and they are undoubtedly precursors to the masks used in eighteenth-century Irish furniture. In contrast with all the movements of the acanthus foliage are the twenty-eight unruffled flower pots, also carved in oak, crowning each newel. Although England is rich in similar staircases, some carved by Edward Pearce or Grinling Gibbons, this Irish example excels in its exuberance.[304] Whereas the staircases at Beaulieu and

301 T.J. Clohosey, 'Dunmore House', *Old Kilkenny Review*, iv (1951), pp 44-8, at p. 47.
302 William Kenn to John Perceval, 3 Aug. 1665, *Egmont*, ii, pp 14–15. A later version of the stairs at Burton House was to have a 'strong raile, hand raile, posts, heads and pendants as also bannisters, all well turned and to be framed in' (BL, Add. MS 46947 B-734C).   303 The yew stairs at Birr Castle, built between 1660 and 1681, are of a completely different design (M. Girouard, 'Birr Castle, Co. Offaly, I and II', *Country Life*, iv & xxv (5 Feb. & 11 March 1965). Thomastown also had a massive oak staircase (M. Bence-Jones, 'Thomastown Castle, Co. Tipperary', *Country Life*, 2 Oct. 1969).   304 The staircase at Thorpe Hall (Lincolnshire) has similar inverted brackets to the one at Eyrecourt (Hill & Cornforth, *English country houses*, Plates 160–1). The new building (1687) at Dublin Castle also had 'a noble staircase', as described by John Dunton (*Anal. Hib.*, (1931), p. liii). Peter Delalis, a carver, was responsible for work (on the staircase?) in the Tholsel in Dublin in 1685 (*CARD*, v, p.371). Other woodcarvers in Dublin were the French Huguenots James and Louis Tabary (admitted to the franchise respectively in 1682 and 1685). James Tabary was responsible for

Figure 4.16 Front hall and staircase at Eyrecourt, County Galway 1900 (C. Bancroft).

Kilcreene were completely disconnected from the hall, the one at Eyrecourt was almost completely integrated into the hall, with only a carved screen of two arches suspended from the ceiling separating the two (Figure 4.16).

At Eyrecourt, an elaborate bracketed cornice at the second-floor landing elevated the eye to a plaster ceiling, executed in rectangular panels, decorated with elegant curly branches, complete with pendants. This ceiling, though less Baroque than that of the chapel in the Royal Hospital, showed supreme craftsmanship. Nearer the Pale, Beaulieu still exhibits a different style of ceiling. Here a heavy oval floral garland is set in the midst of four similar quarter circles. Contrasting with the light hue of the plaster, a skewed perspective painting in the centre – in the style of the Baroque mural painter Antonio Verrio (1636–1707) – shows a gallery opening into a clouded and cherubimed sky, unlikely to deceive even the most casual of observers. Other examples of this type of ceiling must have existed in Ireland: the banqueting room in the Waterhouse near Kilkenny Castle also had 'a painted skye roof with angells'.[305]

Late seventeenth-century houses often had panelled rooms with heavy bolection mouldings (a raised moulding, usually with flat edges and a raised centre, for framing panels, doorways and fireplaces),[306] surrounding the projecting panels.[307]

carvings in the chapel of the Royal Hospital, Kilmainham. John Tabary, sculptor, was admitted to the franchise in 1685 (*CARD*, v, pp 259, 367, 373).   **305** Dineley, 'Observations 1675–1680'. For seventeenth-century plasterers in Dublin, see C. Curran, *Dublin decorative plaster work* (London, 1967).   **306** As at the upper landing at Eyrecourt.   **307** Both at Beaulieu and Eyrecourt. At Eyrecourt, some doors had simple but highly projecting bolection frames (Figure 4.16, this page). The door frames of the principal rooms were also embellished at Burton House.

Doors, which interrupted the rhythm of the panels, were sometimes flanked with pilasters, also carved in wood,[308] or occasionally set into wooden arches.

Late seventeenth-century buildings sometimes housed interior features from older houses. The marble doorcases and chimney pieces from the dilapidated seat of Lord Strafford at Jigginstown (Kildare) were to be brought over to Kilkenny for the use of Ormond.[309] Similarly, the carved gallery (by Edmund Tingham) of the earl of Cork's house in Dublin was purchased in 1657 by Lord deputy Henry Cromwell, possibly for incorporation into Phoenix House, to which he added a wing.[310]

Marble was frequently used in country houses. Floors were sometimes executed in black and white marble, as at the Waterhouse at Kilkenny and the chapel of Blessington (Wicklow).[311] Forty tons of marble arrived at Lord Conway's estate in 1671, presumably for the embellishment of Portmore (Antrim).[312] He had a marble chimney piece made by a Dutchman, Francis Cavenburghe,[313] which the earl of Essex regarded as 'well wrought', but of poor quality marble. Little is known of the appearance of these chimney pieces. One, formerly at Eyrecourt, was very tall and showed heavy bolection mouldings, all executed in black marble.[314] At that time, chimney pieces contained portable grates, some valuable: the Duchess of Ormond had them removed from Dublin Castle (together with their locks and keys) when Ormond lost the Lord lieutenancy in 1669.[315] Chimney pieces were sometimes adorned with paintings,[316] as were doorways, executed according to the required size.[317] Irish marble must have attained some fame in the reign of Charles II, as it was exported to England for the manufacture of chimney pieces,[318] and commissioned for the rebuilding of St Paul's Cathedral in London, and the decoration of Hampton Court.[319]

Furniture

Although furniture inventories for houses such as Dunmore, Kilkenny Castle,[320] Rathcline,[321] and other places,[322] show large numbers of items, few pieces of this

---

308 Duchess of Ormond to Dr Hall, 3 Dec. 1664, *Ormond*, n.s., iii, p. 357. It is unclear whether these marble doorcases and chimney pieces were actually removed to Dunmore or Kilkenny Castle.   **309** Randal Clayton to John Perceval, 30 Oct. 1657, *Egmont*, i, p. 587. **310** [P. Luckombe], *A tour through Ireland* (Dublin, 1780), pp 66–7. At Kilkenny Castle, marble piers were used (John Baxter to Duchess of Ormond, 20 March 1680, *Ormond*, n.s., v, p. 292). Marble was also to be used for 'the four coynes' (coigns) of Burton House (Cork) (BL, Add. MS 46947b-734c).   **311** George Rawdon to Conway, 19 Sept. 1671, Conway papers, PRO, S.P. 63/330, No. 204.   **312** *CSPD, 1673–5*, pp 42, 52.   **313** Surviving chimney pieces from Kilcreene (Kilkenny) are similar.   **314** Countess of Ormond to George Mathew, 16 Feb. 1668–9, *Ormond*, n.s., iii, p. 441.   **315** A fireback of 'cast gold' from Chichester House, Dublin is illustrated in *Country Life*, 13 Jan. 1972, p. 97.   **316** As at Beaulieu, where the chimney piece is made of wood.   **317** C. Smith to [John Perceval], 19 Jan. 1685, *Egmont*, ii, p. 145.   **318** *Ormond*, n.s., iv, p.170.   **319** *Walpole Society*, xv, p. 8, and iv, p. 59.   **320** For Dunmore, *Ormond*, n.s., vii, pp 509–13; for Kilkenny Castle, *Ormond*, n.s., vii, pp 501–8.   **321** MacLysaght, *Irish life in the seventeenth century*, pp 412–3.   **322** For Phoenix House (Dublin), see *Ormond*, n.s., vii, pp 500–1; for Dublin Castle, *Ormond*, n.s., vii, pp 497–9. See also the inventory for Castlemartyr (Cork) in *Orrery papers*, pp 168–79.

period have survived in Ireland. These inventories convey little idea about the craftsmanship, but one's imagination is stirred when encountering 'a silver table and stands',[323] and eleven chairs in the bedroom of a lady.[324] Tapestry hangings in profusion were present in the rich Ormond houses, but also in less well known houses such as Sir William Domville's at Loughlinstown (Dublin).[325] Walls were usually decorated with paintings, which could be purchased in Dublin,[326] or imported from England.[327] Thematically, the pictures varied greatly, from 'a woman making sausages', hanging in the dining room at Burton,[328] to views of Versaille and Windsor.[329]

At a time when servants' beds were occupied by two or three people, the beds of the gentry were very luxurious, with damask hangings and 'plumes of feathers'.[330] One formerly at Belan (Kildare) excelled in reputation because ('with an imagination that supplies a tradition for everything')[331] James II and William III both allegedly slept in it in 1690.[332]

From 1660 to 1680, at least seventeen watch and clockmakers were active in Dublin.[333] This city (and also presumably Cork, Limerick, Galway and Waterford) provided employment for cabinetmakers, upholsterers and other furniture makers.[334] The importation of furniture from England, and perhaps other countries, is documented. The famous scientist Robert Boyle sent a clock to his brother Lord Orrery in 1671,[335] while Lord Herbert of Cherbury had furniture sent over from England for his seat at Castleisland (Kerry).[336] Similarly, when Lord Conway planned to stay at Portmore (Antrim) in 1683, he was advised that 'furniture for a lodging chamber or two and linnen will be necessary to be sent over', but he also heard that 'table linen may be better provided here'.[337]

The quality of some of the furniture and silver must have been considerable: plate valued at £1,000 was stolen from Kilkenny Castle,[338] while Tyrconnell's

323 *Ormond*, n.s., vii, p. 499. **324** Inventory of Castlemartyr (Cork), *Orrery papers*, pp 68–79. **325** Ball, *History of Dublin*, i, p. 91. **326** Sir John Perceval went to Dublin to visit some painters in February 1686 (*Egmont*, iii, pp 365–6). See A. Crookshank & Knight of Glin, *Irish portraits 1660–1860* (Dublin, 1969) for painters of this period. Before 1690, at least eighteen painters were working in Dublin (compiled from Strickland, *Dictionary of Irish artists*). **327** On the painting of Sir George Lane by Sir Peter Lely, see James Buck to George Lane, 3 March 1663, *Ormond*, n.s., iii, p. 44. **328** *Egmont*, ii, p. 16 [1665]. **329** MacLysaght, *Irish life in the seventeenth century*, pp 412–13. **330** Countess of Ormond to George Mathew, 6 Feb. 1674, *Ormond*, n.s., iii, pp 453–3. **331** As J.P. Prendergast mocks these allusions in his *The Cromwellian settlement of Ireland* (Dublin, 1922). **332** T. Cromwell, *Excursions through Ireland* (London, 1828), iii, p. 8. **333** K. Hoppen, *The common scientist in the seventeenth century: a study of the Dublin Philosophical Society 1683–1708* (London, 1978), p. 113. **334** The following were admitted to the franchise of Dublin: William Hill, upholsterer, 1653; Benjamin Archer and Thomas Arden, turners, 1655; Nicholas Wray, turner, 1660. Others mentioned include John Quelch, upholsterer, 1669; William Young, upholsterer, 1681; Thomas Tirrell, upholsterer, 1685 (who made furniture for the Tholsel): *CARD*. Two Englishmen who obtained letters of denization in Ireland were Herbert Rowe, upholsterer, 1669 and John Foulkes, turner, 1671: Shaw (ed.), *Letters of denization*. **335** Robert Boyle to Orrery, 2 Dec. 1671, *Orrery papers*, p. 94. See also *Egmont*, ii, p. 22. **336** Lord Herbert to Richard Herbert, 18 March 1673, Smith (ed.), *Herbert correspondence*, p. 210 **337** George Rawdon to Conway, 14 Feb. 1683, *CSPD, 1683*. **338** Longford to Ormond, 23 Sept. 1685, *Ormond*, n.s., vii, p. 362.

troops robbed Antrim Castle of money, plate and furniture valued at £4,000.[339] This account of furniture is hampered by the rarity of surviving Irish examples of the period, although we can assume that the craftsmanship was comparable in standard to that of the interiors.[340]

Sculpture

Sculpture during the late seventeenth-century was much practised by foreign artisans. The Dutch 'marble dresser' Francis Cavenburghe produced chimney pieces. In the north, two Polish sculptors worked in local alabaster, 'making statues and many fine things' for Lord Donegal.[341] It is unclear whether the statues enriched the exterior of one of his seats, as at Blessington (Wicklow).[342] Less extravagant stone carvings can still be found at Killyleagh (Down) in the form of the arms of Charles II.[343]

A statue adorned the City Exchange of Limerick, built in 1673. Although it is not known whom this figure represents, the Tholsel in Dublin was decorated with Portland stone statues of Charles I and Charles II, carved by the Dutchman Willem De Keyser.[344] These crude and inelegant figures are still preserved in the basement of Christ Church, Dublin.[345] De Keyser also executed a fountain, possibly for Kilkenny Castle, which 'will exceed all works of that kind' in England.[346] The gardens of Kilkenny Castle were embellished with four large statues and sixteen smaller ones, copied from Charles II's Privy Garden, while the superlative carver Grinling Gibbons submitted a design for an iron gate.[347] Foreign and native sculptors carved monuments in churches, such as that of the Southwells in Rathkeale (Limerick). This displays classical features of a pediment supported by baseless Doric pilasters, executed in reddish brown and black marble.[348]

Outbuildings

Although accounts often mention the erection of brew houses, wash houses, bake houses and other outbuildings, it is unclear whether these were designed to match the main house. At Burton (Cork), the outbuildings were projected symmetrically inside the enclosure (Figure 4.8). At Old Carton (Kildare), a regular Palladian outline existed, with two outbuildings placed at the end of two curved walls, projecting symmetrically from the house, possibly containing the kitchen and stables. Whereas these particular buildings were executed in stone, the paucity of information on outbuildings does not exclude the possibility that others were executed in timber (Figure 4.17).

339 Hill (ed.), *Montgomery MSS*, p. 279.   **340** Known pieces include the oak chairs of archbishops Bramhall and Magretson in St Patrick's Cathedral, Armagh.   **341** George Rawdon to Conway, 24 Dec. 1667, *CSPI, 1666–9*, p. 530.   **342** These statues were placed above the arcade in the centre of the house.   **343** *Arch. sur. Down*, Plate 415.1.   **344** *CARD*, v, pp 271, 291, 319, 354, from 1683–5. His father was the famous Dutch architect/sculptor Hendrik de Keyser (1565–1621).   **345** Photographs are in R. Loeber, 'An introduction to the Dutch influence in seventeenth- and eighteenth-century Ireland', *Bulletin Ir. Georgian Soc.*, xiii (1970), pp 20–1. One statue was incorrectly identified as James II.   **346** Longford to Ormond, 24 Dec. 1681, *Ormond*, n.s., vi, pp 279–80.   **347** Longford to Ormond, 24 Dec. 1681, *Ormond*, n.s., vi, pp 279–80.   **348** I am indebted for this information to Col. S. O'Driscoll. It was erected by Sir Thomas Southwell in 1676.

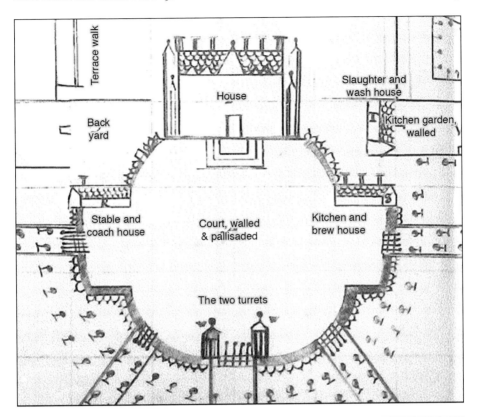

Figure 4.17a–b Old Carton, County Kildare, as shown on *c.*1680 map and in *c.*1738 by the Dutch artist Johann Van der Hagen (1675-1745). Old Carton was rebuilt by Richard Castle from 1739 onwards.

The prestige attached to horses and horse breeding in the reign of Charles II can hardly be overestimated. 'I begin to be the greatest breeder of horses in the King's dominions', wrote Colonel Daniel O'Brien from Carrigogaline (Clare) in 1670, 'for I keep about my house 16,000 acres (6,500ha) for my mares, colts and deer, which shows the bareness of my land' (a reference to the Burren?).[349] An idea of the impact of a horsey obsession on the household might be gleaned from the

---

349 Colonel Daniel O'Brien to Arlington, 26 July 1670, *CSPI, 1669–70*, p. 206.

lady who wrote, 'I believe we shall be eaten out of house and home for my Lord's horses and dogs'.[350] A love of horses moved landowners to establish race courses and to build impressive stables.[351] Ralahine (Clare) had 'the fairest stable of the countrye'.[352] Indeed, it was a pretty building of one storey, with dormers and a scroll-pedimented doorway.

Another correspondent extolled Lord Conway's stable at Portmore (Antrim) as 'the nonsuch [unparalleled example] of a stable in all the kingdom': it was so vast that it was joked that Conway would have to enlarge his house 'to make it suitable to that fine building'.[353] This stable of two storeys was 140 feet x 35 feet and 40 feet high (42.7m x 10.7m x 12.2m); it could accommodate two troops of horse and it was probably designed by William Hurlbut.[354] Even Ormond, a moderate man in building, intended to pull down the stables at Kilkenny Castle to build new ones which would resemble Ampthill Lodge, at that time a royal building.[355]

Gardens

The development of gardens accelerated greatly in the reign of Charles II. Almost every new seat was surrounded by deerparks, pleasure gardens and waterworks. The frequent references to the importation of gardeners from England, beginning in 1653,[356] demonstrates again the overwhelming English influence. Sometimes, this influence went amiss, as in the case of Francis Hartley, the gardener at Lisburn Castle. After his death, the agent George Rawdon claimed that 'none of the workmen he employed here understand anything, for he would not show anybody any of his skill'.[357] Conway's seats displayed the simultaneous development of Irish and English estates, where workmen and gardeners were shuttled to and fro from one country to the other.[358]

Usually, the most extensive element of the surrounding demesne lands was a deerpark, found near almost all the larger houses.[359] The mania for deerparks reached an unsurpassed height with the laying out of the Phoenix Park, which covered over 2,000 walled-in acres (800ha) in its heyday.[360] Deerparks provided ample opportunity for the gentry to chase the bucks, which were sometimes imported, as were Highland swine for the park at Portmore.[361]

---

350 Lady Broghill (daughter-in-law of Lord Orrery), quoted in C. Philips, *A history of the Sackville family, earls and dukes of Dorset* (London, 1930), i, p. 432. Her husband, Lord Broghill, had a house called Mallow Park (*CSPD, 1672–3*, p. 164).   **351** As at the Curragh in Kildare, and by Lord Conway at Lambeg in Antrim.   **352** Dineley, 'Observations 1675–1680'.   **353** Joseph Stroud to Conway, 8 July 1671, *CSPD, 1671*, p. 375.   **354** *Topog. dict. Ire.*, i, p. 112.   **355** Colonel Edward Cooke to Lord Bruce, 12 Nov. 1662, *15th Report*, app. iii, p. 168. Ampthill Lodge was then a royal hunting lodge in England.   **356** Valentine Savage to John Perceval, 2 Dec. 1653, *Egmont*, i, p. 528. See also George Rawdon to Conway on sending over a Dutch gardener in 1656: *CSPI, 1647–60*, p. 621; John Read to Richard Bowen, 18 March 1672–3, Smith (ed.), *Herbert correspondence*, p. 211.   **357** George Rawdon to Conway, 3 July 1672, *CSPD, 1672*, p. 310.   **358** Lady Conway to her husband, 9 Sept. 1664, Nicholson (ed.), *Conway letters*, p. 227; George Rawdon to Conway, 17 Feb. 1677, *CSPD, 1676–7*, p. 561.   **359** For example, at Portmore (Antrim), Harristown (Kildare), Dunmore (Kilkenny), Glenarm (Antrim) and Bunratty Castle (Clare).   **360** Craig, *Dublin*, p. 14.   **361** *CSPD, 1678–80*, pp 229, 241 & 258.

Another diversion was catching birds by use of decoys. Lord Arran (son of the Duke of Ormond) and Lord Conway were each erecting decoys in 1665.[362] At Conway's estate near Portmore, this involved digging three to four acres (1.2ha–1.6ha) for a pond,[363] after an English example,[364] and at a considerable expense. When it was finished, the Dutch fowler imported 200 tame ducks, assuring Conway that 'with the help of God I shall katch [wild] fowl enough'.[365]

The gardens at the richest seats – Kilkenny Castle, Dunmore, Portmore – also included bowling greens. Bowling was a favourite recreation in Dublin, where there was a much-frequented green at Oxmanstown, conducive to socialising.

Pleasure gardens could comprise an integral part of fortified enclosures, such as at Burton House and Rathcline. Their usual design was in rectangles or squares, separated from each other by walks. The rectangles were often bordered by box hedges and close walks of cinders, as could be seen at the Royal House at Chapelizod,[366] where the gardens were laid out by the Duchess of Ormond in 1668,[367] after she had started the gardens at her house Dunmore (Kilkenny).[368] The walls surrounding Irish gardens provided ornament and shelter for a great variety of trees and flowers as at Longford Castle.[369] The flowers were often displayed in pots of Irish manufacture,[370] or imported from Flanders (greatly disliked by Francis, the gardener at Portmore, who deplored their frivolous 'fashions').[371]

Extensive pleasure gardens graduated into the landscape by the planting of rows of trees along radiating avenues, which finally dissolved into surrounding nature. In this way, seen from the air, the manor house was the focus of cultivation and fine gardening, which decreased proportionate to the distance from the house. The intermediate state of tree planting along walks could be extensive, as shown in the gardens of Castle Waterhouse (Fermanagh) in 1688 (Figure 4.18).[372] The central axis of the trees in front of the house led the eye to the newly built church of the neighbouring settlement, integrating the house, the demesne and the estate village.[373]

Many landlords spent time and money in laying out these gardens; Lord Massereene's 'greatest entertainment' was planting, especially experimentation

362 Rawdon to Conway, 12 April 1665, *CSPI, 1663–5*, p. 569. Lord Arran had his seat at Maddenstown (Kildare), near the Curragh. 363 *CSPI, 1663–5*, p. 569. 364 Rawdon to Conway, 20 May 1665, *CSPI, 1663–5*, p. 582. 365 *CSPI, 1663–5*, pp 569, 637. 366 Countess of Clarendon to John Evelyn, 8 Feb. 1686, S. Singer (ed.), *State letters of Henry, second earl of Clarendon* (London, 1828), i, p. 237. 367 Ball, *Dublin*, iv, p. 170. 368 John Bryan to Duchess of Ormond, 18 Dec. 1667, *Ormond*, n.s., iii, pp 282–3. 369 Co. Longford in 1682, TCD, MS 1.1.3. 370 Shannon to John Perceval, 13 March 1683, *Egmont*, ii, pp 128–9. Shannon had his seat at Shannon Park (also called Ballinrea) near Carrigaline (Cork). 371 Daniel Arthur to Conway, 25 June 1667, *CSPI, 1666–9*, p. 385; George Rawdon to Conway, 24 Dec. 1667, *CSPI, 1666–9*, p. 530. 372 TCD, MS 1209.82. This was the estate of Dr John Madden. 373 As at Blessington (Wicklow) and Burton (Cork). A similar axis at Castleisland (Kerry), leading to a bridge, was to be planted with two rows of 'Dutch willows, sycamore or other spreading trees' (Samuel Wilson to Lord Herbert, 21 May 1678 in Smith (ed.), *Herbert correspondence*, p. 244). At Burton (Cork), a 'firr grove' was laid out in March 1686 (*Egmont*, iii, p. 371).

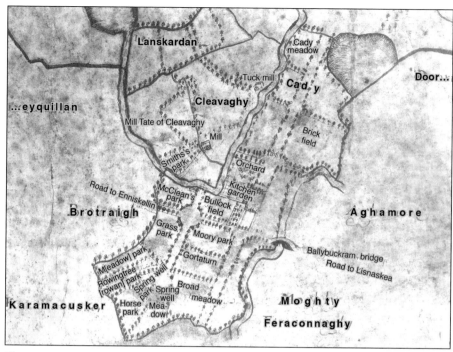

Figure 4.18 The landscaped grounds of Castle Waterhouse, County Fermanagh, in 1688. The field names have been superimposed to ease legibility (Trinity College, Dublin).

with pines.[374] As Ireland did not offer all the fashionable trees required, it was necessary to turn to other countries. As early as 1653, John Perceval imported fruit trees from England,[375] setting a pattern subsequently much repeated,[376] which led to the importation of French seed and trees from Bordeaux.[377] This was often an intellectual and scientific interest,[378] which also extended to the desire by some landlords to erect glasshouses to raise exotic and delicate plants, with surprising success.[379] Some gentry devoted time to their orchards, importing various fruit trees in an effort to brew the best possible cider.[380]

The greenery and flowers of the gardens usually contrasted with the waterworks, often mentioned in contemporary descriptions. At Longford Castle (Longford),

---

374 MacLysaght, *Irish life in the seventeenth century*, p. 136. Petty wrote a short note on the cultivation of timber in Ireland (Lansdowne (ed.), *Petty papers*, pp 126–7).   **375** *Egmont*, i, p. 531.   **376** *Egmont*, ii, pp 129, 130, 137; *CSPI, 1666–9*, p. 587.   **377** George Rawdon to Conway, 3 March 1669, *CSPI, 1666–9*, p. 693. See *Ormond*, n.s., iii, p. 132.   **378** Sir John Perceval, for example, had Nehemiah Grew, *Anatomy of plants* (London, 1682) sent to him from England (Christopher Crofts to Sir John Perceval, 26 Oct. 1683, *Egmont*, ii, p. 135).   **379** 'Glasses' are mentioned at Castle Forbes (Longford) in 1682, (TCD, MS 1.1.3). Thomas Bellingham, visiting Sir Arthur Rawdon's seat at Moira (Down), in 1690, mentioned 'the conservatory' there (A. Hewitson (ed.), *Diary of Thomas Bellingham, an officer under William III* (Preston, 1908), p. 123). Bernard de Gomme's map of Dublin also shows a glasshouse, now near the site of Westland Row Station (J. Simms, 'Dublin in 1685', *IHS*, 14 (1964–5), p. 216).   **380** George Rawdon to Conway, 21 Oct. 1665, *CSPI, 1663–5*, p. 653.

these consisted of 'most pleasant fishponds and canalls in which are tench in great plenty, and carp with store of trout, roach &c'.[381] Rathcline (also Longford) had extensive fishponds, for which long canals were dug to obtain the necessary water.[382] If a lake was near the house, as at Harristown (Kildare), one might discern a miniature ship, 'perfectly rigged, sufficiently large for a pleasure yacht'.[383] Several fountains stood in the gardens of Kilkenny Castle, including one with a Triton and shell, disgorging water from its mouth.[384] Another fountain in the Waterhouse was fed by an 'engine of curious artifice', driven by a horse to raise the water.[385] The Kilkenny gardens were further embellished by a grotto, of which little is known. [386] For one structure, probably in the garden of Portmore, 12,000 painted tiles from Ostend were imported by Lord Conway, of which only two-thirds arrived unbroken.[387] The gardener, Francis, commented that he could not use half of these, inducing George Rawdon to lament 'a very dear commodity they prove'.[388] Whether these tiles were meant for a grotto or garden building remains an intriguing question. Other typical garden buildings included a pigeon house, an icehouse and an aviary.[389] The erection of icehouses in Ireland was solely entrusted to the earl of Carlingford in 1665.[390]

CONCLUSIONS: THE WILLIAMITE WAR

Shortly after the accession of the Catholic King James II in 1685, a proclamation was issued for securing the firearms of the militia. This alarmed Protestant settlers because it hampered them in defending themselves against the Irish. The ousting of the Protestant Clarendon as Lord lieutenant, quickly followed by the 1687 arrival of the Catholic Richard Talbot (first earl of Tyrconnell), was perceived as proof that the Protestant interest was waning rapidly. This resulted in a stampede to England, leaving 1,100 houses empty in Dublin alone as early as August 1687.[391] In 1688, the exodus intensified.[392] Consequently, the building of houses almost completely stopped,

381 Shannon to John Perceval, 13 March 1683, *Egmont*, ii, pp 128–9.   382 NLI, MS 8646 (6), map of Rathcline (Longford). A trench to bring 'the water from Agaheel into Arther lough' was dug near Portmore (Antrim) in 1679–80 (*CSPD, 1678–80*, p. 241).   383 J. O'Flanagan, *The lives of the Lord chancellors and keepers of the great seal of Ireland* (London, 1870), i, p. 376. Shortly after 1684, Petty built his famous double-bottom ship, in partnership with John Skeffington, second Viscount Massareene. Massereene had been granted the fishing of Lough Neagh provided that he build a barque for the lake (*Ormond*, n.s., iii, pp 246–8). He wanted to deploy the double-bottom boat for his own use, which precipitated a long dispute with Petty, which Petty finally won (Fitzmaurice, *Petty*, p. 112). In another case, the fowler of Lord Conway proposed to build him a pleasure boat (George Rawdon to Conway, 17 March 1667, *CSPI, 1666–9*, p. 585).   384 Longford to Ormond, 24 Dec. 1681, *Ormond*, n.s., vi, pp 279–80.   385 Shirley & Graves (eds), 'Dineley'.   386 John Baxter to Duchess of Ormond, 20 March 1680, *Ormond*, n.s., v, p. 292.   387 George Rawdon to Conway, 18 June 1667, *CSPI, 1666–9*, p. 382.   388 George Rawdon to Conway, 18 July 1667, *CSPI, 1666–9*, p. 392.   389 George Rawdon to Conway, 13 April 1667, *CSPI, 1666–9*, p. 345.   390 *CSPI, 1663–5*, p. 632.   391 Petty to Sir Robert Southwell, 4 Aug. 1687, Lansdowne (ed.), *The Petty-Southwell correspondence 1676–1687* (London, 1928), p. 280.   392 Simms, *Jacobite Ireland*, p. 43.

with the exception of optimistic Catholics, like Sir Valentine Brown, who erected an addition to Ross Castle in 1688.[393] Rebuilding Dublin Castle continued until late in 1687 under William Molyneux, although not all the projected buildings were started. James II had a mint erected in Dublin,[394] which was wide-eaved, a common feature for that time. Although several churches were built in the reign of James II, it is likely that the overall volume of construction decreased considerably after 1685.

In 1688, James II fled to Ireland, after William III was acknowledged as king in England. The first parliament to sit in Ireland for more than twenty years urged James II to repeal the Act of Settlement and to restore the dispossessed Catholics. James II, however, supported a more limited Act of Attainder, forfeiting only the estates of those ostentatiously disloyal to him.

The subsequent destruction in Ireland during the Williamite War undermined the rebuilding of the previous decades. Allegiances in this war were determined by the question of landownership. William III had already announced that he would confiscate the lands of his opponents for the benefit of his supporters.[395]

The accounts of agents and stewards, who had the difficult task of safeguarding properties deep in a hostile countryside, conveyed the anxieties experienced by many. 'All here in this kingdom ... in a manner is destroyed', wrote William Taylor from Burton (Cork) in 1689: 'our stock in this country is likewise destroyed, ... so that I fear there will be a famine ... Those of us that have not lost all expect to lose every minute'.[396] From Dunmore (Kilkenny), Ormond's steward John Baxter reported that 'most are fleeing from danger; but God be thanked, fear hath not yet seized me, and I hope never shall'.[397] A few days later, hurried attempts were made to ship all the really valuable portable goods from Kilkenny Castle to England, 'if it is not too late'.[398]

Ultimately, these fears were warranted, for destruction of houses occurred on a large scale. As early as 1688, the renovated Castlemartyr (Cork) was wrecked by Justin McCarthy, because of the rebellion of Captain Boyle.[399] During the Williamite War, devastation reached a climax. The Duke of Wurtemberg advised the Danish king: 'The enemy under the Duke of Berwyck has carried out frightful burnings [which have] done damage to the country to the value of several millions and burned down more than twelve fine towns and very many beautiful castles, including Charleville, which was the finest in Ireland, and all such places in the counties of Cork and Tipperary'. A message had been sent to the Duke of Berwick to intimidate him, warning him that if he continued his burning campaign, the Irish prisoners, including the officers, 'would be burned alive'.[400]

---

393 MacLysaght (ed.), *Kenmare manuscripts*, p. 404. Ashbrook (Derry) was built in 1686 (Burke, *Visitation*, ii, p. 130). Old Carton (Kildare) may have been erected by the earl of Tyrconnell in the same period. Viscount Gormanstown erected a chapel at Gormanstown in 1687.   **394** For a picture of James II's mint in Dublin, see *Georgian Society records*, ii, p. 61.   **395** Simms, *Jacobite Ireland*, p. 84.   **396** William Taylor to Edward Lloyd, 24 April 1689, *Egmont*, ii, p. 190.   **397** Baxter to Henry Gascoigne, 15 Jan. 1689, *Ormond*, n.s., viii, pp 15–16.   **398** Henry Gascoigne to Gerard Bor, 17 Jan. 1689, *Ormond*, n.s., viii, p. 29.   **399** J. Murphy, *Justin MacCarthy, Lord Mountcashel* (Cork, 1959), p. 16.   **400** Wurtemberg to Christian V, 29 Oct. 1690, Danaher & Simms (eds), *Danish force in Ireland*, p. 90. See also H.J Lawlor (ed.), 'Diary of William King,

These burnings were certainly not limited to Cork and Tipperary. 'God direct his judgement', wrote Sir Donough O'Brien in July 1690, 'for there is great destruction in the county of Limerick, Broof [Bruff] demolished, Balligirana walls, Caraffa, Carless House all burnt'. The devastation was not only due to the Jacobite army; they undoubtedly found active allies in the tories, who did 'enormous damage to the persons and property of both soldiers and civilians'.[401] Furthermore, newly built suburbs in Galway and Limerick were pulled down to make room for improvised fortifications and to create a clear line of sight for firing from inside the walls. In Ulster, Tyrconnell's army plundered Hillsborough, Lisburn, Belfast and Antrim.[402] The destruction was exacerbated by the practice of stripping lead from roofs to manufacture bullets.[403]

The greater part of the Big Houses that survived the Williamite War suffered unfortunate fates thereafter. Lady Ormond's Dunmore (Kilkenny) and Lord Conway's Portmore (Antrim) were neglected and subsequently pulled down in the eighteenth century. Boyle's seat at Blessington (Wicklow) went up in flames in 1798. Other houses, such as Old Carton (Kildare) and Kilruddery (Wicklow), were altered beyond recognition. Kilcreene (Kilkenny) and Mosstown (Longford) were levelled more recently. Eyrecourt (Galway) was dismantled prior to 1930. A tiny number remain, of which only Beaulieu (Louth) still shows the unchanged splendour and refinement that once distinguished late seventeenth-century architecture in Ireland.[404] It embodies a turning point in Irish architecture, when the metamorphosis of medieval dwellings into comfortable and architecturally ambitious houses occurred.

D.D., Archbishop of Dublin, during his imprisonment in Dublin Castle, II', *JRSAI*, xxxiii (1903), pp 255–83 at p. 273.   **401** Simms, *Jacobite Ireland*, p. 198.   **402** Hill (ed.), *Montgomery MSS*, p. 279.   **403** Hewitson (ed.), *Diary of Thomas Bellingham*, p. 139.   **404** Finnebrogue (Down) still exists but is much altered. Richhill (Armagh) retains more of its original state.

CHAPTER FIVE

Early Classicism in Ireland:
architecture before the Georgian era

INTRODUCTION

THE EMERGENCE OF IRISH ARCHITECTURE in the classical fashion is conventionally regarded as starting with the appearance of Edward Lovett Pearce's Palladian buildings in the late 1720s and 1730s, followed by the tidal wave of neo-classical architecture by architects such as Richard Castle, Thomas Ivory and James Gandon. Was wide acceptance of Classicism in eighteenth-century Ireland due to the architects' ability to sway their patrons, or were the patrons already predisposed to favour classical styles? Were Pearce's patrons the first in Ireland to be confronted with all the paraphernalia of Classicism, or could the parents of his patrons have taught them the essence of classical art?

Classical Irish architecture before the eighteenth century is little known because so little has survived to the present day. A succession of internal revolts, culminating with the 1922 burnings, eradicated much of the evidence of early Classicism. The damp Irish climate and the decline of landed families contributed to this toll. As late as the 1960s, Eyrecourt Castle (Galway) lost its princely staircase and wainscotting (sold to the newspaper millionaire William Randolph Hearst, and later gifted by him to the Detroit Arts Institute). Of numerous houses known to have been built in the late seventeenth century, only Beaulieu (Louth) survives intact. The countryside is also pockmarked with the ruins of the plantation houses of the early part of the century. Again, the survival of any building with an intact interior is extremely rare.

Historical context

In the middle of the sixteenth century, English hegemony was largely limited to Dublin and surrounding counties. Outside that small area, Irish customs and culture prevailed, and these were usually considered as barbaric and devoid of 'civility'. The poorer tenants lived in thatched cabins made of wattles and clay and lacking chimneys. Wealthier dwellings still made a poor impression in the seventeenth century. A contemporary English doggerel mocks two cavaliers who mistook their host's residence for a stable:

> Ned, he alights and leads (God bless us all)
> His horse into his Worship's very hall
> And looking round about, cries in great anger,
> 'Zowns, here's a stable has no rack nor manger'.

'Peace Ned', (quoth I) 'prithe be no so gasty;
This room's no stable though it be as nasty;
I see a harp and chimney too, and dare
Say there was fire in't before the war;
So this is no place for a horse you see'.
'Tis then for very beast, I'm sure', quotes he.[1]

English sovereignty was only nominal in most of the Irish territories. Successive monarchs, each in their own piecemeal way, sought to expand English rule and plant Englishmen in these territories. The rebellion or alleged treason of great Irish lords and their followers provided a justification to confiscate large tracts of land. The government then sponsored the settlement of British undertakers who were tasked to attract British tenants. These schemes for settlement, called plantations, were first small as in the counties Laois and Offaly. Subsequently, the Munster and Ulster plantations extended over vast tracts. In the absence of rebellions, the government confiscated further areas in Leinster through 'proving' that existing land titles, which had often not been challenged for centuries, were legally invalid. A voluminous influx of settlers took place, and buildings were erected at an unprecedented rate. Two major revolts of the Irish, one from 1593–1603, the other in 1641, largely unravelled the process of settlement. However, these revolts also prompted renewed confiscations and grants of lands to soldiers and settlers. They came from every stratum of English and Scottish (and to a lesser extent Welsh) society, each bringing with them their own particular interpretation of contemporary British architecture. The Cromwellian settlement of Ireland was confirmed and extended after Charles II ascended the throne in 1660. Thirty years of peace and reconstruction ended in 1689 when the Williamite campaigns once more inflicted widespread destruction. In the end, the conquerors further claimed large tracts of lands and founded new plantations. A prolonged period of peace followed in which artistic tastes developed, leading to the acceptance of the mature classical architecture of Edward Lovett Pearce in the early 1730s.

Catholic influences
Although the earlier introduction of classical themes into Ireland was related to the influx of British settlers, there is considerable evidence that various Irishmen developed a taste for classical art. A small part of this development emanated from the rise of the Counter-Reformation in Ireland. Whereas in England, Catholic missions organised from the Continent remained largely hidden from public view, the Counter-Reformation was successful in Ireland, especially in the early seventeenth century, and it inspired the founding of numerous churches, some embellished with baroque designs. In secular architecture, many eighteenth-century classical themes in Ireland had their precursors in the preceding century. The emergence of the eighteenth-century classical tradition of architecture in Ireland formed much less of a break with the past than has often been asserted.

---

1 Quoted in T.C. Croker (ed.), *Tour of M. Boullaye le Gouz in Ireland in 1644* (London, 1837), p. 132.

Classical ideas reached Ireland in a variety of ways.[2] First of all, Irishmen of some means travelled to Europe, often to join either religious orders or foreign armies. Others, especially the sons of the nobility, were educated abroad from the sixteenth century onwards. In a tract of 1613, it was noted that 'Sir Patrick Barnewall (*fl.* 1534–1622), now living, was the first gentleman's son of quality that was ever sent out of Ireland to be brought up in learning beyond the seas'.[3] Yet the numbers educated abroad had become so alarmingly large that Trinity College was founded in 1592 to keep them from foreign contamination. Despite Trinity College and government restrictions, many young Catholics continued to receive their education on the Continent. They belonged to Irish or Old English families and they sought a university education denied them in Ireland in the various Catholic colleges in the Spanish Low Countries, France, Spain and Italy. Some sons of British settlers were sent on the Grand Tour to France, Italy and other continental countries. The young Roger Boyle, who later became an amateur architect, travelled to Geneva with his tutor in the 1630s, where he was taught 'the knowledge of the sphera and of the architecture'.[4] In a travel journal of 1605, Henry Piers, son of an English immigrant, described twenty-seven churches in Rome, including St Peter's:

> The chauncell of the churche is newly builte and is made in the forme of a crosse beinge tenn score yardes [183m] longe everye waye, the highe altar is sett iuste in the middeste of the crosse and right over is builte a statelye bye towre in the form of a lanterne, and is double vaulted from the height of the churche up to the tope of saide towre, in the which is placed a mightie boule of brass, which will well containe twenty men.[5]

The first known Irish architect who travelled in Italy was Captain Nicholas Pynnar (director-general of fortifications and buildings). During his stay in Venice from 1606 to 1608, the English ambassador Sir Henry Wotton introduced Pynnar to the Doge and his Court, who employed him as an engineer.[6] Almost five decades later, Captain James Archer, a Catholic architect and engineer, returned to Ireland

---

2 For a general introduction to classical influences in Ireland, see W. Stanford, *Ireland and the classical tradition* (Towata, NJ, 1976). Early Irish heraldic books were occasionally decorated with classical designs. See, for example, Daniel Molyneux, 'Visitation begonne in the Cittie of Dublin', 1607 (GO, MS 46). On early classical themes in Irish book decorations, see M. Pollard, 'The woodcut ornament stocks of the Dublin printers 1500–1700', thesis submitted for the Fellowship of the Library Association, 1966, copy in TCD. Another example is Caesar's head on the 1670 charter of Dublin bricklayers (BL, Add. MS 11,268, f. 98).   **3** Quoted in 'A brief relation of the passages in the parliament summoned in Ireland anno 1613' in J. Lodge (ed.), *Desiderata curiosa Hibernica* (Dublin, 1772), i, p. 418. Sir Patrick Barnewall of Crickstown sat in the parliament of 1585 and was buried at Lusk (J. D'Alton, *History of the county of Dublin* (Dublin, 1838), p. 306).   **4** L. Stone, *The crisis of the aristocracy 1558–1641* (Oxford, 1965), p. 698. Details about Roger Boyle and other architects in Ireland of this period can be found in Loeber, *Biographical dictionary*.   **5** Henry Piers, 'A discourse of his travels written by himself, 1605', Bodl., Oxford, Rawlinson MS D. 83. Copy in Pearse Street Library, Dublin, Gilbert MS 177.   **6** *CSPI, 1606–8*, p. 651; *Cal. of state papers, Venice, 1603–7*, pp 403, 413–14, 417. Pynnar brought Italian architectural drawings from Sir Henry Wotton to the earl of Salisbury, who was then building Hatfield House.

after fifteen years in France to execute works for the Duke of Ormond.[7] The Duke himself, forced into exile during the Commonwealth, had visited the Netherlands and France.

Many early architects, craftsmen and architect-engineers in Ireland came from England, where Classicism was accepted on a far wider scale.[8] The great variety of buildings in Ireland once attributed to Inigo Jones, however, ranging from Jigginstown (Kildare),[9] Portmore (Antrim),[10] Joymount (Antrim),[11] the portico at Lismore Castle (Waterford),[12] to even William Robinson's Royal Hospital, Kilmainham,[13] have all remained unsubstantiated. Dr John Westley, son-in-law of Jones's successor John Webb, however, was both a lawyer and an architect with a large practice in Ireland, of which nothing more remains than some tantalising documentary evidence.[14]

Architectural treatises

The foreign influences on Irish architecture were reinforced by the increased distribution of architectural treatises, both in published and manuscript form. One of the most prolific builders of the early seventeenth century, Richard Boyle, first earl of Cork, owned a little book with hand-drawn designs of famous monuments in perspective, which he gifted to the connoisseur the earl of Arundel in 1628.[15] More influential were printed pattern books from France, Italy and the Low Countries. The first recorded collection of architectural pattern books, in the library of Lord Conway in County Antrim, was confiscated in 1641.[16] Another very large collection of these books was in the hands of several generations of the Molyneux family, who were successively clerk of the Royal Works, master gunner of Ireland and surveyor-general.[17] The Molyneux collection consisted of thirty-seven books on architecture and fortifications that included Andrea Palladio's *Quattro libri dell' architettura* (Venice, 1601), Hendrik De Keyser's *Architectura moderna* (Amsterdam, 1631) and Androuet Du Cerceau's *Les trois livres d'architecture* (Paris, 1559), and later works such as Pierre Le Muet's *Art of fair building* (London, 1670) and John Evelyn's *Parallel of architecture* (London, 1680).

The earliest known examples of classical decoration can be found in the English Pale. Arabesque details embellish a stone table that belonged to the Lord deputy, the earl of Kildare. It carries the date 1533 and is now at Kilkea Castle (Figure 5.1). Not far from there, at Moore Abbey (Kildare) (Figure 5.2), a window surround

---

7 *Sixth report*, p. 731.   **8** For a review of these groups, see the introduction to Loeber, *Biographical dictionary*.   **9** M. Craig, 'New light on Jigginstown', *UJA*, xxxiii (1970), pp 107–10.   **10** R. Heber, *The life of the Right Rev. Jeremy Taylor D.D.* (Huntington, CT, 1832).   **11** S. MacSkimin, *History and antiquities of Carrickfergus* (Belfast, 1823), p. 119.   **12** Bence-Jones, *Country houses*.   **13** J. Gandon & T. Mulvany, *The life of James Gandon, Esq.* (Dublin, 1846), p. 261.   **14** Bodl., Carte MS 31, f. 440.   **15** A.B. Grosart (ed.), *Lismore papers* (1886–8), series 1, ii, p. 285.   **16** W.G. Wheeler, 'Libraries in Ireland before 1855: a bibliographical essay' (Dip.Lib., University of London, 1957, revised 1965, vol. i, copy in TCD). He refers to a catalogue of the Conway collection in the Public Library in Armagh.   **17** [S. Molyneux], *A catalogue of the library of the Honourable Samuel Molyneux, deceased, which will be sold by auction the 20th of January, 1729–30* (copy in TCD, vvi–45).

Figure 5.1 This elaborate stone table at Kilkea Castle, Co. Kildare, was commissioned in 1533 by Gerald Fitzgerald (1487-1534), ninth earl of Kildare. The inscription reads 'Geraldus Comes Kildariensis' – meaning Gerald earl of Kildare. He was also known as 'Gearóid Óg'. He moved in different cultural worlds, and was an art connoisseur and a bibliophile.

shows an accumulation of putti, vases and Roman armour, oddly combined with Gothic tracery. It could very well date back to the late sixteenth century, when the old abbey there was granted to Lord Audley (1551–1617), who had been in Holland as governor of the city of Utrecht. It is in this fashion, in small isolated decorations, that Classicism unfolded in Ireland. Judging from surviving artefacts, that development was slow in the sixteenth century. Only after the Nine Years' War ended in 1603 did the use of classical themes in building spread significantly.

Simultaneously, the division of labour within the architectural profession started to evolve. The craftsman-architect who submitted designs to his patrons and who also took care of their execution continued to work in this way. He might have a book available with a choice of his own or someone else's designs. In 1681, a carpenter called Fisher was asked to bring 'his book of draughts' to Sir John Perceval.[18] Alongside the craftsman-architect, a distinct group of 'architects' entered the scene in Dublin in the late 1620s, when twelve were admitted to the freedom of the city.[19] Little is known about these individuals: it is unclear whether they merely provided designs and left the execution to others. The first known gentleman-architect was

18 BL, Add. MS 46,958 B, f. 68.   19 R. Loeber (ed.), 'Architects and craftsmen admitted as freemen to the city of Dublin 1464–85 and 1575–1774', unpublished MS, copy in the National Gallery of Ireland, Dublin. Architects in a wider sense are mentioned in the city of Waterford in 1646 (*Tenth report*, app. v, p. 279).

Figure 5.2 Right jamb of the late sixteenth-century bay window, at Moore Abbey, Monasterevin, County Kildare. The designs are clearly derived from those of the Milanese engraver Giovanni Pietro de Birago (*fl*. 1471–1513) (Irish Architectural Archive).

Sir Thomas Roper, first Viscount Baltinglass, who made a design for the earl of Cork's Dublin house in 1631.[20]

The next logical step, the sending over of ready-made designs for Irish buildings from Italy, did not occur any earlier than 1707, when designs for Burton House were to be sent from Rome to Cork.[21] Classicism in Irish architecture changed drastically

20 Huntington Library, San Marino, California.   **21** BL, Add. MS 47,025, ff 80–1.

after the middle of the seventeenth century; no longer were only relatively small classical details introduced, but entire elevations and plans came to be classically inspired. At the same time, certain Gothic features in architecture lingered on, mainly in ecclesiastical settings.

EARLY CLASSICISM

Door surrounds

Early seventeenth-century classical door surrounds and chimney pieces undoubtedly stood out upon largely undecorated walls. An early example of a classical door surround was the old main entrance to Trinity College, Dublin, erected *c*.1592. It had caryatids (a sculpted female figure serving as an architectural support taking the place of a column or pillar) that carried an architrave and frieze probably of the Doric order, crowned by a pediment and decorative strap work.[22] Two decades later, Richard Boyle (created earl of Cork in 1620), contracted with two English masons, Richard and John Hamond, to erect a classical gate at his residence, the College at Youghal. This elaborate structure no longer exists, but documents indicate that it was decorated with pediments, columns and architraves, and included such Jacobean mannerist details as 'pyramids' and 'diamonds', all executed in alabaster and red marble.[23] It must have been an exceptional if eccentric feature, and it probably did not set a trend.

The use of pedimented doorways did not become popular until the second half of the seventeenth century; instead, more decorative stonework was preferred, as at the front door of Portumna Castle (Galway, 1618) (Figure 5.3).[24] Here, obelisks on consoles frame an oval window supported by strap work, a design typical of English Jacobean art. In Ireland, this kind of doorcase has always been more numerous than is recognised nowadays.[25] Not far from Portumna, the doorways of the wealthy families of French and Brown in Galway displayed exuberant classical features almost Baroque in effect, although still very Jacobean in their detail. The doorway of the French house, with its banded pilasters, resembled designs published by Serlio

---

22 Visible on a late sixteenth-century view of Trinity College, published by J.P. Mahaffy in *An epoch of Irish history: Trinity College, Dublin*, second ed. (Dublin, 1906), title page.   23 Chatsworth, Lismore, MS 3, f. 131. Anne Crookshank allowed me to quote from documents which she and Irene Calvert abstracted at Chatsworth.   24 M. Craig, *Portumna Castle* (Dublin, 1976).   25 Apart from the examples in the text, other early seventeenth-century classical door surrounds include those at Dromaneen (Cork), Manor Hamilton (Leitrim, 1638), Loughcrew (Meath) and Newtown (Down) where both entrances are now incorporated into garden gates, Dunluce Castle (Antrim), Rathcline (Longford), Killyleagh Castle (Down) and Moore Hall (Kildare, late sixteenth century?). Gone are the classical main entrances of Bunratty Castle (which consisted of a segmentally pedimented surround, probably dating from *c*.1617 (Dineley, 'Observations 1675–80', p. 173) and Menlough Castle (Galway, *JGAHS*, viii (1913–14), p. 155). Classical doorsurrounds of early seventeenth-century churches are at Tullynakill (Down, 1639) and Rathrea (Longford). Rathrea has Doric pilasters, a proper frieze and a pediment. (Information kindly provided by Maurice Craig.)

Figure 5.3 Front door of Portumna Castle, County Galway, erected in 1618.

and Dietterlin.[26] However, these doorways may also have derived from Spanish examples, for Galway had some commercial contacts with that country.

Such doorways were not confined to the Galway area. One of the first-known classical door surrounds erected for an Irish landowner, Diarmuid Mac Eoghan

---

26 For the Browne and French doorways, see *JGAHS*, iv (1905–6), pp 37–9, 62–4.

Figure 5.4 Gate of Killyleagh Castle, County Down, erected after 1610.

Mac Cártaigh (Dermot MacOwen McCarthy), probably dates from 1609. It adorns the ruins of Kanturk Castle (Cork) and it displays a robust architrave supported by unusual pillars standing on pedestals decorated with a diamond pattern. The whole composition is notably free in its interpretation of classical proportions. A more conventional example is at Killyleagh Castle (Down), erected after 1610 by a Scottish planter, James Hamilton, earl of Clandeboy (Figure 5.4). This doorcase, now dismantled and removed to the garden, had Ionic pillars with a correct entablature,

Figure 5.5 North door of Newtownards Priory, County Down, erected between 1608 and 1618 (Northern Ireland Archaeological Survey).

topped by a cartouche set into strap work. The preceding examples contrast greatly with the doorway of Newtownards Priory, also in Down (Figure 5.5). That priory had been converted by another Scottish settler, Sir Hugh Montgomery, between 1608 and 1618.[27] He employed Scottish craftsmen, who were probably responsible

27 Hill (ed.), *Montgomery manuscripts*, p. 59; *Arch. sur. Down*, p. 260.

Figure 5.6 Plaster work, Ormond Castle, Carrick-On-Suir, County Tipperary, executed in 1565. 'E R' in the design means Elizabeth Regina (Queen Elizabeth). She had ascended the throne in 1558. The figure on the top right is a representation of Justice – Ivsticia (Dúchas).

for a much flatter and more diverse type of decoration such as foliage attached to ribbons, masks and strap work, crowned by an imitation of a segmental pediment. Works of this kind are exceedingly rare in Ireland.

Most Irish country houses or castles of the period lacked classical door surrounds. Gothic features lingered on for a long time. A doorway at Dunmore

Castle (Kilkenny) has a pointed arch dating from the late 1610s. Similar examples abound in Ulster, Leinster and Munster.

Classical features often exhibited a certain whimsicality. At Blarney Castle (Cork), an exceptional brick construction of several storeys of half columns decorated a round projection above a doorway of an addition to the castle. Bricks were the main building material of Jigginstown (Kildare), built for the Lord deputy Wentworth (first earl of Strafford) in 1636. At this building, classically inspired features were incorporated: window surrounds executed in bricks of two colours, voussoirs (wedge-shaped elements, typically stones, used in building an arch or vault) alternating with strange egg-shaped boulders, and Tuscan base-mouldings to the chimneystacks.[28] Apart from these details, the building lacked symmetry, and with its external chimneystacks was decidedly old-fashioned.

Chimney pieces

Isolated classical elements are also evident in Irish chimney pieces and plaster work. Among the earliest surviving classical chimney pieces is one from 1565 inserted in the house at Carrick-on-Suir built for 'Black' Tom, tenth earl of Ormond. It has short tapering pilasters on pedestals decorated with a radiating pattern. The plaster work in the gallery and other rooms of the house (Figure 5.6) is close to contemporary work in the Low Countries and in England. A variety of cartouches are divided by 'antique' interlacing bands and half-figures; fluted Doric pilasters are supported by mannerist consoles which carry segmental arches under which stand classical figures in high relief with their Latin names above their heads. Glass for this building and wainscot (still intact in the early 1900s) was ordered in 1566 by the earl of Ormond from Antwerp and Amsterdam respectively. His intermediary was an agent of Sir Thomas Gresham, who was at that time organising the building of the Exchange in London, the design and materials of which came largely from Antwerp.[29] Whereas Piers, ninth earl of Ormond, brought Flemish tapestry weavers to Kilkenny in the early sixteenth century, his successor 'Black Tom' may have employed English artisans for his plaster work.

A great number of English craftsmen were employed by Sir Richard Boyle (first earl of Cork), the most wealthy and energetic of all the early seventeenth-century planters in Ireland. In March 1612, he signed a contract for a chimney piece with the masons Richard and John Hamond, who were then erecting the classical gate at Youghal in Cork. They bound themselves to execute the chimney piece as follows:[30]

> Impr. I am to make into the under storey ii columns of black stone with base and capitall of alabaster, and above the paire I am to make archatraves, freeze and cornise, the architrave and cornice of black and white stones and the freeze of redd. In the second storey I am to make 3 [the three crossed out] columns of black stone with pilasters of the same behind the [unintelligible]

28 Craig, 'New light on Jigginstown'.   29 J. Burgoa, *The life and times of Sir Thomas Gresham* (London 1845), ii, p. 117.   30 Chatsworth, Lismore MS 3, ff 131, 139, gives the full contract for the chimney piece, signed by the mason Richard Hamond and his son John.

Figure 5.7 Wooden chimney piece, the College (also known as Myrtle Grove), Youghal, County Cork (William Lawrence photograph, NLI).

> between each pilaster of redd stone and in the [unintelligible] of the same
> Morteestiment shall stand the mayne armes of (alabaster) under mantelling
> helmet and crest to be cutte iii foote [0.9m] square. On the topp I am to make
> an architrave and cornice of redd stone the freeze of black.

This work does not survive. However, a wooden chimney piece, probably made around this period, at the College in Youghal (Figure 5.7) still shows allegorical figures of Hope and Charity between elaborate cartouches decorated with strap work, a typical derivation from Flemish mannerism with its scrolls and central lion's head.[31] Another version of these curly cartouches can be found at Donegal Castle (Figure 3.15) where stone pilasters support the chimney piece inserted in 1610, although they lack capitals of any sort.[32] Contemporary funeral monuments show similar features.[33]

31 Part of a contemporary wooden chimney piece was reinserted in the convent adjoining the College. A third wooden example partially survives at Ballyseedy (Kerry).   32 A large fragment of a singular chimney piece of a different design can still be found at Ormond Castle in Carrick-on-Suir: it was supported by two large scrolls, not unlike a design by the Italian architect Serlio (S. Serlio, *Tutte l'opere d'architettura et prospettiva* (Venice, 1619), p. 157). Another early (1603) classical chimney piece is at Carrigaholt (Clare) (drawing in RIA, MS 3 A 49).   33 Loeber, 'Early seventeenth-century monuments to the dead'. See also A. Crookshank, 'Lord Cork and his monuments', *Country Life*, cxlix (1971), 1288 f.

Figure 5.8 Castlelyons Castle, County Cork, in 1950 (National Monuments Service, Department of Culture Heritage and the Gaeltacht).

Façades

The early seventeenth century saw a slow evolution in the façades of buildings. When Lord deputy Wentworth was welcomed to Limerick in 1637, wooden triumphal arches were erected. He described them: 'Architecture and invention not asleep, as appeared in their arch-triumphals, with their ornaments and inscriptions; the ingenious accommodation of their Cupids, their Apollo, their ancient genii, their laureate poets ... and even the seven planets reciting several verses' in his praise telling him 'What we ought to be [rather] than what we were'.[34] Such structures may have been rather sophisticated in comparison with the average elevation of new buildings of that time. The decline in building towerhouses was accompanied by the erection of two- or three-storeyed houses on a rectangular or T-plan. Most houses showed façades with uneven window spacing. When Wentworth promoted the erection of a mint in Dublin in 1635,[35] its plan was not based on classical principles: windows were placed at regular intervals within each room, but their external spacing was highly asymmetrical. An early exception was Roscommon Castle, where large windows were inserted in a symmetrical and uniform pattern soon after 1587.[36]

In the early seventeenth century, patrons and artisans became more aesthetically aware. The beauty of the location and a fine prospect from a country house was mentioned by Lady Barrymore in 1641, when she was rebuilding Castlelyons (Cork) (Figure 5.8).[37] When the first earl of Cork agreed in 1631 with the builder

34 *CSPI, 1633–47*, p. 168.   **35** Sheffield Public Library, Strafford MS, plan of proposed mint, undated but probably constructed *c.*1634–5.   **36** R. Stalley, 'William of Prene and the Royal Works in Ireland', *Journal of the British Archaeological Association*, xli (1978), pp 30–49, Plate xvi.   **37** F. Verney & M. Verney (eds), *Memoirs of the Verney family* (London, 1892), i, p. 210.

Figure 5.9a–b Clogrennan Castle, County Carlow, as drawn by Thomas Dineley (NLI), and an early twentieth-century postcard by Duggan, Carlow (NLI).

Edmund Tingham to re-erect three ranges of the square court of Maynooth Castle (Kildare), he stressed that the work must be built in a fair and uniform manner.[38] The Butler family renovated Clogrennan Castle (Carlow) before 1615 (Figures 5.9a–b).[39] A drawing of its original appearance showed regular spacing of windows and chimneystacks. As part of this development, buildings shed their defensibility. These features are evident at another vanished building, Charlemont Castle (Armagh). It was built for Sir Toby Caulfeild between 1620 and 1624,[40] within the protection of a fort with four bastions: it had large windows in symmetrically projecting bays on all sides. Whereas corner turrets would have previously provided defence, here ranges of chimneystacks rose, in one of the first instances of the planned silhouette and massing of an Irish building in different planes. Charlemont may also be the first instance of a 'sham' castle in Ireland. This type of design did not become typical of this period in Ireland, though loosely connected with Charlemont Castle is another vanished house, Joymount (Figure 5.10), which formerly stood within the walls of Carrickfergus. Built in 1616 by Sir

38 Grosart (ed.), *Lismore papers*, series 1, ii, p. 135.   39 *11th Report*, app. vii, p. 75.
40 Marshall, *Charlemont and Mountjoy Forts*, pp 13–14.

Figure 5.10 Joymount House, Carrickfergus, County Antrim: detail from a drawing by Thomas Phillips in 1616. Chichester's new house was built within the precincts of the confiscated Franciscan friary (NLI MS 3137 (42)).

Arthur Chichester, Joymount had three massive bow windows facing the sea, and it was crowned by a flat balustraded roof.[41]

Early churches

The limited development of classical themes in early seventeenth-century residences was replicated in Protestant churches. During the early seventeenth century, many Protestant churches were rebuilt or newly erected by native or immigrant craftsmen. Under the auspices of the Companies of London, the English builder William Parrott constructed St Columb's cathedral in Londonderry from 1627 onwards. The building featured windows of a depressed-arched Gothic design; classical details were absent.[42] A series of smaller Protestant churches had some classical detail, but none could boast of a classically inspired plan. Newtownards

41 Detail of a view by Thomas Phillips in 1685, NLI, MS 3137, f. 42.   42 *Historic buildings ... in the city of Derry* (Belfast, 1970), p. 7.

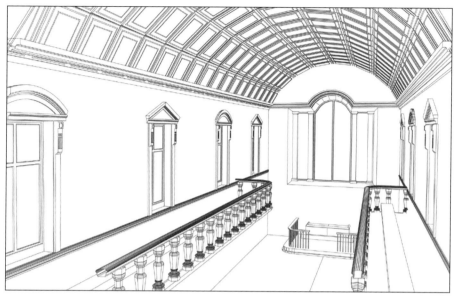

Figure 5.11 Jesuit chapel, Back Lane, Dublin, one of the first and finest classical structures in Ireland. The Jesuits, a new order, abandoned the Gothic and built their churches in a neo-classical style. This chapel was built in 1628 under the patronage of the dowager Countess of Kildare. Elizabeth Nugent had married Gerald, the fourteenth earl: his death in 1612 left her a free hand. The complex consisted of a college, novitiate, sodality, main chapel and her private residence, Kildare Hall. The chapel had two-storey rectangular galleries, a raised pulpit and a railed altar. Adopting Renaissance principles of architecture, the chapel was built on the plan of a triple cube with a coffered ceiling and gallery. It compares favourably with the chapel at St James' palace in London, designed by Inigo Jones in 1623. Kildare Hall was closed down definitively in 1641. This reconstruction drawing is by the distinguished Dublin architect Niall McCullough.

church (Down, 1632) was typical: its only classical feature was the aisle arcade of four 'handsome' stone arches of the Doric order.[43]

The limited deployment of classical detail in Protestant churches was surpassed by at least one Catholic church. During the 1620s and 1630s, religious toleration was more widespread in Ireland than in England. The establishment in 1622 of Propaganda de Fide in Rome accelerated an Irish Catholic mission that was largely orchestrated from the Continent. Religious orders such as the Jesuits and Franciscans became active, and renovated older churches or built new ones.[44] The most astonishing Counter-Reformation church was the Jesuit chapel at Kildare Hall, Dublin, built in 1628. It stood in Back Lane on the site of the present Tailors' Hall. Although long disappeared, its interior features are known from a detailed description by the first earl of Cork.[45]

---

43 [Luckombe], *Tour 1779*, p. 335. Other examples include the simple round-headed west door of Lismore cathedral and another at Tullynakill church (Down, 1639) that has pilasters and an architrave. As early as 1617, St Mary's church in Youghal received a 'compaste [compassed] inbowed roof' (Grosart (ed.), *Lismore papers*, series 1, i, p. 169).   **44** W. Phillips (ed.), *History of the Church of Ireland*, 3 vols (Oxford, 1933–4); C. Meehan, *The rise and fall of the Irish Franciscans* (Dublin, 1877).   **45** *CSPI, 1625–32*, pp 509–10.

It was seated round with an altar with ascents, a curious pulpit and organs, and four places for confession neatly contrived, galleried above round about with rails and turned ballasters, coloured, a compass roof, a cloister above with many other chambers, all things most fair and graceful, like the banquetting house at Whitehall.

RENEWED CLASSICAL IMPULSES AFTER 1660

Kildare Hall was spared during the Rebellion of 1641 and the Cromwellian aftermath. Multitudes of other buildings, however, were burned or stripped for firewood and lead. After the country regained a sullen peace imposed by Cromwell, a rebuilding process started early in the 1650s. However, little is known about this activity. Contemporary records fail to indicate the emergence of more mature classical architecture during this period, as was evident in England. It was only after Charles II's restoration in 1660 that a significant new development in Irish architecture took place. One of the first known classical elevations erected in Ireland was the townhouse of the Lord justice, Sir Maurice Eustace, built between 1660 and 1665. It formerly stood in Dame Street in Dublin, and it is known only from an eighteenth-century description:[46]

> The front was most uncommonly ornamented with regular pilasters between the windows, from the capitals of which an arch was carried over each window, and in the void space formed by the turn of the arch were oval stones, the only ones to be seen in the building. Half of the front was several feet further back than the line of the street, which made it appear as if it was a wing – if so, there must have been a similar one on the other side.

It may have been designed by Dr John Westley, son-in-law of John Webb, who was sent by Sir Maurice Eustace to England in 1661 with a wooden model of Phoenix House, the royal lodge.[47] The curious oval stones of Eustace House inserted between the pilasters may have been adapted from an illustration in Serlio's seventh book of architecture (Figure 5.12).[48]

Eustace House with its giant pilasters was an exception; otherwise it resembled the country houses that architects such as Hugh May and Roger Pratt were developing in England. Such houses certainly existed in Ireland but only Beaulieu (Louth) survives intact. Even though most of these houses were built in the relatively peaceful period between 1660 and 1689, they were surrounded by enclosures of palisades or stone walls with corner turrets from which the flanks could be protected. Such a layout was designed by the builder Thomas Smith for Burton House (Cork, 1671). This house was erected for Sir Philip Perceval but, as he was still a minor, his uncle Sir

46 I am indebted to Peter Walsh for drawing my attention to an eighteenth-century description of this house by Austin Cooper (*Dublin Penny Journal* (1902), p. 276).   47 BL, Add. MS 15,893, f. 243.   48 Serlio, *Tutte l'opere*, Libro settimo, p. 69.

Figure 5.12 Eustace House, Dame Street (opposite Eustace Street), Dublin, built of brick in 1671.
This reconstruction is based on a detailed dairy entry by the antiquarian Austin Cooper in December
1782, when the house was being demolished to make way for the widening of Dame Street. Briefly
occupied by the Fitzgeralds, it was also called Kildare House. A 1685 lease passed it between Walter
Harris and Michael Mitchell, both merchants (Rolf Loeber's 1974 reconstruction drawing).

Robert Southwell acted as the patron. Unlike Irish enclosures of preceding decades,
strict symmetry was observed here, even when partitioning walls and outbuildings.
An even more curious enclosure was planned in that same year in County Antrim.
The earl of Conway was in an advanced stage of finishing surprisingly extensive
stables at Portmore. This building was closely modelled on Hugh May's classically
inspired stables at Cornbury (Oxfordshire). Both house and stables at Portmore
were to be encompassed by a wall which the English architect William Hurlbut[49]
had planned on an 'ovall figure'. Even in England, such a large layout on an oval
plan was unknown. Conway disliked it and changed it to a 'sexangular' plan to make
it more defensible.[50] Thus at both Burton and Portmore, classical planning was still
subordinated to the need to withstand the attacks of native inhabitants.

Much closer to Dublin, Old Carton (Figure 5.13) was erected in 1687 for Richard
Talbot, earl of Tyrconnell. Here the enclosures no longer presented a defensive

49 Colvin, *Biographical dictionary of British architects*, p. 440.   50 Hastings MSS 14,491 and
14,506, Huntington Library, San Marino, California.

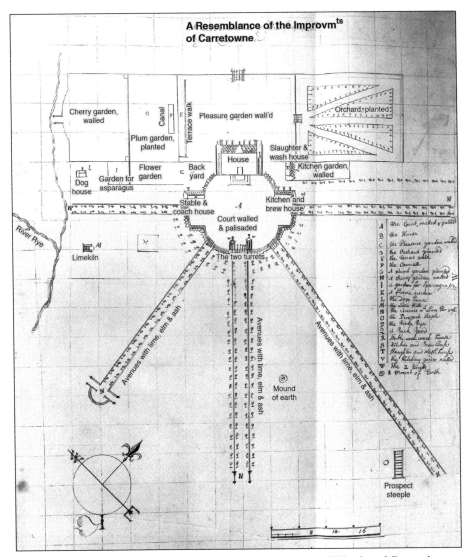

A Resemblance of the Improvm^{ts} of Carretowne

Cherry garden, walled

Canal

Terrace walk

Pleasure garden wall'd

Orchard, planted

Plum garden, planted

House

Slaughter & wash house

Flower garden

Back yard

Kitchen garden, walled

Dog house

Garden for asparagus

Stable & coach house

Kitchen and brew house

Court walled & palisaded

River Rye

Limekiln

The two turrets

Avenues with lime, elm & ash

Avenues with lime, elm & ash

Avenues with lime, elm & ash

Mound of earth

Prospect steeple

Figure 5.13 'A resemblance of the improv[e]m[en]ts of Carretown'. This plan of Carton demesne c.1680 shows the careful integration of the house and gardens into a wider formal landscape setting. Enclosures walled with warm brick protected the orchards and gardens from damaging wind and frost. Carton had multiple walled enclosures close to the house, including a cherry garden, a plum garden, a pleasure garden, orchard, a garden for asparagus, flower garden and kitchen garden. Fruit trees were often trained against sheltering south-facing walls. Redrawn by Matthew Stout (Holkham Archive).

appearance. A semi-circular wall extended in front of the main house, whose main block was connected by curtain wings to two symmetrically disposed pavilions. It is the earliest Palladian layout of an Irish country house in which the buildings and landscape were purposefully related.

Eyrecourt Castle (Galway) illustrates the evolution towards a more symmetrical plan (Figure 5.14). Early seventeenth-century houses – and some dating from later

Figure 5.14 Eyrecourt Castle, County Galway, built before 1677.

in the century – featured a main hall positioned to one side. At Eyrecourt, built before 1677, the plan of the house, featuring a recession at the rear, resembled Robert Hooke's plan for Sir Walter Young's house in Devon.[51] The main hall and imperial staircase were centrally placed, occupying a third of the whole house. Hidden from public view for a century, this massive, exquisitely carved staircase was ripped out of Eyrecourt Castle by its cash-strapped owner, and sold in 1927 to the American newspaper magnate William Randolph Hearst, with the intention of installing it in his fantasy castle in California. The mercurial Hearst changed his mind and donated it to the Detroit Institute of Art.

This staircase, constructed in the 1670s, is the only surviving example from that period in Ireland. It is truly monumental in scale – six by seven metres, and two storeys high. Compared to the circular staircases of Irish towerhouses, the Eyrecourt staircase marks a major departure from late medieval methods of getting 'upstairs'. Its enormous size and its monumental but detailed carvings constituted a ceremonial entrance to the upper storey of the main reception rooms (*piano nobile*) of the house. Having made a grand entry by this impressive staircase, visitors could then enjoy the vista over the formal garden, the parkland and the distant Burren. The layout of the staircase consists of two separate sets of steps, turning 180 degrees at the half-way point and then merging into a single flight that reached the upper landing. The ascent is easy and gradual, much less steep than a modern staircase. As seen

---

51 M. Batten, 'The architecture of Dr Robert Hooke', *Walpole Society*, xxv (1937), p. 109.

Figure 5.15 Staircase, main hall, Eyrecourt Castle, County Galway (Detroit Institute of Arts).

from the downstairs hall, the staircase is partly screened by the Eyre family's coat of arms, flanked by two arches ingeniously suspended from the ceiling (Figure 4.16). On the first steps, the balustrades and newel posts with their wealth of botanical detail become visible, including many carved vases with flowers. At the half-landing, the full extent of the staircase first becomes visible, showing contrasts between the straight lines of the massive bannisters and the rolling down of the carved acanthus leaves from the railings.

The gradual ascent continues to the first floor, where a wall of decorative panelling with superimposed pilasters on each side of the double doors announced

Figure 5.16 Doorway at Beaulieu House, County Louth (photo by Cara Konig-Brock).

the saloon. The high point of the staircase is its rich carving dedicated to nature. The newel posts alone carry thirty carved vases of flowers, mostly freestanding, while others adjoin the walls. Two carved heads of 'green men' at the top of the staircase spout acanthus leaves from their mouth, with the leaves rolling down the foliated frieze below the massive bannisters. Other faces of 'green men' feature up and down the staircase.

The Eyrecourt staircase is of exceptional quality, combines different designs, and supplies a crucial (and until now hidden) link in the evolution of Irish decorative

Figure 5.17 Two-component chimney piece in the dining room at Eyrecourt Castle, County Galway (NLI).

arts. Clearly, the Eyrecourt staircase must be the product of a master designer and a set of experienced carvers working in lime, chestnut, oak and pine. Similarities in design with the Royal Hospital, Kilmainham point to the involvement of the architect and surveyor-general William Robinson and the carvers who worked at Kilmainham's main hall (and presumably the chapel) during the early 1680s.

The staircase fuses several major art styles. Its symmetrical layout and its supporting pillars are clearly classically inspired. The acanthus leaves reflect designs published in seventeenth-century pattern books. The 'green men' hark back to the Middle Ages, but they are also the earliest surviving example of the distinctive masks that became central to the design of Irish carved side-tables of the eighteenth century.

The superb superimposed pilasters at the *piano nobile* level contrast strongly with the curious arrangement of pilasters flanking the front door and the oval window above it, decidedly old-fashioned when compared with the more assured neo-classical doorway at contemporary Beaulieu (Louth) (Figure 5.16).

The interiors of late seventeenth-century country houses, apart from their elaborate staircases, heavy panelling and plaster work, were often remarkable because of their refined classical chimney pieces. At Eyrecourt, the two-component chimney piece (Figure 5.17) followed closely a design in Serlio's seventh book. Elsewhere, Italian Baroque is reflected in a chimney piece that most likely came from Old Carton. Here spiral columns carried an acanthus frieze (Figure 5.18) hiding a Roman bust, and the capitals assumed the form of grotesque masks.

Figure 5.18 Baroque-style wooden chimney piece from Old Carton, County Kildare (now in the shell house on the demesne). The style is influenced by the Manueline style (Portuguese late Gothic), a sumptuous, eclectic form of architectural ornamentation of the early sixteenth century, incorporating maritime elements and representations of exotic discoveries. This innovative style marked the transition from late Gothic to Renaissance. Its exuberance did not suit sober Protestantism, which abandoned it quickly in favour of a chaste neo-Classicism.

The erection of complete classical structures in Ireland is not recorded prior to 1681 when the Duke of Ormond obtained a design from Hugh May (1621–84), the English architect, for building a waterhouse (Figure 5.19).[52] This circular building, long demolished, stood in the garden of Kilkenny Castle and it was decorated with giant pilasters all round. Porticos are recorded at several houses. For instance, the Duchess of Ormond rebuilt Dunmore Castle (Kilkenny) in 1663–4. Her architect, Captain John Morton, built a (classical?) portico with pillars in front.[53] Around this time, the architect William Dodson prepared grandiose plans for the Royal Lodge, the Phoenix House, which included a projecting portico of Portland stone.[54] Another Doric portico embellished the courtyard of Lismore Castle, seat of the earl of Cork and Burlington.[55] All these early porticos have vanished. Although some may have been giant porticos, one cannot conclude this for certain. At Blessington

---

52 NLI, MS 2417, f. 237. This document is partly misquoted in *Ormond*, n.s., vi, pp 279–80.
53 *Ormond*, n.s., iii, p. 201.   **54** NLI, MS 2487, ff 23–4.   **55** C. Smith, *The ancient and present state of the county and city of Waterford* (Dublin, 1746), p. 56.

Figure 5.19 Francis Place, 'The Duke of Ormond's house att Kilkenny taken from the bridg'. Hugh May's circular water house building of 1681 in the garden of Kilkenny Castle. Hugh May (1621–1684) was an English architect who worked in the era between the introduction of Palladianism into England by Inigo Jones, and the full flowering of English Baroque under John Vanbrugh and Nicholas Hawksmoor. May worked extensively on Windsor Castle and Ormond enticed him to work for him.

(Wicklow),[56] a one-storey arcade with pillars was built (prior to 1676) on the garden side of the house, and this might well then have been called a portico.

Public buildings
The evolution of Classicism in Irish country houses was paralleled by similar developments in public buildings. Here too buildings varied in sophistication: some were obviously the product of craftsmen with a basic but often shaky knowledge of classical themes, while others showed more balanced design. For example, the old Tholsel in Dublin[57] (Figure 5.20), erected from 1676 onwards, followed a loose understanding of classical composition. Other tholsels built in Irish towns at this time largely follow this informal pattern. They contrast strongly with the design of the Exchange in Cork (Figure 5.21), erected in 1708,[58] which displayed a highly balanced sense of proportion and detail, and which may have been modelled on the Royal Exchange in London.

The main front of Trinity College, Dublin (Figure 5.22) was erected from 1672 onwards. The left portion of the building was designed by the craftsman-architect Thomas Lucas,[59] and it again displayed an adaptation of classical and British themes. Its pavilions carried Holborn gables (Dutch Billies) and were decorated

---

56 Bence-Jones, *Country houses*, p. 44.   57 Dineley, 'Observations 1675–80'. Demolished. Compare this building with the old exchange of Limerick and the session house at Naas (Kildare), both of which had galleries with classical pillars, and an accumulation of mannerist details (Dineley, 'Observations 1675–80', p. 140).   58 The Knight of Glin kindly gifted me this photograph of the Cork Exchange from the Holkham Collection.   59 Loeber, this volume, p. 238.

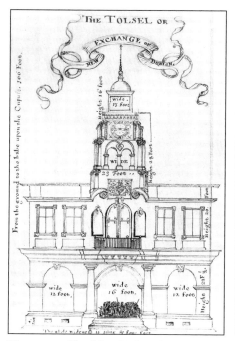

Figure 5.20 The 'New Exchange' (now known as the old Tholsel) in Dublin, erected from 1676 onwards. Drawn and measured by Thomas Dineley in 1681 (NLI MS 392).

Figure 5.21 The 'New Exchange of Corke' built from a design by Twiss Jones between 1705 and 1710. It was demolished in 1837 (Holkham Collection).

Figure 5.22 The front of Trinity College, Dublin, erected from 1672 onwards (Brooking's map, 1728).

with two storeys of pilasters. The central portion of the building, although also pilastered, generated a totally different appearance with its tall roof and widespread chimneystacks. The central element of Trinity College imitated the central pavilion of the newly erected Hotel des Invalides in Paris. This military hospital also served as the model for the Royal Hospital Kilmainham, although there the architect William Robinson followed its conception in rough outline only and not in detail as at Trinity College.

Figure 5.23 Baroque columns and pilasters, main chapel altar, Royal Hospital, Kilmainham, built from 1682 onwards. The work is by the gifted French carver James Tabary.

Figure 5.24 Gothic rosette, detail of the main window of the chapel, probably by William Robinson, *c.*1682, Royal Hospital, Kilmainham.

James Tabary, a Huguenot carver, was responsible for the highly French interior to the chapel of the Royal Hospital.[60] This chapel, built from 1682 onwards, was developed in a way that lacked any good comparison elsewhere in Great Britain and Ireland. The main altar is an accomplished Baroque composition with clusters of columns and pilasters (Figure 5.23). The decorative details in the chapel show consistently high craftsmanship. It was once thought that the main window of the chapel (Figure 5.24) with its Gothic rosette was recycled from the medieval priory on the site; closer inspection reveals that it is integral with the concave surround that is typical of William Robinson's work.[61] Later work by Robinson at St Mary's church in Dublin showed clearly that he knew how to combine classical and Gothic details (Figure 5.25). However, Robinson's contemporaries favoured classical themes over Gothic ones. Irish architecture in this respect and in many other ways in the seventeenth century echoed developments in English architecture. Many of Robinson's churches have been altered. His work at St Carthage's cathedral (Lismore, Waterford) shows again his use of concave mouldings and round-headed windows with segmental tracery. The latter is most likely based on examples of Dutch church designs published in Hendrik de Keyser's *Architectura Moderna*,[62] which may also have inspired Hugh May's windows at Windsor Castle.

Domes were already evident on Irish buildings more than fifty years before the erection of the dome at the Parliament House on College Green by Edward Lovett Pearce, *c.*1730. An early Dublin dome is visible on a drawing by Francis Place of the north side of Dublin, which includes St Andrew's church, erected in 1672 after a

60 NAI, RHK 1/1/1, under the date 27 January 1686/7.   61 R. Loeber, 'Sir William Robinson', *Ir. Georgian Soc. Bull.*, xvii (1974), pp 3–9.   62 See, for example, the engraving of Hendrik de Keyser's Zuiderkerkin (Amsterdam) in *Architectura Moderna* (1631).

Figure 5.25 East window, St Mary's church, Dublin by William Robinson, 1701.

design by William Dodson.[63] The oval plan and dome could easily have been copied from Serlio.[64] St Andrew's was unique for its time in Great Britain and Ireland, for Wren only designed the oval St Antholin's (London) six years after St Andrew's was started. The oval plan of St Andrew's must have been strikingly novel for many Dubliners, for it was always called the 'round' church. Another octagonal dome was erected in 1695 by William Robinson to crown the Four Courts,[65] at that time situated close to Christ Church cathedral.

63 R. Loeber, 'An unpublished view of Dublin in 1698 by Francis Place', *Ir. Georgian Soc. Bull.*, xxi (1978), pp 7–15; Wheeler & M. Craig, *Dublin churches*, p. 9.   **64** Serlio, *Tutte l'opere* (1619), Libro quinto, p. 204.   **65** Loeber, 'William Robinson', p. 8.

POST-WILLIAMITE ARCHITECTURE

Before the outbreak of the Williamite War in 1689, Ireland had already witnessed
the introduction of a variety of classically inspired architectural themes, some
derivative from English and Flemish examples, others originating in Renaissance
Italy. One would think that the pace had been set for ever more advanced classical
structures. Rebuilding after the war offered opportunities for that; nevertheless, a
different development took place.

Although the rebuilding process after the Williamite War was widespread, few
innovative designs were used for country houses. Some, such as Castlecor (Cork)
and Buncrana Castle (Donegal),[66] were built with attached pavilions projecting
from the main block. Apart from such variations, the houses largely resembled other
late seventeenth-century examples. Formal houses prior to 1720 were only rarely
decorated with giant pilasters, for instance at Castle Durrow (Laois)[67] and Castle
Bernard (Cork),[68] but these houses still retained late seventeenth-century features.
An extravagant classical scheme by the surveyor-general, Thomas Burgh, for his own
house near Naas,[69] proved financially reckless and it remained unrealised apart from
its pavilions. At Clonmannon (Wicklow),[70] a small pedimented frontispiece featured
a rusticated ground floor and Doric pilasters on the first floor, all executed in brick.
One of the pavilions of Palace Anne (Cork), executed in rubbed brick, also survives.
It dates from 1714,[71] and it offers a good example of a regional interpretation of
classical themes in conjunction with a revival of the curvilinear gable.

Entrance doorways became stereotyped: swan-neck pediments usually crowned
a simple broad moulding. Examples include country houses such as Buncrana
(Donegal) and Castlemartin (Kildare). Occasionally, large gateways were built. The
most impressive example, at Kilkenny Castle, erected after 1698 for the second duke
of Ormond by William Robinson,[72] formed a balanced design of giant pilasters,
niches and a pediment, all executed in fine ashlar.

The lack of innovation in country house design in the early eighteenth century
is hard to explain. Some Irish landowners such as Edward Southwell focused more
on their English estates. He employed Sir John Vanbrugh for the building of Kings
Weston near Bristol. His relative, Sir John Perceval (later earl of Egmont), made
plans in 1707 to rebuild the burned-out shell of his Irish residence, Burton House

---

66 Castlecor, built in 1723, according to a date stone, was demolished some decades ago (for an
illustration, see J.P. Neale, *Views of seats of noblemen and gentlemen in England and Wales, Scotland
and Ireland* (London, 1818–29), I, n.p.). For Buncrana Castle, see M. Craig, *Classic Irish houses
of the middle size* (London, 1976), pp 64–5. The pavilions at Buncrana Castle are presumably
contemporary with the house; this is less certain for Castlecor.   67 A drawing of its original
appearance was published in R. Loeber, 'Castle Durrow', *Ir. Georgian Soc. Bull.*, xvi (1973), p.
104.   68 C. Smith, *The ancient and present state of the county and city of Cork* (Dublin, 1774),
i, p. 248. Demolished.   69 A drawing originally among the collection of Major J.H. de Burgh
of Oldtown (Naas, Kildare) was lost some years ago. Only a photograph is preserved, published
by Bence-Jones, *Country houses*, p. 229.   70 Craig & Knight of Glin, *Ireland observed*, p.
32.   71 G. Bennett, *The history of Bandon* (Cork, 1869), p. 485.   72 Loeber, 'William
Robinson', p. 9.

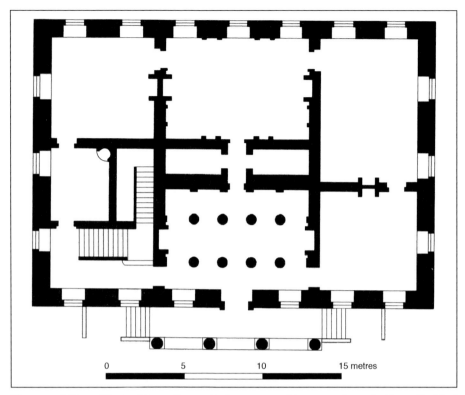

Figure 5.26 Plan of Burton House, County Cork, as proposed in 1707: redrawn by Conor Rochford from J. Anderson, *A genealogical history of the house of Yvery* (London, 1742).

(Cork) and he discussed this project in Rome with unidentified architects. The dimensions of the ruins were sent to Rome[73] to allow designs to be prepared, and a plan of a porticoed house at Burton (Cork) (Figure 5.26) may well date from this time. Although one would expect that an Italian architect was commissioned to make a design, the young James Gibbs, then in Rome, may have received instructions from Perceval.[74] Perceval later encouraged Gibbs to visit Ireland, but (after much hesitation) Gibbs declined.[75] Perceval was not discouraged, and he commissioned plans before 1715 from another newcomer, Colen Campbell, who based his design on Palladio's Pojana and Villa Cornaro plans.[76] Financial difficulties inflicted by the South Sea Bubble prevented Perceval from executing this purely classical building. It took another seven years before Ireland saw its first genuinely classical country house, Castletown, built for Speaker Conolly by the Italian architect Alessandro Galilei and Edward Lovett Pearce.[77]

73 BL, Add. MS 47,038, ff 111, 112, 119; J. Anderson, *A genealogical history of the House of Yvery* (London, 1742). The engraving of Burton House was inserted in only some copies of this book.   74 BL, Add. MS 47,025, ff 80–1.   75 *Egmont*, ii, pp 235–6.   76 Published in C. Campbell, *Vitruvius Britannicus, or the British architect*, 3 vols (London, 1715), i, pp 95–7.   77 M. Craig, Knight of Glin & J. Cornforth, 'Castletown, Co. Kildare', *Country Life*, 27 March, 3 & 10 April 1969.

Figure 5.27 St Werburgh's church, Dublin,   Figure 5.28 St Ann's church, Dublin, begun
begun *c*.1718 (Brooking's map, 1728).   *c*.1718 (Brooking's map, 1728).

A major development in classical architecture occurred in Dublin in the 1710s. By one of those quirky Irish contradictions, designs of Jesuit origin were chosen for two churches erected by the Protestant Church of Ireland. The rebuilding of St Werburgh's (Figure 5.27) started in 1715. The surveyor-general, Thomas Burgh, designed it and supervised its erection.[78] The façade is derived from Vignola's Gesu in Rome, and it is probably based specifically on Francesco da Volterra's design for the Jesuit church of S. Chiara (Rome). A few years later, St Ann's church was

78 R. Loeber, 'Biographical dictionary of engineers in Ireland 1600–1730' in *Ir. Sword*, xiii (1977–9), p. 115.

begun. Here the façade (Figure 5.28) was transposed rather mechanically from Rossi's engraving (1683) of S. Giacomo degli Incurabili, another Roman church by Francesco da Volterra.[79] Nothing now remains of this intriguing attempt to impose a Catholic design on a Protestant church.

CONCLUSION

Whereas in England the early eighteenth century was marked by an upsurge in Baroque architecture under the leadership of architects such as William Talman (1650–1719) and John Vanbrugh (1664–1726), building in Ireland consolidated features of the late seventeenth-century style. Irish patrons with vision such as Sir John Perceval and Edward Southwell turned towards England, while others lacked both vision and finances. Baroque ideas only rarely found architectural expression in Ireland. William Robinson's design for the east window of St Mary's church in Dublin of 1703 (Figure 5.25)[80] is among the first examples in Ireland in which a new and freer use of classical themes was expressed. Robinson departed Ireland soon afterwards, spending most of his life in a self-imposed exile in England. Captain Thomas Burgh (1670–1730), his successor as surveyor-general, remained conservative in building; it was only during the 1720s, when the gifted Edward Lovett Pearce (1699–1733) emerged, that true Palladian ideas transformed Irish villas.

79 Illustrated in H. Hibbard, *Carlo Maderno and Roman architecture 1580–1630* (University Park, PA, 1971), Plate 14c.   80 Loeber, 'William Robinson', p. 9.

CHAPTER SIX

The architecture of Irish country houses 1691–1740: continuity and innovation

(co-authored with Livia Hurley)

INTRODUCTION

BETWEEN THE WILLIAMITE WAR (1689–91) AND 1739, over 160 new country houses were built in Ireland, only a portion of which survive. This was a period of major shifts in landownership, when landed and commercial incomes gradually improved, allowing owners to remodel existing seats as well as to build anew. Early forms of Palladianism were introduced and a new era of sophisticated architecture appeared alongside the more provincial adaptations of classical ideas. The study of the architecture of Irish houses of this particular period has received relatively modest attention from architectural historians.[1] While these fifty years have been depicted as somewhat of a vacuum, it was in fact a time of continuity, experimentation and innovation, ultimately setting the stage for the mature, classically-inspired architecture of the remainder of the eighteenth century.[2]

This survey of the period engages with three critical areas. Firstly, how did the post-Williamite confiscations and economic conditions impact on estate ownership, the architectural profession and country house building? Secondly, what are the characteristics and innovations of house architecture that materialised during this period and before the practice of Richard Castle[3] (*fl.*1728–50)? And thirdly, did Irish houses of this period differ greatly from those in England?

Analysis of the architecture of this period is particularly challenging. Relatively few contemporaneous travellers' accounts of Ireland exist, county survey texts are rare, and government surveys cover confiscated properties only. Unlike England, few collections of Irish architectural drawings survive and building accounts for the period are also relatively scarce. The documentation

---

1 Craig, *Classic Irish houses*; Craig, *Architecture of Ireland*, pp 177–99; B. de Breffny & R. ffolliott, *The houses of Ireland* (London, 1975), pp 83–100; Bence-Jones, *Burke's guide to country houses*, p. xix; T. Barnard, *Making the grand figure: lives and possessions in Ireland 1641–1770* (New Haven, 2004), pp 49–187, 188–225; P. McCarthy, 'The planning and use of space in Irish houses 1730–1830' (PhD, TCD, 2008). 2 T. Barnard, *Improving Ireland: projectors, prophets and profiteers 1641–1786* (Dublin, 2008). 3 Castle's first documented country house commission was in 1728.

of surviving buildings has improved over recent decades because of architectural surveys and inventories, However, numerous houses have been erased or rebuilt, obscuring their original appearance.

The dating of structures without documentation still remains difficult and this also applies to the earliest identification of architectural features. The literature is riddled with dating attributions, but firm evidence is often wanting. In reality, house construction was usually prolonged, particularly if the owner's finances and economic conditions fluctuated, or because of absenteeism, both internally (not living on the estate but close to Dublin) and externally (living in England). Despite these reservations, their construction accelerated only after 1710, allied with the notion that the income of estate owners only gradually improved after the end of the war.[4] The absence of many of these houses from the period reinforces the need to expand on earlier studies, and to combine field evidence with scant documentary records. This chapter addresses the three questions posed, and while the limitations of space hinders a more thorough architectural analysis, the intention is to create a gazetteer of examples which can stimulate further study in the area.

ARCHITECTURAL INNOVATION

The architecture of houses throughout the seventeenth century developed in several revolutionary ways. Whereas towerhouses continued to be built in the early decades, they soon vanished and non-defensive houses appeared subsequently. In the late century, a new generation of quadratic, compact double-pile houses emerged. Beaulieu (Louth), having been rebuilt, may partly belong to this period. The development of this type appeared very shortly after those in England.[5] Ruined examples include Eyrecourt Castle (Galway), the later rebuilt Burton House (Cork) and Old Carton (Kildare). All these houses featured tall prominent hipped roofs and overhanging eaves supported by classical modillions (ornate brackets or corbels supporting a cornice). Façades slowly gained symmetrically-positioned window openings.[6]

The new building tradition continued during the early peaceful years of the reign of James II (1685–9) when Jacobites built additions in the late seventeenth-century style at Kilcash Castle (Tipperary) and Ross Castle (Kerry).[7] Activities, however, came abruptly to a halt with the threat of a war. Many patrons and their architects fled the country for England in the late 1680s, to return after the war in 1691. Military campaigns were mostly fought out on the battlefields rather than through sieges of cities or defensive Big Houses. The exception was north-west Munster which became the seat of war, lying 'not far from Lymerick and in the enemy's quarters' and where 'about fifty substantial houses' were reduced to 'ashes'.[8]

4 L.M. Cullen, 'Economic development, 1691–1750' in *NHI*, iv, pp 143ff.   5 Craig, *Classic Irish houses*, p. 5.   6 Loeber, this volume, chapter 5.   7 J. Flood & P. Flood, *Kilcash: a history 1190–1801* (Dublin, 1999); J. Larner (ed.), *Killarney: history and heritage* (Cork, 2005), p. 70. 8 BL, Add. MS 47,041, f. 26.

Our understanding of the architecture that succeeded the war relies heavily on what occurred as a result of the confiscation and sale of properties owned by Catholics. While improving economic conditions facilitated investments in estates and their attendant architecture, recovery was slower in some instances, particularly because of the lack of livestock. The period between 1691 and 1704 was characterised by great uncertainty concerning the properties of those Catholics involved in the war. Some were regranted their lands, but many lost out. Eventually, half-a-million plantation acres (330,000ha) were granted to Irish and English Protestants. Ambiguity about the fate of a large number of properties owned by Catholics was resolved in 1702–3 when an auction was held at Chichester House in Dublin, which included lands owned by the defeated James II.[9] Unsurprisingly, the period prior to this legal certainty saw limited house construction on confiscated lands. In fact, these areas experienced the gradual decay of many existing buildings due to anxiety over ownership and suspended maintenance.[10] The economic calamities caused by the war were unequally distributed across the country. In essence, the concentration of confiscations in the east and south-west of the country, and their absence in the highly Protestant north, must have contributed to wide geographic differences in uncertain ownership, derelict country seats, delays in economic recovery and new building work.

Relatively few of the nobility built any substantial domestic architecture between 1691 and 1739. Several were content with their seventeenth-century or older houses, notably the earl of Clanrickarde at Portumna (Galway) and the earl of Kildare who re-acquired Carton (Kildare). Some Jacobite Catholics, such as the Talbots, turned Protestant and returned to their ancestral homes, in their case Malahide Castle (Dublin).[11] Government-instigated exclusion of Catholics from employment (army, church, courts) and the forced division of Catholics' estates among their children limited their income and their descendants' ability to enhance their estates.[12] Some former Jacobites chose to repair their existing homes or to build relatively small houses. Examples of the latter are Ballyconra (Kilkenny, 1724), a modest seven-bay, two-storey gabled house of the former outlaw, the sixth Viscount Mountgarret, and Lieutenant Colonel Mathias Everard's equally modest seven-bay hip-roofed Randlestown (Meath), which shows some advanced features for its time such as the defining cornice between floors.[13] Everard had fought under James II but he recovered his estate under the articles of Limerick. Conversely, the third Viscount Kenmare, forced to vacate his ancestral Ross Castle (Kerry) for use as a government barracks, built the substantial new seat of Kenmare House at Killarney (Kerry) in the early decades of the eighteenth century. The Jacobite James Cotter, descended from a

9 W. Maguire (ed.), *Kings in conflict 1689–1750* (Belfast, 1990), pp 139–56; J.G. Simms, *The Williamite confiscation in Ireland 1690–1703* (London, 1956), pp 148–57, 177–92. 10 A survey of confiscated properties in Meath in 1700 showed wide expanses of often empty land: A. Horner & R. Loeber, 'Landscape in transition: descriptions of forfeited properties in Counties Meath, Louth and Cavan in 1700', *Anal. Hib.*, xlii (2011), pp 59–180. 11 P. Somerville-Large, *The Irish country house: a social history* (London, 1995), pp 111–15. 12 Maguire, *Kings in conflict*, p. 156. 13 Bence-Jones, *Burke's guide*, p. 237.

Figure 6.1 Castle Mary, County Cork was built by the Jacobite James Cotter/Séamus Mac Éamonn Mhic Coitir (1630–1705) (Irish Architectural Archive).

long-established Catholic family, regained his family estate to build the architectural gem of Castle Mary (Cork, demolished) (Figure 6.1).[14] Another individual with Jacobite leanings, the second Duke of Ormonde, fled Ireland in 1716 to join his exiled king. Subsequent confiscation of his properties and some regrants to his son, Lord Arran, led to the decay of Kilkenny Castle and Dunmore (both in Kilkenny).

In the realm of the Protestant nobility, noteworthy are the works of the earl of Inchiquin at Rostellan (Cork) in 1710,[15] and the earl of Orrery, whose unnamed structures on his wife's estate of Caledon (Tyrone) were alluded to in a satirical verse 'written on the front of a mock castle, erected by the 5th earl of Orrery, near the ancient palace of the great and illustrious O'Neill'.[16] Improvements among the more prosperous Protestants are also distinguished, such as Castle Durrow (Laois, from 1716) built by William Flower. One of the largest landowners, John Perceval, had ambitious plans for the rebuilding of Burton House (Cork) from the 1710s onward, but these never advanced beyond construction of the stables.[17] The architect of Lord Tyrone's rebuilt Curraghmore (Waterford, 1707) is unknown, but its massing is uncannily similar to the Dutch country seat of Middachten (1694–7) for Godard van Reede, first earl of Athlone, who commanded a vanguard of the Williamite army in Ireland.[18]

14 Craig, *Architecture of Ireland*, pp 143, 146. Although treated by Craig as a late seventeenth-century house, Annsgrove (also Annegrove) is clearly more early eighteenth century in its detail. 15 Michael Gould to Donat O'Brien, 19 Sept. 1710, Ainsworth (ed.), *Inchiquin manuscripts*, p. 104. 16 BL, Add. MS 20,719, f. 13. 17 Barnard, *Improving Ireland*, pp 120–42. 18 TCD, MS 4024, f. 46. A date stone of 1701 indicates that rebuilding had started earlier.

CONFISCATED ESTATES

Most purchasers of confiscated Jacobite estates after the Williamite War were already landowners in Ireland and only a few were Englishmen or English consortia.[19] Those who were granted or purchased forfeited estates, and built upon them, came from the mercantile and professional classes. Gustavus Hamilton, the former soldier and future Lord Boyne, received 3,482 Irish acres (2,298ha) of forfeited lands and he erected Stackallen (Meath, *c.*1712) in a retro late seventeenth-century style, while William Conolly (speaker of the House of Commons), who made his fortune buying confiscations, built the palatial Castletown House (Kildare, 1722). As guardian to the young Conyngham, heir of the former Fleming estate at Slane (Meath), Conolly is the likely candidate for the selection of the architect John Curle (*fl.*1690s–1722) to draft plans *c.*1709–10 for extending and squaring-off the old Fleming castle. In the same county, Alderman William Graham's Platten, a nine-bay, three-storey brick house with a courtyard, was possibly one of the largest houses of this period.[20] Amongst those with foreign links was Bartholomew Vamhomrigh, a Dutch merchant, who erected Celbridge Abbey (Kildare); its subsequent rebuilding obscured any Dutch stylistic ideas if they ever existed. John Allen, a descendant of an Anglo-Dutch merchant family, built a house at Stillorgan (Dublin) that was allied to late seventeenth-century English and Irish architecture rather than to Dutch examples.[21] Despite the cultural and religious differences of those who built during this period, there were no appreciable distinctions in the building styles adopted by Catholics, Protestants, newcomers and grantees of confiscated estates. English rather than continental influences dominated.

THE ARCHITECTURAL PROFESSION

While the architectural profession certainly matured in the early stages of the eighteenth century, attributions to architects far outweigh the evidence and relatively few houses can be firmly linked to specific professionals. This is exemplified by the major players in the fraternity at that time. William Robinson (1645–1712), engineer, surveyor-general and designer of the Royal Hospital Kilmainham (Dublin), planned his own residence at Islandbridge near Dublin, the rebuilding of Kilkenny Castle (Kilkenny) and, possibly, his country seat at Sherwood Park (Carlow).[22] He left Ireland in 1709 to live permanently in England. Attributions to his colleague Thomas Burgh (1670–1730), architect of some of the greatest works of the eighteenth-century in the capital, are equally scant, with Oldtown (Kildare, *c.*1721), Dromoland (Clare, 1717–18) and possibly Barbavilla (Westmeath) attributed to his hand.[23] Edward Lovett Pearce (1699–1733), architect of the new parliament building on

---

19 Simms, *Williamite confiscation*, pp 177–92.   **20** NLI, MS 6486.   **21** Celbridge Abbey is sometimes known as Marlay, not be confused with Marlay House in Dublin.   **22** Loeber, *Biographical dictionary*, p. 95.   **23** For the architects and builders mentioned here, www.dia.ie/works; Loeber, *Biographical dictionary*.

Figure 6.2 James Malton's 1789 depiction of Castle Durrow, County Laois, built from 1716 onwards (Victoria and Albert Museum, London).

College Green in Dublin (the most significant addition to the city's architectural canon during this period), also designed country houses but his portfolio extends only to Bellamont Forest (Cavan, 1730s), the unexecuted remodelling of Stillorgan (Dublin), and possibly Summerhill (Meath, 1730s, completed subsequently by Richard Castle). His influence on Irish Palladian architecture in particular was certainly much greater as judged by the many attributions of buildings to him. The mysterious John Curle was behind Old Castle Coole (Fermanagh, 1709), as well as works at Beaulieu (Louth, *c*.1710–20). His drawings for the remodelling of the aforementioned Conyngham Hall (later Slane Castle, Meath) depict turrets against a Baroque-style roof, more widespread in Bavaria than in Ireland, and a string of oval windows, formerly seen at Castlemartin (Kildare).[24]

The term 'architect' is possibly too narrow for this period and the origins of some designs might better be sought among builders and landowners themselves. The builder Benjamin Crawley is known for his work on Castle Durrow and the mason John Rothery began Mount Ivers (Clare) using English designs. The employment of the same builders and artisans on disparate sites was common. The steward of the Burton estate in Cork advised John Perceval in 1711 that he knew two or three 'that have built several good houses in ye countys of Clare and Lymerick and performd very well'.[25] Stonemason Barnaby Demane, who executed the fine

24 L. Hurley, 'Public and private improvements in eighteenth-century Ireland: the case of the Conynghams of Slane 1703–1821' (MLitt, TCD, 2008), pp 22–4.   25 William Taylor to John Perceval 30 Aug. 1711, BL, Add. MS 46,964, f. 107v. This may refer to the mason John O'Brien who built Shannon Grove (Limerick) from 1709 onwards (Loeber, *Biographical dictionary*, p. 81).

ashlar façade and giant pilasters of Castle Durrow (Figure 6.2), also provided chimney pieces at Dromoland,[26] and his contemporary who worked on Barbavilla (Westmeath) was employed subsequently at Castle Forbes (Longford).[27] Their widespread employment might explain the spread of architectural innovations across the country.

Estate owners sometimes sought out foreign architects, but very few have been clearly identified. Those that are known generally left the country after failing to find sufficient patronage to stay. The Florentine architect Alessandro Galilei (1691–1737) was brought to Ireland by the Molesworths in 1718 and he advised the viscount on improvements at Breckdenstown (north Dublin).[28] Later he produced designs for the main façade of Conolly's seat at Castletown, which may have been executed under the supervision of Pearce in 1722.[29] Two English architects who never set foot in Ireland but who contributed architectural designs were William Kent, who sent plans in 1727 to Henry Boyle (who was then building at Castlemartyr, Cork),[30] and James Gibbs, who made designs for Newbridge (Dublin) sometime after 1749.[31] In the long history of construction plans for Burton House, the Dutch military engineer Captain Rudolph Corneille (*fl.*1690) was mentioned to Perceval as a 'contriver' willing to rebuild there in 1711, yet there are no documented houses by his hand.[32] The arrival of the German architect Richard Castle sounded a new era, but his transformative work falls outside the chronological scope of this chapter.

EXTERNAL INFLUENCES

Several estate owners turned to England rather than to Ireland for their architectural activities: most notably, the immensely wealthy Richard Boyle, third earl of Burlington (1694–1753), who advanced Palladian architecture in England only despite his status in Ireland.[33] The irony was that the earl and other contemporaneous absentees could not have built in England were it not for the massive annual income extracted from their Irish estates. Architectural pattern books certainly wielded some influence, although very few of these were published in the early eighteenth century and none in Ireland. The most influential was *Vitruvius Britannicus*, published in London in three volumes (1715; 1717; 1725) followed by a delayed fourth volume in 1739. Among the subscribers were several prominent members of the peerage such as

26 R. Loeber, 'Castle Durrow', *Ir. Georgian Soc. Bull.*, xvi (1973), p. 106.   **27** Barnard, *Making the grand figure*, p. 28.   **28** E. McParland, 'Edward Lovett Pearce and the new junta for architecture' in T. Barnard & J. Clark (eds), *Lord Burlington: architecture, art and life* (London, 1995), pp 151–67.   **29** Loeber, *Biographical dictionary*, pp 54–5.   **30** Barnard, *New anatomy*, pp 224–5.   **31** A. Cobbe & T. Friedman, *James Gibbs in Ireland: Newbridge, his villa for Charles Cobbe, archbishop of Dublin* (Dublin, 2005).   **32** Another foreigner was Leuventhen, who built Red House (also known as Uniacke House) in Youghal (Cork). An unidentified, possibly French, architect made a rather crude drawing for 'Ahadoe' (Aghadoe, Kerry), also known as Supple Court, *c.*1700 (Irish Architectural Archive, *Irish architectural drawings: an exhibition catalogue* (Dublin, 1963), p. 29).   **33** Barnard & Clark (eds), *Lord Burlington*.

Ormonde, Arran, Orrery, Burlington, Castlecomer, Kingsale and Perceval and some with smaller holdings like Edward Southwell, Richard Tighe, William Monck, the bishop of Waterford, Dr Pratt of Trinity College and William Maynard of Curryglass (Waterford).[34] No subscriber was drawn from the ranks of the Catholic families who returned to their ancestral estates after the war. Three Irishmen had designs for their houses published in *Vitrivius Britannicus*, but for their English rather than their Irish seats: Southwell's Kings Weston (near Bristol); Perceval's unexecuted design; duke of Ormonde, Richmond Lodge (near London).

While designs published in the *Vitrivius Britannicus* were for houses situated in England, the volumes influenced Irish architecture in several ways, most obviously through illustrated elevational treatments. The front façade of Belvoir (Antrim) was largely inspired by Kings Weston,[35] while the elevations of two other houses, Kenmare House and Mount Ivers, were gleaned from seventeenth-century English houses (Burlington House, London, 1665–6; Chevening, Kent, *c.*1630s). At Antrim Castle (Antrim, *c.*1710 onwards), the entrance door surround and window above were duplicated from a house at Twickenham outside London.[36]

EARLY EIGHTEENTH-CENTURY HOUSE FORMS

In the late seventeenth century, houses were usually of two storeys (sometimes over basement) with a breakfront, a wide-eaved, high hipped roof supported on modillions and a row of dormers (Eyrecourt Castle).[37] This type continued to be built well into the next decades,[38] but only a few survive – notably Shannon Grove (Limerick) and Stackallan (Meath, *c.*1712) (Figure 6.3).[39] A larger type, echoing earlier styles, was composed of a seven- to thirteen-bay façade with a recessed centrepiece of three bays.[40] In addition to Castletown House, several even more

---

34 Most but not all subscribed to the three volumes. **35** Drawing in private collection. **36** See vol. i, Plates 48, 77, 95–6; vol. ii, Plate 85; vol. iv, Plates 6–10. The eighteenth-century mansion house in Cork was also based on a design from vol. 1, Plate 50. The elevation of Santry Court (Dublin, demolished) compares well with Roger Pratt's Horseheath Hall (Cambridgeshire, 1663–5) (iii, Plate 91) but Santry dates from *c.*1700 and was probably inspired by means of this or some other English example. **37** For houses with dormers, see also Stillorgan (demolished), Mount Merrion (demolished), Loughlinstown (all Dublin); Bogay (Donegal); Mountainstown (Meath); Dromana (Waterford); Castle Durrow (Laois); Kilcreene (Kilkenny); Camolin Park and Loftus Hall (both Wexford, both demolished); Knocktopher (Waterford, altered); Morristown Lattin (Kildare, demolished). **38** Most early eighteenth-century examples of this old-fashioned tall-roofed country house have been lost during the last century or were altered at some point, including Ardfert Abbey and Old Kenmare (both Kerry); Ballyburley (Offaly); Kilcreene (Kilkenny); Loughlinstown (Dublin); Kilmacurragh (Wicklow); Ashgrove (Tipperary); Old Tourin (Waterford); Old Castle Coole (Fermanagh); Moyrisk (Clare); Old Slane (Meath); Ballinlough (Westmeath, roof later lowered). **39** This probably included Beaulieu (Louth), which has proved particularly difficult to date. The house was possibly remodelled in the early eighteenth century when its L-plan was transformed into a rectangular plan. **40** Also Ardfert Abbey (Kerry, demolished); Kilcreene (Kilkenny, demolished); Rathaspeck (Wexford); Stillorgan (Dublin, demolished); Old Stradbally (Laois, demolished).

Figure 6.3 Stackallan House, County Meath, *c.*1712. An aerial photograph from 1960.

palatial models like Kenmare House (Kerry, demolished), Barne (Tipperary) and
Gloster (Offaly) were built in the first decades of the eighteenth century.

This period also saw the emergence of a small number of three- to five-bay
houses, as high as they were wide, resembling the larger Georgian townhouses
in Irish cities. Two of these have been attributed to the architect-painter Francis
Bindon (1690–1765): Clermont (Wicklow) and Furness (Kildare).[41] Invariably, this
category had three storeys (again sometimes over basement) in which the upper
storey, unlike previous forms, had regular window openings rather than dormers,
thus amplifying space and light.[42] Following a typical *piano nobile* arrangement,
principal reception rooms were usually located on the first floor. This became less
common in the following century when they were commonly located on a slightly
elevated ground floor level.

Early eighteenth-century country houses were often still gabled, a building
tradition emanating from former times[43] with curvilinear gables becoming more
popular in later decades.[44] A single, central curvilinear gable could be found at
Old Gowran Castle (Kilkenny, demolished), The Turrets (Limerick) and probably

41   dia.ie/architects/view/477/BINDON-FRANCIS#tab_works.   42   Also in this category
are Rossana (Wicklow), Mount Ivers (Clare) and Riddlestown (Limerick).   43   Also Belan
(Kildare, demolished); Ballyconra (Kilkenny, demolished) and Woodsfield (Offaly).   44   Loeber,
this volume, chapter 5. A late seventeenth-century example was Blessington (Wicklow).

Figure 6.4 Buncrana Castle (County Donegal) (Dúchas). The plaque over the main door commemorates the fact that Theobald Wolfe Tone was brought here after his arrest in 1798.

formerly at Celbridge Abbey (Kildare). A curious instance was Old Castle Leslie, also known as Glaslough (Monaghan, *c.*1720, rebuilt), where a semi-circular gable was flanked by pointed gables, but perhaps the most original was Palace Anne (Cork) with its row of three curvilinear gables crowning the main block, flanked by two pavilions, each one with a slightly differently styled gable. [45] An English counterpart is Moulton Hall (north Yorkshire, 1654). The gabled, symmetrical pavilion theme continued at Moone Abbey (Kildare) and Shannon Grove (added in *c.*1723), providing undulating counterpoints to the horizontal features of the main block – a construct reminiscent of Palladio's Villa Barbaro in the Italian Veneto.

An unusual arrangement of a shallow U-plan with two small projections (for example, Buncrana, Donegal) (Figure 6.4) was not unique to Ireland; it could also be found in England after 1691 and it may have had French counterparts. [46] The type was quite different from the U- and H-plans prevalent in Ireland during the 1600s in that the projections were narrow – only one bay wide and one bay deep. Typically, they were roofed at a slightly lower pitch than the main house. [47] Unlike the narrow flankers which characterised medieval towerhouses (such as those in Louth and Meath) and those dating from the late sixteenth and early seventeenth centuries,

45 E.P. Shirley, *The history of the county of Monaghan* (London, 1879), p. 147. **46** English examples include: Schomburg House (Pall Mall, London), Tickencote (Leicestershire) and Bexston Hall (Cheshire). **47** Sometimes the roofs of the projections were integrated with the roof of the main house (Ballykilcavan, Laois) or detached as in the case of a gabled main house (Buncrana, Donegal).

these projections (usually only two)[48] did not perform a defensive purpose.[49] Plans depict service for chimneys but contemporary accounts do not reveal the rooms' true function: they may have contained closets, dressing-rooms or gentlemen's studies. Their windows tended to be of similar scale to those in the main house, providing views over the demesne or formal gardens beyond.

Seventeenth-century fortified houses typically accommodated more chimney stacks than towerhouses, but by the next century the number of stacks of the average country house had been reduced and, as a consequence, their placement had become more prominent. This had little to do with a reduction of the number of fireplaces serving different rooms. Their typical position on the outer walls was sustained but there was a move towards internal spinal walls and centrally placed clusters, as at Castle Durrow.[50] Flues were combined at some stage, a technological advance resulting in fewer stacks and less clustering of independent flues serving individual fireplaces.[51] Fire-proofing methods advanced with several houses provided with vaulted basements and much of their internal panelling was executed in fire-proof plaster or stuccowork rather than in timber as at Castletown and Ballyhaise (Cavan).[52] At the same time, waterworks in country house gardens proliferated and with it the practice of hydraulics. It is possible that water supplies within the house also benefitted from this development.

CLASSICAL ARCHITECTURAL LANGUAGE

The slow emergence of the classical language of the late seventeenth century continued. Pediments were placed over three-bay centrepieces, their apexes lower than the main roof line, much in the tradition of the architecture of England and Europe.[53] Subsequently, a more dominant version appeared; its pinnacle was now

---

48 A few houses had four projections. Borris (Carlow) may have originated earlier than the eighteenth century. However, Castle Mary (Cork, demolished) appears to have been newly built in the early eighteenth century.   **49** Surviving examples of this period are at Buncrana (Donegal) and Ballykilcavan (Laois). See also Blandsford (Laois, at the rear); Linsfort Castle, also known as Mount Paul (Donegal, tablet 1720, Craig, *Classic Irish houses*, p. 66); Old Kilruddery (Wicklow), known from a painting; Cahirguillamore (Limerick, demolished); Morristown Lattin (Kildare, demolished); Old Courtown (Wexford); Charlestown (Roscommon, demolished), known from a painting in W. Laffan (ed.), *Ireland's painters: topographical views from Glin Castle* (Tralee, 2006), p. 197; Garryhinch (Offaly); front to Antrim Castle (Antrim); Swift's Heath (Kilkenny); Castlecor (Cork); Waringstown (Down); Crotto (Kerry); Portavo (Down); three storeys over basement, tympanum plus high stairs in front, P. Carr, *Portavo: an Irish townland and its people* (Belfast 2003), frontispiece showing painting. The rectory at Clonegal (Carlow) is of the same type. It has projections at the rear on the garden side (R. Loeber & K. Whelan, 'An early-eighteenth century house: Clonegal rectory, County Carlow', *Jn. Wexford Hist. Soc.*, xiii (1990–1), pp 135–41). **50** Examples at Shannon Grove and Riddlestown (both Limerick) and Kiltullagh (Galway). **51** For example, at Castlecor (Cork), Dysart (Kilkenny) and Castletown (Kildare) (Craig, *Classic Irish houses*, pp 6, 18–19). **52** Barnard, *Making the grand figure*, p. 23. **53** Late seventeenth-century examples include Old Carton and Eyrecourt Castle (Galway). Similar early eighteenth-century examples were formerly at Slane Castle (Meath), Mount Merrion (Dublin) and Old

as high or almost as high as the roof behind it, as at Kilmacurragh (Wicklow) and Yeomanstown (Kildare). In exceptional instances, a main façade had two pediments (Old Ashford, Galway) or one over five bays such as at Ballyburley (Offaly, demolished); this was a favoured approach taken by Burgh, and Ballyburley is possibly by his hand. During the same period, the rhetoric was expressed through the giant order (where columns or pilasters span two or more storeys) and most eloquently in designs for Corinthian pilasters at Drumcondra (Dublin), ascribed to Pearce, and Burgh's new front for Dromoland.[54] Kilkenny Castle followed suit with its main gates, with similar examples on the façades of Castle Bernard (1715)[55] and of Bantry House (both Cork). A variant where full-height pilasters defined the building edges, rather than just the bays, occurred at Castle Durrow, Moira (Down) and Mountainstown (Meath). Inigo Jones is recalled at Old Clonmannon (Wicklow, *c.*1710) where one-storey Doric pilasters sit above a rusticated base in the central breakfront, all executed in brick.[56]

The central one- and two-storey portico popularised by Palladio in Italy in the late sixteenth century never became popular during this particular period in Ireland. An exception is Pearce's Doric entrance portico at Bellamont Forest, often recognised as the first of its kind in Ireland. Still, a portico was planned at an earlier date for Burton House (Kildare), but it was never executed (Figure 5.26), and a portico at Seafield (Dublin) may also belong to this period. Although the movement towards symmetrisation of façades, window and door openings accelerated, there were still many exceptions. This all changed in the late seventeenth and early eighteenth centuries when symmetry of openings and decreasing scale from first to upper floors became practically the norm.

Decorative elements

Gradually, the main façades, as well as the wings, were designed with semi-circular and ocular niches, usually for displaying decorative urns (Burton Hall, Carlow, *c.*1712). Niches were not necessarily responsive to the introduction of a window tax in 1696 as often implied. Urns and eagles adorned parapets;[57] half-faced urns crowned the aedicule at Marlay (Dublin) and they were placed above the hall windows on either side of the entrance at Mountainstown (Meath).[58] Typically, niches were in pairs on higher storeys – on each side of the central vertical axis[59] or in the central vertical axis of the front and rear façade.[60] Less common were the more

---

Stradbally (Laois), and can still be seen at Barbavilla (Westmeath) and Stackallan (Meath). This feature was also prominent at the now ruined old stables of Belan (Kildare).   **54** F. O'Kane, 'Leamaneh and Dromoland: the O'Brien ambition: Part II: Obliges me to dip my hands in mortar: Catherine O'Brien's influence at Dromoland' in *Ir. Arch. & Dec. Studies*, vii (2004), pp 86–9, at p. 88.   **55** C. Smith, *The ancient and present state of the county and city of Cork* (Dublin, 1774), i, p. 284.   **56** Originally, the building was symmetrical: see drawing in Laffan (ed.), *Painting Ireland*, p. 223.   **57** Surviving examples include Castle French (Roscommon) and Bantry House (Cork).   **58** Also at Turvey (Dublin, demolished) and several other early eighteenth-century houses like Dawson's Grove (Monaghan, demolished).   **59** Such as at Drumcree (Meath, demolished); Cuffesboro (Laois); Burton Hall (Carlow, demolished) and Gloster (Offaly).   **60** For example, at Tudenham Park (Westmeath, demolished) and Dunmore (Laois, demolished).

costly sculpted figures; their existence at Donnycarney House (Dublin) proved fatal when one toppled and killed Dr Thomas Molyneux's son in May 1715.[61] While little is known about the craftsmen responsible for these embellishments, it is quite likely that they were also involved in the execution of contemporary funerary monuments: the English sculptor William Kidwell, for example, produced very distinguished work while working in Ireland during this period.

Masonry
Although scholars have disputed the prevalence of brickwork in the early decades, it was widespread in reality.[62] Remarkably few examples have survived.[63] Bricks were likely to have been made locally, close to the site, and sometimes within the landowner's own demesne.[64] Certainly there were some imports, and the proximity of brick houses to coastal towns is unsurprising. Those used at Mount Ivers (Clare) and Palace Anne (Cork) may have been imported from Bristol. However, records indicate that importation was on a small scale due to high costs, so the use of foreign brick was often reduced to facings and embellishment. This period also saw the introduction of ashlar façades, a substantially more expensive alternative to the earlier rough-cut stone façades, revealing the swelling status of the new ascendancy. Outstanding examples are Stackallan, the two new fronts to Dromoland (1714, 1717–18), Castle Durrow and Castletown (1722).

Roofs
Godfrey Richards's English translation of Palladio's *First book of architecture* in 1663 triggered a decline in medieval carpentry practices. While high roof profiles remained common,[65] roof pitches were gradually lowered and hipped ends appeared as Palladianism slowly advanced. Whereas a steep pitch was used on the extension of Dromoland (Figure 6.5) in 1714, Burgh proposed a much lower pitch for his new works there in 1717, effectively eliminating the attic storey.[66] Generally, these structural changes relegated servants' quarters to the lower levels of the house, most likely to the basement, while upper floors were often reserved for a range of large bedrooms; a nursery (Castletown); or a gallery for the owner's family and guests as at Mount Ivers (Clare) and Bowen's Court (Cork).[67] Parapets replaced wide-eaved

61 Molyneux, *Sir Thomas Molyneux*, p. 42. Donnycarney House was on the current Marino Estate.   62 Maurice Craig (*Architecture of Ireland*, pp 177, 331) challenged J.P. Mahaffy's assertion (*Georgian Society records* (Dublin, 1913), v, pp 9, 22) that only 'an occasional country house' was built of brick. Good examples are at Mount Ivers (Clare); Clonmannon (Wicklow, partly surviving); Rossana and Clermont (Wicklow); Swift's Heath (Kilkenny) and Stackallen (Meath), both now plastered.   63 Those that have been lost include: Stillorgan and Santry (Dublin); Dawson's Grove (Monaghan); Belvoir (Down); Dollardstown and Platten Hall (both Meath); Palace Anne and Castle Bernard (both Cork); Bilboa Court (Limerick); Belvoir (Antrim) and Camolin Park (Wexford).   64 For use of brick in Irish architecture in the seventeenth and eighteenth centuries, see S. Roundtree, 'A history of clay brick as a building material in Ireland' (MLitt, TCD, 2000).   65 Examples include Kiltullagh (Galway), Ashgrove (Tipperary, demolished) and Stillorgan (Dublin, demolished).   66 O'Kane, 'Leamaneh and Dromoland', pp 86–9.   67 Somerville-Large, *Irish country house*, p. 117.

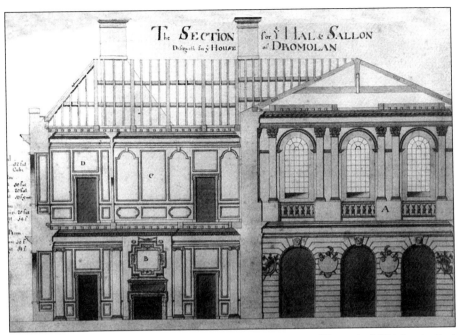

Figure 6.5 'The section for ye hall & sallon designeth for ye house of Dromolan'. This longitudinal drawing by Thomas Burgh featured a steeply pitched roof, forming part of his building proposal for the extension of Dromoland, County Clare in 1714 (Irish Architectural Archive).

roofs; their introduction gave primacy to the architecture of the façade and altered elevational proportions. Where parapets were not employed, heavy stone cornices supported the roof rim, as championed by Curle at Old Castle Coole.[68] Internally came radical changes in the structural framing process and roof truss profile.[69] Amongst them was the insertion of tie-beams at wall plate level to withstand outward thrust, for which collar-beams were applied as structural braces at a higher level (Kilmacurragh, Wicklow, *c*.1700).[70]

Viewing platforms (where the valley between two roof ridges supported a railed open area) were an important feature of the late seventeenth century (Eyrecourt) and proved popular for contemplating the landscape and following the spectacle of the hunt. Only a few houses had a central lantern or roof-gazebo (Woodlands, formerly Luttrellstown, Dublin; Gola and Ancketill's Grove, Monaghan). It is likely that changes at roof level represented a fundamental shift in the choice of sites for house building. In the late seventeenth century, houses tended to be constructed on plains and their gardens featured long avenues, canals and other axial features, best observed from a height. In contrast, as part of the picturesque movement, country houses in the next decades were often located in rolling parkland, providing more

68 Also at Cuba Court (Offaly) and Doneraile Court (Cork). 69 H. Louw, 'Anglo-Netherlandish architectural interchange *c*.1600–*c*.1660', *Architectural History*, xxiv (1981), p. 13. 70 L. Hurley & R. Loeber, 'The development of timber construction in the seventeenth and eighteenth centuries' in Loeber et al. (eds), *Architecture 1600–2000*, pp 61–6.

Figure 6.6 Ardfert Abbey, County Kerry (William Lawrence photograph, NLI).

varied views from within the house itself. Houses elevated on a raised basement, enjoyed even more advantageous views of the surrounding landscape. Much still needs to be gleaned about the relationship between the arrangement of internal spaces and carefully contrived vistas over avenues, gardens and follies.

Doors and windows

Sash windows were introduced into Ireland in the 1680s (Kilkenny Castle) to replace the heavy transom-and-mullion window which nonetheless remained the typical window arrangement until the end of the century. They were also planned for Burton House in 1703 but this project was never realised.[71] Loveday observed in 1732 that 'even thatched houses are sashed in Ireland'.[72] Eighteenth-century windows were usually elegantly proportioned, high and narrow, with heavy glazing bars and relatively small window panes, like the nine-over-nine sashes at Dromana (Waterford). Some later houses such as Ardfert Abbey (Kerry, demolished) (Figure 6.6) and Ballyburley (Offaly, demolished) (Figure 6.7) had six-over-six sashes.[73] Camber-headed windows embellished with a scrolled keystone – a rare enough Baroque detail – survive in the basement of Bonnettstown (Kilkenny) and at Haystown (Dublin).[74] The articulation of doorways came in diverse forms of carved

---

71 N. Roche, 'The development of the window in Ireland *c.*1560–1860' (PhD, Edinburgh College of Art, 1998); BL, Add. MS 46,978, f. 49.   72 Loveday, *Diary of a tour in 1732*, p. 58. 73 Ballyburley was described as 'a fine old mansion in the Elizabethan style roofed with bog oak' and with five-feet thick walls, when it was razed by an accidental fire in 1888 (*King's County Chronicle*, 28 June 1888).   74 Craig, *Classic Irish houses*, pp 68–9. Such window surrounds were used in an urban context by William Robinson at St Mary's Church, Dublin, in 1701 and by Thomas Burgh at the lower yard of Dublin Castle a year later.

Figure 6.7 Ballyburley House, County Offaly (*King's County Directory*, 1890, p. 80).

pediment profiles, resembling those appearing on funerary monuments of the same period. The highly popular swan-neck scroll pediments, first introduced in Ireland in the late seventeenth century, are depicted in Dineley's drawings of Bunratty Castle and Ralahine (both in Clare).[75] Triangular and segmental pediments were also typical and possibly the least used in Ireland were hooded forms.[76] Aedicules[77] without pediments but with single and double columns (Clermont, Wicklow; Randlestown, Meath; Ballyconra, Kilkenny) or rusticated pilasters such as at Rathaspeck (Wexford), were also favoured; their cornices were usually executed in masonry although the more economical option of carved timber was used at Ballyburley and Kilmacurragh (both demolished).

Overlights to doorways were typical but rather small in contrast to their contemporaries in urban settings. Pedimented windows were rare – Old Dromana (Waterford) – and alternating segmental and triangular pediments even rarer.[78] One of the earliest Venetian windows[79] in Ireland may have been at Killester (Dublin), built from 1694–1706, which had some associations with Burgh. Doorways with

75 NLI, MS 392, ff 167, 179. Examples at Buncrana (Donegal); Lisduff and Damer House (both Tipperary); Doneraile Court (Cork).   **76** Triangle examples: Ballykilcavan (Laois); Cuba Court (Offaly, demolished); Castle Mary (Cork); Castle Morris (Kilkenny, demolished). Segmental examples: Barbavilla and Drumcree (both Westmeath); Oakley Park (Kildare) and Rathaspeck (Wexford). Hooded examples: Shannon Grove (Limerick); Turvey (Dublin, demolished); Gloster (Offaly).   **77** An aedicule is a surround to a door, window or niche consisting of pilasters or columns usually supporting a pediment.   **78** Also at Castle Durrow and formerly at Gowran Castle (Kilkenny, demolished).   **79** Venetian windows are tripartite, the central light arched and wider than the sidelights which are flat-headed. They are also also known as Serliana windows after Serlio's treatise *Architettura* (1537).

Figure 6.8 Turvey House, County Dublin, as photographed in 1967 (demolished in 1987).

Palladian motifs soon followed during the 1720s and 1730s.[80] Diocletian windows (segmental arched windows divided into three lights by heavy mullions) appeared by 1720 when used at the old house at Adare (Limerick),[81] and in the uppermost floor of the front of Turvey House (Dublin, demolished) (Figure 6.8).[82] Rusticated voussoir[83] surrounds are recorded on later houses – Brianstown (Longford, 1731) and Bonnettstown (Kilkenny, 1737).

FORECOURTS AND STABLES

Between 1690 and 1740, some significant changes took place in the relationship between the main house and its auxiliary structures. Defensive bawns, a recognised element of the early and late seventeenth century, disappeared in the next decades. This is remarkable considering the threat of rapparees post-1691 and subsequent

---

80 At Elphin Palace (Roscommon, demolished); Belan (Kildare, demolished); Dollardstown (Meath, demolished); Syngefield (Offaly, partly demolished); Old Stradbally (Laois, demolished).   81 J. Hill, 'Gothic in post-Union Ireland: the uses of the past in Adare, Co. Limerick' in T. Dooley & C. Ridgeway (eds), *The Irish country house* (Dublin, 2011), p. 63. The term Diocletian derives from the Thermae Diocletiani (Baths of Diocletian) in ancient Rome. The central light of the window is often wider than its two adjacent sidelights.   82 Turvey was the ancestral estate of the Barnewalls, Lords Trimblestown. The original mansion, built from materials recycled from the Convent of Grace Dieu, was built in 1565, according to a tablet: 'The arms of Christopher Barnewall and Dame Marion Sharle, alias Churley, who made this house in Anno 1565'. The eighteenth-century house likely incorporated portions of the former structure, as it contained secret hiding places, passages and staircases (J. Kingston, 'The Barnewalls of Turvey', *Reportorium Novum*, 1:2 (1956), pp 336–41).   83 A voussoir is a wedge-shaped or tapered stone used to construct an arch.

foreign invasions in the ensuing decades.[84] The bawn was superseded by one of the more prominent features of Palladian planning to take hold in Ireland – the formation of a *cortile* or forecourt with symmetrically placed twin pavilions, one on either side of the residence and usually set forward at some distance from the main block.[85] The addition of colonnades formalised this further and emphasised the architectural language and form of the ranges. In most instances, the pavilions were positioned length-wise, parallel to the front façade, creating a well-proportioned extended profile of a taller main block flanked by the lower, one-storey pavilions.[86]

Old Carton exemplified this with long narrow pavilions connected to the main residence by curved screen walls with an undulating profile. Van der Hagen's painting of the demesne illustrated in some detail the forecourt and turning circle as highlighted by the six-horse carriage. An anonymous design for the pavilions at Barbavilla (Westmeath, *c.*1730) shows curved, Baroque screen walls, which was sadly unexecuted and never set a trend.[87] At Castletown, the two-storey pavilions are remarkably generous, one accommodating kitchens and storage spaces, and the other the stables. Their connection to the main house in the form of curved Ionic colonnades was exceptional and a possible first for Ireland.[88] In a variant Palladian scheme at Tentore (Laois, demolished), pavilions, placed perpendicular to the main residence, generated an elongated rectangular forecourt, flanked by two long ranges of ten bays, each with a central gateway.[89] There were several instances of pavilions built lengthwise in line with the front façade of the main residence, thereby eliminating the sense of enclosure but nonetheless maintaining the essence of the forecourt in the threshold between the grounds and the house (Castle Durrow; Stillorgan; Palace Anne).

In 1707, the steward at Burton House advised John Perceval to follow the example of other gentlemen and build his stables prior to building the main house.[90] Stables could provide temporary accommodation for the owner until his main residence was complete and this sequence of building works probably implied that the overall design of the complex had already been determined. At Bellamont Forest, the stable complex is situated at some distance from the main house, at a lower level, and connected through an underground tunnel with two curious holding cells mid-way, lit by skylights in the yard above.[91]

---

84 What did change, however, was the protection offered by the large number of barracks built across the country, although this occurred after 1714. É. Ó Ciardha, *Ireland and the Jacobite cause 1685–1766* (Dublin, 2002), pp 82ff; D. Fleming, *Politics and provincial people: Sligo and Limerick 1691–1761* (Manchester, 2010), pp 199–201.   85 An early example was at Old Carton (Kildare), built in the late 1680s.   86 Examples are Old Castle Dillon (Armagh) and Oldtown (Kildare). Less common were the L-shaped pavilions that can still be seen at Shannon Grove (Limerick).   87 Barnard, *Making the grand figure*, p. 206.   88 Screen walls with a convex curvature were the classical norm: other exceptions include the concave curtain walls at Moone Abbey (Kildare).   89 Barnard, *Making the grand figure*, p. 35. Other examples are Ardfert (Kerry, demolished) and Bridestown (Cork), which possibly dates from the early eighteenth century.   90 William Taylor to John Perceval, BL, Add. MS 46,978, ff 139–41.   91 Also at Mount Merrion (Dublin). Coote, the owner of Bellamont, was a magistrate in a remote part of the countryside, which might explain the existence of the cells.

CONCLUSION

The building of country houses resumed in the late 1690s and accelerated subsequently, in particular after 1703, when the last of the confiscated estates had been sold. Very few Englishmen purchased Irish Jacobite estates after the Williamite War, and it is unlikely that foreign immigration exercised a major influence on Irish architecture between 1691 and 1739. Although the architectural profession became more distinct during this period, only three major Irish architects (Francis Bindon, Samuel Waring, Edward Lovett Pearce) are known to have made the grand tour in Europe and only Pearce adopted Palladianism as a model. Protestant rather than Catholic patrons were in the vanguard of Irish architectural innovation, and several Catholic patrons favoured a retro late seventeenth-century style over a more contemporary approach.

Large Irish landowners, such as the Perceval, Southwell and Boyle families, rejected the opportunity to invest in Irish lands and they were underrepresented among the buyers of the confiscated estates. Conolly was a notable exception. Several members of the nobility invested heavily in what became the disastrous South Sea bubble, creating pressure to curtail the planned building of elaborate houses or to sell portions of their Irish estates to raise cash. The case of John Perceval (later Lord Perceval) illustrates the gradual transition from Irish residency on a large estate towards English orientation and absenteeism. Several affluent Irish landowners spent large amounts of their Irish income on building projects in England: the third earl of Burlington at Burlington House and Chiswick; Edward Southwell at Kings Weston (near Bristol); and the Duke of Ormonde, who lived part of the time in England, at Richmond Lodge (near London). These individuals showed an appreciation of 'modern' Palladian-inspired and Italian architecture on a scale that remained absent in Ireland within the domestic canon (with the exception of Castletown). Other than perhaps Edward Lovett Pearce, Irish architects did not necessarily exert any impact on English architecture.

The period from 1691 to 1739, even before Castle made his mark, was a time of architectural innovation, characterised by several technical developments. Classical elements (pediments, pilasters, Palladian motifs, lower roof lines), virtually unknown in Irish architecture of the late seventeenth century, proliferated during the early eighteenth, and fully replaced the mannerisms that flourished in the preceding century. Palladian configurations of classical elements became more common, including the tripartite grouping of houses (the main residence with twin pavilions connected by single-storey curved colonnades or convex walls), a central pediment over a breakfront, full-height pilasters, pedimented windows and doors, and the raising of the main residence over a semi-excavated basement. Nevertheless, the placement and proportions of these decorative classical elements was not always faithful to Palladio and the result could be somewhat incoherent, revealing a flexibility that often bordered on randomness. Another remarkable feature of the fifty years after the Williamite War was the fact that Irish patrons rejected the Baroque architecture of virtuosi such as John Vanbrugh and William Talman, who practiced in England only.[92] The evolution of the Irish house was accompanied by similar developments in the glebe houses of the clergy – Red House in Youghal (Cork) – and the townhouses of the gentry, such as Molyneux House, Moira House and Dawson House in Dublin.

Whether we consider country houses or townhouses of the early eighteenth century, it is evident that no clear Irish style of building had been produced during this time. The development of Irish house architecture then remained largely insular and influences (with the exception of absentee landlords) were almost solely from Britain to Ireland. This also applied to the influence of pattern books, but with a twist. The publication of *Vitrivius Britannicus* lacked examples of Irish architecture, but the architecture of several Irish patrons in England was represented in these influential volumes.

The major distinction between Irish and English country houses is that most Irish examples of this period were modest in size and that the shallow U-plan was common in Ireland, but not always exclusively so. Most Irish houses were five to seven bays wide, with houses of nine bays or more remaining the exception. Truly grand Irish houses such as Castletown were a rarity. The reasons for the emergence of the smaller house, often executed in brick, remain unclear. The break-up of several extensive estates after the Williamite confiscations may partially explain this preference. Economic uncertainties and depressed income from leases may be another reason. Robert Molesworth of Breckdenstown emphasised that expenditure on construction rather than on hospitality was to be preferred.[93]

All these reasons are plausible but the fact remains that many landowners before 1740 expended vast sums on landscaping their demesnes, digging canals, arranging water-works, and laying out avenues and gardens. At the same time, however, expenditure for ostentation may have been limited. When the sculpture and treasures collected by Perceval in Italy were seized by the French, Bishop Berkeley consoled him by writing that 'I question if your neighbours in the county of Cork relish that sort of entertainment' of 'old medals and antique statues ... the finest collection is not worth a groat where there is no one to admire and set a value to it, and our country seems to me the place in the world which is least favoured with virtuosi'.[94] This lack of appreciation for finesse may have applied to architecture as well. Perhaps this is the crux of the architectural history of Irish country houses of this period, which needed patrons, fresh ideas from inside and outside the country, skilled architects and builders, and a society willing to engage with architectural advances and ready to generate a dialogue on aesthetics and function.

92 J. Lees-Milne, *English country houses: Baroque 1685–1715* (London, 1970).   **93** F. O'Kane, *Landscape design in eighteenth-century Ireland: mixing foreign trees with natives* (Cork, 2004), pp 42–3.   **94** Bishop Berkeley to John Perceval, Dublin, 22 Dec. 1709 in B. Rand (ed.), *The correspondence of George Berkeley, afterwards bishop of Cloyne, and Sir John Perceval, afterwards earl of Egmont* (Cambridge, 1914), p. 57.

Publications on Irish history, art history and literature by Rolf Loeber

BOOKS

1967   R. Loeber, *Moderne Ierse verhalen* [Modern Irish stories] (Amsterdam: Polak & Van Gennep, 1967).

1981   R. Loeber, *A biographical dictionary of architects in Ireland 1600–1720* (London: Murray, 1981).

1992   R. Loeber, *The geography and practice of English colonisation of Ireland from 1534 to 1609* (Athlone: Group for the Study of Irish Historic Settlement, 1992).

2006   R. Loeber & M. Stouthamer-Loeber (with A. Burnham), *A guide to Irish fiction 1650–1900* (Dublin: Four Courts Press, 2006).

2007   R. Loeber & M. Stouthamer-Loeber, *Irish poets and their pseudonyms in early periodicals* (Blackrock: E. de Búrca, 2007).

2014   R. Loeber, H. Campbell, L. Hurley, J. Montague & E. Rowley (eds), *Architecture 1600–2000. Art and architecture of Ireland. Volume* II (New Haven CT: Yale University Press, 2014).

ARTICLES

1970   R. Loeber, 'An introduction to the Dutch influence in seventeenth and eighteenth century Ireland: an unexplored field', *Ir. Georgian Soc. Bull.*, xiii (1970), pp 1–28.

1973   R. Loeber, 'Irish country houses and castles of the late Caroline period: an unremembered past recaptured', *Ir. Georgian Soc. Bull.*, xvi (1973), pp 1–69.

1973   R. Loeber, 'Castle Durrow', *Ir. Georgian Soc. Bull.*, xvi (1973), pp 103–6.

1974   R. Loeber, 'Sir William Robinson', *Ir. Georgian Soc. Bull.*, xvii (1974), pp 3–9.

1977   R. Loeber, 'Biographical dictionary of engineers in Ireland 1600–1730', *Ir. Sword*, xiii (1977–79), pp 30–40, 106–122, 230–55, 283–314.

1978   R. Loeber, 'An unpublished view of Dublin in 1698 by Francis Place', *Ir. Georgian Soc. Bull.*, xxi (1978), pp 7–15.

1979   R. Loeber, 'Early Classicism in Ireland: architecture before the Georgian era', *Architectural Hist.*, xxii (1979), pp 49–63.

1980   R. Loeber, 'The rebuilding of Dublin Castle: thirty critical years 1661–1690', *Studies*, lxix (1980), pp 45–69.

1980   R. Loeber, 'Civilisation through plantation: the projects of Sir Mathew De Renzi' in H. Murtagh (ed.), *Irish midland studies: essays in commemoration of N.W. English* (Athlone, 1980), pp 121–35.

1981   R. Loeber, 'English and Irish sources for the history of Dutch economic activity in Ireland 1600–89', *Ir. Econ. & Soc. Hist.*, viii (1981), pp 70–85.

1981   R. Loeber, 'Sculptured memorials to the dead in early seventeenth-century Ireland: a survey from *Monumenta Eblanae* and other sources', *PRIA*, lxxxi:11, C (1981), pp 267–93.

1983   R. Loeber, 'A gate to Connacht: the building of the fortified town of Jamestown, County Leitrim, in the era of the plantation', *Ir. Sword*, xv (1983), pp 149–52.

1986   R. Loeber, 'Arnold Quellin's and Grinling Gibbon's monuments for Anglo-Irish patrons', *Studies*, lxxii (1986), pp 84–101.

1987   R. Loeber, 'Carvings at Moore Abbey, Co. Kildare', *Irish Arts Review*, iii (1987), pp 56–7.

1987   R. Loeber & M. Stouthamer-Loeber, 'The lost architecture of the Wexford plantation' in K. Whelan (ed.) *Wexford: history and society* (Dublin: Geography Publications, 1987), pp 173–200.

1988   R. Loeber & J. O'Connell, 'Eyrecourt Castle, Co. Galway', *Irish Arts Review Yearbook* (1988), pp 40–48.

1989   R. Loeber, 'New light on Co. Wexford architecture and estates in the seventeenth century', *Jn. Old Wexford Soc.*, xii (1988–9), pp 66–71.

1990–1 R. Loeber & K. Whelan, 'An early eighteenth-century house: Clonegal Rectory, County Carlow', *Jn. Wexford Hist. Society*, xiii (1990–1), pp 135–41.

1992   R. Loeber, 'Early Irish architectural sketches from the Perceval/Egmont collection' in A. Burnelle (ed.), *Festschrift in honour of Dr. Maurice Craig* (Dublin: Lilliput Press, 1992), pp 110–20.

1992   E.J. Bok & R. Loeber, 'Het geslacht Wybrants', *Jaarboek van het Centraal Bureau voor Genealogie*, 46 (1992), pp 74–114.

1994   R. Loeber & M. Stouthamer-Loeber, 'Do historical novels inspire Irish historical studies?', *Bulletin of the Early Modern Ireland Committee*, i:2 (1994), pp 34–50.

1994   R. Loeber, 'Settlers' utilisation of natural resources in the seventeenth century' in K. Hannigan (ed.), *Wicklow: history and society* (Dublin: Geography Publications, 1994), pp 267–304.

1995   R. Loeber, 'The reorganisation of the Irish militia in 1678–81: documents from Birr Castle', *Ir. Sword*, xix (1995), pp 197–224.

1995   R. Loeber & G. Parker, 'The military revolution in seventeenth-century Ireland' in J. Ohlmeyer (ed.), *From independence to occupation: Ireland 1641–1660* (Cambridge: Cambridge University Press, 1995), pp 66–88.

1998   R. Loeber, 'The changing borders of the Ely O'Carroll lordship' in W. Nolan & T. O'Neill (eds), *Offaly: history and society* (Dublin: Geography Publications, 1998), pp 287–317.

1998   J.H. Andrews & R. Loeber, 'An Elizabethan map of Leix and Offaly: cartography, topography and architecture' in Nolan & O'Neill (eds), *Offaly*, pp 243–85.

1998   R. Loeber, 'Preliminaries to the Massachusetts Bay Colony: the Irish ventures of Emanuel Downing and John Winthrop Sr' in T. Barnard, D. Ó Cróinín & K. Simms (eds), *A miracle of learning* (Cambridge: Cambridge University Press, 1998), pp 164–99.

1999   R. Loeber & M. Stouthamer-Loeber, 'Fiction available to and written for cottagers and their children' in B. Cunningham & M. Kennedy (eds), *The experience of reading: Irish historical perspectives* (Dublin: Rare Books Group, 1999), pp 124–72.

1999   R. Loeber, 'Warfare and architecture in County Laois through seventeenth-century eyes' in P. Lane & W. Nolan (eds), *Laois: history and society* (Dublin: Geography Publications, 1999), pp 379–413.

2001   R. Loeber, 'An architectural history of Gaelic castles and settlements 1370–1600' in P. Duffy, D. Edward & E. FitzPatrick (eds), *Gaelic Ireland c.1250–c.1650* (Dublin: Four Courts Press, 2001), pp 271–313.

2001   R. Loeber, H. Murtagh & J. Cronin, 'Prelude to confiscation: a survey of Catholic estates in Leinster in 1690', *JRSAI*, cxxxi (2001), pp 61–139.

2002   R. Loeber, 'The reception of foreigners: Dutch merchants in Dublin and its Liberties in the early seventeenth century', *Dutch Crossing: Journal of Low Countries Studies*, xxvi (2002), pp 155–68.

2002   R. Loeber & M. Stouthamer-Loeber, 'Dublin and its vicinity in 1797', *Ir. Geog.*, xxxv (2002), pp 133–55.

2003   R. Loeber, M. Stouthamer-Loeber & M. Stout, 'The rare survival of a defensive mud enclosure at Castletown Clonyn Rahyn (Co. Offaly)', *Offaly Heritage*, i (2003), pp 12–21.

2003   R. Loeber & M. Stouthamer-Loeber, 'The publication of Irish novels and novelettes 1750–1829: a footnote on Irish Gothic fiction', *Cardiff Corvey*, x (June 2003), pp 17–44.

2004   R. Loeber, M. Stouthamer-Loeber & J. Leerssen, 'Early calls for an Irish national literature 1820–1877' in N. McCaw (ed.), *Writing Irishness in nineteenth-century British culture'* (London: Ashgate, 2004), pp 12–33.

2004   R. Loeber, Entries on 'Sir William Robinson' and 'Thomas Burgh', *Oxford dictionary of national biography* (Oxford: Oxford University Press, 2004).

2004   R. Loeber & M. Stouthamer-Loeber, Entries on 'Cecilia Maria Cadell' and 'Selina Bunbury', *Oxford dictionary of national Biography*.

2004   R. Loeber & M. Stouthamer-Loeber, 'The documentation of architecture and sites in Irish gazetteers and road-books 1647–1875' in H. Clarke, J. Prunty & M. Hennessy (eds), *Surveying Ireland's past: multidisciplinary essays in honour of Anngret Simms* (Dublin: Geography Publications, 2004), pp 329–51.

2005   R. Loeber, M. Stouthamer-Loeber & A. Burnham, 'Literary absentees: Irish women authors in nineteenth-century England' in J. Belanger (ed.), *The Irish novel in the nineteenth century* (Dublin: Four Courts Press, 2005), pp 167–86.

2006 R. Loeber & M. Stouthamer-Loeber, 'The Countess of Kildare, a Jesuit chapel (1628), and pastoral care in the Dublin parish of St Audoen's' in C. Doherty, E. FitzPatrick & R. Gillespie (eds). *The parish in medieval and early modern Ireland* (Dublin: Four Courts Press), 2006, pp 242–65.

2006 R. Loeber & M. Stouthamer-Loeber, 'Irish subscribers to poetry published in Edinburgh in 1731: new light on readers and Presbyterians in Offaly, Tipperary and Dublin', *Offaly Heritage*, iv (2006), pp 57–72.

2009 T. Clavin & R. Loeber, 'Elizabeth, countess of Kildare' in J. Maguire & J. Quinn (eds), *DIB* (Cambridge, Cambridge University, 2009), iii, pp 338-9.

2009 R. Loeber, 'Miles Symner' in *DIB*, ix, pp 207–8.

2009 M. Stouthamer-Loeber & R. Loeber, 'Anna Maria Chetwode' in *DIB*, ii, p. 488.

2009 R. Loeber, '"Certyn notes": biblical and foreign signposts to the Ulster plantation' in J. Lyttleton & C. Rynne (eds), *Plantation Ireland: settlement and material culture 1550–1650* (Dublin: Four Courts Press, 2009), pp 23–42.

2011 A. Horner & R. Loeber, 'Landscape in transition: descriptions of forfeited properties in Counties Meath, Louth and Cavan in 1700', *Anal. Hib.*, xlii (2011), pp 59–180.

2011 R. Loeber, 'Maurice Craig: an appreciation in point and counterpoint' in M. Craig, *Photographs 1940–1957* (Dublin: Lilliput Press, 2011).

2011 R. Loeber & M. Stouthamer-Loeber, 'New findings: addendum to the *Guide to Irish Fiction* for the period between 1756 and 1830', *Irish University Review*, xli (2011), pp 202–15.

2011 R. Loeber & M. Stouthamer-Loeber, 'Popular reading practice 1800–1900' in J. Murphy (ed.), *The Oxford history of the Irish book*, iv (Oxford: Oxford University Press, 2011), pp 211–39.

2011 R. Loeber & M. Stouthamer-Loeber, 'James Duffy and Catholic nationalism' in Murphy (ed.), *Oxford history of the Irish book*, iv, pp 115–22.

2011 R. Loeber & M. Stouthamer-Loeber, 'The survival of books formerly owned by members of Old English and Gaelic Irish families in the sixteenth and seventeenth centuries' in T. Herron & M. Potterton (eds), *Dublin and the Pale in the Renaissance* (Dublin: Four Courts Press, 2011), pp 280–91.

2011 R. Loeber & T. Reeves-Smyth, 'Lord Audley's grandiose building schemes in the Ulster plantation' in B. Mac Cuarta (ed.), *Reshaping Ireland 1570–1700: colonisation and its consequences* (Dublin: Four Courts Press, 2011), pp 82–100.

2012 R. Loeber, 'The early seventeenth-century Ulster and Midlands plantations: Part I: Pre-plantation architecture and building regulations: Part II: The new architecture' in O. Horsfall Turner (ed.), *'Theatre of empire': the seventeenth-century architecture of Britain and her colonies* (New York: Spire Books, 2012), pp 73–99, 101–37.

2012   R. Loeber & L. Hurley, 'The architecture of Irish country houses 1691–
        1739' in R. Gillespie & R. Foster (eds), *Irish provincial cultures in the
        long eighteenth-century: making the middle sort: essays for Toby Barnard*
        (Dublin: Four Courts Press, 2012), pp 201–19.

2012   R. Loeber, D. Dickson & A. Smyth, 'Journal of a tour to Dublin and the
        counties of Dublin and Meath in 1699', *Anal. Hib.*, xliii (2012), pp
        47–66.

2013   M. Stouthamer-Loeber & R. Loeber, 'Lays from Killiskey: 1847 'blackface'
        songs about Famine relief in north County Wicklow', *Anal. Hib.*, xliv
        (2013), pp 79–98.

2014   R. Loeber & M. Stouthamer-Loeber, 'The visual worlds of the Edgeworth
        family: private sketches and literary illustrations', *Ir. Architect. & Dec.
        Studies*, xvii (2014), pp 80–107.

2014   R. Loeber, 'Edgeworth family of writers and artists' in N. Figgis (ed.),
        Painting in Ireland 1600–1900. Art and architecture of Ireland. iv (New
        Haven, CT: Yale University Press, 2014), p. 242.

2015   A. Horner & R. Loeber, 'The built environment of late seventeenth-century
        County Meath as seen through the eyes of the Trustees' surveyors of
        1700' in A. Crampsie & F. Ludlow (eds), *Meath history and society*
        (Dublin: Geography Publications, 2015), pp 245–81.

2016   R. Loeber, 'Demesnes on the shores of Lough Ree and Lower Lough Erne
        from the sixteenth to the nineteenth centuries' in B. Cunningham &
        H. Murtagh (eds), *Lough Ree historic lakeland settlement* (Dublin: Four
        Courts, 2016), pp 131–62.

2016   G. Stout, R. Loeber & K. O'Brien, 'Mellifont Abbey, Co. Louth: a study of
        its post-dissolution architecture 1540–1727', *PRIA*, cxvi, C (2016), pp
        191–226.

2016   R. Loeber & B McGrath, 'The legacy of Humphrey Farnham (d. 1624), a
        Dublin builder and architect', *JRSAI*, cxlvi (2016), pp 33–61.

2017–18 R. Loeber & Magda Stouthamer-Loeber, 'The Annals of Ballitore by Mary
        Leadbeater (1766–1824): expanded and revisited', *Áitreabh: Group for
        the Study of Irish Historic Settlement Newsletter*, xxii (2017–18), pp 5–8.

Tabula amicorum

Michael & Giancarla Alen-Buckley, Strancally, Co. Waterford.

Nicholas Allen, Director, Willson Center for Humanities & Arts, University of Georgia, USA.

Niall Allsop, Publisher, Clare Books, Ennis, Co. Clare.

Alexandrine Ameziane, Publisher, Paris/Dublin.

John H. Andrews, Emeritus Professor of Geography, TCD.

John Balfe & Marg Paul, North Bay, Ontario, Canada.

Toby Barnard, Emeritus Fellow in History, Hertford College, Oxford, UK.

Patty Barnett, Laguna Beach, California, USA.

Ted Barron, Executive Director, DeBartolo Performing Arts Center, University of Notre Dame.

Kevin Barry & Aoife Feeney, Dublin/Galway/Montpeyroux.

Terry Barry, Emeritus Fellow, School of History, TCD.

Tom Bartlett, Emeritus Professor, Department of History, University of Aberdeen, Scotland.

Justin Basquille, Consultant Psychiatrist, Snugborough, Castlebar, Co. Mayo.

Carol Baxter & Marc Caball, Terenure, Dublin.

Fiona Beglane, Lecturer in Archaeology, Institute of Technology, Sligo.

Amanda Bell & Patrick Gageby, Dublin.

John Belmore, Castle Coole, Enniskillen, Co. Fermanagh.

Alan Bluett, Partner, The Panel Search & Selection, Dublin.

Jim & Jackie Bolger, Coolcullen, Co. Kilkenny.

Ciarán Brady, Professor of Early Modern History & Historiography, TCD.

Niall Brady, Director, Archaeological Diving Company.

Brian Bredeman, Senior Consultant, Chicago, USA.

Bridget Bredeman, VP, Bank of America Merrill Lynch, Chicago, USA.

Martin Breen, Publisher, Co. Clare.

Colm Brennan, Sculptor, Gorey, Co. Wexford.

John Brennan, Park Hotel, Kenmare, Co. Kerry.

Kate Ward Brennan, CEO & Founder, Ward Design, Philadelphia, Pennsylvania, USA.

Anthony & Mary Browne, Ballyeighan, Birr, Co. Offaly.

Bernard Browne, Old Ross, Co. Wexford.

Victoria Browne & Raymond Hurley, Percy Place, Dublin.

Éamonn de Búrca, Rare Books, Blackrock, Dublin.

William de Búrca, Rare Books, Blackrock, Dublin.

Thomas Burish, Provost, University of Notre Dame.

James & Anne Mullin Burnham, Pittsburgh, Pennsylvania, USA.

Deirdre Burns, Heritage Officer, Wicklow County Council, Co. Wicklow.

John J. Burns Library, Boston College, Chestnut Hill, Massachusetts, USA.

Jack Burtchaell, Slieverue, Co. Kilkenny.

Kevin Burtchaell, President & Founder of Keltia Design.

Patrick Butler, Lawyer, New York.

Brian Byrne, Entrepreneur, Wexford town.

Frances & Jim Byrne, Clovass Manor, Enniscorthy, Co. Wexford.

Michael Byrne, Tullamore, Co. Offaly.

Tom Byrne, Wexford/Dublin.

Donough Cahill, Greystones, Co. Wicklow.

Susan Calandra, Fellow, Distinguished Careers Institute, Stanford University.

Steve & Suzanne Cameron, San Juan Capistrano, California, USA.

Hugh Campbell, Professor of Architecture, UCD.

Mary Balfe Campeau, Kingston, Ontario, Canada.

Michael Campion, Colonel, Military Judge, Defence Forces Ireland.

Daniel Carey, Director, Moore Institute, NUI Galway.

Philip Carney, Managing Director, The HR Company, Dublin.

Andrew Carpenter, Emeritus Professor of English, UCD.

Clare Carroll, President, Renaissance Society of America, New York, USA.

Joe Carroll, Enniscorthy/Dublin.

Larry Carroll, Global Real Estate Brokerage, Cushman & Wakefield, Enniscorthy/New York.

Christine Casey, Professor, Department of History of Art & Architecture, TCD.

Gary L. Cavanaugh, Stockton, California, USA.

William M. Chace, President Emeritus, Emory University, Atlanta, Georgia, USA.

Kathleen James-Chakraborty, Professor of Art History, UCD.

Clare County Library, Ennis, Co. Clare.

Howard Clarke, Emeritus Professor of Medieval Socio-Economic History, UCD.

Aedín Ní Bhróithe Clements, Irish Studies Librarian, University of Notre Dame.

Brian Clingen, Entrepreneur, Chicago, USA.

Terry Clune, founder & CEO, TransferMate & Taxback, Dublin/Kilkenny.

Patrick Cody, Coole, Portroe, Nenagh, Co. Tipperary.

John Coleman, Eighteenth-Century Specialist, Ballymote, Co. Sligo.

Lucy Collins, Associate Professor, School of English, Drama & Film, UCD.

Claire Connolly, Professor of Modern English, UCC.

Sean Connolly, Emeritus Professor of Irish History, QUB.

Jane Conroy, Professor Emerita, French, NUI Galway.

Malachy Conway, National Trust, Northern Ireland.

Marie-Louise Coolahan, Professor of English, NUI Galway.

Brian & Sara Corrigan, Jacksonville, Florida, USA.

Martin Costello, Murphy Jewellers, Kilkenny.

Vandra Costello, Demesne Historian, Dalkey, Co. Dublin.

Sarah Covington, Professor of History, CUNY & Director of Irish Studies program, Queens College, New York, USA.

Neil Crimmins, Architect, Dublin.

John & Deirdre Crowley, Pittsburgh, Pennsylvania, USA.

Michael Cullinan, Urban Agency Architects, Dublin.

Bernadette Cunningham, Deputy Librarian, Royal Irish Academy.

George Cunningham, Roscrea, Co. Tipperary.

James Stevens Curl, Professor, Architectural Historian.

Daniel Curley, Rathcroghan Visitor Centre, Co. Roscommon.

Máirtín D'Alton, Architect, Groarke Works, Dublin.

Tony Daly, Parknasilla Hotel, Sneem, Co. Kerry.

Sara Day, Washington, USA.

Seamus Deane, Emeritus Professor of Irish Studies, University of Notre Dame.

Karen McCartan DeSantis & Victor DeSantis, Washington, USA.

Bríona Nic Dhiarmada, Thomas J. & Kathleen M. O'Donnell Professor of Irish Studies, University of Notre Dame.

David Dickson, Emeritus Professor of History, TCD.

Luke Dodd, Strokestown/London.

Charles Doherty, Senior Lecturer (retired), School of History & Archives, UCD.

Linda Doran, School of Irish, Celtic Studies & Folklore, UCD.

Rosanne Dowling, Buncrana, Co. Donegal/Eyrecourt, Co. Galway.

Mike & Kaitlyn Doyle, Entrepreneurs, Chicago, USA.

Pierre de la Ruffinière du Prey, Emeritus Professor, Department of Art History, Queen's University, Kingston, Canada.

Patrick J. Duffy, Emeritus Professor, Department of Geography, Maynooth University.

David Edwards, Department of History, UCC.

Sandra Elliott, Claremont, California, USA.

Máirín Nic Eoin, Ollamh Emerita le Gaeilge, Scoil na Gaeilge, DCU.

Martin Fanning, Publisher, Four Courts Press, Dublin.

Honora Faul, Assistant Keeper, National Library of Ireland.

W. Ross Federgreen, Physician, Entrepreneur, Forward Thinker, Florida, USA.

John Feehan, geologist, botanist, author & broadcaster, Birr, Co. Offaly.

Jane Fenlon, Bray, Co. Wicklow.

Paul Ferguson, Map Librarian, TCD.

Pearse Ferguson, Finance Director, SIAC Construction, Ráth Chairn, Contae na Midhe.

Nicola Figgis, Associate Professor, Art History, UCD.

Barbara Sweetman FitzGerald, Dublin.

John Fitzgerald, University Librarian, UCC.

Elizabeth FitzPatrick, Personal Professor, School of Geography & Archaeology, NUI Galway.

James D. Fitzpatrick, Assistant Vice-President, Fairfield University, Connecticut, USA.

Siobhán Fitzpatrick, Librarian, Royal Irish Academy.

Elizabeth & Michael Flanagan, Ennis, Co. Clare.

Christopher Fox, Professor of English, University of Notre Dame.

Daniel Gahan, Professor of History, University of Evansville, Indiana, USA.

Joan Killian Gallagher, The Home Place, Fermoyle, Co. Longford.

Michael J. Gallagher, Justice (retired), Illinois Appellate Court, Chicago, USA.

Brendan J. Gardiner, Chief Litigation Counsel, Archer-Daniels-Midland, Chicago, USA.

Patrick Garvey, Tech Entrepreneur, Dublin.

Patrick Geoghegan, speechwriter for An Taoiseach & Professor in Modern History, TCD.

Rev. Steve Gibson CSC, Fr Peyton Centre, Attymass, Co. Mayo.

Raymond Gillespie, Professor of History, Maynooth University.

Glucksman Ireland House, New York University, New York, USA.

Glucksman Library, University of Limerick.

Rob Goodbody, Historic Building Consultant, Bray, Co. Wicklow.

George Gossip, Ballinderry Park, Co. Galway.

Anita Ormond Gough, Hamilton, Ontario, Canada.

Derry Gray, Partner, BDO, Dublin.

David Griffin, Emeritus Director, Irish Architectural Archive, Dublin.

Liam Griffin, Ferrycarrig Hotel, Co. Wexford.

Patrick Griffin, Director, Keough-Naughton Institute of Irish Studies, University of Notre Dame.

Desmond Guinness, Leixlip Castle, Co. Kildare.

Frank J. Hall V, Department of Archaeology, NUI Galway.

Hubert Hamilton, Moyne, Durrow, Co. Laois.

Mary Hanafin, former Minister of Education, Dublin.

Peter Harbison, Honorary Academic Editor, RIA; Professor of Archaeology, RHA; Honorary Fellow, TCD.

Amy Louise Harris, Scholar of Early Modern Memorials, Dublin.

Jennifer Harrison, School of Historical & Philosophical Inquiry, University of Queensland, Australia.

Nathan Hatch, President, Wake Forest University, Winston-Salem, North Carolina, USA.

Bob & Donna Haugh, Orland Park, Illinois, USA.

Jerry Healy, Senior Counsel, Dublin.

Martin Healy, Publisher, Four Courts Press, Dublin.

Ken Hemmingway, Tomona, Kiltealy, Co.Wexford.

Hesburgh Libraries, University of Notre Dame.

Mother Máire Hickey, Abbess, Benedictine Community, Kylemore Abbey, Co. Galway.

Jim Higgins, Heritage Officer, Galway City.

Arnold Horner, Former Lecturer in Geography, UCD.

Audrey Horning, Professor of Archaeology, QUB.

Andrew & Bridget Hoyt, South Bend, Indiana, USA.

Livia Hurley, Design Fellow in Architecture, UCD.

John Hussey, historical geographer, Dublin.

Peter Hynes, Chief Executive, Mayo County Council, Castlebar, Co. Mayo.

Irish Architectural Archive, Merrion Square, Dublin.

Irish Georgian Society, Dublin.

Dale & Debra Jenkins, Raleigh, North Carolina, USA.

Hank Jenkins, Business Analysis Manager, Starbucks, Seattle, USA.

Fr. John Jenkins CSC, President, University of Notre Dame.

Thomas Jensen, Connaught Whiskey Distillery, Ballina, Co. Mayo.

Pierre Joannon, Consul General of Ireland, south of France.

Dan Jordan & Barbara Isaacs Jordan, Brooklyn/Kildavin (Carlow)/ Cruttenclogh (Kilkenny).

Patrick Joy, Founder, Suretank Group, Dunleer, Co. Louth.

Art Kavanagh, Ballsbridge, Dublin.

Sandra Kavanagh, UCC.

Stephen Kavanagh, Director, Aer Lingus, Dublin.

Loughlin Kealy, Emeritus Professor of Architecture, UCD.

Martin Kehoe, Enniscorthy/New York.

Margaret Kelleher, Professor & Chair of Anglo-Irish Literature & Drama, UCD.

Kelliher family, Walpole, Massachusetts, USA.

Eva Kelly, New Ross, Co. Wexford.

James Kelly, Professor of History, DCU.

Bill Kennedy, London, UK.

Brandon Kennedy, Patent Attorney, Chicago, USA.

Peter & Michelle Kenny, Octagon Credit Investors, New York, USA.

Clodagh Keogh, Paris, France.

Daire Keogh, Deputy President, Dublin City University.

Declan Kiberd, Donald & Marilyn Keough Professor of Irish Studies, University of Notre Dame.

John Kirwan, Inistiogue, Co. Kilkenny.

Kathleen Krah, Researcher, National Renewable Energy Laboratory, Denver, Colorado, USA.

Kylemore Global Centre, Connemara, University of Notre Dame.

William Laffan, Monkstown, Co. Dublin.

Felix Larkin, Dublin.

Karen Latimer, Ballynahatty Road, Belfast, Co. Antrim.

Robert Lawson & Shelia Geoffrion, Rockport, Maine, USA.

Joe Lee, Emeritus Professor of History, New York University, USA.

Joep Leerssen, Professor, Europese Studies, Universiteit van Amsterdam, Netherlands.

Colm Lennon, Emeritus Professor of History, Maynooth University.

Mark Leslie, Founder, Martello Narrative Architects, Dublin.

Sammy Leslie, Castle Leslie Estate, Glaslough, Co. Monaghan.

William Little, Lawyer, Waxahachie, Texas, USA.

Patrick Lonergan, Professor of Drama & Theatre Studies, NUI Galway.

Larry & Shaina Lynch, San Bruno, California, USA.

Gerald J. Lyne, Emeritus Keeper of Manuscripts, National Library of Ireland. RIP.

Marian Lyons, Professor of History, Maynooth University.

James Lyttleton, Senior Heritage Consultant, AECOM, Bristol, UK.

Ronald McCaffrey, Professor of Medicine, Harvard Medical School, Boston, USA.

Joe McCann, bookseller, Maggs Brothers, London, UK.

Dermot McCarthy, emeritus Secretary General, Government of Ireland & Secretary General, Department of An Taoiseach.

Patricia McCarthy, Architectural historian, Dalkey, Co. Dublin.

Donald R. McClure, Assistant Professor of Education, St John's University, New York, USA.

Ellen MacConnell, USA.

Turlough McConnell, founder, Turlough McConnell Communications, New York, USA.

Finbar McCormick, Killough, Co. Down.

Barry McCrea, Donald R. Keough Family Professor of Irish Studies, University of Notre Dame.

Niall McCullough & Valerie Mulvin, Architects, Dublin.

Timothy McDonald, Managing Director, Eastdil Secured, Washington, USA.

James Paul McDonnell, Dublin.

Adrian McGennis, CEO, Sigmar, Dublin.

Sister Cathy Nerney, Director of Institute for Forgiveness & Reconciliation, Chestnut Hill College, Pennsylvania, USA.

Tom Nerney, Chairman, CEO & President, United States Liability Insurance Company Philadelphia, Pennsylvania, USA.

Offaly Historical Society, Tullamore, Co. Offaly.

Donnchadh Ó Baoill, Údarás na Gaeltachta, Gaoth Dobhair, Contae Dhún na nGall.

Séamus O'Brien, Mullingar, Co. Westmeath.

Robert O'Byrne, The Irish Aesthete.

Ciarán O'Carroll, Rector, Irish College, Rome, Italy.

Enda O'Coineen, Kilcullen Kapital, Dublin.

Barbara O'Connell, Schull Books, Co. Cork.

Damien O'Connor, Eyrecourt, Co. Galway.

Rory O'Connor, Wexford hurler/DCU Business student, Piercestown, Co. Wexford.

Thomas O'Connor, Director, Arts & Humanities Institute, Maynooth University.

Tim O'Connor, Former Joint Secretary North/South Ministerial Council, Consul General (New York), Secretary-General to President of Ireland.

Kieran O'Conor, School of Archaeology & Geography, NUI Galway.

Conchubhar Ó Crualaoich, Oifigeach Logainmneacha, An Brainse Logainmneacha, Baile Átha Cliath.

Mick O'Dea, Emeritus President, Royal Hibernian Academy, Dublin.

Brendan O'Donoghue, Emeritus Director, National Library of Ireland. RIP.

Barry O'Dowd, Emeritus Senior Vice-President, IDA, Dublin.

Mary O'Dowd, Emerita Professor of Gender History, QUB.

Cóilín Ó Drisceoil, Kilkenny Archaeology, Co. Kilkenny.

Proinsias Ó Drisceoil, Scríbhneoir, Cill Chainnigh.

Offaly County Council, Heritage Office.

Colette O'Flaherty, Keeper of Special Collections/Chief Herald, National Library of Ireland.

Angela O'Grady, Co-Founder & Operations Director, The HR Company, Dublin.

Jane Ohlmeyer, Erasmus Smith Professor of Modern History, TCD.

Finola O'Kane, Professor, School of Architecture, Planning & Environmental Policy, UCD.

P.J. O'Kane, Seabank, Dromiskin, Co. Louth.

Tadhg O'Keeffe, Professor, School of Archaeology, UCD.

Teresa O'Leary, Dublin.

Gearóid Ó Lúing, Assistant Keeper, National Library of Ireland.

Rory O'Mahony, Ormonde Military History Society, Kilkenny.

Mairead O'Malley, Cambridge Innovation Center, Boston, Massachusetts, USA.

Pat O'Malley, Executive Vice-President, Seagate Technology, San Jose, California, USA.

Kevin O'Neill, History, Boston College.

P.J. O'Neill, Moygara Castle Research & Conservation Project, Co. Sligo.

Timothy O'Neill, calligrapher, Sandymount, Dublin.

Donal O'Reagan, Templemore, Co. Tipperary.

Seán O'Rourke, Broadcaster, RTÉ.

Nora O'Sullivan, Camelot Illinois, Chicago, USA.

Patricia Padian, New York, New York, USA.

Valerie & Thomas Pakenham, Tullynally Castle, Co. Westmeath.

Parkmore Press, Roscrea, Co. Tipperary.

Michael Potterton, Department of History, Maynooth University.

Joseph A. Power Jr., Chicago, Immediate Past President, Inner Circle of Advocates, USA.

Mossy Power, Carrick-on-Suir, Co. Tipperary.

Nicholas Prins, Beltra, Co. Sligo.

Gerry Quinn, Business Consultant, Edgeworthstown/Dublin.

Stephen Rea, Actor, Donabate, Co. Dublin.

Michael Redding, Attorney, Sacramento, California, USA.

Terence Reeves-Smyth, Archaeologist, Architectectural & Garden Historian.

Eileen Reilly, Co. Longford.

Ian Reither, Co-Founder, Telnyx, Chicago/Dublin.

Representative Church Body of Ireland Library, Dublin.

Ann Rigney, Professor, Comparative Literature, University of Utrecht, Netherlands.

Killian Robinson, Cardiologist, Sligo.

Kevin & Patty Ronan, Minnesota, USA.

Emmet Root, Omaha, Nebraska, USA.

Alison, Countess of Rosse, Birr Castle, Co. Offaly.

The Earl of Rosse, Birr Castle, Co. Offaly.

William Roulston, Research Director, Ulster Historical Foundation, Belfast, Co. Antrim.

Susan Roundtree, Conservation Architect, Dublin.

Peter & Briad Rowan, Antiquarian Booksellers, Belfast, Co. Antrim.

Ellen Rowley, Research Fellow in Architecture, UCD.

Royal Irish Academy Library.

Fearghal Ryan, SAP, London, UK.

Stephen Ryan, Colonel, Defence Forces Ireland.

Christopher & Elizabeth Sanders, Chicago, USA.

Eithne Scallan, Wexford.

School of Irish Studies, Concordia University, Montreal, Canada.

Thomas S. Schreier, Jr., Founding Director, Inspired Leadership Initiative, Notre Dame.

Eoin Shanahan, Clare/Dublin.

Rev. John-Paul Sheridan, lecturer, Maynooth College.

Anngret Simms, Professor Emerita, Geography, UCD.

Ellen Skerrett, Historian, Chicago, USA.

Nicholas, Rebecca & Grace Smith, Glen Ellyn, Illinois, USA.

Paul Gerard Smith, TCD.

William J. Smyth, Emeritus Professor of Geography, UCC.

Stanford University, California, USA.

Jacob Stanton, Chicago, USA.

Frank & Mary Steele, Cork.

Martin Steer, Emeritus Professor, School of Biology & Environmental Science, UCD.

Geraldine & Matthew Stout, Julianstown, Co. Meath.

Helen & Nóra Stout, Altadena, California, USA.

Justin Dolan Stover, Professor of History, Idaho State University, USA.

Bob & Jeanne Sullivan, Tulsa, Oklahoma, USA.

Bobby & Jennifer Sullivan, Naples, Florida, USA.

Eoin Sullivan, Gort Archaeology, Co. Laois.

Jim Sutton, New Ross, Co. Wexford.

Glascott & Adrienne Symes, Durrow, Co. Laois.

Barbara Talbot, Chevy Chase, Maryland, USA.

Mary Thompson, Dublin/New York.

Jerry Tillery, Defensive Tackle, Los Angeles Chargers, Los Angeles, USA.

Martin A. & Mary B. Timoney, Keash, Ballymote, Co. Sligo.

Alan Titley, Emeritus Ollamh le Gaeilge, UCC.

Patrick Toole, Connecticut, USA.

Isabelle Torrance, Associate Professor, Aarhus Institute of Advanced Studies, Aarhus University, Denmark.

Eugene Trani, Emeritus President, Virginia Commonwealth University, Richmond, Virginia, USA.

Pauric Travers, Emeritus President, St Patrick's College, Drumcondra, Dublin.

Brendan & Valerie Twomey, Dublin.

University of Notre Dame Dublin Global Gateway, Merrion Square, Dublin.

Kathleen Villiers-Tuthill, Clifden, Co. Galway.

John Waddell, Emeritus Professor, Archaeology, NUI Galway.

Aidan Walsh, Castlepollard, Co. Westmeath.

Martin Walsh, Malahide, Dublin.

Julian Walton, Co. Waterford.

Robert Welsh, Emeritus Vice-Chairman, Board of Trustees, University of Notre Dame.

Kevin Whelan & Anne Kearney, Heytesbury Street, Dublin.

John B. White Jr., Atlanta, Georgia, USA.

Andrew Whitefield, lecturer, School of Geography & Archaeology, NUI Galway.

Garry Wilson, Belvelly Castle, Co. Cork.

Daphne Dyer Wolf, Drew University, Madison, New Jersey, USA.

C. J. Woods, Royal Irish Academy.

Wordwell Publishers, Dublin.

Charles Wylie, Santa Barbara, California, USA.

Karina Kloos Yeatman, Stanford University, California, USA.

Bibliography

Primary published sources

J.Y. Akerman (ed.), 'Moneys received and paid for secret services of Charles II and James II from 30 March 1679 to 25 Dec., 1688', *Camden Society*, clii (London, 1851).

J. Anderson, *A genealogical history of the house of Yvery in its different branches of Yvery, Luvel, Perceval and Gournay* (London, 1742).

Annála Connacht: the annals of Connacht AD 1224–1544, ed. and trans. A.M. Freeman (Dublin, 1944). CELT.

Annals of Ulster/Annála Uldh (to A.D. 1131) eds and trans, W. Hennessey & B. MacCarthy, 4 vols (Dublin, 1887–1901). CELT.

Annals of the kingdom of Ireland by the Four Masters, ed. and trans. J. O'Donovan, 7 vols (Dublin, 1848–51). CELT.

[H. Bagnall], 'Marshal Bagenal's description of Ulster, anno 1586', *UJA*, ii (1854), pp 137–60.

[T. Bellingham], *Diary of Thomas Bellingham, an officer under William III*, ed. A. Hewitson (Preston, 1908).

G. Benn, *A history of the town of Belfast* (London, 1877).

G. Bennett, *The history of Bandon* (Cork, 1869).

[G. Berkeley], *The correspondence of George Berkeley, afterwards bishop of Cloyne, and Sir John Perceval, afterwards earl of Egmont*, ed. B. Rand (Cambridge, 1914).

Books of survey and distribution, iii: County Galway, ed. B. Mac Giolla Choille (Dublin, 1962).

[T. Brett], *A letter sent by T[homas] B[rett] gentleman ... conteining a large discourse of the peopling and inhabiting the c[o]untrie called Ardes* (London, 1572), reprinted in G. Hill, *An historical account of the MacDonnells of Antrim* (Belfast, 1873), pp 405–15.

J. Burgoa, *The life and times of Sir Thomas Gresham*, 2 vols (London, 1845).

J. Burke, *A visitation of the seats of the noblemen and gentlemen of Great Britain and Ireland*, second series, 2 vols (London, 1853).

Calendar of ancient records of Dublin, ed. J. Gilbert, 18 vols (Dublin, 1889–1922).

Calendar of Carew manuscripts preserved in the archiepiscopal library at Lambeth 1515–1574, eds J. Brewer & W. Bullen, 6 vols (London, 1867–73).

'Calendar of the Irish Council book 1581 to 1586', ed. D. Quinn, *Anal. Hib.*, xxiv (1967), pp 91–180.

Calendar of the patent and close rolls of chancery in Ireland of the reigns of Henry VIII, Edward VI, Mary and Elizabeth, ed. J. Morrin, 3 vols (Dublin, 1861–3): 1514–75, 1576–1603, 1625–33.

Calendar of state papers preserved in the Public Record Office, domestic series, 1547–1695, 81 vols (London, 1856–1972).

Calendar of state papers relating to Ireland 1509–1670, 24 vols (London, 1860–1911).

J.A. du Cerceau, *Les trois livres d'architecure*, 3 vols (Paris, 1559–82).

[Clarendon], *State letters of Henry, second earl of Clarendon*, ed. W.S. Singer, 2 vols (London, 1828).

A. Collins (ed.), *Letters and memorials of state in the reigns of Queen Mary, Queen Elizabeth, King James, King Charles the first, part of the reign of King Charles the second, and Oliver's usurpation*, 2 vols (London, 1746).

H. Colvin, J. Summerson, J. Hale & M. Merriman, *The history of the King's works, iv, 1485–1660 (part II)* (London, 1982).

'Commonwealth state accounts: Ireland 1650–56', ed. E. MacLysaght, *Anal. Hib.*, xv (1944).

The composition book of Conought, ed. A.M. Freeman (Dublin, 1936).

[Conway], *Conway letters: the correspondence of Anne, viscountess Conway, Henry More and their friends 1642–1684*, ed. M. Nicholson (London, 1930).

C. Coote, *General view of the agriculture and manufactures of the King's County* (Dublin, 1801).

[R. Cox], 'On a manuscript description of the city and county of Cork written by Sir Richard Cox', eds S. Johnson & T. Lunham, *JRSAI*, cxxxii (1902), pp 353–76.

T.C. Croker, *Researches in the south of Ireland* (London, 1824).

T. Cromwell, *Excursions through Ireland* (London, 1828).

E. Curtis (ed.), 'The survey of Offaly in 1550', *Hermathena*, xx (1930), pp 312–52.

J. D'Alton, *History of the county of Dublin* (Dublin, 1838).

K. Danaher & J. G. Simms (eds), *The Danish force in Ireland 1690–1* (Dublin, 1962).

J. Davies, *Historical tracts*, ed. G. Chalmers (Dublin, 1787). CELT.

Description of Ireland and the state thereof as it is at this present in anno 1598, ed. E. Hogan (Dublin, 1878).

[T. Dineley], 'Extracts from the journal of Thomas Dineley, giving an account of his visit to Ireland in the reign of Charles II', eds E.P. Shirley & J. Graves, *JRSAI*, xvi (1867), pp 176–204.

P. Dwyer, *The diocese of Killaloe* (Dublin, 1878).

[J. Dymmok], *A treatice on Ireland by John Dymmok, now first published from a MS preserved in the British Museum, with notes*, ed. R. Butler (Dublin, 1843). CELT.

[Essex], *Essex papers 1672–5*, ed. O. Airy (London, 1890).

[J. Evelyn], *Diary of John Evelyn*, ed. E. de Beer (Oxford, 1955),

[Fitzwilliam], *Fitzwilliam accounts 1560–65 (Annesley collection)*, ed. A. Longfield (Dublin, 1960).

The Georgian Society records of eighteenth-century domestic architecture and decoration in Ireland, 5 vols (London, 1913).

J. Gilbert, *History of the city of Dublin*, 3 vols (Dublin, 1854–9).

J. Gilbert (ed.), *History of the Irish confederacy*, 7 vols (Dublin, 1882–91).

V. Gookin, *The great case of transplantation discussed* (London, 1655).

[le Gouz], *Tour of M. Boullaye le Gouz in Ireland in 1644*, ed. T.C. Croker (London, 1837).

[Granard], *Memoirs of the earls of Granard*, ed. Earl of Granard (London, 1868).

[D. Grose], *Daniel Grose (c.1766–1838): the antiquities of Ireland*, ed. R. Stalley (Dublin, 1991).

J. Hamilton, *The Hamilton manuscripts containing some account of the settlement of the territories of Upper Clandeboye, Great Ardes and Dufferin in the county of Down* (Belfast, [1867]).

[Herbert], *Herbert correspondence: the sixteenth and seventeenth century letters of the Herberts of Chirbury, Powis Castle and Dolguog, formerly at Powis Castle in Montgomeryshire*, ed. W. Smith (Dublin, 1963).

J. Hessels (ed.), *Epistulae ecclesiae Londino-Batavae* (Cambridge, 1880).

G. Hill, *An historical account of the MacDonnells of Antrim* (Belfast, 1873).

G. Hill, *An historical account of the plantation in Ulster at the commencement of the seventeenth century 1608–1620* (Belfast, 1877).

G. Hill, *Plantation papers*, 2 vols (Belfast, 1889).

E. Hogan (ed.), *The history of the war of Ireland from 1641 to 1653 by a British officer of the regiment of Sir John Clottworthy* (Dublin, 1873).

J. Hogan (ed.), *Letters and papers relating to the Irish rebellion between 1642–46* (Dublin, 1936).

J. Hogan & N. McNeill O'Farrell (eds), *The Walsingham letter-book, or register of Ireland, May 1578 to December 1579* (Dublin, 1959).

J. Hooker, 'The description, conquest, inhabitation, and troublesome estate of Ireland 1586' in R. Holinshed, *The chronicles of England, Scotland and Ireland* (London, 1574).

P.H. Hore, *History of the town and county of Wexford*, 6 vols (London, 1900–1911).

[Inchiquin], *The Inchiquin manuscripts*, ed. J. Ainsworth (Dublin, 1961).

Irish fiants of the Tudor sovereigns: during the reigns of Henry VIII, Edward VI, Philip & Mary, and Elizabeth I, ed. J.J. Digges La Touche, 4 vols (Dublin, 1994).

Irish patent rolls of James I: facsimile of the Irish Records Commissioners' calendar prepared prior to 1830 (Dublin, 1966).

[Kenmare], *The Kenmare manuscripts*, ed. E. MacLysaght (Dublin, 1942).

[W. King], 'Diary of William King, D.D., archbishop of Dublin, during his imprisonment in Dublin Castle, Part II', ed. H. Lawlor, *JRSAI* (1903), pp 255–83.

D. Laign (ed.), *Royal letters, charters and tracts relating to the colonisation of New Scotland* (Edinburgh, 1867).

T. Lee, 'The discovery and recovery of Ireland [*c.*1600]'. CELT.

Letters of Denization and Acts of Naturalisation for aliens in England and Ireland 1603–1700, ed. W. Shaw (Lymington, 1911).

[Lismore], *Lismore papers*, second series, ed. A.B. Grosart, 10 vols (London, 1886–8).

J. Lodge (ed.), *Desiderata curiosa Hibernica*, 2 vols (Dublin, 1772).

J. Lodge, *The peerage of Ireland*, ed. M. Archdall, 6 vols (Dublin, 1789).

[London Companies], *Londonderry and the London Companies 1609–1629*, ed. D. Chart (Belfast, 1928).

J. Loveday, *Diary of a tour in 1732 through parts of England, Wales, Ireland and Scotland* (Edinburgh, 1840). CELT.

[P. Luckombe], *A tour through Ireland in 1779* (Dublin, 1780).

[E. Ludlow], *The memoirs of Edmund Ludlow*, ed. C. Firth (Oxford, 1894).

[T. Macaulay], *Macaulay's essay on Sir William Temple*, ed. G. Twentyman (London, 1905).

Maps of the escheated counties in Ireland 1609 (Southampton, 1861).

S. MacSkimin, *The history and antiquities of Carrickfergus* (Belfast, 1823).

Miscellaneous Irish annals AD 1114–1437, ed. S. Ó hInnse (Dublin, 1947). CELT.

Miscellany of the Irish Archaeological Society (Dublin, 1844).

C. Meehan, *The rise and fall of the Irish Franciscans* (Dublin, 1877).

[C. Molyneux], *An account of the family and descendants of Sir Thomas Molyneux* (Evesham, 1820).

D. Molyneux, 'Visitation begonne in the Cittie of Dublin' (GO, MS 46, 1607).

[S. Molyneux], *A catalogue of the library of the Honourable Samuel Molyneux, deceased, which will be sold by auction the 20th of January, 1729–30*.

J. Monahan, *Records relating to the diocese of Ardagh and Clonmacnoise* (Dublin, 1886).

[T. Monk], 'A descriptive account of the county of Kildare in 1682', *JKAS*, vi:4 (1910), pp 339–46.

[Montgomery], *The Montgomery manuscripts*, ed. G. Hill (Belfast, 1869).

F. Moryson, *An itinerary*, 4 vols (Glasgow, 1907–8). CELT.

T. Mulvany, *The life of James Gandon Esq.* (Dublin, 1846).

J.P. Neale, *Views of seats of noblemen and gentlemen in England and Wales, Scotland and Ireland* (London, 1818–29).

[T. Ó Cianáin], *The flight of the earls by Tadhg Ó Cianáin*, ed. P. Walsh (Maynooth, 1916). CELT.

[L. Ó Clerigh], *The life of Aodh Ruadh Ó Domhnaill transcribed from the book of Lughaidh Ó Clerigh*, ed. P. Walsh (Dublin, 1948). CELT.

C. O'Conor Don, *The O'Conors of Connaught* (Dublin, 1891).

J. O'Donoghue, *Historical memoirs of the O'Briens* (Dublin, 1860).

J. O'Hart, *Irish pedigrees or the origin and stem of the Irish nation*, 2 vols (Dublin, 1892).

[Ormond], *Calendar of Ormond deeds*, ed. E. Curtis, 6 vols (Dublin, 1932–43).

T. O'Rorke, *The history of Sligo: town and county*, 2 vols (Dublin, [1878–90]).

[Orrery], *The Orrery papers*, ed. Countess of Cork and Orrery, 2 vols (London, 1903).

[Orrery], *Calendar of Orrery papers*, ed. E. MacLysaght (Dublin, 1941).

[O'Sullivan Beare], *Ireland under Elizabeth ... by Don Philip O'Sullivan Beare*, ed. M. Byrne
(Dublin, 1903).

Pacata Hibernica or a history of the wars in Ireland during the reign of Queen Elizabeth, ed. S.
O'Grady, 2 vols (London, 1896).

[Perrot], 'The Perrot papers', ed. C. McNeill, *Anal. Hib.*, xii (1943), pp 1, 3–65.

[Perrot], *The chronicle of Ireland 1584–1608 by Sir James Perrot*, ed. H. Wood (Dublin, 1933).

W. Petty, *Political arithmetike* (London, 1687).

[W. Petty], *The economic writings of Sir William Petty*, ed. C. Hull (Cambridge, 1899).

[W. Petty], *The Petty-Southwell correspondence 1676–1687*, ed. Lansdowne, marquis of
(London, 1928).

Public records, Ireland, *Eleventh report of the deputy keeper of the public records in Ireland*
(1879).

Public records, Ireland, *Twelfth report of the deputy keeper of the public records in Ireland* (1880).

[Rawdon], *The Rawdon papers, consisting of letters on various subjects, literary, political, and
ecclesiastical, to and from Dr. John Bramhall, primate of Ireland: including the correspondence
of several most eminent men during the greater part of the seventeenth century*, ed. J. Bramhall
(London, 1819).

Report on the manuscripts of lord de l'Isle & Dudley, ed. C.L. Kingsford, 2 vols (London, 1925).

P.P. Rubens, *Pallazzi di Genova* (Genoa, 1613).

[Salisbury], *Calendar of the manuscripts of the marquis of Salisbury*, 2 vols (London, 1883).

S. Serlio, *Tutte l'opera d'architetura et prospetiva* (Venice, 1584).

E.P. Shirley, *Some account of the territory or dominion of Farney* (London, 1845).

E.P. Shirley, *The history of the county of Monaghan* (London, 1879).

[Sidney], *Letters and memorials of state ... written and collected by Sir Henry Sidney ..., Sir
Philip Sidney and his brother Sir Robert Sidney*, ed. A. Collins, 2 vols (London, 1746).

[Sidney], *Sidney state papers 1565–1570*, ed. T. Ó Laídhin (Dublin, 1962).

C. Smith, *The ancient and present state of the county and city of Waterford* (Dublin, 1746).

C. Smith, *The ancient and present state of the county and city of Cork* (Dublin, 1774).

E. Spenser, *A view of the present state of Ireland*, ed. W. Renwick (London, 1934).

[R. Stanyhurst], 'The plain and perfect description of Ireland' in R. Holinshed, *The chronicles
of England, Scotland and Ireland*, 3 vols (London, 1577). CELT.

R. Stanyhurst, *De rebus in Hibernia gestis* (Antwerp, 1584).

[R. Stanyhurst], *Holinshed's Irish chronicle: the historie of Ireland from the first inhabitation
thereof until the yeare 1509: collected by Ralph Holinshed and continued till the yeare 1547
by Richarde Stanyhurst*, eds L. Miller & E. Power (Dublin, 1979).

State papers of Henry VIII, 11 vols (London, 1830–52).

R. Steele, *A bibliography of royal proclamations of the Tudor and Stuart sovereigns and of others
published under their royal authority 1485–1714*, 2 vols (Oxford, 1910).

[Strafford], *The earl of Strafford's letters and dispatches*, ed. W. Knowler (Dublin, 1740).

[Strafford], *The Strafford inquisition of County Mayo*, ed. W. O'Sullivan (Dublin, 1958).

[J. Stevens], *The journal of John Stevens containing a brief account of the war in Ireland 1689–
91*, ed. R. Murray (Oxford, 1912). CELT.

[J. Taylor], *The life of the Right Rev. Jeremy Taylor D.D.*, ed. R. Heber (Huntington, CT, 1832).

[J. Thurloe], *A collection of state papers of John Thurloe*, 7 vols (London, 1742).

W. Trevelyan & C. Trevelyan (eds), 'Trevelyan Papers part III', *Camden Soc.*, cv (London, 1872).

[Ulster], 'Ulster plantation papers 1608–1613', ed. T.W. Moody, *Anal. Hib.*, viii (1938), pp 179–298.

[Ulster], *Ulster and other Irish maps c.1600*, ed. G.A. Hayes-McCoy (Dublin, 1964).

[J. Ussher], *The whole works of the most Rev James Ussher D.D.*, (ed.) C. Elrington, 7 vols (Dublin, 1847).

F. Verney & M. Verney (eds), *Memoirs of the Verney family*, 3 vols (London, 1892).

P. Vingboons, *Af beeldsels der voornaamste gebouwen*, 2 vols (Amsterdam, 1648–74).

P. White, *History of Clare and the Dalcassian clans of Tipperary, Limerick and Galway* (Dublin, 1893).

T. Wood, *An inquiry concerning the primitive inhabitants of Ireland* (Cork, 1821).

H. Wotton, *The elements of architecture* (London, 1624).

T. Wright, *Louthiana: or an introduction to the antiquities of Ireland* (London, 1748).

Theses

N.D. Atkinson, 'The plantation of Ely O'Carroll' (MA, TCD, 1955).

T. Cronin, 'The foundations of landlordism in the barony of Athlone 1566–1666' (MA, UCG, 1976).

M. D'Alton, 'The architecture of the Leix and Offaly plantations 1540–1600' (MLitt, TCD, 2009).

A. Empey, 'The Butler lordship in Ireland 1185–1514' (PhD, TCD, 1970).

N. Fennelly, 'An analysis of the towerhouses in a County Offaly study area' (MA, UCC, 1997).

E. FitzPatrick, 'The practice and siting of royal inauguration in medieval Ireland' (PhD, TCD, 1997).

D. Gallagher, 'The plantation of Longford 1619–41' (MA, UCD, 1968).

L. Hurley, 'Public and private improvements in eighteenth-century Ireland: the case of the Conynghams of Slane 1703–1821' (MLitt, TCD, 2008).

J.D. Johnston, 'The plantation of County Fermanagh 1610–1641: an archaeological and historical study' (MA, QUB, 1976).

J. Lyttleton, 'Native and newcomer in post-medieval Ireland, changing cultural identities in County Offaly: an archaeological perspective' (PhD, UCC, 2006).

P. McCarthy, 'The planning and use of space in Irish houses 1730–1830' (PhD, TCD, 2008).

H. Murtagh, 'Tudor, Stuart and Georgian Athlone' (PhD, UCG, 1986).

M. O'Dowd, 'Landownership in the Sligo area 1585–1641' (Ph.D, UCD, 1980).

M. Pollard, 'The woodcut ornament stocks of the Dublin printers, 1500–1700' (Fellowship, Library Association, 1966).

T. Ranger, 'The career of Richard Boyle, first earl of Cork' (DPhil, Oxford, 1959).

P. Robinson, 'The plantation of Co. Tyrone in the seventeenth century' (PhD, QUB, 1974).

N. Roche, 'The development of the window in Ireland 1560–1860' (PhD, Edinburgh College of Art, 1998).

W. Roulston, 'The provision, building and architecture of Anglican churches in the north of Ireland 1600–1740' (PhD, QUB, 2003).

S. Roundtree, 'A history of clay brick as a building material in Ireland' (MLitt, TCD, 2000).

W.G. Wheeler, 'Libraries in Ireland before 1855: a bibliographical essay' (DipLib, University of London, 1957).

D. White, 'Tudor plantations in Ireland before 1571' (PhD, TCD, 1968).

Secondary sources.
F.H.A. Aalen, K. Whelan & M. Stout (eds), *Atlas of the Irish rural landscape* (Cork, 2011).
M. Airs, *The making of the English country house 1500–1640* (London, 1975).
M. Airs, *The Tudor & Jacobean country house: a building history* (Godalming, 1998).
J.H. Andrews, 'Geography and government in Elizabethan Ireland' in Stephens & Glassock (eds), *Irish geographical studies*, pp 178–91.
J.H. Andrews, *Irish maps* (Dublin, 1978).
J.H. Andrews, *Plantation acres: an historical study of the Irish land surveyor* (Belfast, 1985).
J.H. Andrews, 'Mapping the past in the past' in C. Thomas (ed.), *Rural landscapes and communities* (Blackrock, 1986), pp 31–64.
J.H. Andrews, 'Plantation Ireland: a review of settlement history' in T. Barry (ed.), *A history of settlement in Ireland* (London, 2000), pp 140–57.
J.H. Andrews, 'The mapping of Ireland's cultural landscape 1550–1630' in Duffy, Edwards & FitzPatrick (eds), *Gaelic Ireland*, pp 153–80.
J.H. Andrews & R. Loeber, 'An Elizabethan map of Leix and Offaly: cartography, topography and architecture' in Nolan & O'Neill (eds), *Offaly*, pp 243–85.
K. Andrews, N. Canny & P. Hair (eds), *The westward enterprise: English activities in Ireland, the Atlantic and America 1480–1650* (Liverpool, 1978).
Archaeological survey of Northern Ireland, *An archaeological survey of County Down* (Belfast, 1966).
P. Bagenal, *Vicissitudes of an Anglo-Irish family 1530–1800* (London, 1925).
R. Bagwell, *Ireland under the Stuarts*, 3 vols (London, 1909–16).
F.E. Ball, *The judges of Ireland 1221–1921*, 2 vols (London, 1926).
T. Barnard, *Making the grand figure: lives and possessions in Ireland 1641–1770* (New Haven, 2004).
T. Barnard, *Improving Ireland: projectors, prophets and profiteers 1641–1786* (Dublin, 2008).
T. Barry, *Medieval moated sites of south-east Ireland* (Oxford, 1977).
T. Barry, *The archaeology of medieval Ireland* (London, 1987).
M. Batten, 'The architecture of Dr Robert Hooke', *Walpole Society*, xxv (1937), pp 83–113.
J.C. Beckett, *Protestant dissent in Ireland 1687–1780* (London, 1948).
M. Bence-Jones, 'Springhill', *Irish Times*, 2 July 1963.
M. Bence-Jones, 'Thomastown Castle, Co. Tipperary', *Country Life*, 2 Oct. 1969.
M. Bence-Jones, *Burke's guide to country houses, i: Ireland* (London, 1978).
B. Blades, '"In the manner of England": tenant housing in the Londonderry plantation', *Ulster Folklife*, xxvii (1981), pp 39–56.
F.R. Bolton, *The Caroline tradition of the Church of Ireland with particular reference to Bishop Jeremy Taylor* (London, 1958).
E. Borrowes, 'Tennekille Castle, Portarlington and glimpses of the MacDonnells', *UJA*, ii (1854), pp 32–43.
K. Bottigheimer, 'Kingdom and colony: Ireland in the westward enterprise 1536–1660' in Andrews, Canny & Hair (eds), *Westward enterprise*, pp 45–65.
B. Bradshaw, *The dissolution of the religious orders in Ireland under Henry VIII* (London, 1974).
B. Bradshaw, 'Manus "The magnificent" O'Donnell as renaissance prince' in A. Cosgrove & D. McCartney (eds), *Studies in Irish history* (Dublin, 1997), pp 15–36.
B. Bradshaw, *The Irish constitutional revolution of the sixteenth century* (Cambridge, 1979).
B. Bradshaw, 'Sword, word and strategy in the Reformation in Ireland', *Historical Jn.*, xxi (1978), pp 475–502.
C. Brady, 'Spenser's Irish crisis: humanism and experience in the 1590s', *Past & Present*, cxi (1986), pp 21–49.

C. Brady, 'The decline of the Irish kingdom' in M. Greengrass (ed.), *Conquest and coalescence* (London, 1991), pp 94–115.

C. Brady & R. Gillespie (eds), *Natives and newcomers: the making of Irish colonial society 1534–1641* (Dublin, 1986).

C. Breen, *An archaeology of south-west Ireland 1570–1670* (Dublin, 2007).

C. Breen, 'The maritime cultural landscape in medieval Gaelic Ireland' in Duffy, Edwards and FitzPatrick (eds), *Gaelic Ireland*, pp 418–35.

B. de Breffny, *Castles of Ireland* (London, 1977).

B. de Breffny & R. ffolliott, *The houses of Ireland* (London, 1975).

C. Brett, *Buildings of Belfast 1700–1914* (London, 1967).

A. Brindley, *Archaeological survey of County Monaghan* (Dublin, 1986).

V. Buckley, *Archaeological inventory of County Louth* (Dublin, 1986).

G. Bushnell, *Sir Richard Grenville* (London, 1936).

W. Butler, *Confiscation in Irish history* (Dublin, 1917).

W. Butler, 'The policy of surrender and regrant', *JRSAI*, ii (1913), pp 47–65; 3, pp 99–128.

R. Butlin, 'Irish towns in the sixteenth and seventeenth centuries' in R. Butlin (ed.), *The development of the Irish town* (London, 1977), pp 61–100.

C. Cairns, *Irish towerhouses: a County Tipperary case study* (Athlone, 1987).

G. Camlin, *The town in Ulster* (Belfast, 1951).

C. Campbell, *Vitruvius Britannicus, or the British architect*, 3 vols (London, 1715).

N. Canny, 'The ideology of English colonisation: from Ireland to America', *William & Mary Quarterly*, xxx (1973), pp 575–98.

N. Canny, *The formation of the Old English elite in Ireland* (Dublin, 1975).

N. Canny, *The Elizabethan conquest of Ireland: a pattern established 1565–1576* (Hassocks, Sussex, 1976).

N. Canny, 'Dominant minorities; English settlers in Ireland and Virginia 1550–1650' in A. Hepburn (ed.), *Minorities in history* (London, 1978), pp 51–69.

N. Canny, *The upstart earl: a study of the social and mental world of Richard Boyle, first earl of Cork, 1566–1643* (Cambridge, 1982).

N. Canny, *From Reformation to Restoration: Ireland 1534–1660* (Dublin, 1987).

N. Canny, 'The permissive frontier: the problem of social control in English settlements in Ireland and Virginia 1550–1650' in Andrews, Canny & Hair (eds), *Westward enterprise*, pp 17–44.

N. Canny, 'The Irish background to Penn's experiment' in R. Dunn & M. Dunn (eds), *The world of William Penn* (Philadelphia, 1986), pp 139–56.

N. Canny, *Making Ireland British 1580–1650* (Oxford, 2001).

P. Carr, *Portavo: an Irish townland and its people* (Belfast 2003).

D. Chart, E. Evans & H. Lawlor, *Preliminary survey of the ancient monuments of Northern Ireland* (Belfast, 1940).

D. Chart, 'The break-up of the estate of Con O'Neill, Castlereagh, Co. Down, temp. James I', *PRIA*, xlviii:3, C (1942), pp 119–51.

A. Clarke, *The Old English in Ireland 1625–1642* (London, 1966).

A. Clarke, 'Sir Piers Crosby, 1590-1646: Wentworth's "tawney ribbon"', *IHS*, xxvi (1988), pp 142–60

T.J. Clohosey, 'Dunmore House', *Old Kilkenny Review*, iv (1951), pp 4–8.

A. Cobbe & T. Friedman, *James Gibbs in Ireland: Newbridge, his villa for Charles Cobbe, archbishop of Dublin* (Dublin, 2005).

P. Cockerham & A. Harris, 'Kilkenny funeral monuments 1500–1600: a statistical and analytical account', *PRIA*, ci:5, C (2001), pp 135–88.

B. Colfer, 'Anglo-Norman settlement in county Wexford' in Whelan (ed.), *Wexford*, pp 65–101.

H. Colvin, *A biographical dictionary of English architects 1660–1840* (London, 1954).

A. Cooper, 'Town House, Dame Street, Dublin', *Dublin Penny Journal* (1902), p. 276.

N. Cooper, *English manor houses* (London, 1990).

J. Cornforth, 'Dublin Castle, I', *Country Life*, 30 July 1970.

L. Cox, 'The Mac Coghlans of Delvin Eathra', *Ir. Geneal.*, iv:6 (1973), pp 534–46.

M. Craig, *Dublin 1660–1860* (Dublin, 1969).

M. Craig, 'New light on Jigginstown', *UJA*, xxxiii (1970), pp 107–10.

M. Craig, *Classic Irish houses of the middle size* (London, 1976).

M. Craig, *Portumna Castle* (Dublin, 1976).

M. Craig, *The architecture of Ireland from the earliest times to 1880* (London, 1982).

M. Craig, Knight of Glin & J. Cornforth, 'Castletown, Co. Kildare', *Country Life*, 27 March, 3 & 10 April 1969.

M. Craig & Knight of Glin, *Ireland observed* (Cork, 1970).

A. Crookshank, 'Lord Cork and his monuments', *Country Life*, cxlix (1971), 1288 f.

A. Crookshank & Knight of Glin, *Irish portraits 1660–1860* (Dublin, 1969).

T. Cronin, 'The Elizabethan colony in Co. Roscommon' in Murtagh (ed.), *Irish midland studies*, pp 107–20.

B. Cunningham, 'The composition of Connacht in the lordships of Clanricard and Thomond 1577–1641', *IHS*, xxiv (1984), pp 1–14.

B. Cunningham, 'Natives and newcomers in Mayo 1560–1603' in Gillespie & Moran (eds), *Mayo history 1500–1900*, pp 24–43.

G. Cunningham, *The Anglo-Norman advance into the south-west Midlands of Ireland 1185–1221* (Roscrea, 1987).

J. Cuppage (ed.), *Archaeological survey of the Dingle peninsula* (Ballyferriter, 1986).

J.S. Curl, *The Londonderry plantation 1609–1914* (Chichester, 1986).

C. Curran, *Dublin decorative plaster work* (London, 1967).

J. D'Alton & J. O'Flanagan, *The history of Dundalk* (Dublin, 1864).

O. Davies, 'The castles of Cavan: part II', *UJA*, xi (1948), pp 81–126.

M. Dewar, *Sir Thomas Smith: a Tudor intellectual in office* (London, 1964).

M. Dolley, 'The pattern of Elizabethan coin-hoards from Ireland', *UJA*, xxxiii (1970), pp 77–87.

C. Donnelly, 'The archaeology of the Ulster plantation' in Horning et al. (eds), *Post-medieval archaeology*, pp 37–50.

C. Donnelly, 'Towerhouses and late medieval secular settlements in County Limerick' in Duffy, Edwards & FitzPatrick (eds), *Gaelic Ireland*, pp 315–28.

P.J. Duffy, 'The territorial organisation of Gaelic landownership and its transformation in County Monaghan 1591–1640', *Ir. Geog.*, xiv (1981), pp 1–26.

P.J. Duffy, 'Patterns of landownership in Gaelic Monaghan in the late sixteenth century', *Clogher Rec.*, x (1981), pp 304–22.

P.J. Duffy, 'The nature of the medieval frontier in Ireland', *Studia Hib.*, 22–3 (1982–3), pp 21–38.

P.J. Duffy, 'The evolution of estate properties in south Ulster 1600–1900' in Smyth & Whelan (eds), *Common ground*, pp 84–109.

P.J. Duffy, D. Edwards & E. FitzPatrick (eds), *Gaelic Ireland: land, lordship and settlement c.1250–c.1650* (Dublin, 2001).

S. Duffy (ed.), *Atlas of Irish history* (Dublin, 1997).

S. Duffy, *Ireland in the Middle Ages* (New York, 1997).

R. Dunlop, 'The plantation of Munster 1584–1589', *EHR*, iii (1888), pp 250–69.

R. Dunlop, 'The plantation of Leix and Offaly 1556–1622', *EHR*, vi:21 (1891), pp 61–96.

R. Dunlop, 'Sixteenth-century schemes for the plantation of Ulster', *Scottish Hist. Rev.*, xxii (1924), pp 51–60, 115–26, 199–212.

R. Dutton, *The age of Wren* (London, 1951).

R.D. Edwards, *Ireland in the age of the Tudors* (London, 1977).

S. Ellis, *Reform and revival: English government in Ireland 1470–1534* (New York, 1986).

M. Espinasse, *Robert Hooke* (London, 1956).

J. Feehan, *Laois: an environmental study* (Ballykilcavan, 1983).

J. Fenlon, 'Some early seventeenth-century building accounts in Ireland', *Ir. Arch. & Dec. Studies*, 1 (1998), pp 84–99.

D. Fischer, *Albion's seed* (New York, 1989).

[W. Fitzgerald, duke of Leinster], 'Maynooth Castle', *JKAS*, i:4 (1894), pp 223–39.

W. Fitzgerald, 'Castle Rheban', *JKAS*, ii:2 (1896), pp 176–8.

W. FitzGerald, 'The house and demesne of Monasterevin', *JKAS*, iv:3 (1904), pp 256–7.

W. FitzGerald, 'Baltinglass Abbey, its possessions, and their post-Reformation proprietors', *JKAS*, v:6 (1908), pp 378–414.

W. Fitzgerald, 'The manor and castle of Powerscourt, County Wicklow, in the sixteenth century, formerly a possession of the earls of Kildare', *JKAS*, vi:2 (1909), pp 126–39.

W. Fitzgerald, 'The sculptured stones from the bridge of Athlone, built in 1567, now in the crypt of the Science and Art Museum, Dublin', *JRSAI*, v:3 (1915), pp 115–22.

E. FitzMaurice, *The life of Sir William Petty 1623–1687* (London, 1895).

E. FitzPatrick, *Royal inauguration in Gaelic Ireland c.1100–1600* (Woodbridge, 2004).

E. FitzPatrick & C. O'Brien, *The medieval churches of County Offaly* (Dublin, 1998).

F. Fitzsimons, 'The lordship of O'Connor Faly 1520–1570' in Nolan & O'Neill (eds), *Offaly*, pp 207–42.

D. Fleming, *Politics and provincial people: Sligo and Limerick 1691–1761* (Manchester, 2010).

J. Flood & P. Flood, *Kilcash: a history 1190–1801* (Dublin, 1999).

R. Gillespie, *Colonial Ulster: the settlement of east Ulster 1600–1641* (Cork, 1985).

R. Gillespie, 'Lords and commons in seventeenth-century Mayo' in Gillespie & Moran (eds), *Mayo history 1500–1900*, pp 44–53.

R. Gillespie, 'Destabilising Ulster 1641–2' in B. Mac Cuarta (ed.), *Ulster in 1641* (Belfast, 1993).

R. Gillespie & G. Moran (eds), *A various country: essays in Mayo history 1500–1900* (Westport, 1987).

M. Girouard, 'Lismore Castle, Co. Waterford, I', *Country Life*, 6 Aug. 1964.

M. Girouard, 'Birr Castle, Co. Offaly, I and II', *Country Life*, 4 & 25 Feb. & 11 March 1965.

M. Girouard, *Robert Smythson and the Elizabethan country house* (New Haven, 1983).

M. Girouard, *Elizabethan architecture: its rise and fall 1540–1640* (New Haven, 2009).

R. Glasscock, 'Moated sites and deserted boroughs and villages: two neglected aspects of Anglo-Norman settlement in Ireland' in Stephens & Glasscock (eds), *Irish geographical studies*, pp 279–301.

D. Gleeson, *The last lords of Ormond* (London, 1938).

H. Goff, 'English conquest of an Irish barony: the changing patterns of landownership in the barony of Scarawalsh 1540–1640' in Whelan (ed.), *Wexford*, pp 122–49.

A. Gomme & A. Maguire, *Design and plan in the country house from castle donjons to Palladian boxes* (New Haven, 2008).

M. Gowen, 'Seventeenth-century artillery forts in Ulster', *Clogher Rec.*, x (1979–80), pp 239–56.

B. Graham, 'Anglo-Norman settlement in Meath', *PRIA*, lxxv:11, C (1975), pp 223–49

B. Graham, *Anglo-Norman settlement in Ireland* (Athlone, 1985).

J. Graham, 'Rural society in Connacht 1600–1640' in Stephens & Glasscock (eds), *Irish geographical studies*, pp 192–208.

D. Guinness & W. Ryan, *Irish houses and castles* (London, 1971).

R. Gunther, *The architecture of Sir Roger Pratt* (Oxford, 1928).

A. Gwynn & R. Hadcock, *Medieval religious houses, Ireland* (Dublin, 1970).

P. Harbison, *Guide to the national monuments of Ireland* (Dublin, 1970).

G.A. Hayes-McCoy, 'The early history of guns in Ireland', *JGAHS*, xviii (1938–9), pp 43–65.

G.A. Hayes-McCoy, *Scots mercenary forces in Ireland 1565–1603* (Dublin, 1937).

G.A. Hayes-McCoy, 'Gaelic society in Ireland in the late sixteenth century', *Historical Studies*, 4 (1963), pp 45–61.

G.A. Hayes-McCoy, 'The completion of the Tudor conquest and the advance of the Counter-Reformation, 1571–1603', *NHI*, iii (Oxford, 1976), pp 94–194.

J. Healy, *The castles of County Cork* (Cork, 1988).

P. Henderson, *The Tudor house and garden: architecture and landscape in the sixteenth and early seventeenth century* (New Haven, 2005).

J. Pope Hennessy, *Sir Walter Raleigh in Ireland* (London, 1883).

R. Herbert, 'Antiquity of the Corporation of Limerick', *NMAJ*, 4 (1945), pp 85–130.

H. Hibbard, *Carlo Maderno and Roman architecture 1580–1630* (University Park, PA, 1971).

E. Hickey, 'The Wakelys of Navan and Ballyburley', *Ríocht na Midhe*, v:4 (1974), pp 3–19.

J. Hill, 'Gothic in post-Union Ireland: the uses of the past in Adare, Co. Limerick' in T. Dooley & C. Ridgeway (eds), *The Irish country house: its past, present and future* (Dublin, 2011), pp 58–89.

O. Hill & J. Cornforth, *English country houses: Caroline 1625–1685* (London, 1966).

P. Holland, 'The Anglo-Normans and their castles in County Galway' in G. Moran & R. Gillespie (eds), *Galway: history and society* (Dublin, 1996), pp 1–25.

K. Hoppen, *The common scientist in the seventeenth century: a study of the Dublin Philosophical Society 1683–1708* (London, 1978).

A. Horner & R. Loeber, 'Landscape in transition: descriptions of forfeited properties in Counties Meath, Louth and Cavan in 1700', *Anal. Hib.*, xlii (2011), pp 59–180.

A. Horning, 'Dwelling houses in the old barbarous manner: archaeological evidence for Gaelic architecture in an Ulster plantation village' in Duffy, Edwards & FitzPatrick (eds), *Gaelic Ireland*, pp 375–96.

A. Horning, E. Ó Baoill, C. Donnelly & P. Logue (eds), *The post-medieval archaeology of Ireland 1550–1850* (Dublin, 2007).

R. Hunter, 'Carew's survey of Ulster, 1611: the 'voluntary works'', *UJA*, xxxviii (1975), pp 81–2.

R. Hunter, 'The English undertakers in the plantation of Ulster 1610–41', *Breifne*, iv (1974), pp 471–500.

R. Hunter, 'Plantation in Donegal' in W. Nolan, L. Ronayne & M. Dunleavy (eds), *Donegal: history and society* (Dublin, 1995), pp 283–324.

L. Hurley & R. Loeber, 'The development of timber construction in the seventeenth and eighteenth century' in Loeber et al. (eds), *Architecture 1600–2000*, pp 61–6.

J. Ide, *Some examples of Irish country houses of the Georgian period* (New York, 1959).

Irish Architectural Archive, *Irish architectural drawings: an exhibition catalogue* (Dublin, 1963).

R. Wyse Jackson, *Cathedrals of the Church of Ireland* (Dublin, 1971).

D.N. Johnson, *The Irish castle* (Dublin, 1985).

J. Johnston, 'Settlement and architecture in County Fermanagh 1610–41', *UJA*, xliii (1980), pp 79–89.

F. Jones, *Mountjoy 1563–1606* (Dublin, 1958).

E. Jope, 'Scottish-style castles in the north of Ireland', *UJA*, xiv (1951), pp 31–47.

E. Jope, 'Castleraw near Loughgall, Co. Armagh', *UJA*, xvi (1953), pp 63–7.

E. Jope, 'Mongavlin Castle, Co. Donegal' *UJA*, xvii (1954), pp 169–72.

E. Jope, 'Moyry, Charlemont, Castleraw and Richhill: fortification to architecture in the north of Ireland', *UJA*, xxiii (1960), pp 97–123.

E. Jope (ed.), *Studies in building history: essays in recognition of the work of B.H. St John O'Neil* (London, 1961).

H. Kearney, *The British Isles: a history of four nations* (Cambridge, 1989).

W. Kelly & J. Young (eds), *Scotland and the Ulster plantations* (Dublin, 2009).

P. Kerrigan, 'Seventeenth-century fortifications, forts and garrisons in Ireland: a preliminary list', *Ir. Sword*, xiv:54–5 (1980), pp 3–24, 135–56.

P. Kerrigan, 'Irish castles and fortifications in the age of the Tudors, parts 1–2', *An Cosantóir* (1984), pp 199–203, 275–9.

P. Kerrigan, *Castles and fortifications in Ireland 1485–1945* (Cork, 1995).

P. Kerrigan, 'Castles and fortifications of County Offaly c.1500–1815' in Nolan & O'Neill (eds), *Offaly*, pp 393–438.

J. Kingston, 'The Barnewalls of Turvey', *Reportorium Novum*, i:2 (1956), pp 336–41.

E. Klingerhofer, *Castles and colonists: an archaeology of Elizabethan Ireland* (Manchester, 2010).

B. Lacy, *Archaeological survey of County Donegal* (Lifford, 1983).

W. Laffan (ed.), *Ireland's painters: topographical views from Glin Castle* (Tralee, 2006).

J. Larner (ed.), *Killarney: history and heritage* (Cork, 2005).

H.C. Lawlor, *Ulster: its archaeology and antiquities* (Belfast, 1928).

H. Leask, 'Mallow Castle, Co. Cork', *JCHAS*, ii (1944), pp 19–24.

H. Leask, *Irish castles and castellated houses* (Dundalk, 1946).

H. Leask, 'Early seventeenth-century houses in Ireland' in Jope (ed.), *Studies in building history*, pp 243–50.

H. Leask, *Irish churches and monastic buildings*. i: *The first phases and the Romanesque*; ii: *Gothic architecture to A.D. 1400*; iii: *Medieval gothic and last phases* (Dundalk, 1960).

J. Leerssen, *Mere Irish and fíor-Ghael: studies in the idea of Irish nationality, its development and literary expression prior to the nineteenth century* (Cork, 1997).

J. Lees-Milne, *English country houses: Baroque 1685–1715* (London, 1970).

C. Lennon, 'Richard Stanihurst (1547–1618) and Old English identity', *IHS*, xxi (1978–9), pp 121–43.

C. Lennon, *The lords of Dublin in the age* of *Reformation* (Dublin, 1989).

M. Lindsay, *The castles of Scotland* (London, 1986).

R. Lloyd, *Elizabethan adventurer: a life of Captain Christopher Carleill* (London, 1974).

R. Loeber, 'An introduction to the Dutch influence in seventeenth- and eighteenth-century Ireland', *Ir. Georgian Soc. Bull.*, xiii (1970), pp 1–28.

R. Loeber, 'Castle Durrow', *Ir. Georgian Soc. Bull.*, xvi (1973), pp 103–6.

R. Loeber, 'Biographical dictionary of engineers in Ireland 1600–1730', *Ir. Sword*, xiii (1977–9), pp 30–44, 106–22, 230–55, 283–314.

R. Loeber, 'Sir William Robinson', *Ir. Georgian Soc. Bull.*, xvii (1974), pp 3–9.

R. Loeber, 'An unpublished view of Dublin in 1698 by Francis Place', *Ir. Georgian Soc. Bull.*, xxi (1978), pp 7–15.

R. Loeber, *A biographical dictionary of architects in Ireland 1600–1720* (London, 1981).

R. Loeber, 'The changing borders of the Ely O'Carroll lordship' in Nolan & O'Neill (eds), *Offaly*, pp 287–318.

R. Loeber, 'Civilisation through plantation: the projects of Sir Mathew De Renzi' in Murtagh (ed.), *Irish midland studies*, pp 121–35.

R. Loeber, 'Sculptured memorials to the dead in early seventeenth-century Ireland: a survey from *Monumenta Eblanae* and other sources', *PRIA*, lxxxi:11, C (1981), pp 267–93.

R. Loeber (ed.), 'Architects and craftsmen admitted as freemen to the city of Dublin 1464–85 and 1575–1774', unpublished MS, copy in the National Gallery of Ireland, Dublin.

R. Loeber (ed.), 'Geographical calendar of landownership in Ely O'Carroll in the sixteenth and seventeenth centuries', unpublished document, deposited at the Offaly Historical Society, Tullamore (Offaly).

R. Loeber, 'Settlers' utilisation of natural resources in the seventeenth century' in K. Hannigan (ed.), *Wicklow: history and society* (Dublin, 1994), pp 267–304.

R. Loeber, 'The changing borders of the Ely O'Carroll lordship' in Nolan & O'Neill (eds), *Offaly*, pp 287–317.

R. Loeber, '"Certyn notes": biblical and foreign signposts to the Ulster plantation' in Lyttleton & Rynne (eds), *Plantation Ireland*, pp 23–42.

R. Loeber, H. Campbell, L. Hurley, J. Montague & E. Rowley (eds), *Architecture 1600–2000* (New Haven, 2014).

R. Loeber & G. Parker, 'The military revolution in seventeenth-century Ireland' in J. Ohlmeyer (ed.), *From independence to occupation: Ireland 1641–1660* (Cambridge, 1995), pp 66–88.

R. Loeber & T. Reeves-Smyth, 'Lord Audley's grandiose building schemes in the Ulster plantation' in B. Mac Cuarta (ed.), *Reshaping Ireland 1570–1700: colonisation and its consequences* (Dublin, 2011), pp 82–100.

R. Loeber & M. Stouthamer-Loeber, 'The lost architecture of the Wexford plantation' in Whelan (ed.), *Wexford*, pp 173–200.

R. Loeber & K. Whelan, 'An early eighteenth-century house: Clonegal rectory, County Carlow', *Jn. Wexford Hist. Soc.*, xiii (1990–1), pp 135–41.

H. Louw, 'Anglo-Netherlandish architectural interchange *c*.1600–*c*.1660', *Architectural History*, 24 (1981), pp 1–23.

T. Lunham, 'Some historical notices of Cork in the seventeenth and eighteenth centuries', *JRSAI*, xiv (1904), pp 65–9.

J. Lydon, 'The problem of the frontier in medieval Ireland', *Topic: a Journal of the Liberal Arts*, xiii (1967), pp 9–14.

J. Lydon, *Ireland in the later Middle Ages* (Dublin, 1973).

K. Lynch, *Roger Boyle, first earl of Orrery* (Knoxville, TN, 1965).

J. Lyttleton, 'Faith of our fathers: the Gaelic aristocracy in Co. Offaly and the Counter-Reformation' in Lyttleton & Rynne (eds), *Plantation Ireland*, pp 182–206.

J. Lyttleton, 'Rathcline Castle: an archaeology of plantation in County Longford' in M. Morris & F. O'Ferrall (eds), *Longford: history and society* (Dublin, 2010), pp 135–59.

J. Lyttleton & C. Rynne (eds), *Plantation Ireland: settlement and material culture 1550–1700* (Dublin, 2009).

M. MacCarthy-Morrogh, *The Munster plantation: English migration to southern Ireland 1583–1641* (Oxford, 1986).

M. MacCarthy-Morrogh, 'The English presence in early seventeenth-century Munster' in Brady & Gillespie (eds), *Natives and newcomers*, pp 171–90.

P. McCarthy, *Life in the country house in Georgian Ireland* (Yale, CT, 2016).

E. McCracken, 'Charcoal-burning ironworks in seventeenth- and eighteenth-century Ireland', *UJA*, xx (1957), pp 123–38.

E. McCracken, 'Supplementary list of Irish charcoal-burning ironworks', *UJA*, xxviii (1965), pp 132–6.

B. Mac Cuarta, 'Mathew De Renzy's letters on Irish affairs 1613–1620', *Anal. Hib.*, xxxiv (1987), pp 107–82.

B. Mac Cuarta, 'The plantation of Leitrim 1620–41', *IHS*, xxxii (2001), pp 297–320.

N. McCullough & V. Mulvin, *A lost tradition: the nature of architecture in Ireland* (Dublin, 1987).

M. MacCurtain, *Tudor and Stuart Ireland* (Dublin, 1972).

M. MacCurtain, 'A lost landscape: the Geraldine castles and towerhouses in the Shannon estuary' in J. Bradley (ed.), *Settlement and society in medieval Ireland* (Kilkenny, 1988), pp 429–44.

M. McKenna, 'Evidence for the use of timber in medieval Irish towerhouses: a regional study in Lecale and Tipperary', *UJA*, xlvii (1984), pp 171–4.

K. McKenny, *The Laggan army in Ireland 1640–1685* (Dublin, 2005).

E. MacLysaght, *Irish life in the seventeenth century*, second edition (Cork, 1950).

T. McNeill, *Anglo-Norman Ulster: the history and archaeology of an Irish barony 1177–1400* (Edinburgh, 1980).

T. McNeill, 'The stone castles of northern County Antrim', *UJA*, xlvi (1983), pp 101–28.

T. McNeill, *Castles in Ireland: feudal power in a Gaelic world* (London, 1997).

T. McNeill, 'The archaeology of Gaelic lordship east and west of the Foyle' in Duffy, Edwards & FitzPatrick (eds), *Gaelic Ireland*, pp 346–56.

E. McParland, 'Edward Lovett Pearce and the new junta for architecture' in T. Barnard & J. Clark (eds), *Lord Burlington: architecture, art and life* (London, 1995), pp 151–67.

W. Maguire (ed.), *Kings in conflict 1689–1750* (Belfast, 1990).

J.P. Mahaffy, *An epoch of Irish history: Trinity College, Dublin* (Dublin, 1906).

J. Mallory & T. McNeill, *The archaeology of Ulster from colonisation to plantation* (Belfast, 1991).

C. Manning, 'Maghernacloy Castle and the Hadsors' in C. Manning (ed.), *From ringforts to fortified houses: studies on castles and other monuments in honour of David Sweetman* (Bray, 2007), pp 209–16.

J.J. Marshall, *History of Charlemont and Mountjoy forts* (Dungannon, 1921).

C. Maxwell, *History of Trinity College* (Dublin, 1946).

C. Maxwell, *Country and town under the Georges* (Dundalk, 1949).

C. Milligan, *The walls of Derry* (Londonderry, 1948).

T.W. Moody, 'Sir Thomas Phillips of Limavady, servitor', *IHS*, i (1930), pp 251–72.

M. Moore, *Archaeological inventory of County Meath* (Dublin, 1987).

M. Moore, *Archaeological inventory of County Wexford* (Dublin, 1996).

M. Moore, *Archaeological inventory of County Leitrim* (Dublin, 2003).

H. Morgan, 'The colonial venture of Sir Thomas Smith in Ulster 1571–1575', *Hist. Jn.*, xxviii (1985), pp 261–78.

H. Morgan, 'The end of Gaelic Ulster: a thematic interpretation of events between 1534 and 1610', *IHS*, xxvi (1988), pp 8–32.

H. Morgan, *Tyrone's rebellion: the outbreak of the Nine Years' War in Tudor Ireland* (Dublin, 1993).

T. King Moylan, 'The district of Grangegorman III', *Dublin Hist. Rec.*, 18 (1945), pp 1–15.

M. Mulcahy, 'Elizabeth Fort, Cork', *Ir. Sword*, iv (1959–60), pp 127–34.

T. Mullin, *Coleraine in by-gone centuries* (Belfast, 1976).

J. Murphy, *Justin MacCarthy, Lord Mountcashel* (Cork, 1959).

J.J. Murray, 'The cultural impact of the Flemish Low Countries on sixteenth- and seventeenth–century England', *American Historical Review*, clxii (1957), pp 837–54.

H. Murtagh (ed.), *Irish midland studies: essays in commemoration of N.W. English* (Athlone, 1980).

K.W. Nicholls, 'Gaelic society and economy in the high Middle Ages' in *NHI*, ii (Oxford, 1987), pp 397–438.

K.W. Nicholls 'The Kavanaghs 1400–1700', *Ir. Geneal.*, v (1974–9), pp 435–47, 573–80, 730–4.

K.W. Nicholls, *Land, law and society in sixteenth-century Ireland* (Dublin, 1978).

K.W. Nicholls, *Gaelic and gaelicised Ireland in the Middle Ages* (Dublin, 1972; second edition, 2003).

K.W. Nicholls, 'The MacCoghlans' in *Ir. Geneal.*, vi:4 (1983), pp 445–60.

K.W. Nicholls, 'Gaelic landownership in Tipperary from surviving Irish deeds' in W. Nolan & T. McGrath (eds), *Tipperary: history and society* (Dublin, 1985), pp 92–103.

W. Nolan, *Fassadinin: land, settlement and society in south-east Ireland 1600–1850* (Dublin, 1979).

W. Nolan & T. O'Neill (eds), *Offaly: history and society* (Dublin, 1998).

B. Ó Bric, 'Landholding by Galway townsmen in Connacht 1585–1641', *IESH*, ii (1975), pp 60–1.

C. O'Brien & D. Sweetman, *Archaeological inventory of County Offaly* (Dublin, 1997).

J. O'Callaghan, 'Fortified houses of the sixteenth century in south Wexford', *Old Wexford Soc. Jn.*, viii (1980–1), pp 1–51.

É. Ó Ciardha, *Ireland and the Jacobite cause 1685–1766* (Dublin, 2002).

C. Ó Cleirigh, 'The O'Connor Faly lordship of Offaly 1395–1513', *PRIA*, xcvi:4, C (1996), pp 87–102.

P. Ó Conluain, 'Some O'Neill country maps 1575–1602', *Dúiche Néill*, i:2 (1987), pp 13–24.

K. O'Conor, 'The later construction and use of motte and bailey castles in Ireland: new evidence from Leinster', *JKAS*, xvii (1987–91), pp 13–29.

K. O'Conor, *The archaeology of medieval rural settlement in Ireland* (Dublin, 1998).

K. O'Conor, 'The morphology of Gaelic lordly sites in north Connacht' in Duffy, Edwards & FitzPatrick (eds), *Gaelic Ireland*, pp 329–45.

C. Ó Danachair, 'Irish towerhouses and their regional distribution', *Bealoideas*, xlv–xlvii (1977–9), pp 158–63.

B. Ó Dalaigh (ed.), *The strangers' gaze: travels in County Clare 1534–1950* (Ennis, 1998).

P. O'Donovan, *Archaeological inventory of County Cavan* (Dublin, 1995).

M. O'Dowd, *Power, politics and land: early modern Sligo 1568–1688* (Belfast, 1991).

J. O'Flanagan, *The lives of the Lord Chancellors and keepers of the great seal of Ireland* (London, 1870).

P. O'Flanagan, 'Surveys, maps and the study of rural settlement development' in D. Ó Corráin (ed.), *Irish antiquity* (Cork, 1981), pp 320–6.

J.H. Ohlmeyer, 'Strafford, the "Londonderry business" and the "New British History"' in J. Merritt (ed.), *The politics of Thomas Wentworth, earl of Strafford 1621–1641* (Cambridge, 1996), pp 209–29.

F. O'Kane, *Landscape design in eighteenth-century Ireland: mixing foreign trees with natives* (Cork, 2004).

F. O'Kane, 'Leamaneh and Dromoland: the O'Brien ambition: Part II', *Ir. Arch. & Dec. Studies*, 7 (2004), pp 86–9.

T. O'Keeffe, *Barryscourt Castle and the Irish towerhouse* (Dublin, 1997).

T. O'Keefe & S. Quirke, 'A house in the birth of modernity: Ightermurragh Castle in context' in Lyttleton & Rynne (eds), *Plantation Ireland*, pp 86–112.

P. Ó Mórdha, 'The MacMahons of Monaghan 1603–1640', *Clogher Rec.*, ii:1 (1957), pp 148–69.

N. Ó Muraíle, *The celebrated antiquary Dubhaltach Mac Fhirbhisigh* (Maynooth, 1996).

D. Ó Murchadha, 'Gaelic land tenure in county Cork: Uíbh Laoghaire in the seventeenth century' in P. O'Flanagan & C. Buttimer (eds), *Cork: history and society* (Dublin, 1993), pp 213–48.

R. Oram & P. Rankin, *Historic buildings in and near Dungannon and Cookstown* (Belfast, 1971).

A. Orme, 'Youghal, County Cork: growth, decay, resurgence', *Ir. Geog.*, v (1965–8), pp 121–49.

G.H. Orpen, 'Mot[t]es and Norman castles in Ireland', *EHR*, 12 (1907), pp 228–54, 440–67.

G.H. Orpen, 'Novum Castrum McKynegan: Newcastle, Co. Wicklow', *JRSAI*, viii (1908), pp 137–8.

A. O'Sullivan, *The archaeology of lake settlement in Ireland* (Dublin, 1998).

A. O'Sullivan, *Crannógs: lake dwellings of early Ireland* (Dublin, 2000).

A. O'Sullivan, 'Crannógs in late medieval Gaelic Ireland c.1350–c.1650' in Duffy, Edwards & FitzPatrick (eds), *Gaelic Ireland*, pp 397–417.

M. O'Sullivan, 'The fortification of Galway in the sixteenth and early seventeenth centuries', *JGHAS*, xvi (1934), pp 1–47.

P. O'Sullivan (ed.), *Newcastle Lyons: a parish of the Pale* (Dublin, 1986).

W. O'Sullivan, 'Medieval Meath manuscripts', *Ríocht na Midhe*, vii:4 (1985–6), pp 3–21.

A. Oswald, 'Euston Hall, Suffolk, I', *Country Life*, 10 Jan. 1957.

C. Parker, 'Cavan: a medieval border area' in R. Gillespie (ed.), *Cavan: essays on the history of an Irish county* (Dublin, 1995), pp 37–50.

G. Parker, *The military revolution: military innovation and the rise of the West 1500–1800* (Cambridge, 1988).

H. Pawlisch, *Sir John Davies and the conquest of Ireland: a study in legal imperialism* (Cambridge, 1985).

M. Perceval-Maxwell, *The Scottish migration to Ulster in the reign of James I* (London, 1973).

M. Perceval-Maxwell, *The outbreak of the Irish rebellion of 1641* (Montreal, 1994).

C. Philips, *A history of the Sackville family, earls and dukes of Dorset* (London, 1930).

W. Phillips (ed.), *History of the Church of Ireland*, 3 vols (Oxford, 1933–4).

P. Piveronus, 'Sir Warham St Leger and the first Munster plantation 1568–69', *Éire-Ireland*, xiv (1979), pp 15–36.

D. Power, 'The archaeology of the Munster plantation' in Horning et al. (eds), *Post-medieval archaeology*, pp 23–36.

J.P. Prendergast, 'The plantation of the barony of Idrone, County Carlow', *Kilkenny & South East Ireland Archaeological. Soc. Jn.*, series two, ii (1859), pp 400–28; iii (1860), pp 20–44, 69–80, 171–88, 196–208.

J.P. Prendergast, *The Cromwellian settlement of Ireland* (Dublin, 1922).

L. Price, 'Armed forces of the Irish chiefs in the early sixteenth century', *JRSAI*, lxii (1932), pp 201–7.

L. Price, 'The Byrnes country in County Wicklow in the sixteenth century', *JRSAI*, lxiii (1933), pp 224–42.

D. Quinn, 'Sir Thomas Smith (1513–1577) and the beginning of English colonial theory', *Proceedings Americal Philological Soc.*, lxxxix:4 (1945), pp 543–60.

D. Quinn, *Raleigh and the British empire* (New York, 1949).

D. Quinn, 'Ireland and sixteenth-century European expansion', *Historical Studies,* i (1958), pp 20–32.

D. Quinn, 'The Munster plantation: problems and opportunities', *JCHAS,* lxxi (1966), pp 19–40.

D. Quinn, *The Elizabethans and the Irish* (Ithaca, NY, 1966).

D. Quinn, *Ireland and America: their early associations 1500–1640* (Liverpool, 1991).

T. Rabb, *Enterprise and empire* (Cambridge, MA, 1967).

R. Ramsey, *Henry Cromwell* (London, 1933).

T. Reeves-Smyth, 'Community to privacy: late Tudor and Jacobean manorial architecture in Ireland 1560–1640' in Horning et al. (eds), *Post-medieval archaeology*, pp 289–326.

P. Robinson, *The plantation of Ulster: British settlement in an Irish landscape 1600–1670* (Dublin, 1984).

P. Robinson, *Carrickfergus: Irish Historic Towns Atlas 2* (Dublin, 1986).

N. Roche, 'The manufacture and use of glass in post-medieval Ireland' in Horning et al. (eds), *Post-medieval archaeology*, pp 405–20.

P. Roebuck, 'The making of an Ulster great estate: the Chichesters, barons of Belfast and viscounts of Carrickfergus 1599–1648', *PRIA*, lxxix:1, C (1979), pp 1–26.

W. Roulston, 'Seventeenth-century manors in the barony of Strabane' in J. Lyttleton & T. O'Keeffe (eds), *The manor in medieval and early modern Ireland* (Dublin, 2005), pp 160–87.

W. Roulston, 'The Scots in plantation Cavan 1610–42' in B. Scott (ed.), *Culture and society in early modern Breifne/Cavan* (Dublin, 2009), pp 121–46.

W. Roulston, 'Domestic architecture in Ireland 1640–1740' in Horning et al. (eds), *Post-medieval archaeology*, pp 327–44.

A.H. Rowan, 'Killyleagh Castle, Co. Down', *Country Life*, 19 & 26 March, 2 April & 9 April 1970.

A.H. Rowan, *The buildings of Ireland: north-west Ulster: the counties of Donegal, Fermanagh and Tyrone* (London, 1979).

T. Sadlier & P. Dickinson, *Georgian mansions in Ireland, with some account of Georgian architecture and decoration* (Dublin, 1915).

M. Salter, *Castles and strong houses of Ireland* (Malvern, 1993).

M. Salter, *The castles of Leinster* (Malvern, n.d.).

B. Scott, *Cavan 1609–53: plantation, war and religion* (Dublin, 2007).

St John D. Seymour, *The Puritans in Ireland 1647–1661* (Oxford, 1921).

C. Shammas, 'English commercial development and American colonisation 1560–1620' in Andrews, Canny & Hair (eds), *Westward enterprise*, pp 151–74.

A. Sheehan, 'The population of the plantation of Munster: Quinn reconsidered', *JCHAS*, lxxvii (1982–3), pp 107–17.

A. Sheehan, 'The overthrow of the plantation of Munster in October 1598', *Ir. Sword*, xv (1982), pp 11–22.

A. Sheehan, 'Irish towns in a period of change 1558–1625' in Brady & Gillespie (eds), *Natives and newcomers*, pp 93–119.

A. Simms, 'The influence of classical precedent on English plantation theories in Ireland' in *Convegro internazionale. I paessagi rivali Europei* (Perugia, 1973), pp 483–91.

J.G. Simms, 'Dublin in 1685', *IHS*, xiv (1964–5), pp 212–26.

J.G. Simms, *The Williamite confiscation in Ireland 1690–1703* (London, 1956).

K. Simms, 'Warfare in the medieval Gaelic lordships', *Ir. Sword*, xii (1975–6), pp 98–108.

K. Simms, *From kings to warlords: the changing political structure of Gaelic Ireland in the later Middle Ages* (Woodbridge, 1987).

K. Simms, 'The brehons of later medieval Ireland' in D. Hogan & W.N. Osborough (eds), *Brehons, serjeants and attorneys* (Dublin, 1990), pp 51–76.

K. Simms, 'Native sources for Gaelic settlement: the house poems' in Duffy, Edwards & FitzPatrick (eds), *Gaelic Ireland*, pp 246–67.

A.P. Smyth, *Celtic Leinster: towards an historical geography of early Irish civilisation AD 500 to 1600* (Dublin, 1982).

W.J. Smyth, *Map-making, landscapes and memory: a geography of colonial and early modern Ireland c.1530–1750* (Cork, 2006).

W.J. Smyth & K. Whelan (eds), *Common ground: essays on the historical geography of Ireland* (Cork, 1988).

P. Somerville-Large, *The Irish country house: a social history* (London, 1995).

R. Stalley, 'William of Prene and the Royal Works in Ireland', *Journal of the British Archaeological Association*, xli (1978), pp 30–49.

R. Stalley, 'Irish Gothic and English fashion' in J. Lydon (ed.), *The English in medieval Ireland* (Dublin, 1984), pp 65–86.

R. Stalley, *The Cistercian monasteries of Ireland: an account of the history, art and architecture of the white monks in Ireland from 1142 to 1540* (London, 1987).

W. Stanford, *Ireland and the classical tradition* (Towata, NJ, 1976).

N. Stephens & R. Glasscock (eds), *Irish geographical studies in honour of E. Estyn Evans* (Belfast, 1970).

L. Stone, *The crisis of the aristocracy 1558–1641* (Oxford, 1965).

G. Stout, *Archaeological survey of the barony of Ikerrin* (Roscrea, 1984).

G. Stout & M. Stout, 'Early landscapes: from prehistory to plantation' in Aalen, Whelan & Stout (eds), *Atlas of the Irish rural landscape*, pp 31–65.

J. Summerson, *Architecture in Britain 1530 to 1830* (London, 1970).

D. Sweetman, *The medieval castles of Ireland* (Cork, 1999).

D. Sweetman, 'The hall house in Ireland' in J. Kenyon & K. O'Conor (eds), *The medieval castle in Ireland and Wales* (Dublin, 2003), pp 121–32.

D. Sweetman, O. Alcock & B. Moran, *Archaeological inventory of County Laois* (Dublin, 1995).

C. Tait, *Death, burial and commemoration in Ireland 1550–1650* (London, 2002).

M.W. Thompson, *The decline of the castle* (Cambridge, 1987).

E. Tickell, 'The Eustace family and their lands in Co. Kildare Part II', *JKAS*, xiii (1958), pp 307–41.

J. Tighe, *Moore Abbey* (n.p, nd.).

P. Tohall, 'Charlemont Fort, Co. Armagh', *Ir. Sword*, iii (1957–8), pp 183–6.

D. Tough, *The last years of a frontier* (Oxford, 1928).

V. Treadwell, 'The Irish parliament of 1569–71', *PRIA*, lxv:4 (1966), pp 55–89.

V. Treadwell, *Buckingham and Ireland 1616–1628: a study in Anglo-Irish politics* (Dublin, 1998).

V. Treadwell, *The Irish commission of 1622: an investigation of the Irish administration 1615–22 and its consequences 1623–24* (Dublin, 2006).

W. Trevelyan & C. Trevelyan (eds), *Trevelyan Papers part III* (London, 1872).

Ulster Architectural Heritage Society, *List of historic buildings in the area of Craigavon within the Moira Rural District* (Belfast, 1969).

A. Vicars, 'Notes on Grange Con', *JKAS*, iii (1899–1902), pp 382–5.

W. Wallace, 'John White, Thomas Harriot and Walter Raleigh in Ireland', *The Durham Thomas Harriot Seminar, Occasional Paper*, No. 2 (1985), pp 3–24.

P. Walsh, *The will and family of Hugh O'Neill, earl of Tyrone* (Dublin, 1930).

P. Walsh, *The Ó Cléirigh family of Tír Conaill* (Dublin, 1938).

D. Waterman, 'Some Irish seventeenth-century houses and their architectural ancestry' in Jope (ed.), *Building history*, pp 251–74.

D. Waterman, 'Sir John Davies and his Ulster buildings: Castlederg and Castle Curlews, Co. Tyrone', *UJA*, xxiii (1960), pp 89–96.

S. Weadick, 'How popular were fortified houses in Irish castle building history?' in Lyttleton & Rynne (eds), *Plantation Ireland*, pp 61–85.

T.J. Westropp, 'Notes on the lesser castles or 'peel towers' of the County Clare', *PRIA*, v (1898–1900), pp 348–65.

H. Wheeler & M. Craig, *The Dublin city churches of the Church of Ireland* (Dublin, 1948).

K. Whelan (ed.), *Wexford: history and society* (Dublin, 1987).

D. White, 'The reign of Edward VI in Ireland: some political, social and economic aspects', *IHS*, xiv:55 (1965), pp 197–211.

D. Wilsdon, *Plantation castles on the Erne* (Dublin, 2010).

H. Woodbridge, *Sir William Temple, the man and his work* (New York, 1940).

Index

Irish placenames are listed under their respective counties.
Illustrations are indicated by page numbers in bold.